Utilizing Open Source Tools for Online Teaching and Learning:

Applying Linux Technologies

Lee Chao
University of Houston—Victoria, USA

Information Science REFERENCE

INFORMATION SCIENCE REFERENCE

Hershey · New York

Director of Editorial Content: Kristin Klinger
Senior Managing Editor: Jamie Snavely
Managing Editor: Jeff Ash
Assistant Managing Editor: Carole Coulson
Typesetter: Sean Woznicki
Cover Design: Lisa Tosheff
Printed at: Yurchak Printing Inc.

Published in the United States of America by
Information Science Reference (an imprint of IGI Global)
701 E. Chocolate Avenue,
Hershey PA 17033
Tel: 717-533-8845
Fax: 717-533-8661
E-mail: cust@igi-global.com
Web site: http://www.igi-global.com/reference

and in the United Kingdom by
Information Science Reference (an imprint of IGI Global)
3 Henrietta Street
Covent Garden
London WC2E 8LU
Tel: 44 20 7240 0856
Fax: 44 20 7379 0609
Web site: http://www.eurospanbookstore.com

Library of Congress Cataloging-in-Publication Data

Chao, Lee, 1951-
Utilizing open source tools for online teaching and learning : applying Linux technologies / by Lee Chao.

p. cm.

Includes bibliographical references and index.
Summary: "This book covers strategies on using and evaluating open source products for online teaching and learning systems"--Provided by publisher.

ISBN 978-1-60566-376-0 (hardcover) -- ISBN 978-1-60566-377-7 (ebook) 1. Web-based instruction. 2. Linux device drivers (Computer programs) 3. Operating systems (Computers) I. Title.
LB1044.87.C42 2009
371.33'44678--dc22

2008054193

British Cataloguing in Publication Data
A Cataloguing in Publication record for this book is available from the British Library.

Table of Contents

Section IV:
Trends and Advances

Foreword

How to make better use of open source technologies in learning, teaching, and lab management systems is a matter that is widely discussed in professional meetings and at other formal and informal meetings of faculty, researchers, administrators, and managers of educational institutions, training centers and labs. Mostly the conversations would revolve around the challenges and difficulties encountered, and partial successes. Those with a success story would usually share his or her experiences to other groups of individuals. The value of Li Chao's *Utilizing Open Source Tools for Online Teaching and Learning: Applying Linux Technologies* is greatly enhanced by the fact that it is perhaps the first truly comprehensive and authoritative book to appear on the difficult task of planning, developing, and administering the various components of an online teaching/learning system using only open source technologies. The book has importance that is not only timely but timeless, in that it covers all aspects of the application of open source technologies to online teaching/learning systems, and moreover it discusses many of the underlying instructional and foundational issues besides the nuts and bolts of downloading and configuring the latest systems and technologies. The book provides a wealth of guidance and valuable information on the technologies that are available and what they can do, with a special emphasis on Linux operating systems and related products, and how to develop and administer online teaching systems using them. To its author, whom I have had the pleasure of working with for many years, may every reader render due appreciation, for distilling the wisdom garnered from his experiences and much research that has gone into this work.

May I underscore that this book is not just theory – even though the author has gone to extraordinary measures to describe the methodological underpinnings – but rather based on much practical experience, what we actually use, the result of much trials and tribulations on the author's part, and the ultimate lessons learned. What Li describes here in these pages actually works, and in many instances reflects the best strategies and options that are available for the set of conditions or problems being considered.

I am glad to write the Foreword to this new, innovative, and highly relevant book, written by one of our most popular teachers.

Meledath Damodaran, PhD
Professor of Computer Science, Information Systems and Math
University of Houston-Victoria
Victoria, Texas, USA

Meledath Damodaran *is a professor of computer science and mathematics at the University of Houston-Victoria. He is the coordinator of the Computer Science and Mathematics Programs at UHV. Prior to joining UHV in August 1991, he taught computer science at various universities for over 11 years. His research interests are in software quality management, parallel processing, and neural networks. He is also interested in software engineering, software project management, and computer science and computer information systems education. He teaches a wide variety of courses including operating systems, software project management, software engineering, programming language theory, computer security, database design, artificial intelligence, computer architecture, and information systems. Dr. Damodaran has also worked as a consultant to industries and governmental agencies. He was a Fulbright Scholar in 1992 and a Mellon Visiting Faculty Fellow in the Computer Science Department at Yale University in New Haven in 1989-90. Dr. Damodaran has also served as the president of Applied Computer Consultants, Inc. in Edmond, Okla., from 1984 to 1986. Dr. Damodaran received his doctorate from Purdue University in 1977.*

Preface

Online teaching/learning has become the main stream among higher education institutions. More and more courses in various fields have been offered online. More and more students have enrolled in online courses. On each campus, large or small, online teaching/learning systems are a key component of their education systems. For a number of the higher education institutions, a well-established online teaching/learning system is their lifeline for keeping their classes running. An online teaching/learning system depends heavily on the technologies used in constructing the system's infrastructure. Often, an online teaching/learning system is constructed on a highly reliable network system with adequate performance. Such a system is complicated and expensive. The implementation of such a network system requires a significant amount of budget, the knowledge about various technologies, and the skills to install and manage the technologies used in the online teaching/learning system.

There have been numerous articles and books about online teaching and learning published in recent years. A few of them are about applying open source products to the support of online teaching and learning. However, it is not easy to find one that covers the development of the entire online teaching/learning system with open source products. It is difficult to find one that includes all the phases of the development process, such as requirement investigation, system modeling, system implementation with open source products, open source-based system security, open source-based system deployment, open source-based system management, and open source-based system evaluation. The open source approach has been discussed by many authors. However, the application of open source products to the development of online teaching/learning systems has not been systematically examined. To help researchers and practitioners be better informed, this book reviews studies done in recent years in the related fields.

One of the goals of this book is to improve the understanding of the development of online teaching/learning systems. The book goes through each phase of the development process and provides strategies that will help accomplish the development tasks. Especially, the book focuses on the roles played by open source products in the development process of an online teaching/learning system. For each major component in the online teaching/learning system, the book provides the information about the open source products involved in that component and describes how the open source products are used in that component. While readers make decisions, this book informs them that it is possible to construct an open source-based online teaching/learning system without using proprietary software. To help readers make their decisions, this book also provides examples, case studies, and comments to illustrate the usage of some open source tools.

The development of an online teaching/learning system needs the concepts and theory of instructional design, the skills for dealing with hardware and software, as well as the knowledge of project management and technical support. IT professionals from various fields are involved in the development and management of the online teaching/learning system. Faculty members, staff members, and students are involved in the development of the online teaching/learning system. Administrators of different levels and people who care about education are also involved in the development process.

This book is written for those who participate in the online teaching/learning system development to inform them that there is an alternative open source solution of delivering knowledge and education to the students. This book provides information for decision makers so that they can choose an appropriate online teaching/learning system for their campus.

A sophisticated online teaching/learning system does not have to be expensive. For the project manager, the book illustrates a systematic approach to the design, development, and implementation of an online teaching/learning system. The information provided in this book can also assist the project manager in financial planning, expenditure monitoring, equipment purchasing, and resource allocation. This book shows IT professionals that open source products are available to implement each component of an online teaching/learning system. The book helps the system designer to properly create a model for an online teaching/learning system before the system is implemented. It introduces some of the open source management tools that can make the online teaching/learning management more efficient and flexible.

This book shows instructors how to create online course materials in today's Web-based teaching environment. It also provides technical details for technical personnel on system management, especially, on security management and system update strategies. The book also lets faculty members and students know that an open source-based online teaching/learning system is as good as a proprietary-based online teaching/learning system. All in all, this book is intended to help readers, either a veteran project manager or a new faculty member who has just begun to develop his/her online classes.

To implement a complex project like an online teaching/learning system with open source products, one need to know what open source products are available and what features are supported by these open source products. This book is designed to address these issues too. To better understand the open source products and how they are used to support online teaching and learning, this book closely examines the popular open source products and compares the strengths and weaknesses of these products. The book also provides strategies of selecting the open source products for the tasks in each phase of the development process.

Among the open source operating systems, Linux stands out due to its popularity and merits. This book pays more attention to the Linux operating system for both the server side and the client side. It reviews the major Linux distributions and their operating systems. What makes Linux important to an online teaching/learning system is its security, reliability, and flexibility.

As a server operating system, Linux can be used to manage user accounts and to host remote access servers. The Linux operating system is also capable of hosting all the application software packages that are necessary to support the daily operations of an online teaching/learning system. This book reviews the server-side open source application software such as learning management systems, Web servers, e-mail servers, video conferencing servers, and database management systems.

To deliver knowledge through the Internet, this book reviews various network setups and open source network protocols. For network management, the book introduces various open source network management tools.

Security is one of the top concerns for running an online teaching/learning system. This book examines possible security vulnerabilities of the open source teaching/learning system and security measures that should be enforced. Some open source security management tools are reviewed. This book provides information on how to use these tools to protect the online teaching/learning system.

The Linux operating system can also be used as a desktop operating system on personal computers. The desktop operating system allows students to remotely access class Web sites for course materials and access online computer labs for hands-on practice. The desktop operating system is also used to host application software such as the software used to create and manage online teaching materials. This book examines the popular Linux desktop operating system, compares its features, and lists the application packages included in the operating system.

To help instructors create online teaching materials, this book reviews various open source Web authoring tools, multimedia software, and collaboration utilities.

Of these open source products, the book gives detailed information on what they can do and how they can be downloaded and configured.

Through examples, this book demonstrates how Linux is used in the process of developing an online teaching/learning system. For instance, Linux is used to perform tasks such as managing network resources and student accounts, hosting Web servers, database management systems, and learning management systems, managing security, and providing remote access services. In this book, Linux is also used to create online course materials.

For the future development of online teaching/learning systems, the book gives information about the trends in technology and in e-learning that can potentially improve online teaching and learning. As always, there will be new open source products. This book discusses some new features and new trends among open source server and desktop operating systems, network technologies, database management systems, learning management systems, and security management. The book also provides information about some new technologies that are still under development.

THE CHALLENGES

An online teaching/learning system itself is often a Web-based enterprise-level project. Such a system is complex and versatile. A variety of technologies are involved in the construction of an online teaching/learning system which consists of servers, networks, personal computers, mobile devices, operating systems, system and network management software, security management software, remote access software, data management software, learning management software, multimedia software, collaboration software, Web development software, e-mail service software, and other application software. The daily teaching and learning activities are supported by these technologies. In addition to the support of teaching and learning, these technologies are also part of the course content covered in many technology related curricula. A sophisticated online teaching/learning system allows users to access course materials through the Internet, provides various tools for learning management, and allows students to perform hands-on practice on servers and networks. Often, a university spends a large portion of its annual budget to support such a large system. Developing and maintaining such a system is often a big challenge for many universities.

Not only is an online teaching/learning system complex, it is also a fast changing system. Each year, even each month, new technologies are released, new e-learning ideas and practice are reported, and new course materials are created. To keep up with the IT industry's trends and to teach students the knowledge that is not obsolete, an online teaching/learning system needs to be updated frequently. Many of the proprietary products do not have updates before new versions of the products are released. Once a new version is released, it will cost a university to purchase the upgrades, add additional hardware and software, reconfigure the system, and provide training to users. With a proprietary product, the system upgrade is expensive and time consuming.

Given the fact that an open source-based online teaching/learning system can be the solution for many higher education institutions to support their online classes with minimum cost and with up-to-date technologies, one may assume that most of the online teaching/learning systems should be open source based. However, it is not the case in reality. Most of the higher education institutions are either not aware of the open source solution for online teaching/learning systems or may not have the personnel with the knowledge and skills to implement this type of system. Open source products are often the results of the effort of researchers and programmers. There is very little marketing effort for these products. Although many of these products are compatible with proprietary products, the decision makers and technical staff may not be fully aware of these facts.

For online teaching/learning systems, strong technical support is also a key factor. Open source tools such as those included in the Linux operating system are free and powerful enough to handle tasks such as networking and Web development. Using Linux is a great way to solve budget problems. On the other hand, Linux and other open source tools are less understood by many faculty members and administrators. Also, many technicians in technical support teams have less experience in dealing with these tools. To develop hands-on practice course materials for technology-based courses, faculty members and technical support teams need to know how to know about the features provided by open source products, how to select the open source products to achieve their goals, how to design instructional materials with these tools, and how to use open source products.

THE ANSWERS

For the development of an online teaching/learning system, based on the requirements and budget, universities have come up with various solutions. In most cases, the expenditure on technologies will increase dramatically as online teaching/learning systems become more complex and the requirements for reliability and performance get higher. The shortage of funding often hinders the effort of improving an online teaching/learning system. Among various solutions, using the open source technology to construct an infrastructure to support online teaching and learning stands out as a solution that is inexpensive and able to meet all the requirements.

By using an open source based online teaching/learning system; higher education institutions can significantly reduce the cost of developing and supporting online classes while improving reliability and performance.

For an online teaching/learning system to keep up with the IT industry's trends and to teach students the up-to-date knowledge, open source products provide a viable solution by allowing users to add new components whenever they are available. There is no cost to obtain new versions of the products. Users can also determine which part of the product should be upgraded instead of upgrading the entire package.

To help readers better understand the application of the open source solution to the online teaching/learning system development process, this book provides the information of open source products used in each phase of the development. The book also compares some of popular open source products and their usability in an open source teaching/learning system. Since open source products will be used to support the development of an online teaching/learning system, it is helpful to provide information about this type of system. This book will address each of the key areas in the development of an online teaching/learning system.

In this book, we will discuss the design strategies, implementation methods, and the effectiveness of online teaching/learning systems. The book presents some possible solutions to the challenges encountered in the system construction and management.

ORGANIZATION OF THE BOOK

There are 12 chapters in this book. The chapters are categorized into four main sections, Introduction, Infrastructure Development for Offering Online Courses, Course Material Development for Online Courses, and Trends and Advances. The following is a brief description of each section.

Section I: Introduction. This is an introduction section that includes three chapters. This section provides an overview of open source products. As the title of the book indicates, the open source products are used to support the development of online teaching/learning systems. To help readers understand how to properly apply the open source products to the development of an online teaching/learning system, this section also introduces the theories of instructional design and instructional technology, and the solution development procedure. The instructional design model ADDIE will be used as a guideline for the system's development.

The first chapter provides an overview of the open source technology. This chapter gives the background information of the open source approach. In the overview, this chapter will explain the concept of open source and what open source tools are available for online teaching and learning. It gives a brief history of the open source technology. This chapter also investigates the current usage of open source products in education institutions. It discusses the strengths and weaknesses of the open source products and the roles that can be played by these open source products in developing an open source online teaching/learning system.

The second chapter reviews the instructional technology theory in general. Developing an online teaching/learning system is a complex process that needs to be thoroughly planned. Such a system must be carefully designed before it can be implemented. Since one of the book's goals is to show how to apply the open source tools to the development and management of online courses, the theory of instructional technology is introduced in this chapter as a guideline for the development process. Based on the theory of instructional technology, the development of an online teaching/learning process is divided into five phases, needs analysis, system design, system development, system implementation, and system evaluation. In this chapter, topics related to these five phases are covered.

Chapter III provides the technology requirement analysis. It describes the methods of conducting the requirement analysis. This chapter explains how to collect information and how to analyze the collected information. It covers the requirement analysis for computer systems, networks, learning management systems, application software, collaboration tools, and course material development.

Section II: Infrastructure Development for Offering Online Courses. This section discusses the components in an online teaching/learning system. It includes six chapters. Each chapter covers a major component. Based on the analysis conducted in Chapter III, the open source products are reviewed for each component of an online teaching/learning system.

Chapter IV introduces the network infrastructure for an online teaching/learning system. Based on the technology requirement analysis, Chapter IV examines the network related open source tools that can be used to achieve the design goal. The first topic discussed in Chapter IV is the client-server architecture on which an online teaching/learning system will be developed. Then, this chapter looks into network equipment. The next topic to be covered in this chapter is about the network management related open source tools. Lastly, this chapter demonstrates the network development process for an online teaching/learning system.

Chapter V is devoted to the discussion of server technology. Servers are used to deliver course materials and other services to students. Chapter V discusses the issues related to computer systems on the server side. Linux as a server operating system is the main topic in this chapter. Linux Enterprise Server is an open source network operating system that is used to handle network resources as well as application software. Servers handle remote access through the Internet. This chapter examines some of the server equipment that supports the Linux operating system.

The next topic covered in this chapter is the investigation of open source system management tools, especially those included in the Linux operating system. This chapter also introduces various virtual server technologies that play an important role in online computer lab management. The last part of this chapter demonstrates a server development process with open source products.

Chapter VI is focused on database system development. This chapter starts with the review of open source database management systems. Then, it discusses some of the database design, development, and implementation-related issues. It looks at database management and explores the open source tools for database management. Lastly, this chapter gives an example of installing and configuring the database management system MySQL on a server with the Linux operating system installed.

Chapter VII covers the topics related to open source learning management system (LMS) software packages. An LMS is commonly used to support course setup, management, and assessment. Many LMS software packages can also provide tools for developing multimedia course materials and tools for collaboration. This chapter compares several popular open source LMS packages. The last part of this chapter shows an example of the installation and configuration of an LMS on a Linux server.

Chapter VIII deals with the security management of an online teaching/learning system. Security is very important to online teaching and learning. This chapter examines security policies for online teaching/learning systems. It goes over the process of creating a well defined security policy. This chapter also discusses the issues related to vulnerability assessment. It investigates security vulnerabilities and explores some of the open source vulnerability assessment tools. It also explores other open source security tools used to enforce various security measures. Then, examples are given on the security management with the Linux operating system.

Chapter IX discusses open source computer systems and tools for the client side of an online teaching/learning system. The Linux desktop operating system is the main focus. This chapter also examines the open source tools for the management of the Linux desktop operating system. In addition to the desktop management tools provided by the Linux operating system, the chapter also reviews other open source desktop management tools. The last topic in this chapter is about the open source remote access tools. The configuration of some open source remote access tools is demonstrated.

Section III: Course Material Development for Online Courses. This section covers the issues related to developing course materials with open source products. Two chapters, Chapter X and Chapter XI are included in this section.

Chapter X focuses on the development of course materials with the open source tools. The theories of instructional design and instructional technology are used to guide the development process. By following the instructional design model ADDIE, this chapter illustrates how the open source tools are used to develop course materials. This chapter gives some detailed discussion on the open source Web authoring, multimedia, and collaboration tools. The last part of this chapter presents an example to illustrate how the open source tools are used to develop course materials to meet the objectives required by the instructional design.

Chapter XI deals with the issues of implementation and evaluation which are part of the ADDIE model. After the online teaching materials are developed, the next task is to deploy the teaching materials. Since the Web server and student accounts are managed by the computer service department, the strong support from computer service is the key for a successful deployment. This chapter discusses technical support and training which belong to daily maintenance. The improvement of the online teaching/learning system should be based on the feedback from the users. The response from the instructors and students can be used as a guideline for identifying the areas that need to be improved. The last topic in Chapter XI discusses the evaluation of online courses and course materials.

Section IV: Trends and Advances. This section has one chapter, Chapter XII, which is about the trends in the development of online teaching/learning systems.

Chapter XII provides information about some of the trends in open source products and other technologies that have a potential impact on the development of online teaching/learning systems. This chapter points out some of the recent changes in instructional technology. It describes the possible use of the newly developed open source products for online teaching/learning systems.

Acknowledgment

My thanks go to the book reviewers who have provided comprehensive and critical comments that are valuable contributions to the book. I am grateful to Dr. Mel Damodaran who has written the wonderful foreword for this book. I would like to give my appreciation to my students for their participation in the online learning process and for their constructive suggestions to enhance the quality of the online instruction. I would like to acknowledge the help of my colleagues and the university's technical support team with the online computer labs. I would like to express my deep appreciation to Dr. Jenny Huang for her review on the content of the manuscript and constructive suggestions to enhance the quality of the book. Special thanks go to all the editors and staff at the IGI Global, especially, to Jan Travers, Tyler Heath, Rebecca Beistline, and Mehdi Khosrow-Pour. They have provided great help from the decision on the book title to the final publication of this book.

Lee Chao
University of Houston—Victoria, USA

Section I
Introduction

Chapter I
Introduction to Open Source Products

INTRODUCTION

Web-based teaching has become one of the main stream teaching and learning methods in most of the higher education institutions. To support teaching and learning activities over the Internet, Web-based teaching has been implemented with various technologies. Among the various solutions, using the open source technology to construct a platform for supporting online teaching and learning has attracted a great deal of attention. To better understand the open source technology and how it can be used to support online teaching and learning, we will first take an overview of the open source technology in this chapter. We will investigate the roles played by the open source technology. We will also examine the strengths and weaknesses of the open source technology in general. At the end of this chapter, a framework of the book will be presented to give an overall picture of the discussion in the book.

The overview section will explain what open source is and list some open source tools that are available for online teaching and learning. It will briefly review the history of the open source technology. We will investigate the usage of the open source technology in education institutions.

After the brief overview, we will look at the roles the open source technology plays in the IT industry and in online teaching and learning. Then, we will consider the advantages and disadvantages of the open source technology. We will compare the open source technology with the non-open source technology according to the cost, security, usability, and reliability. Based on the comparison, we will find out the strengths and weaknesses of the open source technology and the measures to be taken to reduce the impact of the disadvantages.

The last topic of this chapter is about the book framework. This book is constructed according to the framework. The book framework lists the topics and summarizes the issues in this book, which will help the reader to follow the discussion throughout the book. The framework of this book is also closely related to the process of developing solutions for online teaching with the open source technology.

The conclusion section will summarize what we have discussed in this chapter. It will also present the findings drawn from the discussions in this chapter.

BACKGROUND

After the rapid development over the past twenty years, online teaching and learning have been widely adopted by higher education institutions. When compared with the overall higher education student population, the enrollment of online classes has been growing considerably faster (CRIENGLISH.com, 2008; Sloan Consortium, 2006). According to Sloan Consortium (2006), almost 3.2 million students were taking at least one online class during the fall 2005 semester, which is nearly 40% increase when compared with the enrollment the year before. The fast increase of enrollment indicates that more and more courses need to be supported by Web-based technology.

Web-based technology is also used to accomplish tasks such as student account management and other knowledge management. The increasing needs of Web-based technology create a great opportunity for the IT industry and higher education institutions. On the other hand, it also creates some challenges. Manufacturers need to improve their products to meet the requirements from the ever changing market. The computer service departments in higher education institutions are facing more and more pressure on improving performance, usability, flexibility, and security of their instructional Web sites. Instructors need to design and implement better materials for online teaching; this requires the instructors themselves to keep learning new technologies and instructional theories. Students need to adapt to new teaching and learning environments which may be a lot different from what they had in high school. They will experience the advantages and disadvantages of online teaching and learning. The administrators of higher education institutions will face increasing demands for funding, technical support, new curricula, and skilled personnel.

All this has generated great research interests in dealing with these challenges. Numerous studies have been done in the area of Web-based teaching technologies. In their book, Horton and Horton (2003) described various technologies that can be used to present course materials online, manage students' accounts, and support collaboration. Many research papers have also been published in this area.

On the history of using computer-assisted instruction, readers can find Hall's (1970) report which stated that computers were used as instructional tools in Pennsylvania in the late 1960's. In the early 1990's, Szabo and Montgomery (1992) reported that the World Wide Web was used to implement the computer-based training classes. Web based training has also been adopted by companies. Through the Web, companies provide distance training for their employees. In the book edited by Berge (2000), distance training case studies are contributed by different authors. Through these case studies, readers can learn a lot about how to plan, organize, develop, deploy, and sustain distance training. The authors indicate that distance training can be a very effective tool for improve employees' skills.

Since the early 1990's, a large number of books and research articles about Web-based teaching have been published. One of the important research areas is the impact of technology on teaching and learning. Kozma (1994) conducted research on how the students interacted in the technological environments and how the media and computers influenced the students' understanding. He argued that the use of technology did have an impact on teaching and learning.

The use of technology in teaching and learning has its positive impact and negative impact. Nott, Riddle, and Pearce's (1995) study indicated that the reaction on the impact of the WWW technology on learning is mixed. One of the weaknesses of Web-based teaching is in the area of collaboration. Chu's (1999) article discussed the development of a real-time interactive Web-based teaching system and analyzed the impact of this system on learning. Based on the factors such as assessment, cost, students' feedback, and collaboration, the research shows that the reaction to the Web-based remote interactive teaching system is also mixed.

As technology advances, the quality of Web-based teaching has been improved significantly. More and more collaboration tools and multimedia teaching materials have been developed to overcome the weaknesses of Web-based teaching. Advanced theories such as artificial intelligence and expert system have also been applied to Web-based teaching. Chau and Sze (2004) developed an artificial intelligence based package for improving the interactivity and effectiveness of online teaching and learning.

For Web based teaching and learning, collaboration is a top concern. Palloff and Pratt (2007) solved the online collaboration problem by creating an online learning community. The instructors and students collaborated in the virtual classrooms through the Internet. Palloff and Pratt (2007) provided many practical tips to guide readers in developing online communities of their own.

As the number of mobile devices is increasing rapidly, wireless and mobile computing technologies have been widely adopted in Web-based teaching to reach out to more students. This has a great advantage if the application interfaces can be automatically generated on mobile devices and PCs. Normally, the hands-on practice requirements by a technology-based course post more challenge for online teaching. Various tools are developed to assist the teaching and learning of such course content. Sarkar (2004) discussed the use of the design tool WLAN-Designer in teaching and learning wireless LAN design.

In various degrees, the open source technology has been involved in the development of instructional technology which has evolved from the traditional mainframe-based technology to today's Web-based technology (Bull & Garofalo, 2002). When the universities started to use computers to assist instruction, all the computing tasks are handled by mainframe computers. Since very little commercial application software was available for a mainframe computer, users needed to write various programs to handle various computing tasks. The source code of these programs was often shared and exchanged among colleagues and students. The openly available source code helped to set up computer-assisted teaching. As the concept of open source code gained popularity, some of the well written programs became open source software. Later, two revolutionary open source software packages reshaped the IT industry. The first one is the World Wide Web invented by Tim Berners-Lee (Stewart, 2001). The World Wide Web is the joint effort of volunteer programmers and is a product of the Internet collaboration. The second significant open source software package is Linux which is an open source version of UNIX (Brashares, 2001).

There are many other open source software tools available for developing and managing the online teaching infrastructure. The purpose of this book is to investigate open source tools and to show how to develop an online teaching/learning system and teaching materials with the open source tools.

OVERVIEW OF OPEN SOURCE TOOLS

The term open source means that the source code of the software is open to the general public with no or minimal copyright restriction. Originally, open source code was available to users in a shared group. The open source code allowed the users to exchange the code and to contribute their effort to improve the code. Later, open source has become a way of software development. In the development process, the software is improved by thousands of users that make the software more stable and versatile. In its short history, the open source software has made several revolutionary changes in the IT industry. Nowadays, the open source concept not only has a tremendous impact on the software industry, but also has become the culture in a manufacturing process that uses the collective effort to gain significant results.

The following will first review some major events in the history of the open source software and then briefly describe the open source related industry and market.

History of Open Source Tools

Using open source materials for teaching and learning has a long history in the field of education. Course materials are always shared among teachers and students. Lecture notes, handouts, lab manuals, and assignments are often developed by using open source materials. Instructors and students can reproduce open source course materials by modifying them to fit their own teaching and learning needs. Education has benefited greatly from the open source approach. This approach is also the main force to motivate the innovation of new technology. In the short history of computer technology development, many of the innovations have been made through the open source approach. The technologies such as the Internet, Web, Linux, and many more are all open source tools. In the following, we will explore some of the major open source tools along with the history of their development.

Internet

The Internet, as we all know, is the backbone of the IT industry. However, the first Internet was the result of the collective effort of an open standard approach. The first significant project done with the open source approach was the Advanced Research Projects Agency Network (ARPANET) project. In the 1960's, a group of researchers were trying to develop a network protocol for the U.S. Department of Defense. By requirements, the new network should be able to stand harsh conditions and keep the communication alive. Certainly, the concept and construction of such a network were new to everyone. The project involved so much knowledge from various academic fields. It was particularly difficult for a small group of people to carry out such a huge project. To make it happen, the researchers adopted the open standard approach to develop the network protocol. Under the open standard, the technologies and resources are available to all the users approved by a committee. These approved users worked for the same project on a consensus basis. As a result, the collective effort created the world's first Internet ARPANET. Although from today's point of view the ARPANET is a bit slower, the project realized a new approach in software development and a legacy of concepts and algorithms that today's Internet industry is still using. The following is the timeline of the ARPANET history.

- **1967:** The first ARPANET design meeting was held in Ann Arbor, Michigan.

- **1968:** Network Working Group was organized to develop protocols for the ARPANET.
- **1970:** Network Control Protocol (NCP), as a host-to-host protocol, was first used by the ARPANET. Also, the first 56kbps cross-country link was installed by AT&T.
- **1972:** The first e-mail program sent messages across the ARPANET.
- **1973:** The first international ARPANET connection to University College of London (England) was established.
- **1975:** The first ARPANET mailing list was created and the first TCP protocol was tested.
- **1982:** The TCP/IP protocol suite was developed for the ARPANET.
- **1985:** The ARPANET was split into two parts, ARPANET and MILNET.
- **1990:** The ARPANET became history.

UNIX

The next significant development of open source software is the UNIX operating system (Hauben, 1994). In the 1960's, AT&T's Bell Labs, General Electric and the Massachusetts Institute of Technology (MIT) jointly created a new operating system called Multiplexed Information and Computing Service (Multics). Later, when the development did not produce the result they had expected, most of the parties withdrew from the project. The remaining developers continued to work on it and renamed the operating system UNICS (or UNIX) instead of Multics. Eventually, UNIX became one of the dominant operating systems for mainframe servers and desktop computers in the 1970's and 1980's. Since then, many different versions of UNIX have been released. However, these versions of UNIX belonged to two different groups, one was proprietary and the other was open source. The proprietary group was led by AT&T. In 1984, AT&T left the open source community and made UNIX a proprietary operating system for mainframe computers. Later, Sun Microsystems, HP, IBM, and Santa Cruz Operation (SCO) became significant members of this group. These companies treated their own versions of UNIX as proprietary products. As a result, the versions of UNIX from different companies are not compatible; this has caused a lot of confusion among customers. Since then, there has been less innovation. The other group was led by the developers of Berkeley Software Distribution (BSD). The developers at University of California, Berkeley have developed some open source UNIX operating systems such as FreeBSD which runs on Intel x86 PCs, NetBSD which runs as a starting point for portability, and OpenBSD which runs as a highly secured operating system. The following is the timeline of the UNIX history.

- **1965:** Bell Labs, General Electric and the Massachusetts Institute of Technology (MIT) decided to jointly create a new operating system called Multics.
- **1969:** AT&T decided to withdraw from the project. Multics was rewritten and was named Uniplexed Information and Computing Service (UNICS or UNIX).
- **1971:** The first edition of UNIX was released.
- **1972:** The programming language C was developed.
- **1977:** The first BSD version of UNIX was released.
- **1982:** Sun developed its version of UNIX called Sun UNIX 0.7.
- **1983:** SCO released its version of UNIX called XENIX System V.
- **1986:** Hewlett-Packard (HP) released its version of UNIX called HP-UX.
- **1990:** IBM released its version of UNIX called Advanced Interactive eXecutive (AIX).
- **1993:** NetBSD 0.8 and FreeBSD 1.0 were released.

Since then, the development of UNIX has been strong. Different versions of UNIX have been upgraded many times. Recently, the BSD versions of UNIX have been upgraded to OpenBSD 4.0, FreeBSD 6.1, and NetBSD 3.0.1. The HP version of UNIX has been upgraded to HP-UX 11i v3 OS; the Sun version of UNIX has been upgraded to Solaris 10 OS; the IBM version of UNIX has been upgraded to AIX Version 6.1. These UNIX operating systems are widely used in various education institutions to support online teaching/learning systems.

World Wide Web

The World Wide Web provides an environment for online teaching and learning. Without the invention of the World Wide Web, e-learning can only be limited to text-style content. The invention of the World Wide Web demonstrates another success story of the open source approach. In 1989, Tim Berners-Lee who worked in CERN was trying to join the hypertext with the Internet, which eventually led to the creation of the World Wide Web. He also invented the first Web server and named it httpd. By 1991, the world's first Web site was presented online. The World Wide Web has no copyright imposed on it. It is available to the general public so that everyone can easily adopt it into their own programs. To make sure that the World Wide Web remains an open source product, the World Wide Web Consortium declared that the World Wide Web is a royalty-free technology (Gillies & Cailliau, 2000). After years of development, the World Wide Web has become one of the most popular ways to exchange information. For online teaching and learning, it is used to present course materials, display students' information, and manage online classes. It can be used to extend a computer lab to anywhere where students can access the Internet. In addition to being used as an online teaching tool, it is also used to build e-commerce. Many successful business models are created on top of the World Wide Web such as Google and Amazom.com. The following briefly describes the timeline of the World Wide Web history.

- **1989:** Tim Berners-Lee proposed the idea to join the hypertext with the Internet.
- **1991:** The World Wide Web was released on central CERN machines and W3 browser was installed on VM/CMS.
- **1993:** CERN decided that the WWW technology is free.
- **1994:** The World Wide Web Consortium was founded.

After years of development, in today's e-learning, the World Wide Web is the technology that online teaching/learning systems have to depend on.

Linux

Another milestone in the development of open source software is the invention of Linux. In 1991, Linus Torvalds, a computer science student, was trying to develop an open source operating system kernel which contained device drivers for controlling hardware devices and a multi-threaded file system for his new PC with an 80386 processor. At that time, there was some other open source software such as GCC - a multiple language compiler, GDB - a debugger, and GNU - a text editor, and so forth. By combining the available open source software, Linus released the first pre-release version of Linux in 1992. In 1994, Version 1 of Linux was released. Licensed under the GNC General Public License, Linux is guaranteed to be free to the general public. Immediately, this new open source operating system attracted a lot of attention from programmers. A year later, thousands of contributions from individuals around the globe were added to the new operating system (Wirzenius, 2003). With these contributions, the size of the Linux operating system grows over 40MB. If the GUI tools and many other utilities are added, a Linux package can take several gigabytes hard drive space. The timeline of the development of Linux is listed below.

- **1987:** MINIX was created for teaching the operating system designed to run on the Intel 8086 microprocessor.
- **1991:** Linux was introduced by Linus to run on the Intel 80386 microprocessor.
- **1994:** The first commercial version of Red Hat Linux was introduced.

- **1996:** The first GUI for Linux/UNIX operating systems K Desktop Environment (KDE) was introduced.
- **2001:** The Linux operating system was introduced in supercomputing.
- **2005:** Four of the top five fastest supercomputers used Linux.

Now, the latest stable version of the Linux kernel has been upgraded to the version 2.6.22.5. Linux has become a popular operating system used on servers, desktop computers, supercomputers, mobile phones, PDAs, and network routers. Linux is now supported by major IT companies such as Dell, Hewlett-Packard, IBM, Novell, and Sun Microsystems.

Java

Another major event in the World Wide Web history is the creation of Java. In the early 1990s, the World Wide Web was widely accepted for exchanging information worldwide. Web site developers need a write-once-and-run-anywhere type of programming language to process data that are generated on the World Wide Web. The open source programming language Java is this kind of programming language. In 1991, a group of researchers, Bill Joy, James Gosling, and several others, from Sun Microsystems were trying to develop a system that could allow electronic devices from heterogeneous networks to communicate with each other. James Gosling's responsibility was to find a programming language for the project. Since the widely used programming language C++ did not meet the requirement, James decided to create a new language, Oak, to get the job done. Since the name Oak had already been used by another programming language, they named the new programming language Java. In 1995, Java 1.0 was available to the general public. At first, Java is a closed source product but is free to the general public (Feizabadi, 2007). In 2007, Java was licensed under the GNU General Public License to make it truly open source. The following timeline briefly describes the development of Java.

- **1991:** A team was formed to create a device-independent programming language named Oak, later named Java.
- **1995:** Java was released and the Java technology was incorporated with the Netscape Navigator Internet browser.
- **1999:** Java 2 with the improved graphical user interface and additional packages was released. Also, the beta version of J2EE designed for enterprise applications was released.
- **2004:** Java 2 Platform, Standard Edition 5 was release.
- **2006:** Java 2 Platform, Standard Edition 6 was release.
- **2007:** Java became open source software.

After years of development, Java is now a platform free, secure, and versatile programming technology.

MySQL

To support e-learning and e-commerce over the Internet, universities and companies need databases to store data. In 1994, a Swedish consulting company called Tcx was trying to use the in-house database management system called UNIREG to manage large databases. Since UNIREG was not designed for Web related tasks, it generated a lot of overhead which was not good for handling dynamic applications such as Web pages. So, Tcx created MySQL which has a client-server system that includes a multithreaded database engine. This kind of database engine allows multiple processes work simultaneously without costing much computation power. In addition to the database engine, MySQL includes user management tools, database servers to host databases, database backup and recovery tools, data presentation tools, and it also supports a wide range of programming languages (Safari, 2007). MySQL is licensed under the GNU General Public License. This makes MySQL open source software. Anyone can download the MySQL source code and use it to suit his/her needs. MySQL API is designed in the way that the third party's code can easily be used with MySQL. In addition, the MySQL database management system is also fast, reliable, and easy to use. These features make MySQL suitable for supporting Web-based applications. After years of development, MySQL is now the most popular open source database management system, which allows the user to add, access, and analyze the data stored in its database. The timeline of MySQL is shown below.

- **1979:** UNIREG was developed for in-house database management.
- **1995:** MySQL was developed for Web related database management tasks.
- **1998:** The Windows version of MySQL was released.
- **2003:** MySQL version 4.0 was released.
- **2005:** MySQL version 5.0 was released.

Currently, MySQL 6 is being developed. The first alpha version of MySQL 6 was released in 2007.

Moodle

To implement online teaching and learning, it is necessary to have a learning management system (LMS) to manage the online teaching and learning related activities. Martin Dougiamas, a former WebCT administrator at Curtin University, is one of the researchers who devoted their time, energy, and intelligence to the development of open source software for e-learning. In 1999, Moodle which is the acronym of Modular Object-Oriented Dynamic Learning Environment was evolved as an e-learning management tool, and Martin Dougiamas is the creator of Moodle. The timeline of Moodle development is shown below.

- **1998:** Some preliminary work was done for developing Moodle.
- **2001:** Moodle was released to early testers.
- **2002:** Moodle version 1.0 was released.
- **2006:** Moodle 1.6 was released.

In the above, we have looked at several major events that are related to online teaching in the history of open source software. There are so many open source tools that have been developed to accomplish various tasks. These tools will be categorized and described later. Next, let us investigate the open source software market and how it impacts the IT industry.

Open Source Market

In the short history, open source tools have been developed from code sharing to an enterprise-level software industry. Often, products that have the fastest development in each branch of the IT industry are open source products. Even in the fast changing condition, open source tools can often maintain their popularity, reliability, and robustness. In the following, we will take a closer look at how the IT market is influenced by the open source products.

The success of the Internet, World Wide Web, Linux, Java, and a lot of other open source software has generated a huge software market to compete with their commercial counterparts. As early as 1999, a memo from Microsoft considered open source software a major competition. Since then, the growth of open source tools has been substantial. Nowadays, open source tools are significant players in e-commerce, e-learning, and e-government. Also, the open source technology is the market leader in portable computing devices such as PDAs and cell phones.

For open source software, the software itself is free. The revenue is from service and support. This indicates that the revenue of the open source market is long term. According to Information Data Group (IDC), the adoption of open source software will accelerate through the year 2011 (Lawton & Notarfonzo, 2007). In the year 2006, the stand-alone open source software market value was about 1.8 billion dollars. By the year 2011, its market value will reach 5.8 billion dollars. Since open source software is free, the actual usage of open source software is much larger than what is indicated by the market value.

Since the invention of the ARPANET, the Internet technology has been improved significantly and the open source technology is the key factor in the Internet improvement. The Internet related open source technologies such as DNS, sendmail, TCP/IP network protocols and the Web programming languages such as Perl are founding stones of today's Internet. In the Web server market, the dominant Web server is Apache which is open source software. The award-winning Web browser Firefox is considered by many users as a faster, safer, and easy-to-use browser.

Originally, Linux is a PC version UNIX-like operating system. After years of development, it is not just a fast and efficient PC operating system any more. Today's Linux kernel has the 64-bit CPU support for symmetric multiprocessing and the support for enterprise-level network management. These features make Linux suitable to work as a server operating system for hosting large databases and large scale network management. Linux is known as a stable, versatile, and secure enterprise-level operating system and it is a major competitor of Microsoft Windows operating system. Among the server operating systems, Linux has been one of the fastest growing software since 1998. In 2006, the Linux server revenue grew 6.1 percent (Shankland, 2006). As mentioned earlier about open source software, the Linux revenue is only from the service and support. There should have been a larger number of Linux servers actually installed. Due to the popularity of Linux, major system vendors such as IBM, HP, and Sun are pushing Linux hard to their customers.

The Linux operating system includes a kernel and a lot of other open source software such as tools for text editing, network management, and GUI. Such an operating system may contain millions of lines of code. Many vendors have realized that they can make profit by synchronizing the tools included in Linux, making installation CDs, writing user's manuals, and providing technical support. These types of companies are vendors of Linux distributions. The well known Linux distribution vendors are Red Hat, SUSE, and Mandriva. They sell their own versions of Linux with a small cost.

Unlike its strong presence on the server market, Linux is relatively weaker on the desktop computer market. However, Linux is catching up. In recent years, in addition to the vendors such as Sun and IBM who have been pre-installing the Linux operating system on their PCs for a long time, other major computer hardware vendors such as Dell, Lenovo, and HP have started to pre-install the Linux operating system on their laptop and desktop computers. Cost efficiency is one of the advantages of Linux, which is the reason why Linux has a strong presence in the developing countries. As Linux is gaining momentum on the desktop operating system market, almost all of the major software producers have been developing Linux versions of their software.

As indicated above that Linux is not just another open source operating system, a significant portion of the IT industry is developed around Linux. A large number of server and desktop hardware devices and many software packages are produced to run on Linux. Based on the prediction of IDC, by the year 2008, the combined worldwide market revenue for desktops, servers, and packaged software that would run on Linux would exceed $35 billion (Keizer, 2004).

One of the objectives of Java is to match the World Wide Web. Therefore, major Web browser vendors quickly adopt Java to enhance the functionalities of their Web pages. In the computing history, Java's adoption rate has been faster than any other programming language. Java is not only a write-once-and-run-anywhere programming language, it is also reliable and secure, which is suitable for network computing. Worldwide, there are over 6.5 million Java software developers, and Java powers over 4.5 billion network devices, hand-held devices, and computers (Java, 2008).

Due to its high performance and reliability, MySQL is the world's most popular open source database management system. According to MySQL.com (2008), there are over 50,000 downloads from MySQL's Web site per day. MySQL is also a fast growing database management system on the DBMS market. As a low cost, secure, and reliable database management system, MySQL has been adopted by various companies sizing from small businesses to leading IT organizations to support their information systems. Now, MySQL has the enterprise-grade reliability. By supporting the advanced features in the SQL 2003 standard, MySQL is the most cost-effective database management system for supporting e-commerce applications.

Since 1999, Moodle has been widely accepted by the e-learning community. Now, Moodle has over 400,000 registered users, speaking over 75 languages in 193 countries. Moodle creates a truly diversified learning environment where different groups of users can learn in different languages (Moodle, 2008).

It is interesting to know that people with experience in open source tools are highly demanded in the IT industry. Brandel (2007) pointed out that job hunters with open source skills would be sure to find employment. She said that there was a rising interest among employers to hire IT professionals who have experience in working with Linux, Apache, MySQL, and PHP, referred to as LAMP.

ROLES OF OPEN SOURCE TECHNOLOGY IN ONLINE TEACHING

As mentioned earlier that the open source technology has been and will play an important role in the IT industry. Undoubtedly, open source software has been involved in many parts of the online teaching infrastructure. In the following, we will look at how open source software is used to meet the requirements of online teaching and learning.

In the previous subsection, we investigated the impact of open source tools on the market and IT industry. The impact has been significant. It is true that the open source tools can be an important player in the development of an online teaching/learning system. To develop a better online teaching/learning system, it is necessary for online teaching designers and developers to understand the roles played by these open source tools in developing and supporting an online teaching/learning system.

To allow students to remotely access online course materials, universities that offer online courses much establish well-developed Web sites and must have well-maintained Internet connection. During the review of the history of the open source tools, we learned that both the Internet and World Wide Web were invented through the open source approach. We cannot imagine that we can offer online courses without these two open source tools. The major Internet communication protocols and the most used Web server software are still open source tools. Even though some of the Web browsers are not open source software, they are free due to the influence of open source software. Linux, as an open source operating system, includes commonly used Internet communication protocols, network management tools, Web servers, Web development tools, and Web browsers.

To manage Internet communication and to host Web servers, we need server operating systems. From the discussion of Linux in the exploration of its history, we know that Linux is a powerful, secure, reliable, and low cost operating system that can handle all the tasks of online courses. Linux can be used to handle the communication over the Internet and manage network security. It provides many open source tools to handle various hardware devices such as those used for the collaboration and multimedia content. It can also be used to host learning management systems, databases, and other application software. In summary, an online teaching infrastructure has the following components that can be implemented by Linux:

- Linux computers are great to be used as Web servers due to its strong secure features.
- Being able to run on older personal computers, Linux can be used to easily convert those older computers to print servers, firewalls, network routers, and many other useful devices.
- Intranet can also take advantage of the cost effective Linux computers. The Linux computers can be used as file servers, VPN servers, and various devices mentioned previously.
- The advantages of Linux make it a great learning tool. With minimum cost, Linux can be used to meet the hands-on practice requirements of many

technology-based online courses such as programming, networking, system administration, and Internet computing.

- Due to its stability, Linux is suitable to be used to support database servers. Oracle has a free version database management system specially designed for Linux.
- The Linux server operating system has been used on network servers. It provides many network management tools to help network administrators to get the job done quickly and easily.
- Linux is great for distributed computing. Often, it is a major player in the grid computing and cluster computing environments.

There are other roles that can be played by Linux in an online teaching/learning system. We will have more detailed discussion in later chapters when we are dealing with specific tasks.

For courses that need the support of a learning management system, there are some open source learning management systems such as Moodle. As an open source learning management tool, Moodle can handle various course and knowledge management tasks. The following are roles that can be played by Moodle:

- Moodle can be used for course Web site management. It can be used to schedule online courses and manage activity modules, quizzes and grades.
- Moodle supports collaboration components such as forums, chats, and workshops.
- Moodle can be used to manage students' accounts. It supports several authentication schemes.
- To enforce security measures, Moodle provides several tools for data encryption, certification, and decryption.
- Moodle supports tools for developing and managing course content.
- Moodle supports a truly diversified learning environment. It allows students to specify their own languages, identify their time zones, and create their own accounts.
- Moodle can communicate with external databases to query and store information from and to those databases.
- Moodle provides remote access tools to help students to remotely access course content.
- Moodle also provides a good performance analyzing tool which can be used to analyze teaching efficiency and students' performance.

As application software, Moodle can be installed on servers with the Linux operating system. Moodle supports the Web browsers installed on the Linux desktop operating system.

In an online teaching/learning system, databases are used to store the user and course related content. MySQL, a popular open source database management system, can be used to accomplish the following tasks in an online teaching/learning system:

- MySQL databases can be used to store student information and course information.
- With the built-in database design tools, MySQL can be used to accomplish database design tasks.
- MySQL provides tools for developing and managing a data warehouse which can hold terabytes of information.
- MySQL provides tools for assisting data transaction between a database and other data sources.
- MySQL is also a database management tool for database administration, database backup and recovery, performance tuning, and troubleshooting.
- MySQL provides a strong support for enterprise-level Web-based database application development.
- To query the information stored in databases, MySQL supports SQL and many other programming languages such as PHP, Perl, Python, Java, C#, Ruby, Groovy, AJAX, and so on.
- As an open source database management tool, MySQL allows the customization of software for better service and performance.
- MySQL provides a data analysis tool to support business intelligence applications.
- The encryption and decryption functions provided by MySQL can be used for data security management. MySQL can manage user accounts down to a client's desktop computer.

As we can see in the above, from design to implementation, MySQL is involved in each step of the development of an online teaching/learning system. MySQL is platform flexible. It supports Linux, UNIX, and Windows operating systems.

The Java technology is the combination of both a programming language and an enterprise-level application development platform. Java is a general-purpose programming language. It is a powerful platform for developing, compiling, and deploying portable application software. In an online teaching/learning system development process, Java can be used to accomplish the following tasks:

- Java is designed for creating network-based applications. Therefore, it is very popular among developers who develop and deploy World Wide Web applications.
- It provides built-in classes for developing applications, managing networks, generating XML code, and accessing databases.
- Java's user interface tools can be used to create sophisticated GUI used by an online teaching/learning system.
- Java's popularity is not just limited to the World Wide Web. Among universities, Java is a popular programming language used in teaching computer programming, data structure, operating systems, Internet computing, and many other courses.

Java is one of the programming languages supported by the Linux operating system. The combination of Linux, Moodle, MySQL, and Java provides a complete solution to construct a fully functioning online teaching/learning system.

Now, we have investigated some important roles played by some of the major open source tools. In later chapters, we will discuss these roles in detail.

Before using the open source tools to develop an online teaching/learning system, let us investigate the strengths and weaknesses of the open source technology. The result of the investigation will help us make a better decision on using the open source tools.

STRENGTHS AND WEAKNESSES OF OPEN SOURCE TECHNOLOGY

In this section, we will analyze the strengths and weaknesses of the open source technology. The reason that the open source software has been so successful is due to the strengths of the open source approach:

- Unlike a commercial software project that requires adequate funding to get the project started, an open source software project can be started with very little funding. If the open source software has a market, other developers will join the project.
- The open source approach does not require a group of experienced developers to provide a total solution to users' IT problems. It adds required components piece by piece based on when a component is needed.
- The installation and deployment of open source software does not require license fees and other service charges.

- Open source software is designed so that it is relatively easy to include other open source software into the software that you are currently using.
- Open source software developers are often those who have the first hand experience. These developers can detect errors in the source code and fix them right away with the open source debugging tools.
- Every open source user can be a developer, which means open source software is supported a very large developer community for error reporting and problem solving.
- Open source software is often the result of research done by researchers in higher education institutions. These researchers not only bring new ideas into the software development project, but also provide analyses and improvement of the software.
- Due to the low cost and availability, the open source technology is very popular among higher education institutions. It is easier for the students to adopt open source software in their work and research after they graduate.
- One of the reasons that open source tools have been adopted by many companies is because of its flexibility. When technology changes, software needs to follow the change. Open source software allows users to add or modify the current code to implement the change.
- After a commercial product is upgraded to a new version, it often means that the older version of the software is less supported and soon it brings the end of the older version of the product. However, for an open source product, there is no such pressure to stop using it since the open source product does not depend on the support team of a product vendor.

Like many things that have pros and cons, the open source approach has its own weaknesses. For many open source products, the following are some of the common weaknesses.

- In general, there is less marketing effort for open source products. There is only minimal spending on advertising open source products.
- There is lack of investment on open source products.
- There is lack of well written user manuals for open source products.

Linux, as an open source operating system, is particularly important since it is related to many other open source products. When compared with other server operating systems, Linux has the following advantages.

- Linux is known as a cost effective operating system. Open source tools have significant lower initial cost. It is basically a free product. Even though some

Linux distribution vendors may charge a small service fee, it is usually less than $100.

- The availability of Linux is another advantage that makes Linux popular. Linux operating system distributions can be conveniently downloaded from the distributions' Web sites. Open source tool providers also allow users to download various useful tools from their Web sites anytime and anywhere.
- Linux has a large user community. When encountering a technical problem, you can always get help from other users who may know better about the problem. Unlike proprietary software vendors whose customers often have to wait for technical support to help since only few people know about the details of their products.
- Due to the fact that Linux is updated by thousands of volunteers constantly, Linux is more portable and much easier to write application software for.
- Linux has a relatively small kernel. It is easy to fit various versions of Linux in different storage media. For portability, the Linux operating system can run on a single CD disk. A simplified Linux operating system can even fit in a floppy disk to convert PCs to network routers. Also, Linux is small enough to be able to fit in various portable devices.
- Another great feature of Linux is that it can be run on older personal computers. It does not require expensive hardware equipment. It can work well on older hardware technologies. This is particularly important for the economically disadvantaged areas. When updating the operating system, people do not have to throw away their older computers. With the Linux operating system, the older computers can also be used as print servers, firewalls, and network routers.
- Due to its simplicity, Linux is very stable and reliable. Compared with other operating systems, Linux seldom needs to be rebooted.
- Due to its stability, Linux is suitable to be used as a database server. As mentioned earlier, Oracle has a free version database management system specifically designed for Linux.

On the other hand, Linux may have the following disadvantages. Some of these disadvantages may be due to lack of marketing effort and others may be due to lack of consistency among Linux distributions.

- Since most of the desktop computers are equipped with commercial operating systems, some users may not be familiar with the Linux technology. They perceive Linux as not easy to use and are reluctant to use Linux.
- When having technical problems, some of the users are accustomed to calling technical support of commercial product providers. They are not used to

finding answers from someone in the Linux user community. They consider Linux as less supported and less reliable.

- Linux from different distributions are not exactly matching each other. This may confuse some users.
- Although the total cost of Linux is less than a commercial product, Linux may not be completely free due to the expense on the support and services. Some of the distributions may also charge fees for tools added to Linux.
- Some of the system administrators may worry about the compatibility with other open source software after a server operating system is updated with a new version of Linux.
- It takes time for someone to write a driver for a new hardware product. Therefore, for some newly developed hardware equipment, drivers may not be available for Linux.

Now that we have investigated the strengths and weaknesses of the open source tools, let us take a look at the topics to be discussed in this book.

BOOK FRAMEWORK

In this section, we will first review the objectives of the book. We will take a look at what is covered in this book. Secondly, we will examine how the book is organized. This section will briefly describe the content of each chapter and how the chapters are related to each other.

Book Objectives

The mission of this book is to help instructors and technical practitioners develop online teaching/learning systems and Web-based teaching materials for online courses with open source tools. The first goal of this book is to provide the technical information about the online teaching related open source tools in general and the Linux technology in particular. The book will discuss two types of open source tools.

The first type includes open source tools that are used for offering online courses. That is, the open source tools that can be used to accomplish the following tasks.

- Tools used to host online courses, such as servers and database tools.
- Tools used to manage online courses, such as learning management systems.

- Tools used to deliver online courses, such as network and remote access tools.
- Tools required by hands-on practice, such as the tools needed by technology-based courses.

The second type includes those tools that can be used to develop course materials. These tools may include Web authoring tools, multimedia tools, and collaboration tools.

The second goal of this book is to show how to use the open source tools to develop and manage online courses.

This book will discuss the hands-on practice requirements and the strategies to use open source tools in instructional design processes. It will provide information on what open source tools are available and where to find them. The book will describe the functionalities of the related open source tools and demonstrate how these functionalities can be used for teaching online courses. The pros and cons of these open source tools will also be discussed. The book will illustrate how to implement online courses with the open source tools. The implementation difficulties of using these open source tools will also be investigated. Moreover, this book will show how the Linux technology and the open source instructional technology can affect and improve teaching and learning.

Book Organization

As the book title indicates, this book is about using open source tools in online teaching and learning. To better understand how the open source tools are used in the development of an online teaching/learning system and to create Web based materials, one needs to thoroughly understand the entire system development process. Therefore, we will use the following approach in this book. We will first go through each phase of the online teaching/learning system development process. While we learn about the requirements for each phase of the development process and the tasks that need to be accomplished to meet the requirements, we will explore the open source tools and discuss how the open source tools can be used to accomplish these tasks.

According to the instructional technology theory, the instructional design model ADDIE can be used as a guideline for the development of an online teaching/learning system and the development of online teaching materials. The ADDIE model has five phases, Analyze-Design-Develop-Implement-Evaluate. This book will follow the ADDIE model to layout its content. Starting from Chapter 2, we will discuss each phase of the development. Along the development process, the application of open source tools will be added into the discussion whenever these tools are needed.

This book is organized into twelve chapters. These chapters are categorized into four general sections, Introduction, Infrastructure Development for Offering Online Courses, Course Material Development for Online Courses, and Trends and Advances. Each section focuses on a different aspect of open source tools for online teaching and learning. The following briefly describes the chapters and how they are related.

Section I: Introduction. This is an introduction section that includes three chapters, Chapter I, Chapter II, and Chapter III. This section provides an overview of open source products. To help readers understand how to properly apply the open source products to the development of an online teaching/learning system, this section introduces the instructional technology theory and the procedure of needs analysis which is the first phase of the ADDIE model.

Chapter II reviews the instructional technology theory in general. Since one of the book's goals is to show how to use the open source tools to develop and manage online courses, the theory of instructional technology can be used to guide the development process. Developing an online teaching/learning system is a complex process that needs to be thoroughly planned. The system must be carefully designed before it can be implemented. The development of online teaching requires the knowledge on project scheduling and management. After the online teaching/learning system is developed, the next task is to implement the system by deploying and maintaining the system to make it available to users. Once the system is implemented, it will need a well designed evaluation plan to get feedback which can be used to further improve the implemented system. This chapter covers the topics such as online teaching/learning system design, development, implementation, and evaluation.

According to the instructional technology theory, the analysis of technology requirements for an online teaching/learning system is a crucial step in the development process. In chapter III, we will get into some details about the technology requirement analysis. Chapter III discusses the requirements for computer systems, networks, learning management systems, application software, collaboration tools, and course materials.

Section II: Infrastructure Development for Offering Online Courses. This section discusses the components in an online teaching/learning system development process. It includes six chapters, Chapter IV, Chapter V, Chapter VI, Chapter VII, Chapter VIII, and Chapter IX. Each chapter covers a major component. Based on the analysis conducted in Chapter III, the open source products are introduced for each component.

Based on the technology requirement analysis, we will investigate the network related open source tools that can be used to achieve the design goals. First, Chapter IV discusses the client-server architecture on which an online teaching/learning system will be developed. Then, this chapter will look into network equipment. The next topic in this chapter is about network management related open source tools. Then, the chapter uses an example to demonstrate the network development process for an online teaching/learning system.

To make a course available online, the course content and course management software need to be supported by various servers. Chapter V discusses the issues related to computer systems on the server side. Linux, as a server operating system, will be the main focus of the discussion in Chapter V. Linux Enterprise Server is an open source network operating system which is used to handle network management; it also hosts databases, learning management systems, and Web servers. It is used to store course materials and students' information. It allows students to remotely access information through the Internet. This chapter also investigates some server equipment that supports the Linux operating system. The next topic in this chapter concerns open source system management tools, especially those included in the Linux operating system. This chapter also introduces various virtual server technologies which play an important role in online computer lab management. The last part of this chapter uses an example to demonstrate a server development process for an online teaching/learning system.

Chapter VI discusses the issues related to database system development. This chapter first explores some of the open source database management systems. Then, it discusses some database design, development, and implementation issues. It covers database management related topics. Lastly, this chapter uses an example to illustrate the installation and configuration of MySQL on a server with the Linux operating system.

Chapter VII introduces the open source tools used for class management. Learning management system (LMS) software is commonly used to support course setup, management, and assessment. While managing online courses, a learning management system keeps the information of students and classes in a database which serves as the data center for information management. Many LMS software packages also provide tools for developing multimedia course materials and tools for collaboration. This chapter discusses these open source class management tools for accomplishing specific tasks. Then, it gives an example of the installation and configuration of an LMS on a Linux server.

Chapter VIII discusses security related issues. Security is very important for an online teaching/learning system. This chapter will first examine the security policy for an online teaching/learning system. It will discuss the process of creating a well defined security policy. The next topic in this chapter is about the issues related to vulnerability assessment. It will investigate the vulnerabilities and explore some of the vulnerability assessment tools. This chapter also explores other open source security tools used to enforce various security measures. At the end, it gives an example of security management for an online teaching/learning system.

Chapter IX discusses computer systems and tools for the client side of an online teaching/learning system. It discusses open source operating systems. Again, the Linux desktop operating system is the main focus in this chapter. Some open source tools for the Linux desktop operating system management are also discussed. This chapter examines the Linux desktop operating system, desktop environment, and desktop management tools. The last topic to be discussed in this chapter is about open source remote access tools. The issues related to the configuration of the remote access tools are investigated and an example is given.

Section III: Course Material Development for Online Courses. This section covers the issues related to developing course materials with open source products. Two chapters, Chapter X and Chapter XI, are included in this section.

Starting from Chapter X, the focus will be on the subjects related to course material development. Since technology-based courses and Web-based teaching all rely heavily on technology, there is no doubt that the instructional technology theory and practice will greatly influence the teaching and learning. The theories of instructional design and instruction technology will be used to guide the development process. Due to the fact that application of the instructional design theory in developing course content has been well studied by many researchers, the chapter will focus more on the technology side of the discussion. It will examine some open source Web authoring, multimedia, and collaboration tools. Then, it will give a comprehensive example to illustrate how to use the open source tools to develop course materials to meet the objectives of the instructional design.

Chapter XI deals with the issues of implementation and evaluation. After online course materials are developed, the next task is to deploy the course materials. Issues related to the online teaching material deployment is discussed. A successful online teaching/learning system also needs a group of experienced computer service personnel who manage the course Web sites and the students who are taking the online courses. This chapter also discusses technical support and training. The development of online course materials takes a lot of effort. The course materials may not be created perfectly at the first time. The improvement of the course materials will depend on the feedback from the users, in our case, the students and instructors. The feedback can be used as a guideline for future improvement. The development of online teaching materials is a cycle of designing, development, implementation, testing, and evaluation. The last topic in Chapter XI is related to the evaluation of courses and course materials.

Section IV: Trends and Advances. This section has one chapter, Chapter XII, which is about the trends in the development of online teaching/learning systems and course materials.

Chapter XII is the last chapter of the book. It discusses the trends in online teaching and learning related technologies and their applications. It describes new features which can significantly improve an online teaching/learning system. Chapter XII also analyzes the impact of new and emerging technologies on online teaching and learning.

CONCLUSION

This chapter has introduced open source tools. It first provided an overview of the open source tools. It reviewed the history of several major open source tools. It also looked at the market impact of these open source tools. It then described the role of the open source tools in developing an online teaching/learning system. It showed that a combination of open source tools such as the Internet technology, Linux, Moodle, MySQL, and Java can provide a powerful solution for developing a sophisticated online teaching/learning system. Then, the chapter analyzed the strengths and weaknesses of the open source tools. The analysis can provide a guideline for making decisions on the selection of technologies for developing an online teaching/learning system. Lastly, this chapter presented the framework of the book. The framework briefly described the content to be covered in this book and how the content is organized.

REFERENCES

Berge, Z. L. (2000). *Sustaining distance training: Integrating learning technologies into the fabric of the enterprise*. San Francisco, CA: Jossey-Bass.

Brandel, M. (2007). 12 IT skills that employers can't say no to. *ComputerWorld*. Retrieved August 6, 2007, from http://www.computerworld.com/action/article.do?command=viewArticleBasic&articleId=9026623&pageNumber=4

Brashares, A. (2001). *Linus Torvalds: Software rebel*. Kirkland, WA: 21st Century Publishing.

Bull, G., & Garofalo, J. (2002). Proceedings of the Fourth National Technology Leadership Summit: Open resources in education. *CITE Journal, 2*(4), 530-555.

Chau, K., & Sze, Y. (2004). AI-based teaching package for open channel flow on Internet. In W. Liu, Y. Shi & Q. Li (Eds.), *Advances in Web Based Learning – ICWL 2004. Third International Conference, Beijing China, August 2004* (pp. 98-105).

Chu, K. C. (1999). The development of a Web-based teaching system for engineering education. *Engineering Science and Education Journal, 8*(3), 115-118.

CRIENGLISH.com (2008). *Rising cost of gas raises online enrollment.* Retrieved July 20, 2008, from http://english.cri.cn/4026/2008/07/10/1361s379210.htm

Feizabadi, S. (2007). *History of Java.* Retrieved August 6, 2007, from http://ei.cs.vt.edu/book/chap1/java_hist.html

Gillies, J., & Cailliau, R. (2000). *How the Web Was Born: The Story of the World Wide Web.* Oxford, England: Oxford University Press.

Hall, K. A. (1970). *Computer assisted instruction: Status in Pennsylvania.* Bureau of Educational Research, Pennsylvania Department of Education.

Hauben, R. (1994). *History of UNIX.* Retrieved August 6, 2007, from http://www.dei.isep.ipp.pt/~acc/docs/unix.html

Horton, W., & Horton, K. (2003). *E-learning tools and technologies: A consumer's guide for trainers, teachers, educators, and instructional designers.* Indianapolis, IN: Wiley.

Java (2008). *Learn about Java technology.* Retrieved July 12, 2008, from http://www.java.com/en/about

Keizer, G. (2004). *Linux to ring up $35 billion by 2008.* Retrieved August 26, 2007, from http://www.techweb.com/wire/showArticle.jhtml?articleID=55800522

Kozma, R. B. (1994). Will media influence learning? Reframing the debate. *Educational Technology Research and Development, 42*(2), 7-19.

Lawton, M., & Notarfonzo, R. (2007). *Worldwide open source software business models 2007-2011 forecast: A preliminary view.* Retrieved August 6, 2007, from http://www.idc.com/getdoc.jsp?containerId=206681

Moodle. (2008). *Moodle community.* Retrieved July 11, 2008, from http://moodle.org

MySQL.com (2008). *MySQL.* Retrieved July 15, 2008, from http://www.mysql.com

Nott, M. W., Riddle, M. D., & Pearce, J. M. (1995). Enhancing traditional university science teaching using the World Wide Web. In I. Selwood, P. Fox, & M. Tebbutt

(Eds.), *Conference Abstracts of WCCE95, the Sixth IFIP World Conference Computers in Education* (p. 12). Birmingham, England: Aston University.

Palloff, R. M., & Pratt, K. (2007). *Building online learning communities: Effective strategies for the virtual classroom.* San Francisco, CA: Jossey-Bass.

Safari (2007). *MySQL*. Retrieved August 6, 2007 from http://safari.oreilly.com/0596002114/msql2-CHP-1-SECT-6#X2ludGVybmFsX1RvYz94bWxpZD0-wNTk2MDAyMTE0L21zcWwyLUNIUC0x

Sarkar, N. I. (2004). WLAN-Designer: A Web-based software tool to enhance teaching and learning wireless LAN design. In *Proceedings of Fourth IEEE International Conference on Advanced Learning Technologies, 2004 (ICALT'04)* (pp. 624-628).

Shankland, S. (2006). *Sun gains server market share.* Retrieved August 6, 2007, from http://news.zdnet.co.uk/hardware/0,1000000091,39281575,00.htm?r=1

Sloan Consortium (2006). *Making the grade: Online education in the United States, 2006.* Retrieved August 15, 2007, from http://www.sloan-c.org/publications/survey/survey06.asp

Stewart, M. (2001). *Tim Berners-Lee: Inventor of the World Wide Web.* Chicago, IL: Ferguson Publishing Company.

Szabo, M., & Montgomery, T. (1992). Two decades of research on computer-managed instruction. *Journal of Research on Computing in Education, 25*(1), 113-133.

Wirzenius, L. (2003). *Linux: The big picture.* Retrieved August 6, 2007, from http://liw.iki.fi/liw/texts/linux-the-big-picture.html

Chapter II
Instructional Technology Theory for Online Teaching/Learning System

INTRODUCTION

In Chapter I, a brief introduction to open source tools is presented. The discussion indicates that open source tools are necessary for an online teaching/learning system. As mentioned in Chapter I, this book will use the ADDIE model as a guideline for the development of an online teaching/learning system and online course materials. Along with the development process, the open source tools will be introduced to accomplish the tasks in each phase of the development.

Chapter I points out that it is possible to use open source tools to develop an entire online teaching/learning system. However, the development process is complicated and involves various technologies. Therefore, before an online teaching/learning system can be implemented, it is necessary to carefully design such a system and the development process should be thoroughly planned. The theory of instructional technology provides a guideline for developing a successful online teaching/learning system. It will be beneficial for the development of an online teaching/learning system if the developers of the system know how to apply the instructional technology theory to the development process.

In this chapter, we will discuss the issues related to planning and designing an online teaching/learning system. A more systematic approach will be discussed for developing online teaching/learning system projects. We will start with the general theory of instructional design. The discussion will show the big picture about an online teaching/learning system development process. We will have an overview of the stages of an online teaching/learning system development process, which provides clues for what to accomplish in the development process.

The first stage in the theory of instructional technology is the design stage. There are three phases at the design stage, conceptual design, logical design, and physical design. The conceptual design phase is about collecting information of users' views and requirements about the project. The users in our project are university administrators, faculty members, staff members, and students. Once the project designers obtain the information they need, the next phase is to translate the users' views and requirements to technical terms and to model an online teaching/learning system based on the collected information. This phase is called logical design. The next design phase is the physical design phase. Its task is to specify the technologies and infrastructure for the project.

The conceptual design will be covered under the topic Online Teaching/Learning Needs Analysis. We will identify the requirements for teaching and hands-on practice. The requirements for an online teaching/learning system depend on the requirements for teaching. This chapter provides you with a systematic way of identifying teaching requirements. The logical design and physical design will be covered by the topic Online Teaching/Learning System Design. In this topic, a conceptual design will be converted to a logical model. Then, the components of the logical model will be specified with technical terms. These technical specifications will allow us to select open source tools in later chapters.

After a system is properly designed, the next stage is system development. At the development stage, the system is physically constructed. Based on the technology analysis, we can figure out what type of online teaching/learning system should be developed. However, system development will be affected by several other factors, such as teaching requirements, cost, ease of learning, and support from the institution. In addition to issues related to system construction, we will discuss the issues related to identifying resources, assessing cost, scheduling the project's timeline, and forming the project's development team. Investigating these topics will help you decide how the online teaching/learning system should be built and what to do to support the online teaching/learning system in the future. The online teaching/learning system to be developed should balance the support, cost, and the complexity of technologies. The development stage will be discussed under the topic Online Teaching/Learning System Development.

After the online teaching/learning system is developed, the next stage is the implementation stage. During the implementation stage, the tasks to be accomplished are online teaching/learning system deployment and management. The goal at this stage is to make the course materials available for teaching whenever and wherever they are needed. We will discuss the issues related to service and support on content delivery, technical support management, resource management, training management, workload management, and security management. The topic Online Teaching/Learning System Implementation will discuss the issues related to system deployment. The issues related to technical support and system management will also be discussed under this topic.

The last stage of the online teaching/learning system development process is the evaluation stage, which will verify if the system meets the requirements. The evaluation result can be used as a guideline for further improvement. As a complex and comprehensive project, the newly implemented online teaching/learning system is far from perfect. Users' feedback is the key for improving the system. This chapter will also discuss the issues of creating a well designed evaluation plan to get feedback from the users such as the students and instructors. The discussion of these issues will be covered under the topic Online Teaching/Learning System Evaluation.

BACKGROUND

In the early days of e-learning, online teaching/learning systems focused on a single subject or an individual course. After years of development, today's online teaching/learning systems can handle the teaching and learning requirements of a globalized university. They can support courses offered on multiple campuses located at many locations of the world. They can manage teaching and learning of different cultures and in different languages. Such an online teaching/learning system can be as complicated as an e-commerce system for a multi-national cooperation. A systematic approach to creating an e-commerce system can be guided by the information technology solution development theory. A solution development process contains five major stages: Analyzing business requirements and identifying the process and infrastructure related to the requirements, designing and validating a solution to meet the requirements, constructing the solution, deploying and managing the solution, and evaluating the solution. A solution development process consists of two components, software development and infrastructure deployment. Solution development processes can be applied to various projects such as modeling a health system (Chong, Clark, Morris, & Welsh, 2005) and designing a grid computing system (Meliksetian, et al., 2004).

An online teaching/learning system development process can be considered a special case of a general solution development process. Similar to the information technology solution development, instructional technology is about the theory and practice of design, development, utilization, management, and evaluation of processes and resources for learning (Seels & Richey, 1994). The development of an online teaching/learning system involves both components of the solution development. Even though it is hard to find publications that directly deal with the design, development, and implementation of an online teaching/learning system with the instructional technology theory, there are some publications that discuss some specific areas. For example, Yu and Liu's (2006) paper illustrates how to make use of scenario, prototype and participatory design principles in an online teaching system design process. Horton's (2000) book gives a comprehensive overview of Web-based training from system design, development, to implementation. In this chapter, in general, we will apply each stage of the instructional technology theory to an online teaching/learning development process. In later chapters, more specific details will be discussed.

The design of an online teaching/learning system also involves the design of course materials. The idea of using a systematic approach to designing instruction is well discussed by Dick, Carey, and Carey (2004). They argue that, in addition to the elements such as teachers, students, and teaching materials, the environment plays a crucial role in a learning system. Building an online teaching/learning system is creating a learning environment and can greatly benefit from the research of instructional design. In instructional design theory, a generic model for designing teaching materials is called the ADDIE model which stands for Analyze-Design-Develop-Implement-Evaluate. The course material development process covered in this book basically fits into this model. Instructional design is a well studied field. Readers can find major results in research from the works of Kruse and Keil (2000) for designing, developing, and delivering a Web-based training system, the works of Reigeluth (1999) for instructional design theories and models, and the works by Dick, Carey, and Carey (2004) for the systematic instructional design theory. Readers who want to learn more about the trends of instructional design theories and practice may consider Reiser and Dempsey's (2006) book. They discuss the trends and issues in the instructional design field and how technology will affect the future of this field.

ONLINE TEACHING/LEARNING NEEDS ANALYSIS

For an online teaching/learning project, there are two types of requirements. The first type of requirement is the need to develop an online teaching infrastructure which is used to host course materials and to support users' access to the online course materials. The second type of requirement is the need of tools to develop course materials including interaction, collaboration, and multimedia. Here, we will analyze the needs for both the development of an infrastructure and the tools used to assist the development of course materials.

In the following, we will first examine some online courses to see what the needs are for delivering online courses and for hands-on practice. We will then identify the requirements for tools used to create online course materials. Lastly, some tips will be provided on collecting information.

Requirements for Delivering Online Courses

Different types of online courses require different kinds of online teaching/learning systems. Some courses only require an Internet connection and a learning management system, and other courses may require additional technologies such as database servers or online programming packages for hands-on practice. The requirements can be categorized into the following types.

Courses that Need Learning Management Systems

It is relatively easy to implement the e-learning platform for a course that only requires the support from a learning management system. For this type of course, all you need is a well established learning management system for posting online course materials and managing students' assignments. Through the learning management system, students can submit their completed assignments. The submitted assignments will be graded by using the tools included in the learning management system. Hosting the learning management system requires a server with a reliable network connection. The server is a relatively powerful computer system. The learning management system can be used to generate the course Web site. The server side also needs a database management system for managing the course and student related data. A college or university may have already installed such a learning management system and a group of trained technicians to manage the learning management system and server. If so, there is no additional infrastructure requirement from each individual course on the server side. On the client side, students and instructors need personal computers equipped with remote access tools, multimedia tools, network devices, portable storage devices, reliable Internet connections, and Web browsers.

It is relatively easier to implement a teaching/learning system for the online courses that do not require much hands-on practice. For courses that require hands-on practice, you will need additional network devices, powerful servers, high capacity network connections, and management software. The following discusses the technology needed for the courses with hands-on requirements.

Courses that Need Hands-On Practice on IT Products

This type of course is often in technology related curricula such as information systems, computer science, and computer technology. Courses in those curricula, in addition to the infrastructure supported by learning management systems, need the infrastructure to support hands-on practice on the IT products covered by the course content. These courses present a challenge to the online teaching and learning platform. They require students to perform hands-on practice on various servers as well as application software through the Internet. These courses also require students to be able to perform duties usually done by a network manager, security manager, or database manager. Because networks, databases, hardware devices, and servers are involved, extra effort is needed for each individual course. We will categorize these courses and discuss the infrastructure requirements of each type of course in the next few paragraphs.

In the technology related curricula, there are a wide range of technology-based courses that need additional technology support for hands-on practice. The dependency on lab support is different based on the content covered by these courses. Based on the needs for an online teaching/learning system, the technology-based courses can be categorized as the following:

- **Courses requiring simulated labs:** Hands-on activities in some science courses and networking courses can be done using a lab simulated by computer simulation software, such as the simulated chemistry labs (Model Science Software, Inc., 2006), simulated biology labs (Virtual Courseware Project, 2006), and simulated computer networks (Lammle & Tedder, 2003). For this type of course, the additional technology requirements are simulation software, Web browsers capable of viewing the simulation, and Web servers to post the simulation and to allow interactivities through the Internet. Most of the simulation software can to be posted on the Internet.
- **Courses requiring computer controlled instruments:** For some engineering courses, some of the hands-on practice can be done remotely through the instruments controlled by computers. Students can instruct the computers how to act through a Web browser. This type of course needs Web-based infrastructure to support online teaching and learning.
- **Courses requiring application software:** Many technology-based courses require hands-on practice on application software. For example, programming language courses, personal productivity improvement courses, Web computing courses, and database application development courses belong to this category. In addition to a well-established learning management system to support the

course management, this type of course also needs to provide programming software and application development software for hands-on practice.

- **Courses requiring client-server structure:** Many e-commerce related courses require hands-on practice on a client-server structure. Courses such as database systems, Internet computing, and application development are in this category. For this type of course, online teaching/learning is constructed on a client-server structure. In a class, usually several client-server structures are created for hands-on practice, one for each group. There are two ways to deal with this type of course. One way is to construct an online computer lab where the entire client-server structure is installed. The other way is to use students' home computers as the client side, and build the middle tier and server in an online computer lab.
- **Courses requiring network and server side operations:** Many courses in the information systems, computer science, and information technology curriculum belong to this category, for example, courses such as system administration and network management. Hands-on practice in these courses requires students to reconfigure operating systems and networks; this means that the networks and servers used for hands-on practice in the lab are unstable and should not be used for other kinds of courses. For this type of course, a computer lab is necessary.

In general, courses that require hands-on practice present most difficulties to an online teaching/learning platform. Like many other online courses, they need a well-established learning management system. Also, they require faster Internet connection, secure protection, better technical support, and more powerful hardware and software. These courses often need an online computer lab to support hands-on practice. In recent development, wireless and hand-held devices are also widely used for online teaching and learning.

For the development of an online teaching/learning system, in addition to the requirement for an infrastructure, tools for developing course materials for online courses are also needed. The discussion for such needs is given in the next paragraph.

Requirements for Creating Online Course Materials

For online teaching and learning, technologies are also required to develop online course materials. To overcome some weaknesses of online teaching and learning, almost all online courses need various technologies to develop audio, video, or life lecture course materials. A sophisticated general purpose learning management system (LMS) is able to handle some of the technology needs for developing online course materials. If the tools supported by an LMS are not adequate, there are open source tools that are available to support the development of collaboration and multimedia course materials. With those course content development tools, instructors can provide video, audio, and interactive course materials to enrich online courses.

Many types of course materials can be created to meet the requirements of online courses. The following are some of the commonly used course materials:

- Lecture notes
- Hands-on demonstration materials
- Lab activity manuals
- Online help
- Collaborative operations
- Class syllabi
- Lab regulations
- Movies
- Games
- Instruction for enforcing security measures

Based on the nature of the courses, the online course materials can be in many different formats such as text only documents, graph enhanced documents, multimedia enhanced documents, collaboration enhanced Web pages, Web conferencing, virtual reality materials, and online education games. In the following, we will briefly discuss the course content that may be represented in these formats:

- **Text only documents:** These course materials often include basic lecture notes, security and account instructions, lab regulations, and class syllabi. They are relatively easy to create. These teaching materials do not require a lot of storage space and do not require high speed Internet service. It is particularly useful when many students in a class do not have the high speed Internet connection to the course Web site. The weakness of this type of content may be boring and difficult to describe graph-based course content such as a computer screen. The document can be directly uploaded to the class Web site for display or download. It can also be converted to an image file by using a scanner or converted to a pdf file, and then uploaded to the class Web site.
- **Graph enhanced documents:** Photos, charts, clip arts, and screen shots can be used to greatly improve the quality of online course materials. A graph enhanced document may also include lecture notes, lab activity manuals, and so on. When combined with text documents, graphs can greatly improve the

quality of online course materials. They are especially useful for graph-based course materials such as a lab manual which includes many screen shots.

- **Multimedia enhanced documents:** To further improve the quality of course materials, audio and video can be added to documents such as lecture notes, remote access instructions, and lab activity manuals. Movies and animations also belong to this type of course material. Although multimedia enhancement can greatly increase the quality of course materials used to present multimedia content, it requires a lot of computing resources and technical support from the computer service department. It also requires a lot of effort from faculty members who create the course materials. It is not suitable for course materials that need to be updated frequently, such as the lecture notes that require instruction on how to use a frequently upgraded computer product. Often, this type of material can only last for one or two semesters before a new version of the product is on the market.
- **Collaboration enhanced Web pages:** This type of course material is often used for group projects, interactive learning, and online tutoring. Learning management systems or live online conferencing products are often used to host these Web pages. Developing this type of course material is a complicated process. It often requires instructors and instruction support teams to work together to create such materials. The interactive Web site may create a security hole in the university's network security system, additional security effort is needed to protect the university's network. Before a collaboration enhanced Web page can be deployed on the Internet, one has to get the computer service department's approval due to security related issues. To manage a class using collaboration enhanced Web pages, the instructor who teaches the class needs to be the administrator of the Web site, which may require directory service tools for setting up user accounts for remote access. If this violates the current security policies, it has to be resolved at the administrative level.
- **Web conferencing:** Web conferencing can be used to exchange live audio and video information through streaming video and audio technologies. It allows universities to offer live online courses so that students and instructors can interact just like they are in a face-to-face class. Therefore, we can consider Web conferencing a sophisticated collaboration tool. In addition to live meetings, a Web conferencing program can also record the video and audio for students to review later. Most of the Web conferencing programs include both the Internet and IP based telephone system. Like many other multimedia based online teaching materials, Web conferencing requires a lot of computing recourses. The Web conferencing server is often managed by the instruction support team. Each semester, based on the requests of instructors, instructor and student accounts will be created for classes. Before the classes start, there

should be some necessary training for the instructors and students on how to use Web conferencing for teaching and learning.

- **Virtual reality:** Virtual reality is another technology that can be used to improve the quality of course materials. It is a computer generated environment by super-imposing graphics, audio, and sense enhancement devices on a real-world surrounding. Virtual reality has been used in gaming, training, and virtual demonstration such as virtual tours used for hotel room reservation. Although virtual reality has been used in training for years, it is not yet widely used in classroom teaching due to the high cost on hand-mounted devices, tracking hardware and software, and portable computing devices that are used to generate three dimensional graphics.
- **Education games:** Games can also be used to improve learning by training students' decision making strategies and hands-on skills. They can motivate students to improve their hands-on skills and collaboration. There has been reported that video games have been successfully used to teach subjects such as foreign languages and mathematics (Kirriemuir, 2002). Some gaming related curricula also require the support of gaming course materials. Creating games requires programming skills and the understanding of art. Often, it is a professional's job to create games for education. Some video games can be played on the Internet where multiple players can play against one another across the world. Online games can be controlled to limit them to a certain geological area or a group of people.

In the above, we have analyzed the requirements for both delivering online courses and developing online course materials. The analysis gives the general requirements for an online teaching/learning system. For each individual project, there will be specific requirements. Next, we will discuss how to collect information about the requirements.

Information Collection

A well-designed online teaching/learning system is based on a thorough understanding of the needs. Each project has its own specific requirements. The designers of the new system should find answers to the following questions in the early stage of a design process.

- Who will be using the online teaching/learning system and how many users will simultaneously log on to the system?
- What courses will be supported by the online teaching/learning system and what hands-on practice is required by these courses?

- What technologies are required for delivering the online courses?
- What technologies are required for performing the hands-on practice?
- What technologies are required for developing the course content?
- What are the security rules and university's regulations on developing the online courses?
- How is the project funded?

To answer the above questions, the designers need to collect information by interviewing the key players who are involved in the online teaching/learning system. They need to examine the existing course materials and university documents. They should also observe each stage of a teaching/learning process such as curriculum setup, course material development, the existing online teaching/learning infrastructure, the configuration of the current learning management system, and how the instructors and students use the course materials. In the following, we will take a closer look at each of the information collection methods:

- **Interview key players:** For an online teaching/learning system, the key players are university administrators, computer service managers, computer service technicians, faculty members, staff members, and students. The following are the roles played by them:
  - *Students:* Students are the direct users of an online teaching/learning system. They can provide valuable information about their feelings towards the existing online teaching system and their experience on using the technologies and online course materials.
  - *Staff members:* Staff members may include degree counselors, secretaries, recruiters, registrars, and other personnel who are involved in the online teaching management. They are also the direct users of the online teaching/learning system. They can provide feedback from the management point of view.
  - *University administrators:* University administrators may include the department head, college dean, university president, and so on. These are the decision makers. They may not know the technical detail, but they can make decisions on the project budget, support personnel, curriculum, faculty evaluation, and facilities.
  - *Computer service managers:* A computer service manager plays an important role in the development of an online teaching/learning system. Often, the manager is also the leader of the project. The manager will plan the project, write proposals, budget the project, allocate resources, organize the development team, draft security policies, organize meet-

ings, and evaluate the project. The computer service manager can provide detailed information about the technology requirements.

- *Computer service technicians:* Computer service technicians are those who actually work on the project. They are the ones implementing the online teaching/learning system infrastructure, installing and managing the learning management system, providing technical support, helping the instructors on using technology tools, offering training to the online teaching/learning system users. They can provide crucial information such as the types of technologies to be used, the special features of each technology, product reliability and security, and installation requirements.
- *Faculty members:* Faculty members play an important role in the online teaching/learning system development. They are the ones who will use the system to teach. They will design the course content, use the teaching tools to develop online course materials, grade the assignments, demonstrate the use of learning tools, and tutor students. They know what the requirements are for hands-on practice. They can provide detailed information about the technologies that can meet the requirements.

By interviewing these key players, the designers can find out what works and what does not in the current teaching/learning process and what is the motivation for developing the new project. They will also be able to find out the technology requirements for the new project. The designers should document the conversations and get clarification from the interviewees. A successful interview depends on careful preparation and good interpersonal and communication skills.

- **Examine documents:** To understand how exactly the technologies will be used in an online teaching/learning system, the designers need to examine the documents used for teaching and classroom management. The documents may include forms, reports, course materials, lab manuals, course catalogs, class schedules, security policies, and university regulations, which are a good source for finding what technologies are needed to convert these documents into electronic formats and place them online. From the university rules and security policies, the designers can also get useful information about the security requirements for the new online teaching/learning system.
- **Observe teaching/learning process:** By observing a teaching/learning process, the designers can gain the understanding on how the system is managed, how the course materials are developed, how the courses are taught, and how the course materials are used. The designers can use a flowchart to document the data in a teaching/learning process. The flowchart is helpful in modeling the online teaching/learning system and implementing the system's activities.

The above three data collection methods will help the designers to gather valuable information for their design tasks. Based on the collected information, the designers can identify the project's objectives to meet the requirements. They need to translate the collected information into technical terms. Then, they should create a model for the online teaching/learning system to be developed. The model can be used to verify if the future system will meet the requirements. Often, the designers have to adjust the project's objectives to comply with the rules and the financial limitation.

A modeling process is often called a design process. The following discusses issues related to the online teaching/learning system design.

ONLINE TEACHING/LEARNING SYSTEM DESIGN

The second phase of a design stage may include system modeling and validation. Modeling an online teaching/learning system is a special case of modeling a service-oriented solution which is a process to convert a system described by users into a logical model with technical terms (Erl, 2005). A modeling process specifies the system's organization, structure, and technical terminologies. Among many possible choices, the designers need to select the solution architecture that can meet the users' requirements (Chevance, 2005). In the following, we will go over the strategies on modeling an online teaching/learning system.

System Components

After the requirement information is collected, the next task is to identify the components that will be included in the system. The following are some of commonly included components in an online teaching/learning system:

- **Data component:** In this component, the designers need to identify what data objects to keep track of by analyzing the requirement information collected in the conceptual design phase. For every object they have identified, they need to further specify the attributes of the object and the data type and volume. The designers will analyze the relationships among the data objects. In addition to the specification of data objects, they need to specify the operations performed on these data objects, such as how the data will be inserted, deleted, updated, and queried. For the online teaching/learning system, the designers also need to specify how the data can be remotely accessed and how the data can be displayed through Web browsers.

- **User interface component:** In this component, the types of user interfaces need to be specified. Based on the requirements, a user interface can be specified as a graphical interface, menu interface, or command interface. The designers need to specify the appearance of an interface and the activities related to the user interface.
- **Business rule component:** Business rules are often used to determine how a data component can be mapped to a user interface. The component here includes the university regulations and the application logic related to these regulations. For example, if the minimum enrollment requirement for a class is ten students, this regulation will lead to the constraint on whether a class can appear on the class Web site after class registration is completed.

The above components are part of the system infrastructure, which is often created on the client-server architecture.

Client-Server Infrastructure

A single-tier system includes all three components, data, user interfaces, and business rules on a single computer. This type of system can be implemented on a personal computer installed with some application software such as word processing software and a personal database.

A two-tier system has the client tier and server tier. Some of the components are placed on the client tier and the others are placed on the server tier. For example, a Web site is a two tier system. The user interface component is placed on the client tier which is the Web browser, and the business rule and data components are placed on the server side. A two-tier system can be implemented on a network that consists of server computers and client computers which include desktop computers, notebook computers, and hand-held devices.

A three-tier system has the client tier, middle tier, and server tier. The user interface component is usually placed on the client tier, the business rule component is usually placed on the middle tier, and the data component is usually placed on the server tier. A three tier infrastructure can be implemented on a network including client computers, middle tier computers which are also called application servers, and server computers which host databases. The three-tier infrastructure has better performance and is more flexible so that it can include various technologies and different versions of software in one system. On the other hand, the three-tier infrastructure requires more equipment, more complex networks, and more development effort. For a complicated infrastructure, multiple middle tiers may need to be constructed. We can call this type of infrastructure an N-tier system. In later chapters, more technical details about creating an infrastructure will be given.

Logical Design Process

The system described by the conceptual design is a system from the user's point of view. The information provided by a conceptual design does not match the technical terms used in physical implementation. Also, it is not clear how the components in a system are related to each other. To physically implement such a system, the designers need to create a model that logically represents the system with technical terms. The model should include all the components containing the objects and activities associated with them. The model should also include the specifications and features of each component in technical terms.

Developing a model to represent a system is the task covered by the logical design process, which will achieve three goals, analyzing the conceptual information with technical terms, creating a logical model, and validating the logical model. To achieve these design goals, the designers first go through the following steps to analyze the information provided by the conceptual design.

- To design the logical model for the data component, the designers need to identify the data objects, object attributes, and relationships among the objects.
- For business rules, the designers need to define the constraints and activities to implement the business rules with technical terms.
- To design user interfaces, the designers should first decide the interface formats based on the requirement information. Then, the designers will develop prototypes for the user interfaces. For each prototype, the designers should specify properties for each control and define the activities to be performed by the control.

The next task in the logical design process is to create a logical model by integrating the user interfaces, objects, and activities identified by the above steps. The objects and activities are integrated through the relationships among them. One of the commonly used tools to create a logical model is the Unified Modeling Language (UML). The UML provides graphical diagrams to represent the objects, activities, and relationships in a logical model. In the UML, objects are defined by states and properties. Properties are the attributes of an object and a state is a set of property values of an object. Behavior, also called operation, is the term used by the UML to define the activities of an object. There are thirteen types of diagrams used by the UML. These thirteen types are categorized below:

- **Structure diagrams:** These diagrams represent the static structure of the system being modeled. The diagrams that belong to this category are the class diagram, component diagram, composite structure diagram, deployment diagram, object diagram, and package diagram. Structure diagrams also include some of the relationships among objects and some internal structures.

- **Behavior diagrams:** These diagrams represent dynamic behavior between the objects in a system model. The diagrams in this category are the activity diagram, state machine diagram, use case diagram, communication diagram, interaction overview diagram, sequence diagram, and UML timing diagram. These diagrams can be used to model how a system gets the job done.

The UML is an object-oriented modeling language. Therefore, it can be automatically transformed to Java representations which simplify the physical implementation. A detailed converge of the UML is beyond the scope of this book. Interested readers can find useful information from the book by Pilone and Pitman (2005).

Once the logical model is created, the next task is to review the logical model by validating and modifying it. The reviewer will use the logical model to match the requirements obtained from the conceptual design. The reviewer will meet the users to explain how the system will work to see if the requirements have been met. If there are mistakes, the reviewer will record the mistakes and give suggestions for change. Based on the reviewer's suggestions, the designers will redesign the logical model. After the model is redesigned, go through another review to validate the model. Repeat the process until no mistake is detected. The last step in the logical design process is to ask the users to approve the model. Often, both the designers and users will sign a contract for agreement.

The model created in the logical design phase can be used to define the physical structure of the online teaching/learning system; that is, the physical design phase in the system design process.

Physical Design Process

Before the online teaching/learning system construction team can physically build the system, they must know the detailed information about the hardware and software that will be used in the system. To provide such information to the construction team, the designers need to provide the hardware and software specifications for each component in the logical model. Such a task can be accomplished in the physical design process. The designers in the physical design process should get the following work done.

- **Infrastructure definition:** The infrastructure identified in the logical design phase need to be physically specified. The designers need to specify the network structure, the equipment to be used, the computer operating system platform, the remote access method, and so on. The designers should specify how each tier will communicate with other tiers and how the computation load will be balanced.

- **Application definition:** Application software specification is part of the physical design. Application software is used for managing the teaching/leaning system, teaching courses, performing hands-on practice, and programming application logics. For the online teaching/learning system, the commonly used application software may include learning system management, programming languages, virtual machines, multimedia tools, collaboration tools, and many other tools required by various courses. Some of the application software, such as a learning management system, needs to be constructed on a client-server structure. In such a case, there must be synchronization between the application software and the system infrastructure.
- **User interface definition:** In the physical design process, the designers define the user interface platform which can be a Web browser, the client end GUI interface of a database product, an e-mail window, in-house developed forms or reports, and so on. The designers also need to specify the technologies to be included in the user interfaces and the programming languages used to generate scripts. As the front-end of the application software, these user interfaces should be specified to match the configuration of the application software installed on the middle tier or back-end.
- **Database definition:** The physical design of a database should be completed in this phase. To physically define the data component in the logical model, the first thing is to select a database management system used to construct the database. In the physical design process, the designers will consider issues such as database system architecture, data storage devices, data accessing schemes, data types, data storage capacity, hosting server configuration, hosting environment requirements, data security measures, data transfer methods, and how the data will be used. The designers should also determine how to implement the business rules on a database, a middle tier as part of the application logic, or a constraint in the application software. It is required that the database configuration at the back end of the online teaching/learning system should be consistent with the learning management software and the user interfaces at the front-end of the system.

Once the hardware and software are identified, the next step in the physical design process is to validate that the system meet the requirements. The validation tasks can be summarized as the following.

- **System availability:** Make sure that the course materials are available to the qualified students. Also, make sure that the class management tools and course material development tools are available to the qualified instructors.
- **System performance:** The selected system structure, hardware, software should provide adequate performance. Sometimes, due to the limit in the budget, the designers have to consider alternative designs to get better performance.
- **System scalability:** As the enrollment grows, the system should be designed to accommodate future growth. Also, the system should be designed so that it is backward compatible to some older versions of technologies.
- **System security:** Security is often the top issue to be considered in the online teaching/learning system design. The designers should make sure that the system authentication function is properly defined so that the people who use the system can only access the data they have permission to access. The security measures such as vulnerability detection, network monitoring, and user auditing should also be addressed.

Validation is a critical step for meeting the requirements of teaching and learning. An online teaching/learning system is often an enterprise-level project. For such a complex project, it is difficult to design a system that meets every requirement at the first time. Some of the specifications may not meet the requirements exactly. Also, there would be some mistakes. There may be some problems when integrating all the components together. There could be some conflicts when multiple classes share the same resources. Also, technology changes at a rapid pace. Something that works with an older version of the technology may not work for a new version. These factors will lead to the redesigning or modification of the originally designed system after the validation process. By identifying problems, the designers can use the validation result as a guideline for improving the design.

After the physical design phase is completed, the next stage of the system development process will be the development stage. Next, we will discuss the issues related to the implementation of the online teaching/learning system.

ONLINE TEACHING/LEARNING SYSTEM DEVELOPMENT

After the online teaching/learning system is properly designed, it is time to develop the system. The system development stage is a complex process which involves various technologies and technical personnel with various skills. To successfully develop the system designed in the design stage, the first thing is to carefully plan the development process.

Project Planning

The planning starts with forming a planning committee that includes representatives from the university administrators, computer service managers, and faculty members. The following are some of the tasks to be carried out by the planning committee.

- The committee's first task is to identify the resources for the project. The results from the physical design will be used to estimate the project financial requirements. The committee will make a decision on the project budget.
- Based on the available resources, the committee will make decisions on the selection of technologies for the project.
- Once the committee has decided on what technologies to use, they will form a construction team that includes a project manager, in-house technicians, instructors, and people from a consulting company.
- To make sure that the project will be completed on time, the committee will draft the project's timeline.
- The planning committee should also draft security policies that will guide the project development during the construction process.
- The planning committee will also analyze the effectiveness of using the technologies, resources, and manpower so that they can speed up the development process.

The following are the descriptions of the above tasks.

Identifying Resources

One of the main tasks of the planning committee is to identify the resources for the project. The resources may include the project's funding, the availability of necessary technologies, the manpower and skills, and the administrative and technical support. The project funding should cover all the costs of equipment and other materials, labor, services, system management facilities, and remodeling. There are two types of costs, the construction cost and maintenance cost. The budget should reflect whether it is one-time spending or annually-based spending. One-time spending is mainly for the purchase of equipment and the labor cost for contracting the system development. Annually-based spending includes the cost for security update, equipment update, software update, course content update, Internet connection and phone service, training, and maintenance labor. The committee will also identify the skills needed to achieve the goals of the project. If a certain skill is lacking, the committee needs to identify training resources or consider outsourcing part of the project to a consulting company. The support from the administrators and the computer service department is critical for developing and implementing the online teaching and learning system. The administrators should be well informed so that they can give support on the budget and personnel. On the technical side, there should be an agreement on what technical support the computer service department should provide. Usually, there is more demand on the technical support for the online hands-on practice.

Technology Selection

The physical design has provided information about servers, client computers, networks, and software. There are many choices in the selection of technologies for these components in a system. In our case, if there are better or equivalent open source products, the choice will be the open source products. For example, for the server operating system, our choice will be the open source Linux operating system. Also, for the database management system, the choice will be MySQL. In later chapters, more detailed discussion will be given on the selection of the open source products. Details about the selected technologies should be documented. You may want to include the information such as the vendor contact information, models, prices, and product technical specifications. It is not necessary to purchase everything for the project, most of the open source tools can be downloaded online and there may be some surplus equipment that can be used for the project. For the selection of an Internet service provider (ISP), you will need to compare providers' options on the Internet speed, cost, technical support, and so on. You will need to document the configuration information provided by the ISP such as the Internet server's IP address, DNS server's IP address, and the IP address for the gateway.

Project Timeline

To decide on the project's timeline, the committee should first identify the tasks to be carried out during the development. It should identify the tasks' dependencies and set a completion criterion for each task. Then, the duration of each task can be estimated. Based on the tasks' dependencies, technical personnel's skills, and completion duration, the timeline can be optimized by scheduling some of the tasks in the same time periods.

Security Policies

Due to the fact that the online teaching/learning system allows students to perform hands-on practice on the server side, the security related issues are a great concern in the development process. For online teaching and learning, there is often a need to release some of the security measures. For example, online hands-on practice may require that the Web browser be able to run ActiveX or Java scripts. Also, the students need to have the administrator's privilege to be able to work on a server. The committee should add the security measures such as:

- Enabling some service and communication ports required by the courses while disabling others.
- Controlling students' access to the virtual local area network (VLAN) with a different level of security configuration.
- Selecting the more secure network protocols to avoid carrying the plain text content during data transmission.
- Enhancing the security measures on the Web server to prevent unauthorized users from penetrating the online teaching/learning system.
- Implementing all the necessary network and computer system monitoring and auditing services.

There are many other security measures that can be added to the above list based on the security policies of a specific project. Knowing what security measures should be enforced is critical for developing a successful system. The planning committee should take the security issues seriously. Document all the decisions made by the committee for future reference.

Project Effectiveness

To effectively develop the online teaching/learning system, the committee need to deal with issues related to skill sharing, time sharing, resource sharing, purchasing, and workload balancing. For example, the technical personnel may also need to take care of other projects, or the same computing resources need to be shared by other departments. To effectively manage the project development, the committee should establish a work order policy which defines the priority of work orders and resource usage. Student workers can also be hired to help with certain work to speed up the development process. Getting feedback and resolving problems encountered in the development process also enhance efficiency.

Project Construction

After the development process is carefully planned, the project construction can be started. The specifications from the physical design will be used as the guideline for the project construction, such as system installation and configuration. During the construction, the following tasks will be performed:

- The facilities used to support the system infrastructure such as a server room equipped with air conditioning, reliable power supply, uninterruptible power supply (UBS), phone lines, WAN or Internet connection should be in place.
- The hardware and computer system software used by each component in the infrastructure will be installed.
- The networks, servers, and client computers will be properly configured so that the client computers can communicate with the servers.
- The learning management system will be configured to allow the upload of course materials and user accounts. For each course, the course Web site, the grading system, the multimedia tools, and the collaboration tools should also be properly configured.
- The database will be created and configured to accept data from various sources. The communication between the learning management system and the database should be established.
- All the user interfaces should be created and dynamic actions related to these user interfaces should be implemented.
- All the business rules and application logics should be programmed and put into operation.
- The online computer labs should be established. The lab hardware and software should be installed and configured to meet the requirements of teaching and hands-on practice.
- Security measures required by the security policies should be in place. The authentication and authorization of the learning management system and database should also be properly configured.
- The course material development tools should be installed and made available to instructors.
- The remote access scheme for the server, learning management system, and database should be configured according to the ISP's requirements and the security policies.

It will take a great deal of effort and skills to get these tasks done. More details on the issues related to installation and configuration will be covered in later chapters. Our next topic is about system implementation. We will discuss issues related to it.

ONLINE TEACHING/LEARNING SYSTEM IMPLEMENTATION

After the online teaching/learning system is constructed, it is time to deploy the system for the students and faculty members and to keep the system running as it should be. The tasks at the implementation stage may include system testing, system deployment, user training, and system management. The following is the description of each task.

System Testing

The goal of system testing is to verify that the physically constructed system meets the requirements described in the system design stage. There are two types of tests, coverage test and usability test. The coverage test is to check individual functions or features to see if the requirements are fulfilled. The usability test is to check the usage of the new system. This test is done after the system is internally deployed.

- **Coverage test:** The objective of the initial test is to make sure that every function and feature specified by the system design is working properly. Before the system is deployed, the system development team will test the network, servers and client computers to make sure that they function properly. The test will also check the application servers such as the learning management system, database, Web server, and VPN server to see if they meet the design requirements. For the user interfaces, the test will make sure that the menus, buttons, and other controls on the user interfaces work as expected. The test will make sure that data entered from the data entry forms can indeed be saved to the proper places in the database. The test will also need to verify that reports can collect requested information from the database. Code stability is also a task to be carried out in the coverage test.
- **Usability test:** After the system is internally deployed, a testing team formed by technical support technicians, faculty members, staff members, and students will test the system for various types of courses, especially for those courses that require hands-on practice. The test will be conducted in the real online teaching/learning environment. The test team will check if the instructors can access and use the learning management tools, upload course materials, and set up online labs. The staff members will test to see if they can upload course manuals to the system. They will check if the online registration system and the grading system work properly. They will also check if they can set up course schedules and accounts for students. The students will be asked to test if they can access the teaching materials, use collaboration tools, and carry out hands-on practice in online labs. They will test the links on the course

Web sites. They will also be asked to check if they can register and pay for the courses online. The technical support team's task is to verify that the help files and the instructions on the usage of the system are available to the users. They will also test the online help tools such as the text messenger, virtual whiteboard, and e-mail to see if they work properly.

- **Testing procedure:** The tasks in a testing process include making a testing plan, creating a procedure on how to test individual requirements, and selecting the courses for usability testing. The testing plan decides testing team members, the requirements to be tested, and the tools to be used in the testing. The testing procedure includes testing instructions and criteria for a successful test. It should include information about the manuals of the testing tools and the testing instruments. It will also provide information necessary for testing such as the tester's authentication information and the bug report procedure. The courses to be used for usability testing should include the typical courses from different departments. The testing should include the labs used for hands-on practice.

Deployment

After all the bugs are fixed and all the requirements are fulfilled, it is time to release the online teaching/learning system to the faculty members, staff members, and students. Most of the online teaching/learning systems are deployed through Web servers, even though some of the client tools can be deployed through DVDs or portable hard drives.

There are several things that the deployment team should do. The first thing is to make sure that all the necessary data have been migrated to the system's database. All the user accounts should be set and ready to accept remote logins. The login information should be clearly written and placed on the cover page of the system's Web site. All courses for the next semester should be set up and the course materials should also be uploaded to the system.

Secondly, the deployment team should make all the downloadable client software available on the system's Web site. The hardware and software requirements for installing the client software should be available. The Web browser security configuration for software download should also be available to the students. The upgrade information and upgrade service packs for the software on the client side should also be available to the students.

Thirdly, the online technical support service should be in place. As soon as the system is released to the students, there will be a large number of requests for help. The online support team members need to provide their e-mail addresses, text messenger addresses, and phone numbers to the users. If it is possible, they should post their schedules, skills, and the subjects that each team member can help with.

Training

After the system is deployed, the next task is training. Most of the users are new to the system and they need training so that they can properly use the system. The following are possible training topics:

- Training staff members to set up online classes and student accounts on the learning management system. The staff members need to know how to upload and update the course catalog and class schedules for each semester. Some of them will also be trained to use the online registration system.
- Training faculty members to manage online classes and to use the grading system. The faculty members need to know how to upload and modify course materials. They need to learn how to schedule assignment due dates and how to tutor students online. They also need to know how to use online computer labs and how to use the multimedia and collaboration tools provided by the system.
- Training students on how to remotely access the online teaching/learning system, how to use the collaboration tools, how to communicate with their instructors and classmates, how to use online course materials, how to download the course materials, how to submit their assignments, how to take quizzes and exams, and how to check their grades.

There are various ways to carry out the training. Some training can be done in a face-to-face meeting and some can be done online. The following are some possible ways to provide the training.

The rapid progress of technology requires students, instructors, and the technical support team to constantly update their skills and knowledge to keep up with the current trend. The possible resources to update skills and knowledge are:

- **Training seminars:** Short training seminars can be organized to train instructors and students. At the beginning of each semester, students who are enrolled in online courses should take an orientation seminar. During the seminar, each participant can have a face-to-face discussion with their trainer and have hands-on practice guided by the trainer. The participants will gain a lot of first-hand experience in using the new system. Most of these training seminars focus on using a general purpose LMS. For the development and usage of online computer labs, the instructors and the technical support team have to get additional training.

- **Web training:** The disadvantage of face-to-face training is that some people, especially online students, will not be able to attend the training. For those who cannot participate in the face-to-face seminars, the university should provide Web-based training. The advantage of online training is that students can participate in the training from anywhere and at any time. The disadvantage of online training is that the students will not able to talk to the trainer. Therefore, training materials need to be clearly written and necessary screen shots should be provided. The Web site should also be updated whenever new training materials are available.
- **Web conference training:** This is one of the best ways to carry out training. The trainees can log on to a Web conference from anywhere at a specific time. They will be able to ask questions and get hands-on practice. If the trainees cannot do the training at a specific time, they can watch the recorded training at anytime.
- **Email training:** Through e-mail, training materials can be sent to all the trainees at once. It is a very efficient way to provide training. The trainer can also provide a link to get responses or questions from the trainees. The only disadvantage is that there are no live questions and answers. Well written training materials can greatly reduce the impact of this disadvantage.

In the above, we have briefly discussed the training related issues. Next, let us consider the tasks of managing and maintaining the online teaching/learning system.

Management

The online teaching/learning system is a complicated and ever-changing system. Keeping the system fully operational is critical to the success of e-learning. The management job is mainly done by the computer service department. Instructors are also involved in the management in many ways. Since they know the requirements for the technology, they will work together with the lab management team to update, troubleshoot or rebuild the system. They will be asked to verify if the results of system rebuilding or troubleshooting still meet the requirements. The management tasks may include:

- Daily maintenance of the online teaching/learning system
- System update
- Security management

- Backup and recovery,
- Performance tuning

Brief descriptions about these tasks are given below.

Daily Maintenance

First, let us look at the issues related to daily maintenance of the online teaching/learning system. Daily maintenance includes tasks that are routinely scheduled to keep the system running. There are three kinds of jobs, system monitoring, technical support and troubleshooting. For the system monitoring job, technicians are asked to observe the status of the system by checking the following items.

- Any performance problem and remote access problem
- The status of the software, hardware and network equipment
- The status of power supply, room temperature, and other room conditions

Technical support is one of the main management tasks. There will be many questions from the users, especially from the new students who are not familiar with the system. The technical support team should expect many unintentional mistakes from these students. Any online teaching/learning system should provide a guideline which can be easily accessed to help the users find technical support information. Technical support can be done in many ways such as face-to-face help, e-mail help, online instruction, help by phone, and text messaging. Usually, the technical support team is able to provide adequate support on using the learning management system. However, the technical support for online labs is much more complicated. It often requires the technical support team to understand the course content. Therefore, to better support the online labs, the technical support technicians need to constantly update their knowledge and skills. Also, the technical support team has to provide support on a variety of technologies used in various online labs and these technologies get updated in a fast rate.

During the system testing and system operation, there will be some technical problems, hardware and software failure, and problems caused by improper operation. There should be some general guidelines on the responsibility for troubleshooting. When problems occur, it usually is the computer service department's responsibility to solve the problems as quickly as possible to reduce negative impact on the system. Also, there should be some budget for equipment replacement. Technicians may also be asked to help with an online computer lab. In the lab, students need help from the lab management team to fix their problems. Once a problem is solved and a change is made, if necessary, the computer service department should e-mail all the students who are using the lab about the change.

System Update

The rapid progress of technology requires instructors and the technical support team to constantly update the online teaching/learning system with new technology. The content of course materials will also follow the change of technology on the market to catch up with the current technology trend. The computer service department needs to dedicate some staff members to help with system upgrade. The dedicated technicians should have the skills implement the upgrade to meet the requirements from the instructors and students. Before each semester starts, all upgrade requirements for the new course materials must be done to get ready for the new semester. The computer service department needs to carefully schedule the purchasing of equipment and the timeline for upgrade.

Security Management

Security related issues are always the top concern of the computer service department. Once an online teaching/learning system is infected by viruses, the viruses can damage files, jam memory, occupy hard disk space, or even take control the CPU. If the online teaching/learning system is not properly protected, hackers may change the system settings, delete system files, or simply crash the system. The following are some common tasks performed by the security management team for routine system management.

- Check if there is any virus infection and if there are any service packs and patches for downloading.
- Test the system's vulnerabilities and identify potential problems.
- Download and install security patches.
- Configure and update security measures.
- Check the system's firewalls, and monitoring, auditing, and logging services.
- Solve and report any security problem, provide measures to block security holes, and recover infected files.

The security measures should be set to balance the system's availability, reliability, integrity, and confidentiality. Once the online teaching/learning system is in place, the internal network is connected to the external Internet through the system and the risk to the university's internal network is increased dramatically. Security management should be carefully carried out to prevent serious security problems.

Backup and Recovery

This task is to perform the scheduled system and database backup, and recover a failed system. During the system operation, the server or network may crash due to various reasons. To quickly recover from the damage caused by a system crash or other disasters, the system management team must have a plan on system backup and recovery. System backup and recovery deal with the issues related to backup plans, tools to be used for system backup and recovery, and system backup procedures.

Performance Tuning

One of the routine management tasks is to improve the system's performance. In general, a Web-based system has slower performance than a system that is constructed on a local area network. In a Web-based computing environment, a single server may be accessed simultaneously by many students through the Internet. In such an environment, the network throughput and the input/output devices for the system can experience bottleneck. The performance of a Web-based system always has a higher priority in system management in order to keep its full potential for delivering online courses. For routine system management, the performance of the system should be monitored. Some of the common ways to solve performance problems are listed below.

- Set up a problem reporting system so that a performance problem can be sent to the system management team as soon as possible. Usually, performance problems and their solutions are listed as part of the technical report service.
- Analyze the performance problem report and identify the bottleneck.
- Based on the identified problem, solve the performance problem by altering configuration, replacing equipment, upgrading software and hardware, installing patches, or changing the network structure.
- To prevent the problem from happening again, document the changes and inform the users about the changes and give instructions on how to properly use the system.

At this point, we have described several commonly performed tasks in system management. As the system is running, there is more work to be done. As we can see, just the above management tasks will keep the system management team busy all year round.

ONLINE TEACHING/LEARNING SYSTEM EVALUATION

In the instructional technology theory, evaluation is the stage to get feedback from users. The result of the evaluation provides a guideline for further improvement and for next year's budget proposal. Not only the teaching and learning can benefit from the project evaluation, but also the technology usage and the design of the system architecture can benefit from the evaluation. An evaluation process often performs the following tasks.

- **Identify what to evaluate:** An evaluation process often includes the evaluation of course materials as well as the online teaching/learning system that supports the delivery of the course materials.
- **Identify who will be evaluated and who will evaluate:** People who participate in the online teaching/learning system's design, construction and management are usually evaluated, and people who use the system will evaluate.
- **Document evaluation:** Prepare the evaluation instrument and instruction on how to evaluate.
- **Deploy evaluation instrument:** The evaluation instrument can be sent to the evaluation participants through Web forms, e-mail, fax, or regular mail.
- **Schedule evaluation:** Often the evaluation of an online teaching/learning system is part of the class evaluation at the end of each semester.
- **Analyze evaluation results:** Data collected from the evaluation can be analyzed with charts, spreadsheets, or other statistical analysis tools. A report should be created to explain the findings by the analysis.

The goal of the evaluation is to determine if the objectives of the online teaching/learning system have been achieved. The evaluation checks if the system can get the job done effectively and identifies places where the system can be further improved.

CONCLUSION

This chapter has discussed the life cycle of solution development which is consistent with the theory of instructional technology. The discussion specifically focused on the development of an online teaching/learning system. This chapter has described each development stage in detail. The first stage is needs analysis which provides a guideline for the next stage. At the system design stage, there are three deign phases, conceptual design, logical design, and physical design. The next stage is about system development. The issues of project planning and project construction have been explored. The implementation stage deals with the issues related to system testing, system deployment, training, and system management. The last stage of the solution development is about evaluation which gets feedback from the users and provides clues for future improvement. As pointed out in this chapter, the discussion in later chapters will explore the open source tools at each of these development stages.

REFERENCES

Chevance, R. J. (2005). *Server architectures: Multiprocessors, clusters, parallel systems, Web servers, storage solutions.* Burlington, MA: Digital Press.

Chong, F., Clark, J., Morris, M., & Welsh, D. (2005). *Web service health modeling, instrumentation, and monitoring: Developing and using a Web services health model for the northern electronics scenario.* Retrieved June 7, 2006, from http://msdn.microsoft.com/architecture/learnmore/learnimpdes/default.aspx?pull=/library/en-us/dnbda/html/MSArcSeriesMCS6.asp

Dick, W. O., Carey, L., & Carey, J. O. (2004). *Systematic design of instruction* (6th ed.). Upper Saddle River, NJ: Allyn & Bacon.

Erl, T. (2005). *Service-Oriented Architecture (SOA): Concepts, Technology, and Design*. Upper Saddle River, New Jersey: Prentice Hall PTR.

Horton, W. (2000). *Designing Web-based training: How to teach anyone anything anywhere anytime*. New York: Wiley.

Kirriemuir, J. (2002). Video gaming, education and digital learning technologies. *D-Lib Magazine, 8*(2). Retrieved September 9, 2007, from http://www.dlib.org/dlib/february02/kirriemuir/02kirriemuir.html

Kruse, K., & Keil, J. (2000). *Technology-based training: The art and science of design, development, and delivery.* San Francisco, CA: Pfeiffer.

Lammle, T., & Tedder, W. D. (2003). *CCNA virtual lab, platinum edition (Exam 640-801).* Alameda, CA: Sybex.

Meliksetian, D.S., et al. (2004) Design and implementation of an enterprise grid. *IBM Systems Journal.* Retrieved June 7, 2006, from http://www.findarticles.com/p/articles/mi_m0ISJ/is_4_43/ai_n9544042

Model Science Software, Inc. (2006). Chemistry lab simulations for the classroom, the laboratory and the Internet. *Model Science Software.* Retrieved April 9, 2006, from http://modelscience.com

Pilone, D., & Pitman, N. (2005). *UML 2.0 in a nutshell.* Sebastopol, CA: O'Reilly Media, Inc.

Reigeluth, C. M. (Ed.). (1999). *Instructional-design theories and models: A new paradigm of instructional theory, Volume 2.* Mahwah, NJ: Lawrence Erlbaum Associates.

Reiser, R. A., & Dempsey, J. V. (Eds.). (2006). *Trends and issues in instructional design and technology* (2nd ed.). Upper Saddle River, NJ: Prentice Hall.

Seels, B. B., & Richey, R. C. (1994). *Instructional technology: The definitions and domains of the field.* Washington, DC: Association for Educational Communications and Technology. (pp 1-9).

Virtual Courseware Project. (2006). Biology labs on-line. Retrieved April 9, 2006, from http://vcourseware.calstatela.edu/BLOL

Yu, Y., & Liu, Z. (2006). Integrated scenario-based design method for interactive online teaching system. In *International Conference on Computational Intelligence for Modelling Control and Automation and International Conference on Intelligent Agents Web Technologies and International Commerce* (pp. 153-153). Sydney, Australia.

Chapter III
Technology Requirements of Online Teaching / Learning Systems

INTRODUCTION

The previous chapter introduced the general instructional technology theory and went through the application of the ADDIE model for the development of an online teaching/learning system and online course materials. It also analyzed the requirements of an online teaching/learning system and provided the procedures to collect the requirement related information. The requirement analysis is covered by the first phase of the ADDIE model. This chapter translates the requirement related information into technical terms.

To meet the requirements, we need to investigate what technologies can be used. An online teaching/learning system is heavily dependent on technology. Various technologies are used to construct the online teaching/learning system and are used as course content to be taught in different technology-based courses. The first type of technology that is used to develop the online teaching infrastructure is the one that hosts the course content and supports users in accessing the online course materials. The second type of technology is the one that can be used to develop course materials including the interactive, collaborative, and multimedia content. In our case, the technologies used to implement the infrastructure and to assist the development of course materials will be the open source technologies. Therefore, our discussion in this chapter is to analyze the technology requirements by both the online teaching/learning system infrastructure and the online course material development.

Let us start with the technology requirements for computer systems. We will include the requirements for network servers, application servers, and client-side computers such as desktop, notebook, and hand-held devices. The requirements for the operation systems and system management tools will also be discussed.

The next topic is the requirements for networks. An online teaching/learning system is a network based system. We will analyze the technology requirements by each type of infrastructure designed for each type of online teaching/learning system. The discussion will include the requirements for network equipment, network protocols, remote access instruments, and network management tools.

Then, we will look at the requirements for a learning management system. We will consider what services should be provided to manage various types of online courses. A learning management system also provides various tools for class management, collaboration, and presentation of course materials. We will discuss how these tools will be used to meet the technology requirements.

After the discussion of the learning management system, our next task is to analyze the requirements for other application software such as database management systems, programming languages, and office production software. The requirements for virtual machine related technologies and management tools are also considered here.

The last topic in this chapter is the analysis of the requirements for collaboration and multimedia tools for the development of online course materials. The needs for commonly used Internet based communication tools such as the media player, text messenger, Web server, Web browser, and Web conferencing will also be briefly talked about under this topic.

For each of the above requirements, the discussion will be based on the type of infrastructure or the type of course material used in the online teaching/learning system. The requirements identified in this chapter can be used as the system configuration guideline in later chapters.

BACKGROUND

Technology is the driving force of an online teaching/learning system. It is often the most challenging part to deal with. Not only does the computer service department need to use technology to construct the system, but also the students, faculty members, and staff members have to depend on it for online teaching and learning. Properly identifying the technology requirements is a critical step in developing an online teaching/learning system that can achieve the design goals (Horton & Horton, 2003).

In the early days, a teaching system was often supported by a mainframe computer. Text-only monitors were used to display information on the screen (Perry, 2000). As technology advances, personal computers have become one of the important learning equipment. Course materials can be created by using computer software and can be downloaded to personal computers. Therefore, personal computers can be used to display the course content and allow students to complete assignments with the software supported by the computers (Bennett, 1999). Personal computers can also host simulation software which can be used to perform some hands-on activities. They support high volume portable storage devices, digital audio and video devices, and many course material development tools such as Web conferencing tools, multimedia tools, collaboration tools, and various Web content authoring tools for Web-based teaching (Garrand, 2006).

The creation of the World Wide Web made Web-based teaching and learning a reality. Web-based infrastructure allows students to access course materials from anywhere at any time. Today's online teaching/learning system is often constructed on a client-server structure or a Web-based structure. Personal computers on the client side can be connected to servers which provide course materials for students. Through a graphical user interface (GUI), users can interact with the servers, download files, use network based software, and so on. Personal computers also provide multimedia tools for handling the multimedia course content. The course material development tools can also be installed on personal computers. These tools can assist instructors in creating materials for teaching various courses (Ivers & Barron, 2005). In a client-server based online teaching/learning system infrastructure, servers are widely used to support network activities and database operations, and used to host online courses.

Researchers in higher education institutions have been actively conducting studies on applying technology to online teaching and learning. Veglis (2000) discussed some Web-based interactive tools and how to teach courses that require a Web-based online teaching lab. There are some studies on using server-side technologies. For example, to distribute sophisticated multimedia content, a delivery server infrastructure was developed by Boer (2002). The delivery server supports interactive distance learning over various infrastructures. Ayala and Paredes (2003) developed a learner model server. The server supports a personalized learning environment by providing a set of applications specially designed for each individual learner based on the learner's learning style.

There are not many studies on using network technologies to support technology based courses. The research done by Correia and Watson (2006) applied the virtual network technology to the instruction of networking courses. The virtual technology was used to construct their teaching labs on campus.

Most of the studies have focused on using some specific technologies for a specific online teaching/learning task. In this book, a wider view about the usage of technologies in online teaching and learning will be presented. We will systematically investigate how open source technologies are used in constructing different system infrastructures and the required technologies used to support the development of online teaching systems. In this chapter, we will start with the investigation of computer system requirements by an online teaching/learning system project.

COMPUTER SYSTEM REQUIREMENTS

A computer system is a computer installed with necessary software and peripheral devices that can be used to accomplish certain tasks. Various computer systems are used for online teaching/learning systems that use computers to accomplish different tasks. Based on the roles they play, computer systems can be briefly categorized as server computers and personal computers (or someone may call them workstation computers and client computers). In this topic, we will first discuss the tasks that can be accomplished by servers and personal computers. Then, we will examine the requirements for the computer systems according to online teaching and learning.

Server Computers

A server computer in an online teaching/learning system is used to host and manage resources that can be accessed by users with proper permissions through a network. To handle multiple users who access the same server, the server is usually a relatively powerful computer equipped with the following basic software and peripheral devices.

- A server operating system which can be used to manage users, computers, and other application software on a network
- A learning management system and the devices to support the software
- Database management software and storage devices
- Security management software and management tools
- Network devices and management tools
- Printing devices and management tools
- Remote access devices and management tools
- Virtual machine development and management software

- E-mail, chat, or text messenger management software and devices
- Web server development and management software and devices
- Uninterruptible power supply (UPS) equipment and management tools

In the above, only some basic server items are listed. There can be a lot more other software and devices to be installed on a server based on the specific needs to deliver online courses. On the other hand, it is not necessary to install all of the above software and devices on a single server. In fact, to improve security, reliability, and performance, server software is often installed on multiple computers and each computer is only responsible for a specific server task. The following are types of servers commonly used in an online teaching/learning system:

- **Network server:** It is used to manage network users, computers, network structures, security, and resources.
- **Database server:** It can be used to manage databases and storage devices, and it allows users to access data through the Internet or intranet.
- **Application server:** In a three-tier client-server structure, the application server is the server at the middle tier to implement business logic. It processes requests from clients and fetches the necessary data from the server that hosts databases.
- **Multimedia server:** This type of server supports multimedia activities on a network such as delivering streaming multimedia content to Web pages.
- **Print server:** It can manage network printers, scanners, and copiers.
- **FTP server:** It is used for transferring and downloading files over the Internet or intranet.
- **Groupware server:** This server is designed to support group collaboration via the Internet or intranet.
- **Mail server:** This server supports e-mail operations over the Internet or intranet.
- **Proxy server:** It is responsible for filtering client requests and share connections. It can also be used to enhance the security of the internal network.
- **VPN server:** This server enables users to remotely log on to the workplace network via the Internet or intranet.
- **Virtual server:** It can be used to develop virtual machines which are used to perform hands-on practice.
- **Web server:** This kind of server delivers course materials to a Web browser. It can also receive requests from Web browsers, process the requests, communicate with other servers, and return the results back to the Web browsers.

So far, we have discussed various types of servers that perform specific tasks. There are other servers used in an online teaching/learning system. Based on the requirements, several servers can be combined to support a specific online course. The discussion about the requirements of these servers will be given later in this chapter.

Personal Computers

Originally, a personal computer was designed for individual use or for hosting client software in a client-server system. Personal computers may include desktop computers, notebook computers, tablet computers, workstations, Personal Digital Assistants (PDAs), and other hand-held devices. As technology advances, personal computers are no longer limited to personal use or used as client computers. Some of the personal computers are powerful enough to host server operating systems. In fact, most of the Linux operating systems are hosted by personal computers. To make the discussion clearer, we use the term "personal computers" for those computers that host client software even though some personal computers are used to host server software. The following are some of the tasks that can be done by personal computers in an online teaching/learning system.

- Personal computers are installed with client operating systems which can be used to manage user accounts created on individual computers and configure network devices.
- Personal computers can also be used to host application software that can be used to get a specific computation task done.
- Through personal computers, users can access Web servers and browse course materials through the Internet.
- Multimedia devices and management tools can be installed on the client-side computers. They can also be used for creating and viewing multimedia course content.
- Personal computers can also be used to host collaboration tools and management tools so that students can work with instructors and other students.
- Users can use personal computers to send and receive e-mail and other graphical and text messages.
- Personal computers can be used to host client-side software such as database client software, VPN client software, virtual machine client software, and Web conferencing client software.

Personal computers can be in a computer lab or at students' homes as client computers. In the computer lab, the client computers are often the same type of computers. It is relatively easy to manage them. It is much harder to manage students' home computers as client computers since the computers at students' homes can have any types of operating systems, with any types of hardware and application software.

Requirements for Computer Systems

Requirements for computer systems vary depending on what types of system infrastructure will be implemented and what types of course materials will be developed. In Chapter II, we categorized online courses into two types, courses that only need the support of a learning management system and courses that need hands-on practice on IT products. In the following, we will examine what types of computer systems can meet the requirements by these two types of courses.

Courses Needing Learning Management System Support

For this type of course, the online teaching/learning system is usually constructed on the client-server structure. One or more server computers are needed to support the system. If you want to create a relatively reliable system, there should be several server computers, two for network management, one or two for hosting the learning management system software, one for hosting the Web server, one for hosting the database server, one for hosting the multimedia server, one for hosting the mail server, one for hosting the VPN server, one for the groupware server, and one for the network print server. Sometimes, multiple server software can all be installed on a single computer; this may cause some bottleneck for performance and is less reliable.

For the server-side software, each server will have a server operating system installed. The choice of the server operating system depends on factors such as total cost, maintainability, security, and capability to support other e-learning software. In our case, Linux is chosen due to its compatibility to host all the open source e-learning software and other factors such as relatively low cost and tight security. On the other hand, running the Linux server requires a team of technical personnel who can handle most of the development and maintenance tasks without depending on the technical support from the vendors. Linux, as an open source operating system, can be used to support the teaching and learning operations on both the server side and the client side. Linux as an enterprise server operating system can provide tools for network administration and security management. Other open source server operating systems can also be considered.

In additional to the server operating system, application software should be installed on the special purpose servers, which can be used to host the learning management system Moodle, the Web server Apache, and the database management system MySQL. A learning management system server needs learning management system software such as Moodle or other open source tools installed on it. A database server requires a database management system such as MySQL to be installed on it. The open source tool Moodle is a qualified learning management system for the server side. Moodle can also work with the open source database management system MySQL to process the daily operation data. For mail servers and groupware servers, the application software Courier mail transfer agent (MTA) can be installed on a Linux computer as an integrated mail/groupware server. The Courier MTA can provide mail services for user accounts on the Linux operating system as well as the accounts managed by LDAP or MySQL. Some of the Linux distributions include the open source virtual machine management tool Xen Virtual Machine. If not included in Linux, Xen can be downloaded for free. Or we can use the free download VMware Server which can be used to create virtual machines. Even without additional application software, the tools included in Linux can be used to configure the host computer as a print server, a FTP server, a VPN server, a proxy server, or a Web server.

To support online teaching and learning, some other application software may also be required. In addition to the learning management system, a Web conferencing program may be required to support online collaboration and to record video and audio for students to review later. Most of the Web conferencing projects may require the Internet or IP based telephone system for live communication. For the development of a Web conferencing project, you may also need a markup language such as XML or other programming languages such as JavaScript. Tools for Flash animation and audio/video streaming may also be needed. Most of these tools are often included in the Web conferencing software. To secure the computer systems and data transferred over a local area network or the Internet, security monitoring and auditing, firewalls, and data encryption and decryption tools are needed for data protection.

On the client side, students and instructors need desktop computers, notebook computers, or some hand-held devices equipped with remote access tools, multimedia tools, network devices, portable storage devices, reliable Internet connection, and Web browsers. Linux can be installed as a client operating system on the client side. As a client operating system, Linux provides remote access tools for Internet connection and Web browsing. It also provides various multimedia tools for playing recorded lectures, participating in online group activities, and audio and video recording. Linux can host a variety of application software such as the programming software Java and PHP, the office management software OpenOffice, the groupware software phpGroupWare, the network management tool OpenLDAP, and so forth. Most of the mentioned application software is either open source software or freeware and can accomplish the tasks that are done by commercial products.

For online teaching and learning, students' home computers can also be used as client computers which can access the server located on campus. If that is the case, the client computers may have different operating systems and most of them are proprietary products. In such a case, it is not necessary to require all the students to install Linux on their home computers. When setting up servers, one needs to make sure that the remote access technology is compatible with the proprietary products on the client home computers. Another solution is to use virtualization technologies such as Xen and VMware to install the Linux client as the guest operating system on students' home computers.

Courses Needing Hands-On Practice on IT Products

In Chapter II, the courses in this category were further divided into five subtypes, courses requiring simulated labs, courses requiring computer controlled instruments, courses requiring application software, courses requiring client-server structure, and courses requiring network and server-side operations. Each of these subtypes has its own special needs of the computer system. In the following, we will take a closer look at the needs.

- **Courses requiring simulated labs:** These courses need personal computers installed with the operating system Linux. To support teaching and learning for this type of course, the needed application software is simulation software. The tool Wine may be useful if the simulation software is Windows based software. Wine can create a Windows environment to run Windows applications. Linux provides the Web browser and Web server which are useful if the simulation software needs to be posted on the Internet.
- **Courses requiring computer controlled instruments:** These courses need server computers to convert requests sent from Web browsers to the control language understood by the instruments. In this case, a computer with the Linux server operating system, Web server, instrument control software will be necessary on the server side.
- **Courses requiring application software:** For these courses, if the application software needs to be accessed through the Internet, the online teaching/learning system infrastructure needs to be constructed on a client-server structure. In addition to a well-established server to support the learning management system, this kind of course also needs to a server to host application software for hands-on practice. The remote access tools must be included in both the server and client computers. Students' computers will be configured

as client computers which will be linked to the servers through the Internet. If the application software needs to be installed on the students' computers, a FTP server or Web server needs to be set up to allow students to download the software. Again, for both the server and client computers, Linux can be used as the operating system. Multiple application software packages can be installed on the server for different courses.

- **Courses requiring client-server structure:** As pointed out in the previous chapter, multiple client-server structures need to be built, one for the online teaching/learning system and several others for hands-on practice. For the client-server structure that supports the online teaching/learning system, we need one or more servers and personal computers as described earlier. For the client-server structures that support hands-on practice, each such structure will need one or more servers depending on the requirements by each individual course. There should also be an instructor server which can be used to manage the other servers in the lab. The personal computers on the client side can be either students' home computers or the client computers in the lab. The system and application software needed on the personal computers will depend on the requirements of the hands-on practice for each individual course. If the students in each group only need to access one server, the students' home computers can be used as client computers. If the hands-on practice is performed on multiple servers, it is better to have a computer lab that is constructed with the client-server structures each with servers and client computers. In the lab, each server is physically link to several client computers through a network. The requirements for the software may include the server operating system, the client operating system, and application software.
- **Courses requiring network and server-side operations:** These course also need to have several client-server structures. The client-server structures used for hands-on practice for this type of course cannot be shared with other courses because the hands-on practice requires students to re-configure operating systems and networks; this makes the systems unstable. To avoid conflict and reduce cost, virtual machines can be used. After Linux is installed as the host operating system, several virtual machines can be created on each of the host computers. Each virtual machine can be installed with a guest operating system. For the virtual machines on a host computer, one of them can have the server operating system and the others can have the client operating system. Virtual machines require a lot of RAM to run properly. Therefore, make sure that the host computers have enough RAM. For example, if a host computer has three virtual machines, it may need to have 2GB RAM to run four Linux operating systems. If the guest operating system is Windows Vista, the requirement for RAM can be three times higher. Usually, for this type of course, application

software is not required; this means that, for both the client and server, only the operating system is needed for each machine.

Now we have briefly reviewed the computer system requirements for each type of course. Note that not all the courses mentioned above have to use open source products. Many proprietary products can also perform the tasks. Linux and other open source products are only some of the options. In an online teaching/learning infrastructure, the computers are connected through a network. The requirements for the network will be discussed next.

NETWORK REQUIREMENTS

Networks are used to support online teaching/learning systems as well as hands-on practice required by some technology-based courses. An online teaching/learning system and some courses require a stable and well established network. Some other courses only need partly established networks so that students can perform hands-on practice to configure their own networks. In the following, we will exam the network requirements for different purposes.

Network Requirements for Online Teaching/Learning Systems

As described in the previous topic, an online teaching/learning system requires several servers such as a network server, database server, and server for the learning management system. To access these servers from personal computers at home, we need a well-established network to connect the personal computers to the servers.

On the client side, students need to subscribe the Internet service. Nowadays, most of the Internet services are broadband high-speed Internet services such as DSL or cable. The students can connect their own local area network at home to the Internet through a DSL or cable router. Most of the routers allow users to create a small network so that several computers at home can share the same Internet connection by using the Network Address Translation (NAT) technology built inside the DSL router. Through the Internet, the students can access the course Web site or VPN server.

On the server side, a campus is usually connected to the ISP service or to other campuses through T1 or fiber optical cables. Firewalls are configured to protect the internal network. Through the Internet, students are allowed to access the servers. For example, students can access Web servers to get university related information and the links to the other remotely accessible servers. They can access VPN servers to log on to online computer labs. To access course materials, they are allowed to access learning management system servers. They can also access some database servers for hands-on practice. Security is a great concern for the servers that allow remote access. These servers are exposed to malicious viruses on the Internet. Hackers may be able to penetrate into a university's networks through these servers. To protect the university's networks, firewalls should be installed and properly configured according to the network security policies. To prevent users from directly accessing the internal networks through the firewall server, the firewall server should be isolated from the internal networks.

An internal network consists of many subnets that are linked through routers and switches. All the computers and network equipment are physically linked to each subnet. Routers should be configured to protect sensitive data. A university's internal network is usually managed by a directory service installed on one or more network servers. All the computers and user accounts on the network are configured to be in the same domain. The university's branch campuses can be configured as sub domains or organizational units. Each of the remotely accessible servers should be given a fully qualified domain name (FQDN). To summarize, Figure 3-1 presents a simplified illustration of a network infrastructure that supports an online teaching/learning system.

Figure 3-1. Network infrastructure for supporting online teaching and learning

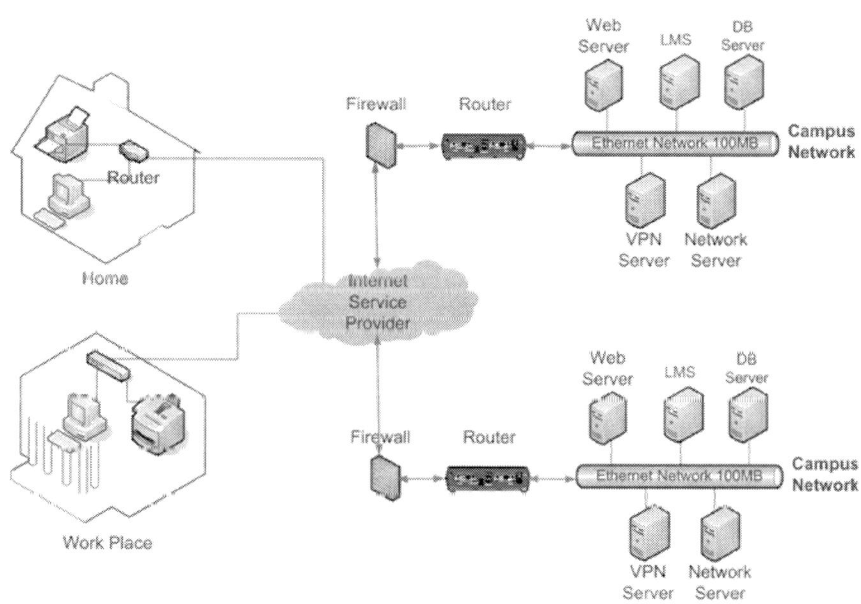

According to Figure 3-1, a student can access the course materials of one of the two campuses depending on which campus the student is registered in. To make the online teaching materials available to students 24 hours a day and 7 days a week, the university's network has to be highly reliable. The reliability of the network can be strengthened by using redundancy and by using well-designed network physical structure. The following discusses these methods.

Redundancy

The network server has to be highly reliable. Redundancy is a commonly used technique to improve reliability. It can be used to prevent the failure of a network component that causes the failure of the network server itself. The following are some of the network server components that can be protected by using redundancy.

- The hard disk system in a network server is one of the most vulnerable components. The redundancy method provides fault tolerance to the hard disk system. The commonly used fault tolerance technique is Redundant Array of Inexpensive Disks (RAID). More details about RAID will be covered in later chapters. Another technique is Self-Monitoring, Analysis, and Reporting Technology (SMART).
- Memory failure can cause data corruption. To prevent memory failure, you need to use the memory that supports Error Correcting Code (ECC). By using additional RAM, ECC is able to correct a single-bit error by itself and report multiple-bit errors.
- The failure of processors will crash the entire network system. Using a network server that has multiple processors greatly improves reliability. In this way, the failure of one processor does not cause the total failure of the network server. Another benefit for the network server to use multiple processors is that it can significantly improve the network server's performance.
- The failure of the network server's network card can disable the communication between the network server and other devices on the network. To prevent the network server's inability to communicate with the rest of the network, the network server can use the network card redundancy technique (using multiple network cards). This can also improve the network server's performance.
- Server redundancy can prevent damage caused by the failure of any components in the network server. Server redundancy can be done by creating a pair of network servers, one as the primary server and the other as the secondary server. Any change on the primary server will be copied to the secondary server. If the primary server fails, the secondary server will continue to op-

erate. To achieve even better redundancy and performance, several network servers can be clustered together.

- Power failure is another main reason that causes the network server to shut down. Using multiple power supplies is the solution. Network servers can be supported by two or three power supplies. In this way, the failure of one power supply will not cause the network server to shut down.

The redundancy method requires more equipment. However, it is an effective way to reduce the network server's downtime. Nothing can be more frustrating than the shutdown of the entire network. Changing the network's physical infrastructure, as described above, can also improve the reliability in the following.

Network Physical Infrastructure

Redundancy can be considered a special case of re-designing the network physical infrastructure. There are some other ways to re-design the network physical infrastructure for better reliability.

- To guarantee the power supply, we should attach the equipment called uninterruptible power supply (UPS) to each of the main network devices. A UPS can be a battery backup system or an emergency generator based backup system. During a power outage, the UPS can still supply power for the network servers. It can also eliminate electric spikes to protect sensitive electronic parts.
- Mesh networks can also improve network reliability. Unlike the other networks, all the nodes in a mesh network are connected to each other via multiple routes. With such a structure, when one part of the connection in the network breaks down, the network can still operate through the other routes. Therefore, such a physical structure forms a very reliable network.
- A grid system that covers each branch campus is another option to make a network server more reliable. In a grid system, the computation result at one node of the network will not immediately affect the other nodes of the grid. In such a way, the breakdown of one node will not affect the normal operation of the other nodes.

Some measures in the daily network management practice can also improve the reliability of a network. The following are some of commonly used measures:

- Timely update routers and other network equipment with patches to fix the operation and security problems.

- For all the critical network equipment, network servers, and applications, make sure to document their configurations. Also, there must be backup facilities in place and there is a backup and recovery plan for daily maintenance.
- For each of the critical components in the network such as routers and switches, make sure to have some spare ones for replacement in case some of them break down.
- Regularly monitoring and auditing the network system can detect problems in the early stage so that the problems can be fixed before they shut down the entire network system.

In the above, we have investigated some of the technical requirements of the networks that support the online teaching/learning systems. For hands-on practice, there may be more requirements for the networks. Next, we will discuss some of the requirements of hands-on practice.

Network Requirements of Hands-On Practice

Many technology-based courses need network support for hands-on practice. As mentioned earlier, some of the courses need fully established networks and some only need partially established networks so that students can perform hands-on practice to configure their own networks. The following describes the networks needed by technology-based courses:

- **Courses requiring simulated labs:** For this type of course, there is no additional requirements on the network structure. The network infrastructure used to support the online teaching/learning system is sufficient for this kind of course. Students can download the simulation software from the learning management system's Web site and run the simulation software on their home computers.
- **Courses requiring computer controlled instruments:** For this type of course, a separate Web site needs to be constructed. The Web site can be created on the university's Web server. If the security concern prevents you from creating the Web site on the university's Web server, you need to have a new Web server to host the Web site. The course Web site provides interactive GUI tools to allow students to control the activities of the computer controlled instruments.
- **Courses requiring application software:** For this type of course, a VPN server may be necessary to allow students to remotely access the application server that is installed on the university's internal network. The VPN server is configured to allow the access by multiple users simultaneously. Not all the programming courses require remote access to the application server.

For example, students in a Java programming class can download the Java development package free from Sun's Web site and install it on their home computers. Therefore, there is no need to remotely log on to the university's application server.

- **Courses requiring client-server structure:** This type of course may need several client-server structures to support hands-on practice. Students are divided into groups and each group has its own client-server structure. Usually, an online computer lab is constructed to support hands-on practice on the client-server structures. In such a case, a VPN server is necessary. After logging on to the VPN server, the students can access their groups' client-server structures for hands-on practice. Routers may be needed if the hands-on practice requires the groups to communicate with each other. If the students' home computers are used as client computers, the students can access the application servers through the VPN server or directly access the application servers which allow remote access. A database server such as Oracle or SQL Server is this type of application server. Figure 3-2 shows the topology of such a network infrastructure. The students can perform their hands-practice on three client-server structures.
- **Courses requiring network and server-side operations:** Similar to the courses that need the client-server structure to support hands-on practice, this type of course needs several subnets to support its hands-on practice. In an online computer lab, several local area networks need to be constructed. However, the local area networks built for this type of course cannot be shared with other courses since re-configuring operating systems and networks will prevent students from other classes to access these networks. This kind of course does not require the network equipment and network servers to be fully configured since students will learn how to configure them. Figure 3-3 shows how the networks should be constructed to support this type of course and other similar courses.

In the above, we have investigated the network requirements for different courses. Some details on the network requirements for hands-on practice are discussed.

The learning management system is a major component in an online teaching/learning system. The requirements for the learning management system will be discussed next.

Figure 3-2. Network infrastructure for supporting client-server hands-on practice

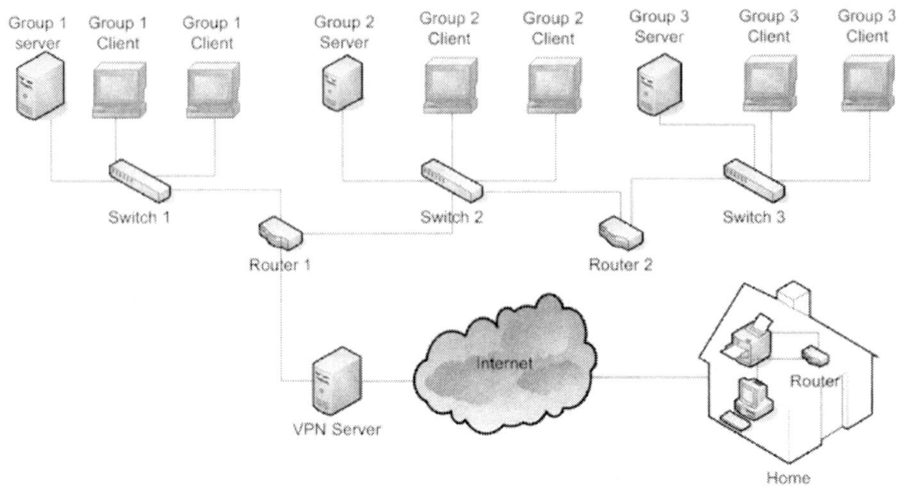

Figure 3-3. Network infrastructure for supporting courses requiring network and server-side operations

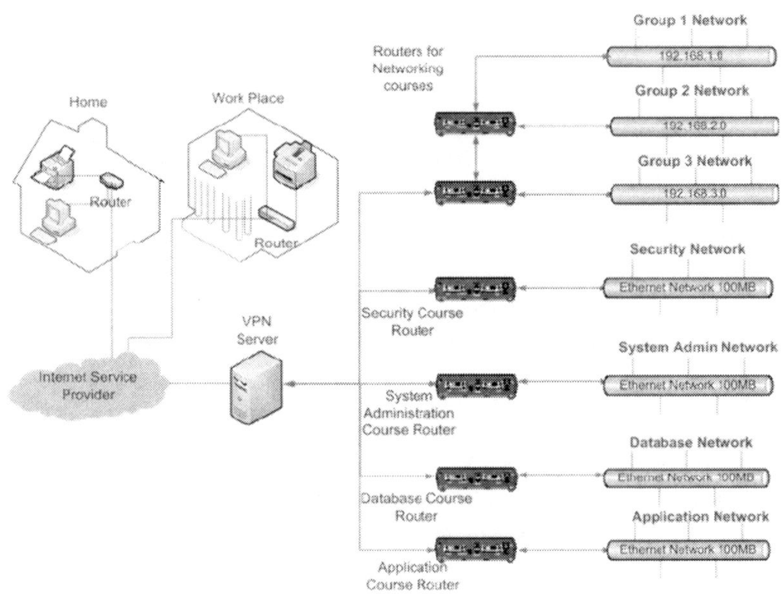

LEARNING MANAGEMENT SYSTEM REQUIREMENTS

Except some online hands-on practice, most of the online teaching activities can be managed by learning management system software. Universities use enterprise-level learning management system software to schedule, track, and report online courses. A learning management system also provides tools for creating teaching materials and managing collaboration for online courses. As such an important component in an online teaching/learning system, a sophisticated learning management system should have the following functionalities.

- To be secure, the learning management system should include tools for enforcing security measures and managing users.
- The learning management system plays an important role in Web-based teaching. To reduce downtime, it should provide tools for system backup and crash recovery.
- To assist instructors in managing their courses, the learning management system should include course management tools for instructors to manage course content, assignments, and grades. It should also include course development tools to help instructors develop Web-based course materials.
- To enhance teaching and learning, multimedia and collaboration tools should be provided by the learning management system for group activities, multimedia presentations, online help and communication.
- The learning management system should provide tools for remote access and online registration for students.
- To assist learning, the learning management system should provide tools to allow students to access course materials, online exams, and grades.

To support these functionalities, a server should be equipped with adequate hardware and software. The following are the hardware requirements for a server computer system to make the learning management system function properly.

- For a server computer system that hosts the learning management system, the requirement for RAM is based on the number of users who simultaneously log on to the same learning management system. For example, if there are one thousand simultaneous user logins, you usually need 10GB to 30GB RAM depending on the learning management system you have installed.
- The learning management system itself usually will not take much hard disk space. However, it requires a database to store the data about users, courses, teaching materials, grades, and so on. For a mid-sized campus, if it is only the learning management system (not counting the database), starting with

10GB hard disk space should be adequate. Later, you may need to add more hard disks as more data are added.

- As mentioned earlier, a server computer system with multiple processors can significantly improve performance and reliability. When there is a large number of simultaneous logins, a server with multiple processors is recommended to host the learning management system.

The requirements for software may vary depending on the courses supported by the learning management system. The following is some basic software that should be included to support the learning management system.

- Usually, a learning management system can be hosted by various operating systems. For example, as an open source learning management system, Moodle is primarily developed for the Linux operating system. It can also be hosted by Windows, Solaris 10, Mac OS X, and Netware 6 operating systems.
- A database is a necessary component for the learning management system. Usually, the learning management system can use databases created by various database management systems. For example, Moodle can be supported primarily by MySQL. In addition, Moodle can also be supported by PostgreSQL, Oracle, and Microsoft SQL Server.
- Programming languages are necessary for creating code for dynamic activities. Some of the learning management systems support multiple programming languages and others support only one programming language. For example, Moodle supports the programming language PHP.
- To allow students to access course materials from various Web browsers, a learning management system supports various Web servers. For example, Moodle primarily supports Apache and also other Web servers that support PHP. Microsoft IIS on the Windows platform is this type of Web server.

In the above we have briefly reviewed the hardware and software requirements for hosting a learning management system. To store and keep track of the data used by the learning management system, databases are used. The technology requirements by a database management system are discussed next.

DATABASE MANAGEMENT SYSTEM REQUIREMENTS

A database is used to store, provide, and manage data for a learning management system. It also supports data analysis for business intelligence. Some of the technology-based courses also need the support of databases for hand-on practice.

For the database to support the learning management system, an enterprise version of a database management system is required. The following are some of the requirements for the database management system to support an online teaching/learning system:

- The database management system should support advanced hardware devices such as a 64-bit CPU, multiple processor computing, and storage area network (SAN).
- Depending on the computing environment, the database management system should be able to adapt to the server platforms supported by Linux, FreeBSD, Solaris, HP-UX, IBM AIX 5L, Windows, and other operating systems.
- The database management system should support new programming features such as SQL 2003 standard-compliant features and Extensible Markup Language (XML), and other programming related tools such as triggers, views, stored procedures, cursors, and schemas.
- The database management system should support database management tools such as user account management, database backup and recovery, data encryption, performance tuning, monitoring and auditing, and metadata management tools.
- A sophisticated database management system should also include tools for business intelligence such as tools for developing data warehouses, and performing data mining and Online Analytical Processing (OLAP).
- To support the online teaching/learning system, the database management system should provide tools such as JDBC and ODBC to manage remote access connection.
- Supporting the technologies such as Java and .NET for developing front-end applications is another requirement for a sophisticated database management system.
- To assist data migration from other data sources into a database, the database management system should include the data migration tools.

In the above, we have investigated some general requirements for a database management system. Depending on the requirements by an online teaching/learning system, there will be some specific needs for the database management system. To support the functionalities of the database management system, some requirements of the hardware and software should be addressed.

- To achieve better performance and reliability, the database should be hosted by a server with multiple 64-bit processors, 1000GB hard disks which are configured with RAID 10, and 16GB RAM. For some small online teaching/learning systems, the above configuration can be modified to use a single processor with a much smaller hard disk and less RAM.

- Although it is not required, it will be nice to include some office product software such as OpenOffice or Microsoft Office.

For the database management system used to support hands-on practice, the above requirements may still be applicable. Since the database management system does not have to support daily operations, the requirements for the server hosting the database can be significantly reduced. Usually, a server computer system with 1GB of RAM and a hard disk of 10GB should be able to handle the needs of hands-on practice.

COURSE MATERIAL DEVELOPMENT REQUIREMENTS

As mentioned in the previous chapter, various types of online teaching materials are created to support Web-based teaching and learning. They can be created in different formats such as text only documents, graph enhanced documents, multimedia enhanced documents, collaboration enhanced Web pages, Web conferencing, virtual reality materials, and online education games. Various technologies are used to create these course materials. The formats of the course materials use different technologies. With those technologies, instructors and online teaching support teams can create video, audio, and interactive course materials to enhance online teaching and learning. In the following, we will take a closer look at the technology requirements for developing course materials in different formats:

- **Text only documents:** The requirement for developing this type of document is low. A good word processing editor should be enough. It needs Internet connection to upload and download course materials. A document can be directly uploaded to the class Web site for display or download. Some software to convert documents and PowerPoint presentations to pdf files may be required if the pdf format is required by the course. For the hand-written course content, a scanner will be needed to convert the document to an image file or a pdf file which can then be uploaded to the class Web site.
- **Graph enhanced documents:** This type of course material requires tools such as photography equipment, an image editor, a chart editor, a computer screen capturer, clip art, and a sophisticated word processor. Often, some of these tools are combined in one software package such as OpenOffice.

- **Multimedia enhanced documents:** Various multimedia technologies are required for this type of course material. The following are some of the equipment and software that may be required to create multimedia course materials.
    - The equipment used to develop audio materials may include a headphone port, speaker port, and a port for a powered or unpowered microphone on a personal computer. Most of these components are usually already built in a personal computer. For the purpose of creating multimedia course materials, these built-in audio devices are good enough.
    - The equipment for creating video materials may include a video card, a monitor, a digital camera or camcorder. The video card generates video signals and sends these signals to the monitor. The digital camera or camcorder can record live-motion video/audio. The recorded materials can be used for Web conferencing or can be edited and archived for later use.
    - To playback multimedia files on a personal computer, a media player is needed. Some Web browsers include a media player. If not supported by a Web browser, one can download a free media player. Audio or video files are often created in various formats. Therefore, some of the media players are able to play audio and video clips, movies, and games that are created in different formats.
    - Web authoring tools are required to create Web pages with multimedia content. These tools allow users to create sophisticated Web pages containing images, animations, and audio and video components. Some Web authoring tools also include a Web page editor that can help with multimedia Web page development. Web authoring tools also provide a remote access utility to configure the connection to a remote database. To assist the development of Web pages, some Web authoring tools also provide templates for some commonly used Web pages.
    - Sometimes, voice recognition software and handwriting identification software can also help create multimedia course materials.
    - Although multimedia enhanced documents can greatly improve the quality of online course materials, they require a lot of computing resources. Keeping the quality of the multimedia materials requires a high speed Internet connection, high quality video card, powerful server and desktop computer, and large hard drives.

The development of multimedia course materials requires a variety of technologies, computation resources, and hands-on skills. It also takes a lot of effort to develop these course materials. More details on developing multimedia course materials will be covered in later chapters.

- **Collaboration enhanced Web pages:** To develop this type of Web page requires a sophisticated Web authoring tool. Such a Web page needs a Web browser that is able to run ActiveX and other scripts. Collaboration tools such as a virtual whiteboard, screen sharing, text messenger, VoIP, and document camera may be needed. The collaboration enhanced Web page also requires fast Internet connection, powerful server and desktop computers, and large hard drives for data storage.
- **Web conferencing:** To create a Web conference, you may need management tools such as meeting management and attendee administration. For live communication, the required tools are audio/video streaming, e-mail, text messenger, and VoIP. For collaboration during a meeting, a Web conference should include tools such as screen sharing management, presenter management, virtual whiteboards, Flash animation, and drawing tools. It is also ideal if a recording tool is included in a Web conferencing package. Most of these tools are often included in Web conferencing software. To secure the live data transferred over the Internet, data encryption and decryption tools are needed for data protection. Like many other multimedia based online teaching materials, Web conferencing also requires a lot of computing resources. The requirements for hardware equipment may include document cameras, camcorders, Webcams, tablets for handwriting, speakers, projectors, and a server computer system to host the Web conferencing server.
- **Virtual reality:** Virtual reality is a computer generated environment by superimposing graphics, audio, and sense enhancement devices over a real-world surrounding. To create the computer generated environment, you will need 3-D simulation software, 3-D drawing tools, and a database generation system. The requirements for the hardware may include a special position detection system, projection system, motion platform, special manipulation system, and 3-D acceleration card in a computer system.
- **Education games:** The development of education games as teaching materials requires tools such as a gaming engine, a programming language, high quality video and audio equipment, a powerful desktop computer, and hand-held devices. In addition to software based computer games, video games can also be played with television-based and hand-held gaming consoles. Video games can also be played on the Internet through a broadband high-speed Internet connection. Some simple games can be played through a modem. Some of the online games may require extra hard disk space, DVD-RAM, interactive TVs, and joy sticks.

In the above, we have investigated the technology requirements for developing course materials for an online teaching/learning system. We have discussed the requirements for the technologies used to create each type of course content. In later chapters, we will further discuss how to use these technologies.

CONCLUSION

In this chapter, we have discussed the technology needs to achieve the design goals. Based on the requirements of an online teaching/learning system, we have identified the technologies that can implement the teaching/learning system to meet the requirements. This chapter first analyzed the requirements for computer systems. We explored various technologies for the servers as well as the client computers. Then, we examined the network technologies that link the client personal computers to the servers installed on the university campus. We discussed two types of networks; one type supports the online teaching/learning system and the other type supports hands-on practice. The requirements for these two types of networks are different, especially on network reliability. After investigating the network technology needs, we looked at the technology needs of the learning management system. We identified the hardware and software needs for supporting the learning management system. We also looked at the requirements of the database management system. As pointed out in this chapter, the technologies are the necessary tools for developing course materials. Therefore, we identified the technology requirements for creating online course materials. In later chapters, we will discuss how to use these technologies to create an online teaching/learning system that fulfills the requirements. We will start with network related open source tools in the next chapter.

REFERENCES

Ayala, G., & Paredes, R. (2003). Learner model servers: Personalization of Web based educational applications based on digital collections. In D. Lassner & C. McNaught (Eds.), *Proceedings of World Conference on Educational Multimedia, Hypermedia and Telecommunications 2003* (pp. 132-135). Chesapeake, VA: AACE.

Bennett, F. (1999). *Computers as tutors: Solving the crisis in education*. Sarasota, FL: Faben.

Boer, A. (2002). A delivery server infrastructure for multimedia distance learning services. In P. Kommers & G. Richards (Eds.), *Proceedings of World Conference on Educational Multimedia, Hypermedia and Telecommunications 2002* (pp. 178-179). Chesapeake, VA: AACE.

Correia, E., & Watson, R. (2006). VMware as a practical learning tool. In N. Sarkar (Ed.), *Tools for teaching computer networking and hardware concepts* (pp. 338-354). Hershey, PA: Idea Group.

Garrand, T. (2006). *Writing for multimedia and the Web: A practical guide to content development for interactive media* (3rd ed.). Burlington, MA: Focal Press.

Horton, W., & Horton, K. (2003). *E-learning tools and technologies: A consumer's guide for trainers, teachers, educators, and instructional designers*. New York: Wiley.

Ivers, K. S., & Barron, A. E. (2005). *Multimedia projects in education: Designing, producing, and assessing* (2nd ed.). Englewood, CO: Libraries Unlimited.

Perry, T. L. (2000). *A history of interactive education and training.* Retrieved April 30, 2006, from http://www.refresher.com/!history2.html

Veglis, A. (2000). Design of a Web based interactive computer lab course. In *10th Mediterranean Electrotechnical Conference, I*, 302-305. Piscataway, NJ: IEEE.

Section II
Infrastructure Development for Offering Online Courses

Chapter IV
Network Development and Management

INTRODUCTION

In the previous chapter, we investigated the technology requirements for an online teaching/learning system. Networks are one of the major components in an online teaching/learning system infrastructure. As mentioned earlier, an online teaching/learning system is often constructed on a client-server structure. A network is used to link the tiers of the client-server structure. Through the network, the client side can send requests to the server side and get response from the server.

A network consists of routers, switches, network adapters, modems, multiplexers, different types of transmission media, network protocols, and network management tools. There are different types of networks such as local area networks, wide area networks, Internet, and so on. Not only does an online teaching/learning system depend on a reliable and secure network infrastructure, many technology-based courses also use networks for hands-on practice.

In this chapter, we will focus on issues related to networks. We will examine how a network works and how it can be used to support the online teaching/learning system. We will also take a closer look at different networks and how they can be used in the online teaching/learning system. We will also investigate what roles can be played by the open source network tools in developing and managing a network infrastructure for the online teaching/learning system.

We will start with the description of the client-server infrastructure. Then, we will investigate various types of client-server structures and compare their features.

We will check into the functionalities of each tier of the client-server structure and how they are able to implement the online teaching/learning system.

After the client-server infrastructure is introduced, we will look at the network equipment used to construct various networks. We will investigate the hardware and protocols used in developing an enterprise-level network. Many of the open source protocols play an important role in various types of network structures. Detailed discussion about these open source protocols will be given in this chapter.

There are various open source network management tools. Many of them can be used to develop online teaching/learning systems. We will categorize these open source tools based on their functionalities. Then, we will discuss them in detail and look into their features and how they can be used in developing and managing the network for an online teaching/learning system.

At the enterprise level, one of the network management tools is Lightweight Directory Access Protocol (LDAP). LDAP is a client-server protocol that can be used for delivering directory services. A directory service defines the namespaces of all the objects on a network. It stores the authentication information about users, computers, and other network resources such as files, printers, and so on. It decides what permissions a user will have and how a computer or other network resources can be accessed. This chapter will demonstrate how to create a directory service with the open source directory service tool OpenLDAP. It will also discuss the configuration issues and the open source tools used in the development process.

BACKGROUND

Constructing networks for an online teaching/learning system is a strenuous project. It often requires tremendous effort and sophisticated skills. First, it needs a careful design on a network's infrastructure to meet the requirements of the online teaching/learning system. Like the development of many IT projects, designing a network infrastructure includes the planning, designing, and implementation phases. For designing large scale networks, readers can find technical details from the book by Cisco Systems Inc., Thomas, and Khan (1999). Readers can find the design of three kinds of networks, campus, wide area, and remote connections from the technical point of view. Some studies on designing networks for universities have been done. Kapadia and Fortes (1998) described Purdue University's network computing hubs' prototype which is a demand-based network computing system for reducing duplicated effort. There are other studies on planning and creating IT infrastructures. Penrod and Harbor (2000) presented a case study on designing and implementing an e-learning system for a large university. They discussed the issues related to the planning and creation of an IT governance structure. They provided an organization structure to overcome barriers while implementing the e-learning system.

A network consists of network devices and protocols. Understanding these devices and protocols requires the knowledge in the fields of computer engineering and computer science. The commonly used network devices include routers, network interface cards, switches, and bridges. The book by Teare and Paquet (2005) examines these hardware devices and how the devices are used in the enterprise-level network design and implementation process. The communication over a network is controlled by network protocols. A comprehensive coverage of network devices and protocols is given by Olifer and Olifer (2006). Studies have also been done on the device and protocol related issues. For example, Parker and Holmes (2007) studied the effectiveness and satisfaction towards the online courses delivered by using the Compressed Video and Internet Protocol.

Wireless technology is also used to construct networks for teaching and learning. To increase mobility and flexibility, Varvel and Harnisch (2001) discussed a wireless campus area network that supported lab based teaching and learning activities on campus.

It requires a network management team to take care of network operations. Often, network management tools are used to assist network management. Readers can find a comprehensive coverage of network management tools of the Linux operating system in Maxwell's (2000) book. For other open source network management tools, readers can find more information in Dubie's (2005) article which introduces several inexpensive, flexible and easy-to-integrate network management tools produced by open source vendors and developers. There are many studies and discussions in the area of network management for e-learning. For example, Uys (2001) discussed the issues related to the management of networked education.

Using the virtual technology can significantly reduce the network management workload. Correia and Watson (2006) conducted a study on using the virtual network technology for teaching networking courses. They showed that the virtual networks created in their labs were easy to maintain and reduced the cost on lab hardware.

A directory service is used to look up information about users and network resources. LDAP is the protocol that allows clients to access the information provided by a directory service through a network connection. OpenLDAP is one of the open source tools for setting up the LDAP service. Jackiewicz (2004) provided detailed information about OpenLDAP. Donzelli, Fontana, Ravaioli, Toppan, Patella, and De Castro (2006) presented an integrated system that combined multimedia broadband services into a common framework. The system is managed by LDAP and SQL servers.

This chapter focuses on network related development with open source tools. We will start with network design related issues. After that, some open source network tools will be introduced and we will discuss how the tools can be used in daily network management.

CLIENT-SERVER ARCHITECTURE

The network development procedure is similar to the development of an online teaching/learning system. It includes the planning, designing, and implementation phases. In this section, we will focus the network infrastructure. First, we will investigate various types of client-server structures and discuss how each of these structures fits in different types of online teaching/learning systems.

In a networked teaching/learning environment, servers are used to manage users and network resources, provide and store course materials, and respond to the requests from clients. The networks are constructed to link the servers to the clients. The client side runs various applications. When the applications need the information stored on the server computer systems, the clients send requests to the servers. The advantages of using the client-server architecture to host the online teaching/learning system are:

- The workload is distributed between the servers and clients; this significantly improves the online teaching/learning system's performance.
- The clients contact the servers only when it is necessary. Part of the application related tasks can be done on the clients' computer systems. In such a way, we can significantly reduce the network traffic.
- A system implemented on the client-server structure is more reliable. The workload is distributed to multiple computer systems. The failure of one computer system will not completely shut down the operation. Also, various measures such as redundancy can be enforced to improve the reliability of the servers.
- The client-server structure is more flexible. It allows the older technology to work with the new technology without replacing the older technology. It also allows the new version of software to work with the older software side by side. One application on the client side can use data from various data sources and one data source can supply data to multiple clients.
- The client-server structure can handle a large number of data transactions and a large number of simultaneous logins.
- The data stored on the servers of the client-server structure are more secure since the servers are better protected by various security measures.

An online teaching/learning system usually supports hundreds and thousands of simultaneous logins. Based on the size of the simultaneous logins and the complexity of the infrastructure, the client-server architecture can be categorized as two-tier architecture, three-tier architecture, or N-tier architecture.

Two-Tier Architecture

If the workload is divided into two partitions, such a computation structure is called two-tier client-server architecture which includes a client tier and a server tier. The two-tier architecture is good for a small online teaching/learning system which usually has less than one hundred simultaneous logins. It is also good for hands-on practice required by some technology-based courses. It is easy to set up and manage. However, for the online teaching/learning system, the two-tier structure has some limitations. Since a client is directly connected to a server, each connection is a keep-alive session. The performance of the two-tier system can be a serious problem when there are many simultaneous keep-alive sessions. Therefore, it often restricts simultaneous logins to less than one hundred. Another disadvantage is that the two-tier structure is not flexible enough when hosting the online teaching/learning system. When the online teaching/learning system is upgraded, the existing system on both the server and client tiers has to be replaced by the new system. Also, since the clients are directly connected to the server, they have to use the same platform that the server uses. For example, when a technology-based course requires Oracle for hands-on practice, a database server is used to host the Oracle database. On the client side, the Oracle client software must be installed for accessing the database server. If later the university decides to use MySQL, the Oracle software on both the client side and the server side has to be replaced by the MySQL software. Due to these limitations, the two-tier structure is often used for hands-on practice and seldom used to host an online teaching/learning system.

Three-Tier Architecture

When the workload is divided into three partitions, such a computation structure is called three-tier client-server architecture which includes a client tier, a middle tier, and a server tier. The three tier client-server structure is designed to overcome the difficulties of the two-tier system by adding a middle tier between the client tier and the server tier. The middle tier can be used to provide services such as Web service, transaction processing service, message service, remote access service, firewall service, business logic implementation service, and so on. These services can make the three-tier client-server system able to handle a large number of simultaneous logins. For example, when there are one thousand simultaneous login attempts, we can create ten middle tier servers, each of them assigned to handle one hundred logins. When a client requests an activity, the middle tier will analyze the request. Depending on the client's request, the middle tier will decide which server to contact and get response from the server. In such a way, a server only deals with a maximum of ten middle tier connections instead of one thousand direct client connections. Also, the transaction processing service allows the clients to share a pool of resources. When requested, the middle tier arranges the connection from a client to a requested resource. When the job is done, the requested resource is returned back to the pool and is ready to handle another request. In such a way, no single connection can hold the resources in its connection session.

Another advantage of the three-tier client-server structure is that it is much more flexible. For example, currently, we have an Oracle database server installed to host databases for hands-on practice required by some of the technology-based courses. If some other courses want to use MySQL for hands-on practice, we can just add a new database server on the server side. There is no need to replace the Oracle database server with the MySQL database server. The middle tier's transaction processing service will decide if a request is for Oracle or MySQL, and then forward the request to the right database server.

The next advantage of the three-tier structure is that the middle tier can share some of the workload on the servers and clients. The calculation of business logic requires a lot of computation power, which can significantly slow down a server's performance. By implementing the business logic on the middle tier computer system, the server can be released to work on other jobs. The middle tier communicates with the server side only when it is necessary. Some middle tier can process a client's request with several resources simultaneously. The middle tier can also be used to host various special purpose servers such as application servers, VPN servers, FTP servers, learning management servers, Web Servers, and firewall servers.

In addition to all the above advantages, the three-tier client-server structure is more secure. The server side is protected by the middle tier. Many security measures can be implemented on the middle tier, such as user authentication and virus detection. The Web server is one of the most vulnerable components in an online teaching/learning system since it directly contacts the Internet. When placed on the middle tier, the Web server prevents clients from directly accessing the back-end servers. The Web server is used to interact with front-end users. In such a way, the Web server can be used to prevent Internet hackers. Instead of letting the clients directly access a database to retrieve information, the middle tier can provide Web services to supply data requested by the clients.

N-Tier Architecture

For an even more complex online teaching/learning system, we can consider an N-tier client-server structure. In the N-tier structure, the tiers are further divided into more specific tiers such as a data tier, presentation logic tier, data access tier, proxy tier, business logic tier, and so on. The functionalities provided by each tier are summarized in the following.

- **Data tier:** A data tier includes storage devices, database servers and other data sources such as text files, spreadsheets, and XML files.
- **Client interface tier:** This tier includes all the interfaces on the client side such as forms and reports for the users on the client side to enter data, view information, and perform some other activities.
- **Presentation logic tier:** This tier includes the presentation logic to support client interfaces such as Web forms and reports.
- **Proxy tier:** This tier controls how a user from the client side communicates with the server. It can be used to analyze the user's request and provide the access to the server based on the permissions given to the user.
- **Business logic tier:** A business logic tier is used to implement business rules. When implementing business constraints, this tier often consumes additional computation power. Therefore, it is usually not placed on the server where the data tier is located.

For a complex system, the distribution of workload to more tiers can make the computation more efficient. On the other hand, too many small tiers can make the networks more complex and hard to manage.

The networks that support the client-server structure often include the Internet, home networks, campus backbone networks, departmental subnets, and networks used for hands-on practice. The communication among these networks is controlled by routers which pass data from one network to another network. In addition to routers, there are many other network devices. Routers also provide various protocols to handle different network related jobs. The following section discusses network devices and protocols.

NETWORK EQUIPMENT AND OPEN SOURCE NETWORK PROTOCOLS

Network devices are used to link computer systems that need to communicate with each other. These devices create paths between the computer systems. The network protocols are used to transfer data from one computer to another. They are also used for managing the communication between computers.

Network Equipment

In the following, let us look at some commonly used network equipment that supports open source network protocols. Many protocols play an important role in network communication. To better understand how these protocols work, we will first investigate the network equipment that uses them:

- **Firewall:** A firewall can be a hardware device or can be built with software. Firewalls are used to prevent intruders from penetrating the internal networks. The online teaching/learning system and the stored course materials should all be protected by firewalls.
- **Gateway:** A gateway is an entrance from one network to another network. A computer system or a network device that controls network traffic from the campus network to the Internet is the gateway. As another example, the server at an Internet service provider (ISP) that controls the network traffic from a student's home computer to the Internet is the gateway. When configuring a network adapter, the information about the gateway is often required. Protocols can commute through the gateway.
- **Router:** Like a gateway, a router is a computer system or a network device that can forward network traffic from one network to another network. The difference is that a router can determine the optimal path for data to travel to a destination. Routers are widely used network devices in an online teaching/learning system. They are used to connect computer networks and the Internet, and then to the students' home networks. On campus, routers are used to join departmental subnets. For hands-on practice, routers are used to link the group networks and the class backbone network. The router itself is also the main network equipment for students to learn about. In a networking class, there are various assignments on router configuration and management.
- **Bridge:** A bridge is another network device that is able to link networks. To make networks work more efficiently, the bridge can block signal collisions and information broadcasts from one local area network to another local area network. Most of the bridge functionalities can be carried out by a router. Although bridges are less expensive than routers, they are not widely used in an online teaching/learning system.
- **Switch:** A switch links several computer systems configured to be on the same network. It serves as a distribution center. When a computer system wants to

send data to another computer system which is located on the same network, the switch allocates the destination system by examining the destination address carried in a packet to be sent and then forwards the packet to the destination system. Switches are widely used network equipment in an online teaching/learning system. They are used to form subnets for departments and offices. They are also used to construct subnets for group activities in a computer lab.

- **Layer 3 switch:** Similar to a router, a Layer 3 switch can be used to forward packets to a destination computer system on another network. The difference between a Layer 3 switch and a router is that the Layer 3 switch is a piece of hardware that implements the software logic built in a router. By doing so, it may lose some flexibility, but gain better performance. Therefore, for network routing, a Layer 3 switch is a high-performance device.

Network devices use various open source protocols that can carry the network traffic to the destinations, control the way a packet should be sent, detect and fix problems during the transmission, and manage the network resources. The discussion of protocols is next.

Network Protocols

Protocols are usually designed to accomplish specific network related tasks and they can be implemented by using software or hardware, or both. During the data transmission over a network, the following tasks can be done by protocols:

- When transmitting information over a network, messages are divided into little chunks called packets which are used to carry the messages to the destinations. Protocols are used to format these packets.
- Protocols can be used to determine the start and end of a packet to be transmitted over a network.
- Protocols can detect a destination end point and determine how to establish a connection to the end point at the destination.
- Protocols can check the messages transmitted to the destinations. If an error occurs during the transmission, they can either correct the error or discard the packet.
- Protocols can reassemble the packets at the ultimate destination to reconstruct the original massages.
- Protocols can also be used to manage connections. They can detect those accidently lost connections and decide what to do with them.

In addition to the above tasks, many open source protocols are created to accomplish specific tasks. In the following, let us take a look at some of the commonly used open source protocols in an online teaching/learning system:

- **Internet Protocol (IP):** IP is a well-known open source network protocol. The communication over various local area networks and over the Internet largely depends on IP, which sends messages from one computer system to another through the Internet and various local area networks. IP can carry messages from one type of network to another type of network. Each computer system or network device that is linked to the Internet or a local area network must have an IP address as the identification of the equipment. Each packet formed for data transmission contains the source address and destination address that are related to the IP addresses of the sender and receiver. IP's job is to carry messages to destinations. Therefore, IP does not have the error checking functionality. It needs to work with other protocols for error detection and correction.
- **Transmission Control Protocol (TCP):** TCP is another famous open source network protocol. It often works with IP for data transmission over the Internet. TCP and IP were the first two network protocols created for data transmission in the 1970's. The creation of these two open source protocols revolutionized network computing. As IP delivers messages to destination computers or network equipment, TCP keeps track of each packet and makes sure that it is efficiently and correctly sent and received. TCP is the protocol that actually formats packets when sending massages and reassembles the packets to get the original messages. The reassembling task can be a complex process. When packets are transmitted, they can take different routes to get to the same destination. When these packets arrive, the order of these packets has been altered. At the destination, TCP waits for all the packets to arrive and reorders these packets to the original sequence. When some of the packets get lost during the transmission, TCP will wait long enough, then discard the entire message, and wait for the sender to resend the message.
  Another main task that can be accomplished by TCP is maintaining the connection between the sender and receiver. TCP keeps the connection between them until the all the messages have been received by the application software on the receiver side. The connection maintained by TCP allows messages to be sent in either direction, which means that the application programs on both sides of the connection can send messages at the same time. To guarantee that connections are established or terminated reliably, TCP uses a three-way handshake scheme to make sure the agreements on connection and disconnection are unambiguous.

The next main task of TCP is checking errors occurred during the transmission. It verifies if any packets get lost during the transmission. Therefore, TCP is known as a completely reliable protocol. It makes sure that anything sent by the sender is delivered to the receiver and there are no duplicated packets.
Another great feature of TCP is congestion control. During transmission, busy traffic or a hardware problem can cause the delay of a packet's arrival at the destination. The delay will in turn cause more resending of messages, which will make the congestion even worse. TCP uses the testing signal to decide how much data should be sent to avoid congestion.
As open source protocols, the combination TCP/IP is not only installed on the open source operating systems such as Linux and BSD, it is also the default network transmission protocol on most of the commercial operating systems such as Widows, Mac OS, and various versions of the commercial UNIX operating system.

- **Hypertext Transfer Protocol (HTTP):** In Chapter 1, it was mentioned that Tim Berners-Lee invented the open source World Wide Web. As part of the World Wide Web, HTTP written by Tim Berners-Lee, is an application protocol that is embedded in TCP for transferring text files, images, audio, video, and other files on the World Wide Web. Being embedded in TCP, the new version of HTTP can keep a connection open and is able to transfer all of the page components. In such a way, HTTP does not need a new connection for each component on the Web page; this can speed up the transmission significantly. A Web browser serves as a HTTP client. While clicking a link or refreshing a URL, the HTTP client can send a request to the Web server which analyzes the request and handles the request with a HTTP daemon program. Later, the response from the Web server will be sent back to the HTTP client.
- **User Datagram Protocol (UDP):** Like TCP, UDP is used to send or receive messages over a network. UDP indentifies application programs by the port numbers used by these programs. UDP also works with IP to transfer messages over the Internet or a local area network. The difference between TCP and UDP is that UDP does not provide error checking and does not form packets for data transmission. These features make UDP not a completely reliable protocol. A message can be lost, duplicated, out of order, or corrupted. On the other hand, UDP is more efficient than TCP and has much less overhead. Even though UDP is not suitable for some high quality transmission, it is very good at transmitting audio and video data which are more tolerant to small transmission errors.
- **File Transfer Protocol (FTP):** FTP is another standard protocol. Virtually every operating system supports FTP; this means that an FTP server can be

hosted by any server operating system and an FTP client can be installed on any personal computer. Software vendors and individual programmers can freely include FTP in their products. FTP is designed to transfer files from one computer system to another over the Internet. Files are stored in an FTP server and FTP clients are allowed to remotely access these files. For example, an FTP client sends a request to the FTP server for a connection. After the connection is established, FTP can upload files from the FTP client to the FTP server or download files from the FTP server to the FTP client. If permitted, the FTP client can also rename or delete files on the FTP server. In an online teaching/learning system, students often use FTP to download course materials.

- **Dynamic Host Configuration Protocol (DHCP):** DHCP is a network protocol that can be used to automatically assign an IP address to a client computer system that is physically networked to a DHCP server. To get an IP address from the DHCP server, the client computer system needs to be configured to take the dynamic IP address. The DHCP server can be configured to distribute a range of IP addresses. It can also decide the lease time and if the client computer can get the same IP address every time the lease is renewed. The use of DHCP has greatly reduced the workload of a network administrator. When a new computer system is linked to the network, it will automatically get an IP address so that it can start to communicate with other computer systems and network devices. Most of the time, students' home computers will get dynamic IP addresses from their Internet service providers. Computer systems for hands-on practice in a computer lab will get their IP addresses from a VPN server or a server set up for distributing IP addresses to the computers in the lab. For security reasons, the computers in a hands-on practice computer lab do not get their dynamic IP addresses directly from the DHCP server on a university's network. For the computer systems in an online computer lab, the DHCP server should be configured to give the same IP address every time a computer system renews its DHCP lease. In that way, students can log on to the same computer system to continue their hands-on practice tasks.
- **Simple Mail Transfer Protocol (SMTP):** SMTP is used to send e-mail from e-mail clients to e-mail servers across the Internet. After an SMTP server receives e-mail from an e-mail client, SMTP sends the e-mail from this e-mail server to the destination e-mail server across the Internet. However, SMTP is not usually used by the destination e-mail client to retrieve e-mail from the destination e-mail server. Other protocols are used to accomplish this task. We will discuss these protocols in the next paragraph. In an online teaching/learning system, the e-mail server that supports SMTP is usually installed

on campus. When students configure their e-mail client software at home, they must provide the outgoing e-mail servers' names or IP addresses. The outgoing e-mail server can be a server provided by one of the popular e-mail service vendors or can be the university's e-mail server. Since SMTP is a simple protocol, it is sometimes included in a Web server or other servers. It also needs to contact a DNS server to identify e-mail addresses. In such a case, make sure that the Web server and the DNS server function properly.

- **Post Office Protocol 3 (POP3) and Internet Message Access Protocol (IMAP):** As mentioned in the previous paragraph, SMTP is a simple protocol; therefore, it does not have much ability to queue messages at the receiving end. Instead of SMTP, the protocols POP3 and IMAP are used to retrieve data. These two protocols allow the client to save messages to the e-mail server. POP3 is a popular protocol for retrieving e-mail. It allows you to download files from the e-mail server to the e-mail client. IMAP can also be used to retrieve e-mail. The difference between IMAP and POP3 is that IMAP has more capabilities of managing e-mail on the e-mail server. As described above, when setting up the e-mail service for an online teaching/learning system, SMTP should be used with either POP3 or IMAP.
- **Secure Shell (SSH):** SSH is a protocol to secure information exchange over a network. When a connection request from a SSH client arrives in the SSH server, the SSH daemon program responds to the request by creating a secure connection. By encrypting the data and authenticating the computer system and the user, SSH creates a secure channel between the sender and receiver. It provides secure remote logins, secure remote command executions, and secure file transfer. Various implementations of SSH have been developed; some of them are proprietary and the others are open source. Among these implementations of SSH, the most popular one is the open source SSH protocol OpenSSH. OpenSSH has been included in a large number of the operating systems such as Linux, Windows, and different versions of UNIX.

In most cases, multiple protocols work together to get a certain task done. The related protocols are grouped together to form a protocol stack. Open System Interconnection (OSI) is a network communication model that divides the protocols and services into seven layers. Each layer represents a protocol stack and performs a special function in network communication. Each computer involved in network communication is equipped with these layers which combine various network protocols and services provided by the operating systems and application software.

OPEN SOURCE NETWORK MANAGEMENT TOOLS

In the above, we have briefly discussed the functionalities of some commonly used network devices and open source network protocols. During the development of a network and after a network is implemented, a team from the computer service department need to manage the network. Some of the network management tasks are carried out with network management tools. There are some open source software packages that can be used for network troubleshooting, analyzing, and monitoring. The following are some of the tasks that can be done by the open source network management tools.

- **Network monitoring:** This type of tool is used to monitor network traffic. From collected information, network administrators will be able to identify possible network problems.
- **Network troubleshooting:** Network management tools can be used to help a network administrator to troubleshoot network problems. These tools can analyze the collected information and provide guidelines for fixing the network problems.
- **Network security:** The network security management tools can be used to detect network security vulnerabilities and enforce security measures. These tools can also handle tasks such as detecting hacker intrusion, configuring firewall properties, downloading and installing anti-virus upgrades and patches, and so on.
- **Remote access:** Some of the network management tools are used to manage remote access. These tools can help network administrators to control who are allowed to remotely access the network resources and what network resources can be accessed by a user.
- **Management reporting:** One of the network management tasks is to write reports about network faults, analyses of observation data, and changes that have been made to fix problems. Some of the network management tools can help network administrators to create network management reports.

Linux, as an open source operating system, includes many of the open source network management tools. There are also stand-alone open source network management tools. Some vendors provide open source network management tools with a service package which includes charges for technical support and maintenance contract. With such a package, the open source network management tools are not really free. However, it is still cheaper than most of the commercial network management tools. In general, open source network management tools provide an inexpensive, easy to use, and flexible option for managing the online teaching/

learning system. In the following, we will examine some of the stand-alone open source or freeware network management tools.

Ethereal

Ethereal is one of the well-known open source network management tools (Ethereal, 2007). The following are some of its features:

- It is used by network administrators worldwide for network troubleshooting and analysis.
- It is a useful tool in protocol development. As an open source product, it allows the network protocol developer to add additional enhancements.
- In network related courses, Ethereal is one of the popular network management tools included in hand-on teaching materials.
- With the filter language included in Ethereal, it has the ability to sort and filter the information captured in the network traffic.
- Ethereal has rich display features. It is able to display all the network traffic through a GUI. The captured data can be displayed in different detail levels.
- Ethereal can capture live data from various types of local area networks such as Ethernet, Token Ring, and FDDI. In addition to capturing data from a wire, Ethereal can capture live data from the wireless IEEE 802.11 network. It can also capture live data that travel through the telephone wire or between cell phones.
- Ethereal can also work with the files containing captured network traffic. The content in the files can be programmatically edited for display and for many other purposes.
- Ethereal can capture and analyze data carried by hundreds of protocols such as the commonly used TCP, IP, HTTP, FTP, SMTP, POP3, IMAP, and so on.
- Ethereal can run on all popular operating systems, such as Linux, Windows, and various versions of UNIX.

Due to its ability to capture network traffic, Ethereal can cause some security vulnerabilities if it is used by the wrong person. We have to make sure that only qualified persons can use the Ethereal tool on a network and do not use Ethereal to capture the traffic in an untrusted network environment.

As a network management tool, Ethereal is very popular. According the survey done by Insecure.Org (2006), Ethereal is the second most popular network management tool. The most popular network management tool is the open source tool Nessus which will be introduced later in this chapter.

Multi Router Traffic Grapher (MRTG)

MRTG is free software available under the terms of the GNU General Public License (MTRG, 2007). To collect information about a network device, MTRG sends a request to the device through the Simple Network Management Protocol (SNMP). After the information is collected, it is transformed back through SNMP. Then MRTG creates an HTML document which contains detailed network traffic with a set of graphics. Originally developed by Tobias Oetiker and Dave Rand for monitoring router traffic, now MRTG is developed into a network management tool that can perform the following tasks:

- MRTG can be used for monitoring and measuring SNMP network devices, such as routers and network adapters. In addition, MRTG can also work with other network related devices.
- MRTG is written in Perl; it can be programmed to collect data automatically in every few minutes.
- MRTG provides HTML pages with text and image files to display the collected information. The collected information can be displayed by day, week, month, and year image files. According to the detail level, MRTG can automatically scale the Y axis to gain the best presenting effect.
- MRTG provides statistic analysis tools to calculate the maximum, average, I/O values, and so on. The result of a statistic analysis can be displayed on the HTML pages created automatically by MRTG. Warnings will be sent via e-mail if some collected values go beyond the normal range.
- As a freeware application, MRTG can run on a majority of operating systems such as Linux, Windows, and various versions of UNIX.

Through the above description, we can see that MRTG is a very convenient network monitoring tool. It can help us find out what the network devices are doing and if there is abnormal behavior during their daily operations.

Nagios

Nagios is also a well-known open source network service tool that can be used to monitor networks (Nagios, 2007). It tests network devices and network servers with intermittent test signals. The status of the network devices will be reported back. When a network problem is detected, it will notify the network administrator. The following are some of the great features provided by Nagios:

- Nagios is able to monitor many commonly used network services and protocols such as SMTP, POP3, HTTP, ICMP, SNMP, FTP, SSH, and so on.
- In addition to monitoring network services and protocols, Nagios is also able to monitor the services provided by network servers such as processor load, disk running processes, and memory usage, and system logs.
- As an open source tool, Nagios is designed to allow users to create their own hosts and service checks depending on the users' needs. In such a way, Nagios can further broaden its monitoring capabilities.
- Originally, Nagios is designed to run on the Linux operating system. Now it can also run on various versions of UNIX. With proper plug-ins, it may be able to run the monitoring service on Microsoft Windows.
- Nagios can notify network administrators about network problems in various ways such as email, instant messages, Short Message Service (SMS), and so on.
- Nagios can display network status information, historical logs, and reports via a Web browser.
- Nagios can define a network host hierarchy and is able to detect which host is down and which host is unreachable.
- To protect the network which is under monitoring, Nagios transmits the collected information through SSH or SSL encrypted tunnels.
- Nagios provides an authorization scheme to help the network administrator to restrict what a user can view and do on the Web interface used to display and configure network status information.
- Nagios is able to define event handlers which can be run during service or host events for searching potential network problems.
- Nagios can even collect the computing environment information, for example, the environment temperature.
- Redundancy and distribution are the techniques often used to improve network system reliability. Nagios can provide services for monitoring redundant and distributed systems.
- By providing an external command interface, Nagios can dynamically configure the monitoring and notification behavior.
- Nagios is able to retain the host and service status across program restarts and automatically rotate the log files.

In addition to the above features, Nagios can also be extended by plugging in additional tools. These tools allow Nagios to be bound to a database, to analyze and graph the data collected by Nagios, to add the PHP programming ability, and so on.

In the above, we have discussed several general purpose network management tools; most of them include functionalities such as network monitoring, information analyses, and reporting. Next, we will look at several network management tools that specialize in network security management.

Nessus

Nessus is an open-source network vulnerability scanner. It has modular architecture with a centralized server that conducts network scanning (Nessus, 2007). The Nessus client can be configured for remote administration interaction. Equipped with Nessus Attack Scripting Language (NASL), Nessus is able to accomplish the following tasks:

- Nessus is built on the Common Vulnerabilities and Exposures architecture which allows it to easily link to other compliant security tools.
- Nessus can be used to scan network vulnerabilities on both local and remote computer systems and networks.
- By using Nessus, the network administrator is able to detect if there are missing security updates and patches.
- Nessus can generate simulated attacking signals to check the network and computer systems' vulnerabilities.
- With NASL, Nessus can describe individual threats and potential attacks. NASL can also be used to create customized scans based on the description of threats and attacks.
- Nessus can test a password by using dictionary and brute-force methods. Many of the vulnerability tests can be conducted in a closed environment.
- Nessus can report the result of a vulnerability scan and save it in a knowledge base in various formats such as plain text, XML, HTML, and so on.
- Nessus allows third party tools to manage vulnerability results. These third party tools can be used with the Linux, UNIX, and Windows platforms.
- The Nessus server is currently able to run on Linux and various versions of UNIX. The Nessus client can run on Linux, UNIX, and Windows.
- With Nessus, the network administrator can schedule a security audit. The auditing process can be configured according to the security policy.

On the network security management market, Nessus is the number one choice. According the survey done by Insecure.Org (2006), Nessus was the most popular vulnerability scanner in the world at the time of the survey and had been used by over 75,000 organizations worldwide.

Zorp GPL

When dealing with network security issues, a firewall is one of the most important instruments to be implemented. The firewall serves as the first line of defense against network viruses and hackers. It can be implemented with hardware or software. Among software based firewalls, Zorp GPL is a well-known open source proxy firewall product (Zorp, 2007). Zorp GPL is built to meet today's demands with the following features.

- Zorp GPL uses an application level proxy which is an application program that runs a firewall between networks. The application level proxy provides highly secured firewall protection and is known to block the widest range of network attacks.
- Zorp GPL is a modular based product. By utilizing modular application gateways, Zorp GPL can easily work with new modules to handle new protocols.
- Zorp GPL allows the network administrator to write scripts with the programming language Python. The scripts can be used to implement security policies and override client actions.
- With Zorp GPL, the network administrator can add or remove the on-demand filter rules.
- Zorp GPL supports a wide range of protocols and services such as HTTP/1.1, FTP, SSL, Telnet, and so on.
- To make the server-side management more efficient, the client-side modification is not required to access the server resources protected by Zorp GPL.
- It is possible to use Zorp GPL to monitor and filter network protocols embedded in SSL and SSH.
- Zorp GPL inspects all inbound and outbound network activities and identifies suspicious patterns that may indicate that there are viruses or hacker activities.
- Zorp GPL can run on ZorpOS with the Debian GNU/Linux woody (version 3.0) installer or any other Linux distributions with Zorp patches.

To properly run Zorp GPL, you need packages such as Python 2.3, Python Extclass 1.2, Glib 2.0, openssl 0.9.7d, Zorp GPL upgrades, and so on. These packages can be downloaded through the Internet.

There are several other open source firewall tools for Linux machines. These open source firewalls can accomplish various security tasks such as protecting a personal computer system, or an enterprise-level network. Firewall filter rules need to be carefully planned. Unlike most e-learning systems, the online teaching/learning system may require more permissions to support hands-on practice. This might conflict with some filter rules that may block some of the hands-on activities. Thoughtfully defined filter rules can often resolve the conflict.

FreeNAC

In many situations, we may need to control the access to a local area network. It is often required that only the authorized computer systems or network devices are able to access the local area network. On other hand, you may want to allow a group of students to access the local area network created on the university's private network for hands-on practice. FreeNAC is such an open source network access control tool (FreeNAC, 2007). The following are some of the tasks that can be accomplished by FreeNAC:

- FreeNAC can track the devices on a network and can control how these devices access the network resources. It can provide a report on the network accessed by these network devices and users.
- FreeNAC can help network administrators to find out how many devices are connecting to an enterprise-level network by querying switches and routers. The query results are automatically documented for later reference.
- A Virtual LAN (VLAN) is a network that consists of computer systems and network devices physically located on different LAN segments. The VLAN is a network constructed by software. Although devices on a VLAN are physically on different LAN segments, logically they are still members of the original VLAN. FreeNAC can be used to manage VLANs.
- For hands-on practice, a group of students may need to access the local area network built in a computer lab on campus. FreeNAC can control the group of students so that they only access the local area network in the lab without accessing the university's private network.
- FreeNAC can be used to configure switch ports through a GUI based utility. With FreeNAC, the network administrator can significantly reduce the time on the configuration of switches.
- The FreeNAC server can run on the Linux operating system. It needs a Cisco switch for creating a VLAN. The FreeNAC client can run on the Windows operating system.

To protect the university's private network, the VLAN is one of the popular technologies that can be used to build a computer lab for hands-on practice. FreeNAC is just the right tool for managing the VLAN created for the computer lab. While allowing students to access the computer systems and network devices on the VLAN, FreeNAC can block the equipment on the VLAN from accessing the private network and network resources. Other functionalities of FreeNAC such as testing and reporting can also greatly reduce the time spent on lab management.

Network Diagnostic Tool (NDT)

There are also some advanced open source network management tools that are available to assist network administrators. NDT is such an advanced open source network management tool that can be used for troubleshooting network performance problems on high-performance networks (NDT, 2007). The following are some of the features provided by NDT.

- NDT is a client-server based network management tool. The server side includes a Web server and a testing engine, and the client side includes a command line interface or Java applet.
- NDT can be installed on a Linux server with a Web100-enhanced kernel. The Web100-enhanced server can communicate with the command line interface or Java applet on the client side. The NDT client (web100clt) can run on Windows and various versions of the UNIX operating system.
- With the Web100-enhanced server, NDT can determine if a network is working properly. It will provide performance tuning information and give suggestions to fix performance problems. To identify a bandwidth congestion, NDT is able to measure the throughput of an Internet connection as well as the throughput of a local area network.
- As a diagnostic tool, NDT can inform the network administrator what the problem is and how the network performance is affected by the problem. Since most network problems happen near the client side, NDT is designed to handle problems such as misconfiguration of the client-side local area network and incorrectly set TCP buffers on client computer systems.
- Through the command line or Java applet interface, the network administrator can run an NDT test of the local area network that has been reported as having problems.
- The test result can be presented in different detail levels so that the network administrator can dig deeper to search for potential network problems. NDT provides plain-text based reports for beginners and detailed system data for experienced network administrators.
- The future NDT will support network performance testing and analysis on IPv6. It will also include more statistics.

As an open source tool, NDT is frequently getting new components from network programmers around the world. As networks become more and more complex, there will be more components added to NDT. In fact, NDT itself is one of the components in the software package called Performance Improvement Performance Environment System (PIPES). There are many other open source tools included in this package for monitoring and analyzing network performance.

To help you accomplish the network management tasks with the open source tools mentioned above, Table 4-1 summarizes the usage of those open source network management tools.

Table 4-1. Usage of network management tools

Network Tool	Usage
Ethereal	Ethereal is a network traffic monitoring tool. With Ethereal, one can capture the data transmitted on a network. During the network troubleshooting process, Ethereal is often used by the network administrator to analyze the network traffic. On other hand, hackers can also use it to capture the encrypted data on a network.
Multi Router Traffic Grapher (MRTG)	MRTG is a sophisticated network monitoring tool. However, it works differently from Ethereal. MRTG collects information from network devices such as routers and network adapters. It can also be used as a device status reporting tool. The statistics program included in this tool can help the network administrator to analyze performance of a network device.
Nagios	Nagios is a network monitoring and troubleshooting tool. For network troubleshooting, it can send out test signals. The testing results can be reported back. If the network administrator needs to test the current status of a network, he/she should consider using Nagios. Nagios can also be used as a network management reporting tool.
Nessus	Nessus is a network security tool. It scans the entire network to identify network security problems. It runs on the client-server structure. To protect a network, a server should be set up to host the Nessus server software and the Nessus client software should be installed on the rest of the computers on the network. The Nessus client software should be available for students to download. As top ranked open source network security software, Nessus can be a competitive alternative to proprietary network security software.
Zorp GPL	Zorp GPL is also a network security tool. Different from Nessus, ZorpGPL is firewall software. It protects a network by filtering communication to allow only the trusted network traffic to pass through the private network. Zorp GPL allows the network administrator to create their own rules to filter network traffic and to handle new network protocols. This feature allows the network administrator to deal with new network viruses without waiting for software companies' updates.
FreeNAC	FreeNAC is a remote access control tool. It can be used to allow a preselected group of users or devices to access the private network from the public network such as the Internet. It also can control what these users can do and report the activities performed by the users. For activity-intensive network-based online courses, FreeNAC is a necessary tool.
Network Diagnostic Tool (NDT)	NDT is a comprehensive network performance analysis tool. It can conduct various network performance analyses and identify network performance problems. For many network administrators, performance problems are often the most difficult problems to solve. Properly using NDT can be a great help.

Linux, as an open source operating system, includes many of the open source network management tools. There are also stand-alone open source network management tools. Some vendors provide open source network management tools with a service package which includes charges for technical support and maintenance contract. With such a package, the open source network management tools are not really free. However, it is still cheaper than most of the commercial network management tools. In general, open source network management tools provide an inexpensive, easy to use, and flexible option for managing the online teaching/learning system. In the following, we will examine some of the stand-alone open source or freeware network management tools.

In the above, only a few open source network management tools are discussed. There are many more open source network management tools available. These tools are also very useful for network administration. Detailed coverage of these open source network management tools is beyond the scope of this book. From the above discussion, it is obvious that the management of networks created for online teaching/learning systems can be done with these open source tools.

NETWORK MANAGEMENT WITH LDAP

The management of users and network resources is a commonly performed network management task. Normally, user account information and network resource information are saved in a directory which is similar to a relational database. The directory is usually hosted by a server computer system. When a user tries to log on to a computer system or a network device on the network, the computer system or the network device will access the user's authentication information stored in the directory. If the login information provided by the user matches the authentication information, the user is allowed to log on to the computer system or network device.

Lightweight Directory Access Protocol (LDAP) is a client-server protocol that is used to deliver the authentication information. LDAP is a light version of X.500 Directory Access Protocol (DAP). Since LDAP is an open source protocol, it is possible to be supported by any application running on any computing platform. Therefore, the LDAP service is not just for Linux/UNIX networks, it is also supported by Windows and Novell NetWare. In the following, we will discuss the directory structure and LDAP process in handling network authentication. Then, we will look at several commonly used open source LDAP management packages.

Directory Structure

For the purpose of directory service, a directory is different from a relational database in several ways. Unlike a relational database, a directory has no rollback and transaction functionalities since it does not frequently add, delete, and update its entries. One of the directory's tasks is to quickly respond to search requests from clients. Therefore, the directory offers a static view of data. It uses network protocols such as LDAP to access data. The future directory may adopt the structure of an object-oriented database which can improve the performance in searching for authentication information.

A directory is constructed on a tree structure. It is often built based on the geographic and/or organizational structure. The top level entry in the tree structure will be the URL of a university or an enterprise. The lower level entries are used to represent campuses, colleges, departments, organizational units, groups, and offices. The lowest level entries will be users, computer systems, and network resources such as network printers and network storage devices.

Each entry in a directory has a unique name called a Distinguished Name (DN) and has a set of attributes which describe the detail levels of the entry. A DN consists of Relative Distinguished Names (RDNs) which are constructed with the attributes' names. For example, a DN can have the following format:

DN: cn=student name,ou=cis,dc=campus,dc=edu

where the attributes Common Name cn and Organizational Unit ou are the RDNs, and Domain Content dc is the parent DN. Each attribute can have one or more values. Starting with the parent DN, the tree structure holds all the subtrees and children. It can also include the reference to other trees hosted by different servers. When searching for the authentication information, client requests may be forwarded to other servers.

LDAP Process

LDAP is a protocol that provides several operations for the client to search and update the directory on the server. An LDAP process starts from a request by a client program. The request is sent by LDAP to the server that hosts the directory. Based on the request, the server searches for or updates the information in the directory. Then, the server sends the response back to the client via LDAP. The following are some of the operations performed during the LDAP process:

- The LDAP process starts by creating a connection from a client to an LDAP server. LDAP uses TCP/IP to transmit data through the default port 389 or another specified port. For a secure LDAP connection, the client can choose to use LDAP SSL which is a SSL tunnel communicating through the port 636.
- Optionally, the client can enable the Transport Layer Security (TLS) service which is used to protect the LDAP connection.
- LDAP defines the authentication operations. The client specifies the authentication operations performed on the server and the search criteria.
- The client submits a request to the LDAP server. When the client's request arrives at the LDAP server, the server checks the client's identification.
- Based on the authentication operation specified by the request, LDAP can specify a particular version of LDAP, add, update, or delete entries in the directory, search for and retrieve entries from the directory, verify if a given attribute value is held by an entry in the directory, and rename an entry.
- Based on the client's instruction, LDAP can recall the previous request by the client, or set the permission for the client to access the directory.
- By combining several basic operations, LDAP can create a new operation.
- After the operations requested by the client are completed, LDAP closes the connection.

Usually, an operating system may include some basic LDAP management tools. For the more sophisticated features, the network administrator may consider using a stand-alone LDAP management tool. The following will introduce some of the open source stand-alone LDAP management tools.

Open Source LDAP

There are three major open source LDAP management tools, OpenLDAP, Fedora DS, and OpenDS. Both OpenLDAP and Fedora DS have been on the market for some time. OpenLDAP can work with many different databases. It can also work with virtual databases as the back-end. The following are some of the features supported by OpenLDAP.

- OpenLDAP is able to handle a 150 million entry database. It can also transfer over 22,000 queries/second or 4,800 updates/second (Chu, 2007).
- OpenLDAP provides many security services such Simple Authentication and Security Layer (SASL), Transport Layer Security (TLS), and Secure Sockets Layer (SSL).
- OpenLDAP supports LDAP Sync Replication which supports pull-based and push-based synchronizations.

- OpenLDAP supports the next generation Internet protocol version 6 (Ipv6) natively.
- To improve manageability, OpenLDAP provides the LDAP-based dynamic configuration engine.
- OpenLDAP provides an overlay mechanism which stacks new features on top of the existing functionalities to improve the capabilities of the existing back-end database.
- OpenLDAP is able to communicate with a system using Inter-Process Communication (IPC) which is a protocol for passing messages between processes to enhance security.
- OpenLDAP provides the LDAP Application Program Interface (API) for software developers to connect to and use a directory server.

In summary, OpenLDAP is a versatile package that can handle the tasks on both the server and client sides. It is a network management tool that is used to configure the services provided by a directory. OpenLDAP is also a fast, reliable, scalable, and easy-to-deploy open source directory server package. Due these features, OpenLDAP is suitable for implementing the LDAP client and server at the enterprise level.

Fedora Directory Server

Fedora Directory Server is another enterprise-level open source LDAP server offered by the Linux distribution vendor Red Hat. Fedora Directory Server is a full-featured LDAP server that is already handling "many of the largest LDAP deployments in the world" (Fedora Directory Server, 2008). Fedora Directory Server is part of the Red Hat community-supported Fedora project. Based on the existing Fedora code, Fedora Directory Server offers a broad range of features such as:

- **Four-way multi-master replication:** Fedora Directory Server can replicate entries to two or more masters at the same time with automatic conflict resolution. In such a way, during the failure of one server, other servers can still provide directory service for both read and write operations. To be more efficient, Fedora Directory Server can also be configured to provide fractional replication which can restrict certain data to be included in a replica.
- **Database:** To store the directory service data entries, Fedora Directory Server uses the high performance Berkeley Database. To ensure Atomicity, Consistency, Isolation, Durability (ACID) data updates, Fedora Directory Service provides utilities to detect incorrectly written data entries. It also provides some

utilities to assist the data replication to multiple databases. Fedora Directory Server can also use any other relational database or any other data source.

- **Security:** Many security measures have been enforced by Fedora Directory Server. For example, Fedora Directory Server provides SSLv3/TLSv1 secure communication over the network. It supports the LDAP extension StartTLS which is used for encryption negotiation. It can work with Kerberos to authenticate to the directory. With Kerberos, the values of individual attributes can be encrypted for better protection.
- **GUI tools:** Fedora Directory Server provides various GUI tools. It supports a graphical console for remote administration. The network administrator can view user data on a tree structure through a Web-based organizational chart. A Web-based search/query interface can also be used for selecting directory server data. The network administrator can use this GUI to insert and update the entries stored in a directory server. Users can use this tool to modify their personal login information. The data stored in a directory can be viewed based on the properties of the entries. For example, the data can be viewed based on the local or employee status on the tree structure. Users can view data by scrolling the search result.
- **Performance:** Fedora Directory Server can sort data entries stored in a directory in several ways to speed up a search. It also provides some tools for high performance logging.
- **Management:** With Fedora Directory Server, most of the server configuration and management tasks such as data import and export, directory backup and restoration, and performance tuning can be done online.
- **Microsoft Active Directory synchronization:** Fedora can synchronize data entries such as users, groups, and passwords stored in Microsoft Active Directory.
- **Programming:** Fedora Directory Server allows developers to extend the functionality of the server using a well defined C/C++ interface. Many of the core features of the server (such as replication, access control, roles, etc.) are implemented as plug-ins.
- **Access control:** Fedora Directory Server attaches the access control information to the data entries. By doing so, the access control information will not be lost after the data are transferred. Fedora Directory Server also supports macros and ad hoc queries for the network administrator to construct access structure. It allows the network administrator to implement a set of rules to manage user accounts and network resources. Through Fedora Directory Service, the network administrator can also disable and enable a user account.

These features make Fedora Directory Server a sophisticated open source directory service package. It can centralize the management of users, computers, and network resources for large companies. With Fedora Directory Server, the tasks of directory service management can be simplified. Fedora Directory Server also improves security and performance.

Sun OpenDS

Sun OpenDS is a directory service tool which was initially developed by Sun Microsystems. Later, it became an open source product developed by developers and other interested parties from around the world (Java.net, 2007). The goal of the project is to construct next generation directory service software. OpenDS is a Java based open source directory server so that it will be able to provide directory related services such as directory proxy, virtual directory, namespace distribution, and data synchronization. Like OpenLDAP, OpenDS is designed to be an enterprise-level directory service. The advantage of a Java based directory service is its portability. Java code can be executed on a wide range of platforms without recompiling. Java's support for networking and concurrent processing, and its exception-handling capabilities make it suitable for developers to create new components for the open source project. The main goal of OpenDS is to gain improvement in providing high performance and data synchronization, being highly secure, being highly scalable, being highly flexible, being highly reliable, and being highly compatible. The following are some details of the design goals.

- **Providing high performance:** Performance is on top of the list. Sun OpenDS is designed to have high performance.
- **Being highly scalable:** Being able to handle a large number of entries is a basic requirement for an enterprise-level directory service. One of the design goals for Sun OpenDS is to handle billions of entries in a single instance. It is required that Sun OpenDS should be able to add servers to the directory server and make effective use of multi-CPU, multi-core machines with several hundreds of GB memory. On the other hand, Sun OpenDS should also be able to run effectively in low-memory environments so that it can handle services on hand-held network devices such as cell phones and PDAs.
- **Being highly secure:** Sun OpenDS is able to provide protection in areas like access control, encryption, authentication, auditing, and password and account management.
- **Being highly flexible:** Sun OpenDS should allow every aspect of the server to be customizable. For example, users can customize password validation algorithms, password generators, logging subsystems, back-end repositories,

protocol handlers, administrative tasks, SASL mechanisms, extended operations, attribute syntax, and matching rules. It is also required that Sun OpenDS be able to run on any platform.

- **Providing data synchronization:** Sun OpenDS is required to support total data synchronization as well as partial data synchronization between instances. It should also provide a means of synchronizing with other applications and data repositories.
- **Being highly reliable:** The failure of a directory service means the failure of an entire system. It is crucial that the directory can still function even when a serious error or an unexpected event occurs.
- **Being highly compatible:** It is required that Sun OpenDS support the features provided by other existing Sun directory services. Sun OpenDS should also be able to migrate entries from other directory servers.

The Sun OpenDS project is still under development. The design goals show that it is a promising open source tool.

As for the concern on which open source directory service product to use, the OpenLDAP is the most popular one. OpenLDAP was available to the user long before the other two directory service products were. OpenLDAP is versatile and can handle user and resource management for almost all online teaching/learning systems. Fedora Directory Server is newer, deigned to handle user and resource management for large companies. It is a good choice for large universities for better performance, security, scalability, and portability. Sun OpenDS is another highly portable, scalable, and reliable directory service. Since OpenDS is still under development, universities should keep an eye on this new and promising open source product.

EXAMPLE: DEVELOPING DIRECTORY SERVICE ON LINUX WITH OPENLDAP

When setting up an online teaching/learning system, one of the first things to consider is the management of user accounts and computer resources for the network based system. An online teaching/learning system consists of multiple network-based application software such as e-mail, learning management system, and database. Also, users need to log on to the system from any of the computers in the computer lab, library, and other public places. It is not practical and convenient to give each student an account on each of the network based application software and for each computer that a student can access on campus. Therefore, the online teaching/learning system must have a centralized user account and computer resource management system. The directory service is such software used to implement the centralized service. With the directory service, each user can log on to various network based application software and log on to the computers on campus that are available to them with only a single account. It is essential for the IT manager and technicians to know how to set up the directory service for their online teaching/learning system. The process of setting up the directory service will be illustrated through the following example.

This example is intended to illustrate a process to create an LDAP service for managing users, computers and network resources with the open source LDAP management tool OpenLDAP. The directory service will be hosted by the Linux operating system. This example will demonstrate how to configure the LDAP server, run the stand-alone LDAP daemon (slapd), populate the directory with user account information, and secure LDAP transactions with the SSL protocol. It will also demonstrate how to access the LDAP server from any client computer system on a campus network. The topics discussed in this example include the description of a campus network, and LDAP server and client configuration.

Description of Campus Network

To illustrate the process of creating a LDAP service for an online teaching/learning system, let us first consider a network system for a fictional campus.

The Wharton University is a medium-sized university with about 10,000 students, faculty members, and staff members. There are about 7000 computer systems and network devices that are connected to the campus backbone network. Sixteen backbone routers are used to link about one hundred twenty departmental subnets with 100-Mbps Fast Ethernet media. There are three high-end switches, and each of them is linked to several backbone routers. The campus also has a number of wireless access points in each building.

The external routing protocol BGP-4 is used by the campus to link to the regional data communication service vendor InternetSouth. The external link uses the high capacity circuit technology known as Synchronous Transport Signal (STS). The currently used STS-3 155.520 Mbps transmission rate can handle 2430 voice circuits.

For the interior routing, the Open Shortest Path First (OSPF) protocol is used. OSPF uses the link-status algorithm to exchange routing information. Each pair of routers on the network periodically sends routing information to each other for routing table updates. Computer labs are created on VLAN for flexibility and security. Several network storage devices and network printers are installed on the campus network.

LDAP Server and Client Configuration

The task to be accomplished by the LDAP server is to manage the information about users, computers, and network resources. The goal of the LDAP server configuration is to make sure that the clients can communicate with the LDAP server.

Before we can start the configuration, we need to make sure that the network is functioning properly. The server computer system has an enterprise version of the Linux operating system installed and the client computer systems from each subnet of the campus can ping the server's IP address. It may help if we do a complete installation which includes all the network management tools. The person who performs the configuration should be given the root privilege. We will also need to make sure that the server computer is connected to the Internet and the DNS server is working properly. Suppose that the domain to be used by the online teaching/learning system is www.wtu.edu. We may also need to verify if an off-campus client computer can access the server through the Internet. Often, for reliability and security, the directory is replicated to multiple servers. If this is the case, we will need to prepare several servers like the above and make sure that these servers can communicate with each other.

Some enterprise versions of the Linux operating system may include the OpenLDAP package. After the installation of the Linux operating system, you may verify if there are folders such as /etc/openldap and /usr/share/openldap/migration. (The term "folder" is not commonly used in Linux documents. Instead, the word "directory" is used. Since the word "directory" has been used for the directory server here, we may use the word "folder" to avoid confusion.) If you have these folders, the OpenLDAP is installed on the server. You are ready to start the LDAP server configuration with the files in these folders.

If OpenLDAP is not already installed, you will need to download the package. You can download the OpenLDAP package from many Web sites. For example, from the following Web sites, your may download the latest version of OpenLDAP:

- http://www.openldap.org/software/download/
- http://ftp.belnet.be/linux/startcom/AS-3.0.6/os/i386/StartCom/RPMS/

You will be asked to choose the release version or the stable version. The release version is the latest version while the stable version is the version that is considered a reliable version. The files to be downloaded have various formats such as tgz or rpm. The installation of each type is slightly different. The following are brief descriptions of these file formats.

- **gz (and z):** A file with the extension gz or z is a file compressed by using GNU gzip. You can use the tool gunzip to unpack the file.
- **tgz:** A file with the extension tgz or tar.gz is a tar file compressed with gzip. A tar file is a single file that is combined by several other files.
- **rpm:** rpm is an open packaging system that packages the source code of certain software into the source and binary forms. The binary form is for installation and the source form is for rebuilding.

The formats tgz and rpm are two commonly used formats for downloadable files. The installation of these files is different. The installation processes of these two types of files are described in the following.

Installation of tgz file: After a tgz file is downloaded, run the following command to unzip the tgz file.

If the tar file is created with GUN tar, use command: `tar -xvzf file.tar.gz`

If not, use the command: `gunzip -c file.tar.gz | tar -xvf -`

After the file is unzipped, you can unpack the tar file by using the following command:

```
tar -xvf filename.tar
```

After the tar file is unpacked, a new folder which contains all the source files will be created. Usually, the next step is to compile the program by using the command:

```
make
```

The next step is to install the program. To do so, enter the command:

```
make install
```

After the installation, you should verify if the folders /etc/openldap and /usr/share/openldap/migration have been created.

Installation of rpm file: This installation is relatively easy. After the file is downloaded, run the command

```
rpm -Uvh filename.rpm
```

You will get the OpenLDAP server installed on the server computer system.

Similar, you may need to install the OpenLDAP client on client computer systems.

To configure the LDAP server, suppose that you have Fedora or Red Hat Linux installed as the server operating system. The next task is to configure the slapd.conf file to enter the suffix and rootdn that match the domain created for your online teaching/learning system. To continue, the next task is to create an encrypted password for the network administrator with the command:

```
/usr/sbin/slappasswd
```

Copy the encrypted password to the file slapd.conf and place it after the entry rootpw. You will also need to configure the permissions that control the access to the LDAP server. For example, you can allow the network administrator to read and write the directory content but only allow others to read the content in the directory. Save the configuration and start the LDAP server with the command:

```
service ldap start
```

After the LDAP server is installed and configured, you can then populate the directory. One way to insert data into the directory is to move user accounts from an existing system to the directory. You may find some tools in the folder /usr/share/openldap/migration to help you get the job done. In the folder, edit the file migrate_common.ph to set the parameters $DEFAULT_MAIL_DOMAIN and $DEFAULT_BASE to match the domain for the online teaching/learning system. The user account information is stored in the files base.pl, passwd.pl, and group.pl. You can use the migration tool ./migrate to move the data from a .pl file to a .ldif files which is the file that can be used by the LDAP server by running the following command:

```
./migrate _ filename.pl > filename.ldif
```

To add the content of the .ldif file to the directory, use the command:

```
ldapadd -D "cn=Manager,dc=wtu,dc=edu" -x -W -f filename.ldif
```

where dc=wtu,dc=edu matches the domain for the online teaching/learning system. Additionally, you can move the data of other types of LDAP objects such as OU to the directory.

To view and manage the data entries stored in the LDAP server, you may download GUI tools to help you accomplish these tasks. There are several open source LDAP editing tools available such as:

- **gq:** A GUI tool for viewing and editing the LDAP server. It can be downloaded from the Web site http://biot.com/gq/.
- **LDAP Browser/Editor:** A Java based GUI tool for editing the LDAP server. It requires the Java JDK software and can be downloaded from the Web site http://www-unix.mcs.anl.gov/~gawor/ldap/.

The above two LDAP server editing tools are good enough for most of the configuration tasks. After one of the above LDAP server editing tools is installed, you will be able to view the data entries transferred to the directory.

The above procedures show you how to set up the LDAP server. Similarly, you can configure the LDAP client so that the client can communicate with the server. Suppose that the operating system installed on a client computer system is Linux. On the client computer, edit the file /etc/ldap.conf to add the server's IP address and the domain name, and then enable the service scope sub. Save the configuration, and the client is ready.

Sometime, the GUI tool for configuring the LDAP client can be used to access the data stored on the server. With the GUI tool, the user can specify the server name and server IP address. Save the configuration and restart the GUI tool, the user will able to view the LDAP data entries stored on the LDAP server with proper permission. The GUI tool included in the Linux operating system can also be used to enable the LDAP authentication on the client computer system. Then, the user can log on to the computer with the centralized LDAP authentication.

Each semester, there will be new students enrolled in the university. These students' accounts should be added to the directory so that they can log on to the online teaching/learning system. One way to do this is to add the new users to the system with the Linux command `useradd` first, and then move the data to the .ldif file and add the content of the file to the LDAP directory. GUI tools such as LDAP Browser/Editor can also be used to add data entries.

After the client and server are configured, the next task is to enforce some security measures.

The LDAP protocol carries the plain text data during the communication. It is possible for someone to capture the data content during the transmission. To fix the problem, the network administrator needs to enable SSL and create a certificate service on the server. This can be done by configuring the file etc/openldap/slapd.conf on the server and the file /etc/ldap.conf on the client to enable SSL. If the SSL package is not included in the LDAP server, you may need to download an open source SSL program and install it.

At this point, we have completed the process of setting up a centralized directory service for the online teaching/learning system. Students can log on to the computers that are linked to the university network. They can also access the computers in the online computer lab through the VPN which may require LDAP authentication. As we can see, the entire directory service can be done by using open source tools.

CONCLUSION

This chapter started with the description of the client-server structures which are commonly used to build an online teaching/learning system. We then discussed several network devices commonly used in constructing the online teaching/learning system. These network devices are the hosts of many open source network protocols and network management tools. This chapter described several open source network protocols and discussed why they are important for today's network based education. For the management of networks, we discussed several open source network management tools. We looked into the features of these open source network management tools and explored how they can be used to manage the network for the online teaching/learning system. To manage users, computers, and network resources, we explored the directory service and the LDAP protocol. Several open source directory service management tools were discussed. An example was given to demonstrate the development process of a directory service which is constructed with open source tools.

A network consists of many servers, client computer systems, and network resources. In next chapter, we will examine the servers and open source server operating systems.

REFERENCES

Chu, H. (2007). *OpenLDAP 2.4 highlights features of the upcoming release.* Retrieved October 30, 2007, from http://www.openldap.org/pub/hyc/LDAPcon2007.pdf

Cisco Systems Inc., Thomas, T., & Khan, A. (1999). *Network design and case studies (CCIE Fundamentals).* Indianapolis, Indiana: Cisco Press.

Correia, E., & Watson, R. (2006). VMware as a practical learning tool. In N. Sarkar (Ed.), *Tools for teaching computer networking and hardware concepts* (pp. 338-354). Hershey, PA: Idea Group Inc.

Donzelli, C., Fontana, C., Ravaioli, A., Toppan, P., Patella, M., & De Castro, C. (2006). An LDAP/SQL-based architecture for broadband services. In *Proc. of IASTED Int. Conference on Communication Systems and Applications*, Banff, Canada.

Dubie, D. (2005). Network management goes open source. *Network World*. Retrieved August 30, 2007, from http://www.networkworld.com/news/2005/051605specialfocus.html

Ethereal. (2007). *The world's most popular network protocol analyzer*. Retrieved September 30, 2007, from http://www.ethereal.com

Fedora. (2008). *Fedora Directory Server*. Retrieved April 25, 2008, from http://directory.fedoraproject.org

FreeNAC. (2007). *Take control of your LAN with FreeNAC*. Retrieved September 30, 2007, from http://www.freenac.net

Insecure.Org (2006). *Top 100 network security tools*. Retrieved May 11, 2008, from http://sectools.org

Java.net (2007). *Open DS*. Retrieved October 30, 2007, from https://opends.dev.java.net

Kapadia, N. H., & Fortes, J. A. B. (1998). On the design of a demand-based network-computing system: The Purdue University Network-Computing Hubs. In *Proceedings of the 7th IEEE International Symposium on High Performance Distributed Computing (HPDC'98)*, (pp. 71-80), Chicago, IL.

Maxwell, S. (2000). *Red Hat Linux Network Management Tools*. New York: McGraw-Hill.

Jackiewicz, T. (2004). *Deploying OpenLDAP*. Berkeley, CA: Apress.

MTRG. (2007). *Multi Router Traffic Grapher*. Retrieved September 30, 2007, from http://www.mrtg.jp/en

Nagios. (2007). *Nagios*. Retrieved September 30, 2007, from http://www.nagios.org

NDT. (2007). *Network Diagnostic Tool (NDT)*. Retrieved September 30, 2007, from http://e2epi.internet2.edu/ndt

Nessus. (2007). *Tenable network security*. Retrieved September 30, 2007, from http://www.nessus.org/nessus

Olifer, N., & Olifer, V. (2006). *Computer networks: Principles, technologies and protocols for network design*. San Francisco, CA: John Wiley & Sons.

Parker, R. & Holmes, J. (2007). Incorporating Compressed Video and Internet Protocol to deliver graduate coursework. In C. Crawford et al. (Eds.), *Proceedings of Society for Information Technology and Teacher Education International Conference 2007* (pp. 472-475). Chesapeake, VA: AACE.

Penrod, J. I., & Harbor, A. F. (2000). Designing and implementing a learning organization-oriented information technology planning and management process. In Lisa Ann Petrides (Ed.), *Case studies on information technology in higher education: Implications for policy and practice*. (pp. 7-19) Hershey, PA: IGI Publishing.

Teare, D., & Paquet, C. (2005). *Campus network design fundamentals*. Indianapolis, IN: Cisco Press.

Uys, P. (2001). Networked educational management: Transforming educational management in a networked institute. In C. Montgomerie & J. Viteli (Eds.), *Proceedings of World Conference on Educational Multimedia, Hypermedia and Telecommunications 2001* (pp. 1917-1923). Chesapeake, VA: AACE.

Varvel, V., & Harnisch, D. (2001). The modern classroom: Using portable wireless computer networking in the classroom. In C. Crawford et al. (Eds.), *Proceedings of Society for Information Technology and Teacher Education International Conference 2001* (pp. 1363-1368). Chesapeake, VA: AACE.

Zorp. (2007). Zorp GPL. Retrieved September 30, 2007, from http://www.balabit.com/network-security/zorp-gateway/gpl

Chapter V
Server Development and Management

INTRODUCTION

In the previous chapter, we discussed the topics related to networks to construct the infrastructure of an online teaching/learning system. A network consists of servers, clients, and network devices. In this chapter, we will investigate how the open source tools are used in the server development for the online teaching/learning system. Servers are computer systems used to host and manage the resources that can be accessed by users with proper permissions through the network. In the online teaching/learning system, servers are used to manage networks, databases, application software, security, and so on. To manage a large number of services needed by the online teaching/learning management system, a server is often run by an enterprise-level server operating system. Many of the open source operating systems, especially Linux, can handle the job. In this chapter, we will discuss server computer systems and enterprise-level open source server operating systems.

This chapter starts with the introduction of server computer systems. We will discuss the server platforms and the technologies used to construct the servers. We will investigate the functionalities of the server components and the utilities of implementing these functionalities. Depending on the requirements, the server configuration can be quite different. Under this topic, we will discuss the strategies of selecting server equipment to meet various requirements by the online teaching/learning system.

After the server platforms and the technologies are introduced, our next task is to examine server operating systems. We will discuss the open source server operating systems in general first, and then our focus will be on the Linux operating system. Several major Linux distributions will be introduced and their features will be examined. We will investigate the services provided by the Linux operating system and how these services are used to support the online teaching/learning system. The configuration of the operating system also depends on the services provided by the server. We will discuss the issues related to the configuration of the server operating system.

Maintaining servers and keep them running in good condition are the major tasks of a computer service department. The server operating system management requires experience and responsibility. It is also very costly. Operating system management with open source tools is one of the solutions that can keep the cost down. In this chapter, we will look at various open source tools provided by the Linux operating system and the services provided by these tools. We will also discuss how to use these tools to solve operating system problems.

Two examples will be used to demonstrate a server development process. In the example, we will discuss how to set up a Linux server and how to configure a Web server to support the online teaching/learning system.

BACKGROUND

Server development and administration are the main tasks performed by the computer service department. Servers play a key role in today's teaching/learning environment; they are used to manage student accounts, to host databases, to support learning management systems, to enforce security measures, and so on. In today's education system, servers are widely deployed in various education institutions from local school districts to global universities.

Servers can be constructed on various platforms such as x86, IBM POWER, Sun SPARC, and Itanium 2. For a small or medium online teaching/learning system, x86 is a popular platform to construct servers. It takes relatively less effort to develop an x86 server due to the fact that the x86 server has a similar structure as that of a personal computer. The x86 platform supports most of the operating systems including the Linux operating system. The book by Buchanan and Wilson (2000) provides more detailed information about PC architecture.

For large campuses, the support for an online teaching/learning system is often done by servers with various platforms such as POWER, SPARC, or Itanium 2. The POWER platform is developed by IBM and it supports the 64-bit computing environment. The enterprise version of Linux supports 64-bit computing which is a desired feature for the virtualization of processors, storage, and networks. The POWER platform fully supports the open source 64-bit Linux operating system.

For more information about IBM servers, readers can refer to the book by Vetter, et al. (2005). The SPARC platform is developed by Sun and it also supports the 64-bit Linux operating system. Readers can get more information about the 64-bit SPARC platform from the book by SPARC International (1994). The Itanium platform is jointly developed by Intel and HP. Itanium 2 supports Windows, Linux, and UNIX. As described above, the Linux operating system is supported by all major server platforms; this means that Linux is platform independent and can be used in any online teaching/learning environment.

The Linux server operating system is the main focus in this chapter. As an open source server operating system, Linux is a popular operating system for supporting teaching and learning. IBM has developed a Linux based e-learning project (IBM, 2007). This project allows users to have experience with hands-on Linux labs on a remote Linux server and learn the Linux operating system. There are many books available to help users to set up Linux servers. The book by Hunt (2002) provides more information about Linux network servers. Configuring the Linux operating system may take longer time for someone who is new to the operating system, but many experienced professionals like Linux because they can have more freedom to configure the system the way they want (Hunt, 2002).

Various open source operating system management tools are used to assist the management of an online teaching/learning system. Readers can find more detailed information in the book by Kavanagh (2004). From his book, readers can learn more about the tools for system administrators, network administrators, and IT project managers.

The server related topics for teaching and learning have been discussed at conferences. Boer (2002) presented a delivery server development process for distributing sophisticated multimedia content. To support interactive distance learning, the delivery server infrastructure was developed to be platform independent so that it could deal with various operating systems and course materials. Ayala and Paredes (2003) demonstrated how a server was used to support a learner model that provided a personalized learning environment. Based on the learner's demand, the server could provide different sets of course materials for the learner.

The Web server is one of the important servers for supporting online teaching and learning. In their paper, Fansler and Riegle (2004) discussed how a Web server was developed to support a data-driven online instructional design analytics system. Atkinson, Cummings, Phillips, and Pospisil (1999) investigated course server software for teaching online courses. They discussed the requirements for a server to support online courses. They demonstrated how servers were used to support online learning management by enabling teaching functions such as presentation of content, discussion groups, class management and related services.

The Linux operating system has been used in schools and higher education institutions. Hoagland, Brewer, and Hoogendyk (2002) investigated how the Linux operating system was compared with other operating systems such as Apple Macintosh and MS Windows. They listed the advantages of using the Linux operating system. They pointed out that Linux was playing an increasingly important role as higher education budgets continued to diminish. They also liked the fact that the Linux operating system could be modified to serve specific needs.

SERVER PLATFORMS AND EQUIPMENT

Server development for an online teaching/learning system requires careful planning. The selection of a server platform and equipment will be based on the needs of the online teaching/learning system as described in the previous chapters. The following lists some of the considerations from the technical point of view for making decisions on the selection of a server platform.

- **Support for the open source operating system:** The first consideration is whether the server platform supports the open source operating system such as Linux. As described earlier, most of the major server platforms support Linux.
- **Cost:** The total cost of the server platform may include the cost of hardware, software, and network equipment. Other costs such as maintenance, training, and consulting should also be considered.
- **Maintainability:** The effort of maintaining a server platform may vary. The measure for maintainability is the average time spent on each server in each semester. The maintainability depends on the reliability of the hardware and software, and the availability of the support from vendors.
- **Reliability:** As a key component in the online teaching/learning system, the server should be highly dependable. The server's reliability is measured by its uptime. The server is considered to be in excellent condition if it has 99% or better uptime. The server hardware and operating system has a great impact on reliability.
- **Technical support:** Some of the server platforms have a wide range of users. The technical support for these server platforms can come from both other users and vendors. The technical support for some other platforms may be mostly from vendors. The support for the older versions of an operating system and the supply of parts for a server computer system are also factors to be considered.

- **Scalability:** Due to the fact that online teaching/learning systems are often fast growing, a server platform is required to support backward and forward scaling as well as horizontal scaling to multiple servers running simultaneously to support cluster computing and grid computing.
- **Deployment:** It will be ideal if a chosen server platform can help to quickly deploy a system to students, faculty members, and staff members. It is important to choose a server platform that requires less training and maintenance effort. It is also desirable if the server platform can be easily mingled with the existing system.

Most of the major server platforms such as x86, POWER, SPARC, and Itanium 2 will meet the majority of these criteria. To be specific, let us examine what the server platforms can provide in the following:

- **x86 platform:** The x86 platform is based on the microprocessors from Intel and AMD. Originally, the x86 platform was created for personal computers. Today's x86 platform includes one or more 32-bit or 64-bit single-core or multi-core x86 microprocessors. It supports most of the popular operating systems such as Linux, Windows, and some versions of the UNIX operating system. It is powerful enough to support most of the online teaching systems. Among the strengths of the x86 platform, the first one is the ease of use due to its similarity to the structure of PCs. The second strength is that it is supported by most software vendors due to its large market share. The third strength is the low cost. The hardware and software supporting the x86 platform are widely available. You can always compare their prices and choose the one that gives the most value. Another strength is that it is relatively easy to get support. The support can come from vendors as well as users. It has a large group of experienced users who can provide help. There are also many vendors, consulting companies, computer stores across the world that sell parts and provide services for the x86 platform.
- **POWER platform:** The POWER platform is based on the microprocessors from IBM. It is built to support Linux, Mac OS, and AIX which is IBM's own version of UNIX. The POWER platform supports both 32-bit and 64-bit operating systems and application software that are mostly supported by IBM and by third party software vendors. One of the strengths of the POWER platform is that it can handle a large project. It can serve up to 4906 or more processors on one platform and can support over 2 terabyte memory. No matter if it is 32-bit or 64-bit, the application software can run equally well on the POWER platform. With the Linux operating system installed, the POWER platform is an attractive technology for a large online teaching system. It is also a good

platform for students to get hands-on practice to learn about Linux and the IBM version of UNIX. Due to its relatively smaller user base, most of the support will directly come from IBM which provides good support through contractors, local agencies, telephones and online. IBM's developing teams often work with universities to develop a large project.

- **SPARC platform:** The SPARC platform is based on the microprocessors from Sun. It is constructed on one or more 64-bit UltraSPARC or SPARC64 microprocessors. The platform can support 128 or more simultaneous microprocessors and over 500GB memory. The SPARC platform supports Linux and Solaris which is Sun's own version of UNIX. The SPARC platform is very reliable and is highly scalable. Many engineering labs have Sun servers installed to handle computation intense tasks. Again, the SPARC platform is suitable for large projects and research. The support for SPARC is also mainly from Sun, contractors, local agencies, telephones and online.
- **Itanium 2 platform:** The Itanium 2 platform is based on the 64-RISC microprocessors developed jointly by Intel and Hewlett-Packard (HP). One of the advantages of Itanium 2 is that, in addition to Linux and various UNIX operating systems such as z/OS, OS390, and HP-UX, Itanium 2 also supports the Windows operating system. This makes Itanium 2 a very flexible platform that gives users more options. Itanium 2 is designed for high-level computation needs. It can support over 512 microprocessors running simultaneously and over 60 terabytes of memory. Many large projects are implemented with the Itanium 2 platform. Unlike POWER and SPARC, Itanium 2 is mainly developed for large projects. Even though the Itanium 2 platform is able to run 32-bit application software, it is much slower when running in the 32-bit mode.

As seen from the above discussion, the x86, SPARC, POWER, and Itanium platforms all support the Linux operating system. Although it has the ability to support some large projects, the x86 platform is mostly used to support small to medium projects due to its low cost and popularity. On the other hand, SPARC, Itanium 2, and POWER have been primarily designed for large projects even though they can handle small projects.

From the above discussion, you can also see that these platforms support both 32-bit and 64-bit microprocessor computation. Although most of the education application software is still 32-bit software, the performance can be significantly improved if a 64-bit operating system or a 64-bit database is used. The use of a 64-bit platform allows a 64-bit operating system to handle more memory and larger files. A 32-bit operating system can only allocate 4GB memory. With the 64-bit system, in theory, an operating system can handle 18 quintillion bytes of memory.

In practice, it can allocate over one terabyte (TB) or more memory. 64-bit processors can also significantly improve the performance of the applications that require high computing power such as audio/video processing, numerical modeling, gaming, querying a massive database. If the application software supports a native 64-bit operating system, a 64-bit CPU can handle twice as much data per clock cycle when compared with a 32-bit operating system. In addition, most of the 64-bit platforms are able to run 32-bit software without sacrificing the performance. Therefore, when a 64-bit platform is available, you should consider using it.

Once the decision on selecting a server platform is made, our next job is to decide how to build a server computer. The server system can be built as a stand-alone server system, a rack system, or a blade system. For a large online teaching/learning system, a combination of stand-alone server systems, rack systems, and blade systems are often used to handle the distributed computation. The following are brief descriptions of these systems:

- **Stand-alone server:** A stand-alone server is a server built on a single computer system. Depending on the usage of the server, the computer system can be a regular personal computer or a computer system equipped with hundreds of gigabyte RAM and several terabyte hard drive disks. Although some of the stand-alone servers can handle some comprehensive projects, they are often used to handle projects to support some specific tasks such as hosting a database management system or serving as a print server. A stand-alone server is an ideal solution for handling small to medium workloads. For a small or medium online teaching/learning system, it is common to use several stand-alone servers to handle different server-side tasks. Each server is built in a mini-tower box and is connected to other servers through the network.
- **Rack system:** Usually, it takes multiple servers to handle the tasks required by an online teaching/learning system. Running multiple servers on many stand-alone computer systems will take more effort to manage these systems. To manage the servers more efficiently, each computer system can be built in a small case and plugged into a rack frame. Servers and other network devices in a rack frame are interconnected. A rack system takes less space and electricity. It has better performance and is more secure. Often a rack system is used with stand-alone servers. It takes care of the main workload and the stand-alone servers take care of specific work such as printing service.
- **Blade system:** An entire computer system can be built on a single board and inserted into a blade enclosure. A blade system is the ultimate solution for the requirements of high scalable performance and capacity. The blade system takes much smaller space than the rack system. It needs fewer network cables and less electricity. For a very large project, multiple blade enclosures can be

inserted to a rack system. Each enclosure can hold 60 or more blade servers and is equipped with multiple power supplies, cooling fans, I/O modules, and so on. The blades in an enclosure share a common backplane and hot pluggable. The features of the blade system make it highly available and easy to manage.

The servers in any of the above system can be developed in any of the major server platforms such as x86, POWER, SAPRC, and Itanium 2. Once the decision is made on what type of server system to use to support the online teaching/learning system, we can select, install, and configure the server operating system. The issues related to operating systems will be discussed in the next topic.

OPEN SOURCE SERVER OPERATING SYSTEMS

Under this topic, we will first examine the open source operating systems. We will discuss the services provided by these operating systems. Then, we will focus on the most commonly used open source operating system Linux. The discussion will start with the introduction of several main Linux distributions. After that, we will investigate the server-side services provided by the Linux operating system and how these services are used to support an online teaching/learning system. Then, we will discuss the configuration of the Linux operating system to support the online teaching/learning system's daily operation.

Open Source Operating Systems

On a server computer, the operating system is the software used to manage users, networks, memory, file systems, data processes, data storage devices, system security, remote access, computer resource sharing, and so on. It controls input and output devices such as a monitor, network interface card, modem, keyboard, USB device, mouse, and so on. The operating system is also used to support application software such as learning management system software, database management system software, programming language software, multimedia software, gaming software, and so on. The commonly used operating systems are Linux, Windows, Mac OS, and various versions of UNIX. Among them, Linux, Mac OS X, and various versions of UNIX are UNIX related operating systems. Windows takes a different approach.

Most of the open source operating systems are UNIX-like operating systems such as Linux, OpenBSD, and OpenSolaris. As open source products, these operating systems open their source code for the general public to contribute their effort to improving the products. These open source operating systems have minimal or no intellectual property restrictions. Users can freely add new components to these operating systems to meet their specific needs. The following are brief descriptions of some commonly used open source operating systems such as Linux, OpenBSD, and so on.

Linux

Linux is one of the most popular open source operating systems. It is licensed under the GNU General Public License and its underlying source code can be freely modified, used, and re-distributed by anyone. Linux has an Internet based development environment. Developers around the world contribute their code through the Internet. The Internet based open development environment makes Linux have the following advantages.

- Linux is one of the favorite operating systems supported by Internet service developers due to its capability in handling Internet based interactivities. Linux is particularly suitable to be used in a client-server system created over the Internet.
- Linux is developed in an environment that allows multiple sessions to run simultaneously. Therefore, it is a multitasking operating system that handles multiple computing tasks simultaneously and allows multiple users to work on the same server computer at the same time.
- Since the World Wide Web and Internet related protocols such as IP are open source technologies, it is convenient for programmers around world to program these technologies into Linux. Therefore, Linux is widely used as a network server to manage various types of networks.
- In addition to being able to communicate through the Internet, the network management by Linux is also able to communicate with other networks managed by other types of technologies such as Novell, Windows, and Appletalk. Therefore, Linux is a good choice to host the directory service.
- In general, Linux requires less hardware resources. Compared with some commercial operating systems, Linux can run on a PC with a small hard drive and less than 32MB RAM. Some versions of the Linux operating system can run on a CD or even on a floppy disk.
- As an open source product, Linux allows programmers to write kernel extensions and drivers for newly published software and hardware. This can make Linux keep updated with new technologies without waiting for the new version.

- Linux is very secure. It provides various security measures to protect sensitive information and to prevent viruses and hackers from invading the network system.
- In general, the total cost of using Linux is low. Since Linux is an open source product, the initial cost of Linux is zero. The cost may come from the service plan offered by Linux distributions. If the technicians on campus know a lot about Linux, then they can keep the service cost down.
- The development environment makes Linux always backward compatible. On the Internet, one can easily find the old drivers and programs to support older equipment. This feature is especially good for universities that have a limited budget and are not able to upgrade their equipment frequently.
- In most cases, it takes less effort to upgrade the Linux operating system. Today's Linux is run on a package system which verifies the dependency of software. If the new application software does not meet the dependency requirement, users will be prompted to download the software that can fix the problem.
- Linux, in general, is reliable. If there is an issue related to reliability, the problem will be quickly posted on the Internet. Programmers around world will work on it and share their experience to fix the problem. Users do not have to wait for a service pack or patch.
- Linux is an enterprise-level operating system. It can meet the requirements for an operating system by a large organization. Linux is often used in the grid system for distributed computing.

In addition to the above features, it is not difficult to find technical support for Linux. Its technical support is provided by Linux distribution vendors, consulting companies, online forums, and a large number of Linux users' groups (LUGs). Many consulting companies, universities, and high schools also provide training.

Besides Linux, there are at least more than thirty open source operating systems. Although not as popular as Linux, these open source operating systems can also handle most of the tasks required of an operating system. The following are some of the significant ones.

Berkeley Software Distribution (BSD)

BSD is a version of UNIX distributed by the University of California, Berkeley. Initially, BSD shared some code with UNIX originally created by AT&T, so it is often called BSD UNIX. Nowadays, there are many operating systems descendent from BSD. Among them, the following are some of the widely used ones.

- **FreeBSD:** This is a descendent of BSD UNIX. The FreeBSD operating system is supported many major platforms such as x86, IA64, SPARC64. POWER, Xen, and so on. Among the operating systems, FreeBSD has a noticeable long uptime and is considered a reliable and robust operating system. FreeBSD is also compatible with Linux; this means that all the application software developed for Linux can also run on FreeBSD. Many network devices also use the derivatives of FreeBSD as their operating systems.
- **NetBSD:** Similar to FreeBSD, NetBSD is also a descendent of BSD UNIX. NetBSD is known by its portability and compatibility with hardware devices. NetBSD is able to run on more than fifty platforms such as x86, POWER, SPARC32, and so on. Due to its portability, many hand-held devices such as PDAs and cell phones use it. NetBSD is also compatible with Linux.
- **OpenBSD:** OpenBSD is a multi-platform descendent of BSD UNIX. It supports the binary emulation of other operating systems such as Linux, FreeBSD, Solaris, and HP-UX. OpenBSD is known by its high security capabilities and well written documents. The security enhancements provided by OpenBSD makes it an operating system that is suitable for firewalls, VPN servers, and servers that must resist cracking and Denial of Service (DoS) attacks.

There are several other BSD descendents which are not as popular as the above three. Next, we will discuss another open source UNIX-like operating system, OpenSolaris from Sun.

OpenSolaris

Unlike Sun's commercial version of the UNIX-like operating system Solaris, OpenSolaris is a powerful open source development platform that creates a community for developers to develop and improve the Solaris operating system. OpenSolaris includes the source code for the Solaris OS core kernel, network support, libraries, commands and many more. Sun provides some advanced development features to OpenSolaris such as Dynamic Tracing, Containers, ZFS, Predictive Self Healing, and so on. These features can be customized by users to meet their specific needs. In 2006, OpenSolaris received the Best Open Source Solution award from SIIA Codie. Today, the world wide OpenSolaris community has over 14,000 members. OpenSolaris is supported by both the x86 and SPARC platforms. It is supported by a variety of hardware devices such as network cards, video cards, SATA and SCSI data buses, USB, and so on. OpenSolaris supports the wireless network standards, gigabit Ethernet, and 10-gigabit Ethernet. As of network protocols, OpenSolaris supports the next generation Internet protocol IPv6 and the secure network protocol SSH.

As discussed above, Linux is the most installed open source operating system and it plays an importance role in an online teaching/learning system. Next, we will look into the Linux operating system and discuss issues related to Linux distributions, services provided by Linux, and Linux configuration.

Linux Distributions

The central part of the Linux operating system, called Linux kernel, was made public by Linus Torvalds in 1991. Since then, Linus and his Linux team at the University of Helsinki in Finland have been improving the Linux kernel. By adding other open source products, Linus and his team made Linux an operating system. The Linux operating system has been upgraded many times by them.

Since Linux is an open source product, the Linux published by Linus and his team can also be packaged and distributed as Linux distributions. The Linux distributions may contain slightly modified kernels. The vendors of the Linux distributions may also add other management software designed to meet different requirements. Nowadays, there are over three hundred Linux distributions. They are commercial or open source Linux related products. Some of these products are designed and developed for the Linux operating system and others for some special purposes such as cluster computing, network routers, or hand-held devices. The commercial products distributed by the distribution vendors are not free. In the following, we will discuss some of the major Linux distributions such as Red Hat, SUSE, Debian, Knoppix, and so on.

Red Hat

Red Hat is the largest Linux operating system distribution vendor (Red Hat, 2007). Founded in 1993, Red Hat has become known as the Linux distribution vendor for supporting enterprise-level computation. Red Hat sponsors an open source version of the Linux operating system called Fedora which is managed by the Linux user community and Red Hat employees. There is another version of the Linux operating system from Red Hat called Red Hat Enterprise Linux. Both versions are open source products. However, they are used for different purposes.

Fedora is a fully functioning operating system. It also serves as a testing platform for many new services and innovation tools. Once a fault in the software is detected, programmers from the user community and Red Hat will work together to fix the problem. It is suitable for developers and inventors to fix problems and to extend Linux functionalities. Fedora is frequently updated, about every four to six months. Fedora is designed for the x86 platform and does not have much support from Red Hat. Red Hat does not provide training for Fedora. Fedora is available through free download.

Although Red Hat Enterprise Linux is also an open source operating system, it is not free for everyone. Most of the users can get this software through subscription. Red Hat Enterprise Linux has less new services and innovation tools but is more stable. After every three new versions of Fedora, there will be a new version of Red Hat Enterprise Linux. Each version of Red Hat Enterprise Linux is fully supported by Red Hat for seven years since its release. Red Hat Enterprise Linux is widely supported by many hardware and software vendors. It is certified by over six hundred computer system vendors such as DELL, HP, IBM, and so on. It also supports over one thousand application software packages from companies such as Oracle, CA, IBM, and so forth. In addition to the x86 platform, it is also supported by other platforms such as Itanium2 from Intel and HP; POWER, zSeries, S/390 from IBM; and SPARC from Sun. Red Hat provides the integrated service for Red Hat Enterprise Linux, including software update and the convenient 24x7 with 1 hour response service. Red Hat and many consulting companies also provide training in various ways including classroom, on-site, and e-learning. It also has three Red Hat Enterprise Linux certification services, Red Hat Architect, Red Hat Engineer, and Red Hat Technician.

SUSE Linux

SUSE Linux is another major Linux distribution owned by Novell (2007). SUSE Linux was originally developed by a UNIX consulting company in Germany. In 2003, Novell acquired SUSE Linux and added the GUI based system management software YaST2 to SUSE Linux. SUSE Linux is distributed in three versions, the "OSS" version which is completely open source, the "eval" version which is a fully featured version that may contain both open source and proprietary programs, and the "retail boxed-set" version which includes a printed manual and CDs. openSUSE is a professional version of SUSE Linux. It is available in a free download open source package or in a retail package which curtains a printed manual, DVD disk, and bundled software including some proprietary components such as Adobe Flash.

Novell also provides two proprietary versions of the Linux operating system, SUSE Linux Enterprise Server (SLES) and SUSE Linux Enterprise Desktop (SLED). These two versions of SUSE Linux are designed for business use. Both of them include technical support from Novell and certified by many hardware and software vendors. SLES can run on servers with platforms such as x86, PowerPC, Itanium 2, and so on. Several major hardware vendors such as IBM, HP, Sun Microsystems, Dell, and SGI sell computer systems with SLES as the operating system and provide technical support for SLES. Based on the customer's request, SLES will be installed, configured and thoroughly tested by these vendors to make sure that it is stable and has high performance for server operations. SLES also supports over two thousand application software packages including Oracle, SAP, Websphere, as well as more than one thousand open source software packages. Roughly, SLES is upgraded to a new version every two years and guarantees that each version will have seven years of life cycle.

SUSE Linux has several features that are great for an online teaching/learning system. It provides virtualization capabilities. It supports Xen virtualization which can host 32-bit virtual machines on 64-bit virtualization host servers. The virtual machines can host operating systems such as MS Windows Server 2003 and XP, SUSE Linux Enterprise Server, and Red Hat Enterprise Linux 4 and 5. For better security and reliability, in an online teaching/learning system, the virtualization technology can be used to support hands-on practice. The combination of SUSE Linux and Xen is a great solution for this purpose. Another useful feature provided by SUSE Linux is that it can work with the Microsoft Windows operating system. SUSE Linux supports the Windows NTFS file system and allows the co-existence of Windows operating systems such as Windows 2000 and XP. It also supports Windows specific modems for remote access. SUSE Linux supports several popular GUI based Linux desktop management tools such as KDE and GNOME. It also includes several multimedia management tools such as K3b for CD/DVD burning, Amarok for audio playback, and Kaffeine for movie playback. RealPlayer is installed on SUSE Linux to handle MP3 files. The very popular office software OpenOffice is also available in SUSE Linux.

Debian GNU/Linux

Debian is another major Linux distribution entity that is strictly following the free software philosophy. Starting as a small Linux distribution entity in 1993, by keeping its open source principle, Debian has now grown into a well-known major Linux distribution entity. Debian combines the Linux kernel and many other open source products licensed to GNU to form an operating system. That is why the Linux operating system from Debian is named GNU\Linux. Unlike the distributions of Red Hat and SUSE, all Debian GNU/Linux products can be freely downloaded from Debian's Web site (Debian, 2007). Although Debian GNU/Linux is free, it is supported by most of the major computing platforms such as x86, POWER, SPARC, HP PA_RISC, and so on. For application software, Debian GNU/Linux supports over 18,000 pre-compiled open source packages from word processing to managing business processes. Debian GNU/Linux is supported by users and Debian. When a user e-mails Debian for help on a certain program, usually the person who developed the program or Debian will respond to the user within 15 minutes. It takes less memory to run the Debian GNU/Linux operating system and still achieve good performance gain. Even though Debian GUN/Linux is free, unlike other distribution entities that let users test the free versions of their products, Debian rigorously tests each new stable version of its operating system before it is released, which means that Debian GUN/Linux is a stable system. Due to its stability, Debian GNU/Linux is suitable to be used as a server operating system. Debian GNU/Linux has been widely used by universities, companies, and government organizations around the world.

Knoppix Linux

Knoppix is one of the most popular Linux distributions. It provides the live Linux operating system on a bootable CD or DVD (Knopper.Net, 2007). It is a Debian GNU/Linux version of Linux and is designed to be run directly from a CD. When booted, the compressed programs are loaded into memory. A CD can hold up to 2GB executable code and a DVD can hold up to 8GB executable code. If a computer system supports bootable USB devices, Knoppix can also be booted from a USB flash drive. In addition to the Debian GNU/Linux software, it also includes programs designed for automatic hardware detection. It supports various peripheral hardware such as graphic cards, sound cards, SCSI and USB devices, and so on. The requirements for a CPU and memory to run Knoppix are minimal. Knoppix only requires an i486 x86 or later CPU and 128MB RAM to operate properly. During the operation, modified or new files are saved to memory, or on a hard drive, or on a USB flash drive. Due to the fact that the Knoppix Linux operating system runs on a CD or DVD, it has to support as many hardware devices as possible. Indeed, it has an extensive hardware detection program which can work with most of the computer systems and network devices with no configuration required. These features make Knoppix Linux a great system recovery tool. If a computer system crashes, one can run Knoppix from a CD and then fix the problem on the troubled operating system, or copy valuable files to a different hard drive, reinstalled the original operating system, and then copy those files back.

In the above, we have discussed some major Linux distributions which are only a small portion of Linux distributions. There are many more of them. The discussion of all of them is beyond the scope of the book. Next, we will examine the services provided by the Linux operating system.

Linux Operating System Services and Management

Now that we have discussed some of the most popular Linux distributions, our next task is to investigate some of common services provided by the Linux operating system. We will look at how these services are used to support an online teaching/learning system. The server-side services provided by the Linux operating system can be grouped into several categories: File system management, software management, system initialization management, system process management, infrastructure service management, Internet service management, security management, and remote administration management. In the following, we will discuss the services provided in each of the categories.

File System Management

A file system in the Linux operating system is used to provide file storage service. An online teaching/learning system generates a large number of files. Storing these files in a proper way is one of the top priorities of the Linux operating system, which supports several file system formats, including the ext2fs, FeiserFS, Directories, and Network File System formats. Brief descriptions of these formats are given in the following:

- **ext2fs:** This is the traditional UNIX file system format that uses the fixed data block size of 1024 bytes.
- **ReiserFS:** This file system can store files more efficiently by using the variable length data blocks.
- **Directories:** This file system format presents the files and their structure information as a table so that one easily figures out where a file is located and other administrative information.
- **Network File System (NFS):** This file system allows the client to access the NFS server regardless of what the local file system is.

The file system on Linux is a hierarchical system that consists of directories and sub directories. The top level of the root directory is denoted by the symbol /. Under the root directory, there are subdirectories such as /boot, /etc/, /home, /usr, /mnt, and so on. The tasks of managing a file system include but not limited to creating, partitioning, configuring, customizing, and checking the file system, and also creating a boot disk, configuring disk quotas, and backing up and restoring the file system. In the following, we will discuss the services provided in each of these categories.

Before we can use the Linux operating system to manage an online teaching/learning system, we need to partition the hard disks installed on the server computer system. Based on the requirements described in earlier chapters, to achieve better security and performance, system files, data files, and index files should be placed on separate hard disks. Therefore, we need to partition the hard disks. The Linux file system has two types of partitions, the primary partition which can be used to start the operating system and the extended partition which occupies the entire remaining hard drive storage and can be subdivided into several logical partitions. If multiple operating systems are installed on the server, each of them should be installed on a separate primary partition. Linux allows a maximum of four primary partitions to be created. There are three tasks in a partition process, creating a partition, editing the partition, and resizing the partition. The tools used for these three activities are:

- **fdisk:** It is a utility used to format a hard disk and logically partition the hard disk for data storage.
- **Logical Volume Management (LVM):** It can be used to create logical volumes. With LVM, you can resize and move logical volumes. By using LVM, you can create a volume and assign a meaningful name to the volume such as college, math, and so on. You can combine several partitions into a large logical volume. With LVM, several hard disks can be configured to form a RAID structure for better performance and reliability.

After a partition is created, you can then create a file system on the partition. The utilities to create and check a file system are:

- **mkfs:** It can be used to create a file system with a format such as ext2, ext3, and MS-DOS. The default format is ext2.
- **mkreiserfs:** This utility is used to create a Reiser file system.
- **mount or umount:** They are used to mount or detach the media on a disk to or from a file system. The mount utility can mount the media on a remote computer and can mount the media to multiple locations.
- **fsck:** It utility can be used to check and repair various types of Linux file systems. By default, it checks and repairs all the file systems listed in the file /etc/fstab.

System administrators prefer to configure file systems in the file /etc/fstab. They can edit files to add, remove, rename, reallocate, and customize a file system. To rescue a failed Linux operating system, the system administrator will need a boot disk or CD which contains the system boot information. Creating a boot disk should be done soon after the Linux operating system is installed. During the installation, you will be prompted to create a boot disk. Some distributions such as SUSE also include the tool YaST to create boot disks for a more sophisticated system structure such as a RAID system.

Once students are assigned accounts to an online teaching/learning system, they can start to upload their files to the system. Usually, there is a limit on how much space each student can get for his or her files. Otherwise, a student can easily take 100GB space if he or she uploads a lot of movies and MP3 music files. The following are some of the Linux tools used to set up the quota for each student.

- **quotacheck:** It is used to check partitions with the quota keyword.
- **edquota:** It is used to set up quotas and copy quotas.
- **repquota:** It is used to generate quota reports.

As mentioned in earlier chapters, to improve the reliability of an online teaching/learning system, we must routinely perform system backup. If the system crashes, the backup will be used to recover the system so that the students' data and course materials will not be lost. The tools used by Linux for data backup are:

- **tar:** This tool is used to archive files. The archived files can be compressed to save storage space.
- **rsync:** This tool can copy a directory and send it to a remote storage device through the network.
- **dd:** It is used to copy and convert files at the byte level, which allows the copying of all the files on a partition including the device files.
- **crontab:** It is a service used to automate routine backup.

For system recovery, the following tools may be helpful.

- **Linux Loader (LILO):** LILO can be used to locate the Linux kernel, load the kernel into memory, and start the kernel.
- **Grand Unified Bootloader (GRUB):** Like LILO, it can boot the Linux operating system. In addition, it can also boot multiple operating systems such as various UNIX-based operating systems and Windows. It can work with a wide variety of hardware devices.
- **Installation CD:** Often, by using an installation CD, the system can be booted to the rescue mode. From there, one can fix the problem or install the backup.

In the above, we have discussed several file system management tools and services provided by the Linux operating system. Besides these basic tools and services, each Linux distribution may include more sophisticated GUI tools to manage the Linux operating system. Interested readers can check the documents of these distributions for more detail.

Software Management

In addition to the Linux operating system, an online teaching/learning system is also supported by many application software packages such as learning management system, database management system, and multimedia tools. The Linux operating system provides various tools to assist software installation and removal. The following are some commonly used tools:

- **Red Hat Package Manager (RPM):** RPM is a utility used by many Linux distributions for installing, uninstalling, verifying, querying, and updating computer software.
- **Debian Package (dpkg):** It is a software management utility developed by Debian. It is similar to the utility RPM and is used to install, remove, and manage the .deb packages.
- **Advanced Packaging Tool (APT):** APT is a high-level software management utility developed by Debian. It simplifies the software management process and is often used by front-end users.
- **YaST Online Update (YOU):** It is a software management utility developed by Novell. The YOU server provides the service that can update all computer systems on a network with the latest patches.

These utilities can significantly reduce the workload of software management. The usage of the package installation tools often depends on which Linux operating system is installed on the server computer. Table 5-1 describes the usage of these installation tools.

System administrators can also install the software packages directly from the source code. The installation process requires the installer to compile the source code by following the instruction in the Readme file.

System Initialization Management

A Linux boot process can be configured in many ways. For example, an online computer often has multiple operating systems installed on it. The configuration of a boot process can specify which operating system is the default operating system. In addition to selecting an operating system, there are some other tasks that can be done during the system boot process such as specifying the system run level, finding the driver for a hardware device, loading the driver into the Linux kernel, and so on. The following are some of the commonly used system initialization management tools supported by the Linux operating system:

Table 5-1. Usage of software installation tools

Installation Tool	Usage
Red Hat Package Manager (RPM)	Developed for Red Hat Linux, RPM can be used to install most of the software packages with the .rpm extension. Most of the software packages developed for Red Hat Linux are packaged with the .rpm extension. These software packages can also be installed on the Linux operating system from other Linux distributions such as SUSE Linux. They are easy to install and manage. Many system administrators prefer to use the RPM formatted software packages for installation if they are available.
Debian Package (dpkg)	Developed for Debian Linux and those Debian related Linux distributions such as Ubuntu, dpkg can be used to install, remove, and manage the software with the .dep extension. During the installation process, dpkg will automatically check software dependencies and detect missing links.
Advanced Packaging Tool (APT)	APT is also developed by Debian for the software with the .dep extension. APT is a high-level software management utility built on top of dpkg. It is created to simplify the software management process. For example, not only can it check software dependencies and detect missing links, it can also automatically download missing packages.
YaST Online Update (YOU)	Created by Novell, YOU can automate software installation and update for an entire network. YOU is mainly used by SUSE Linux which is owned by Novell.

- **init:** It is used to manage run levels. The Linux operating system can run at the levels of a single-text mode, local mode, full multiuser text mode, and full multiuser graphical mode. The init tool can also be used for shutdown and reboot. By using init, one can specify the run level at boot and activate or deactivate services.
- **hwinfo:** After a new hardware device is installed, one needs to install the driver specially designed for that device. hwinfo detects a hardware device and find the driver for the device.
- **modprobe:** It can be used to load or unload modules to or from the Linux kernel.
- **Grand Unified Bootloader (GRUB):** GRUB loads operating systems on the hard drive and then starts the operating systems. If there are several operating systems, GRUB prompts the user and loads the one selected by the user.

Each distribution may also have its own tools to manage the boot process. Also, similar to GRUB, LILO can also be used to load a specific operating system.

System Process Management

During the operation, an operating system deals with a number of processes that are running in memory and the CPU. These processes can be generated by the operating system and launched by users. Some of the processes need to interact with users through a monitor. This type of process is called a foreground process. The other type of process may just run in the background by itself. This kind of process is called a daemon process. Many of the services provided by an operating system are daemon processes. Due to the fact that an online teaching/learning system may need to handle thousands of users and hundreds of online courses, there will be a large number of processes generated during the system's operation. The Linux operating system provides several process management tools to help the system manager to manage those processes. These tools are used to start, stop, or reload a process, prioritize the processes, enable or disable services, and schedule jobs. The following are some of them:

- **ps:** This tool is used to view processes that are currently running on the operating system.
- **nice:** It is used to assign the priority level to a process.
- **kill:** It is used to stop running processes.
- **start:** It is used to start a daemon process or a service.
- **stop:** It is used to stop a daemon process or a service.
- **reload:** It is used to restart a daemon process or a service.
- **cron:** With cron, the system administrator can schedule the processes that need to be done regularly.

The commonly used Linux desktop management software such as KDE and GNOME can also be used to manage processes. Many of the Linux distributions also provide graphical tools for service management.

Infrastructure Service Management

An online teaching/learning system is an enterprise-level system. Many of the services provided by the online teaching/learning system are network-based services such as network printing service, network storage service, and Web-based system administration. Tools are provided by the Linux operating system to manage these enterprise-level services. To manage the printing service, one can use the following tools:

- **kprinter:** It is a utility provided by KDE. It is capable of managing a network-based printer.
- **lpr or lp:** They can be used to submit printing jobs.
- **lpq or lpstat:** They can be used to view printing jobs.
- **lprm or cancel:** They can be used to cancel printing jobs.

An online teaching/learning system is often required to share files and folders. It also needs to communicate with network resources installed on other types of networks. The following are two services that can accomplish those tasks:

- **Network File System (NFS):** An NFS server allows users to access the programs, files, or storage space on the server with the Linux operating system. With NFS, a client can access his or her home directory and any public directory on the server from any computer system on the same network.
- **Samba:** Installed on the Linux operating system, Samba supports the file and printing services for Microsoft Windows clients. It can also be integrated with a Windows Server domain. Being able to communicate with Windows makes Samba very popular. Nearly all distributions of Linux include Samba.

On an online teaching/learning system, there could be thousands of Linux operating systems installed and they are sharing the network resources. It is important that these Linux operating systems, the users using these operating systems, and the network resources are properly managed. The server Linux operating system often includes the service called Network Information Service (NIS) to accomplish the task. Similar to LDAP discussed in the previous chapter, NIS serves as the yellow pages for the Linux based enterprise infrastructure.

On the enterprise-level infrastructure, it is ideal if all the Linux operating systems have consistent time. Tools are provided by the Linux operating system to configure the hardware time and system time. The following are some of them:

- **hwclock:** This tool can be used to access the hardware clock, and display and set the hardware clock time. This tool allows the system administrator to set the system time as the hardware time and vice versa.
- **netdate:** It is used to set the system time.
- **ntpupdate:** This tool can be used to adjust the system time.

Most of these tasks can also be done with the graphical tools provided by the desktop management system installed with the Linux operating system.

Internet Service Management

The Internet is the key component for an online teaching/learning system. The Linux operating system provides many tools and services to support the Internet based computing. The tasks to be accomplished in the process of building an online teaching/learning system may include setting up a Web server, configuring the Internet services, and enabling the FTP server.

As mentioned in earlier chapters, the Apache Web server is commonly used by the Linux operating system. In addition to delivering files, displaying Web pages, and managing Web sites on the Internet, Apache can also execute CGI scripts to carry out more sophisticated computation logic. It can work with programming languages such as Perl, PHP, Python, Ruby, and so on. The tasks of managing the Apache Web server include installing, archiving, and enabling the Apache server. They also include managing users, updating security patches, publishing Web pages, testing Web server configurations, and so on. Apache allows the user to choose which software package to install based on the user's needs:

- **apache2:** This package is for basic installation.
- **apache2-prefork or apache-worker:** These packages are for multiprocessing use.
- **apache2-devel:** To be able to create modules or compile the modules provided by third-party vendors, this package should be installed.

Many of the server-side services provided by the Linux operating system are managed by the Extended Internet Daemon (xinetd). xinetd is a replacement of inetd. xinetd starts the services based on the requirements from clients and removes the services out of memory after the services are terminated. The following are some of the tasks that can be accomplished by xinetd:

- xinetd can control the access to network-based services based on the IP address of a remote host, the name of the remote host, the domain name, and the time of access. By doing so, it can prevent denial-of-access attacks.
- It can stop a server or a service.
- It can log information about system operations.
- It can also bind a service to a specific IP address.

To provide more protection for network-based services, xinetd may also be used with TCP Wrapper which can restrict the access to an individual service.

Security Management

In an online teaching/learning system, students, faculty members, staff members, and technicians need to access the servers remotely from their home computers, office computers, and whatever computers which are able to access the Internet. These users need to access the network server, Web server, VPN Server, learning management system, database management system, and so on. They need to download files from or upload files to the servers. For example, the students should be able to browse the course Web sites. The faculty members should be able to manage the classes and course materials. The staff members should be able to manage class registration. The technicians should be able to remotely manage computer systems and other network devices.

One of the concerns is how we can protect the data transmitted over the Internet. This task can be accomplished by using the open source tool OpenSSH. OpenSSH encrypts the data transmitted over the Internet between computer systems. It supports the following encryption algorithms:

- **Data Encryption Standard (DES):** This is an older version encryption algorithm with a 56-bit encryption key. It is not suitable for encrypting highly sensitive data. Instead, it is often used to construct other encryption algorithms.
- **3DES (Triple-DES):** It is constructed by using three DESs. The key of 3DES has the length of 112 bits to 168 bits.
- **International Data Encryption Algorithm (IDEA):** It is an encryption algorithm with a 128 bit key.
- **Blowfish:** This encryption algorithm allows keys with variable lengths up to 448 bits.
- **Advanced Encryption Standard (AES):** As a successor of DES, AES is a popular algorithm used in symmetric key cryptography.

SSH is constructed on the client-server structure. The tools on the client side can be used to log on to a computer system, shutdown a computer system, securely copy a file from one computer to another computer as well as between two ports, and forward data from one computer to another computer. On the server side, the system administrator can configure OpenSSH to accomplish the following tasks:

- OpenSSH can be configured to allow a group of users to log on with SSH, or deny them from logging on with SSH.
- The system administrator can also specify which version of the SSH protocol to support. There are two versions of SSH, SSH Version 1 and SSH Version 2. SSH Version 1 does not provide integrity verification while SSH Version 2 does. This means that the data transferred through SSH Version 1 can be modified intentionally or unintentionally. The newer version of OpenSSH only supports SSH Version 2.
- OpenSSH can be used to manage public keys. The receiver's public key can be used to encrypt the sender's message. When the encrypted message reached

the destination, only the receiver's private key can be used to decrypt the message.

- OpenSSH can be used to configure public key encryption and generate a key pair.

Operating system security management also includes the management of users, groups, ownership, and permission. Users and groups can be managed by editing several configuration files such as /etc/passwd, /etc/shadow, and /etc/group. The following are brief descriptions of these files:

- The /etc/passwd file contains the records, each of which consists of the user name, UID of the user, GID of the group that the user belongs, comments, the user's home directory, and so on. Although the file name seems to be about passwords, the passwords are actually stored in the /etc/shadow file.
- The /etc/shadow file stores the encrypted user passwords and the information of password expiration.
- The /etc/group file contains group information which includes each group name, group ID, and the members of each group.

Each file or directory in the Linux operating system can be accessed by the file or directory owner, the users from the same group, or the users from other groups. Permissions can be assigned to read, write, or execute. The tools used to manage permissions are:

- **chmod:** It is used to add, remove, or modify permissions.
- **chown:** This tool can be used to change the owner of a file or directory.
- **chgrp:** This tool can be used to change group membership.

Pluggable Authentication Modules (PAM) is an authentication tool for the communication between the user and application software. For an application to be accessed securely, the application using PAM will call PAM which will contact the configuration files and process the request by the application file. The processing result will then be returned to the calling application software.

The Linux operating system often provides various security monitoring tools. For example, the following tools are used to monitor user login activities:

- **who:** This tool is used to display the information such as who is currently on the system, the method used for login, and the time of the last login.
- **finger:** It is used to display the information about users such as login names, full names, terminal types, and idle time.

- **faillog:** As the file name indicates, faillog is used to display the information about login failure such as the name of the user, the number of failed logins, the time of the latest failure, and the terminal type.

Security management is a complex task. It often requires a security policy as the guideline and additional third party tools. More details about security management will be covered in later chapters.

Remote Administration

An online teaching/learning system is a network-based system. It can even be a global system. This requires that network administrators can remotely manage any servers and computer systems on the university's networks. The open source software Virtual Network Computing (VNC) can run on operating systems such as Linux, Windows, and Mac. This means that the network administrator can manage a server with the Windows operating system from a computer system installed with the Linux operating system or vice versa. The same is true for the Mac operating system.

VNC has been included by many Linux distributions. The tasks of server configuration include installing VNC, enabling remote administration, restarting the server, starting the remote access service. After the VNC server is enabled, the VNC technology is established on the client-server structure. The client can initialize a connection by entering the URL http://servername:5801. Based on the thin client concept, the VNC client can send a few requirements to the server. Once the client's requirements are sent to the server, xinetd exports X login dialog windows. If the user is authenticated, xinetd connects the client to the server. Based the client's requirements, VNC allows the server to update the framebuffer which is a video output device. The framebuffer can be used to display a data set representing a window stored in the server's memory. The server's window can now be displayed on the client's monitor. Then, the client uses the GUI tools or run the commands on the server to perform the administration tasks. After the administration job is done, the VNC connection should be terminated for better performance and security.

Network-based software installation is another remote administration task. It requires an installation server with adequate hard disk storage space to hold the installation image. The installation server should be able to communicate with clients through the network. It also needs to make sure that client computers have enough memory and hard disk space for the new software. On the server, it is required that the services such as Network File System (NFS), Hypertext Transfer Protocol (HTTP), and File Transfer Protocol (FTP) should function properly.

To prepare the network-based installation, the software to be installed should be copied to the installation server. To allow clients to access the installation server, the server should be configured to allow remote access. There are three ways to accomplish this task. The system administrator can use one of the services NFS, HTTP, and FTP to perform the network-based installation:

- If the network-based installation is done through NFS, the directory that contains the installation software should be made available to clients by configuring NFS. The portmap server should also be enabled in NFS.
- If FTP is used to perform the network-based installation, then FTP should be configured to allow clients to access the installation directory on the server. The system administrator can either set up an account for each of the clients or allow all the clients to access the installation directory by using an anonymous account.
- If the network based installation is done through a Web server, the system administrator should enable the HTTP access to the installation server. Then, clients can access the installation directory through a symbolic link which contains the path to the installation directory.

The main Linux distributions such as Red Hat, SUSE, and Debian also provide graphic based tools for network-based installation. With these tools, the system administrator can configure the installation server to allow client access to the server.

Once the server is configured, the next task is to configure the client computer system. The system administrator will first need to create a configuration file for the installer for the client computer system to read. The configuration file contains the installation specifications for the client computer system. The information may include the specifications of the network card, monitor, mouse and keyboard, and the information about the client computer. The creation of the configuration file is usually done with the graphical tools supported by the Linux distributions. For example, the package AutoYaST provided by SUSE Linux can be used to create the configuration file. Similarly, kickstart provided by Red Hat can also be used to create the configuration file. The installation format is established in the configuration file. Later, the content in the configuration file can be modified to customize the installation.

After the configuration file is created, the system administrator needs to create a boot floppy disk and copy the configuration file to the floppy disk. On the client computer system, make sure that the first boot drive is the floppy drive. Insert the boot floppy disk into the floppy drive and boot the system. You will be prompted to start the automatic boot process. While the automatic installation is started, the floppy disk can be used to start the installation process on another client computer system.

The automatic installation can also be done through the network or by using a bootable CD. Some of the Linux distributions may also provide extra boot options for less commonly used hardware devices.

Server Virtualization Technologies

Since 2007, the support of virtualization technologies, such as Xen, has been added to the released Linux kernel. With the virtualization technologies, the functions of hardware and software can be simulated by the software called a virtual machine. The advantages of the virtualization technologies are listed below:

- Lower the cost for hardware by sharing the hardware with its host computer.
- Increase security and reliability. Students can perform their administrative tasks on virtual machines.
- Improve portability and flexibility. With virtual machines, multiple operating systems can run simultaneously on the same host.
- Simplify lab preparation and maintenance. The lab manager does not have to reinstall the operating system and application software semester after semester.

There are also some disadvantages of using virtual machines. A virtual machine runs slower than its host computer. When a server hosts multiple virtual machines, there must be enough RAM installed on the server. For example, suppose that a host server requires 1GB RAM and each of its five virtual machines requires 512MB RAM. To run the server and the five virtual machines simultaneously, at least 4GB RAM should be installed on the host server. Despite the disadvantages, virtual machines are great for lab activities. There are also some third party virtual machine products such as VMware.

In the above, we have discussed the issues related to the Linux operating system. Several major Linux distributions have been introduced. We have also explored the services and tools provided by the Linux operating system. Brief discussions about the needs of an online teaching/learning system are given. We have also discussed how the services and tools provided by the Linux operating system are used to meet those needs. Next, we will look at the configuration of a Web server and the security enforcement for Internet based computing.

EXAMPLE 1: INSTALLATION OF LINUX SERVER

This example illustrates how to install a Linux server on a virtual machine. As mentioned above, using virtual machines has several advantages. Suppose that the Linux server is used to support the online teaching lab. Using virtual machines can significantly improve security, flexibility, and maintainability. With the virtualization technology, each computer in the lab can host several virtual machines, each of which is designed to meet the requirements of a specific course. Also, the virtual machines can be distributed to the students, so these students can load them on their own computers for hands-on practice without changing the host computers. The following are the major steps for the installation process:

- Download and install a virtual machine such as the free VMware Server.
- Based on the course requirements, specify the hardware for the virtual machine.
- Configure the virtual machine to meet the specified hardware requirements.
- Install the Linux server on the virtual machine as the guest operating system.
- Install the application software on the guest operating system.
- Install VMware Player to run the virtual machine.

VMware Server installation: VMware Server can be downloaded from the Web site: http://www.vmware.com/download/server.

Before the installation, make sure that you have enough RAM to run the virtual machine. For example, the host computer needs a minimum of 1GB to run the Windows Vista operating system and the virtual machine requires 512MB RAM, you may need 2GB RAM on the host computer. The installation of the virtual server is a simple process. All you have to do is to follow the instructions provided by the installation wizard.

Virtual machine hardware requirements: Before you can create a virtual machine on the virtual server, you need to know the hardware requirements for the virtual machine. Suppose a networking class requires the Ubuntu Linux server to be installed for hands-on practice. The reason to choose the Ubuntu Linux server is that it is a 100% open source Linux operating system. Based on the course requirements, the Ubuntu Linux server will also be used to host the network based application software such as the database server, learning management system server, Web server, programming languages, and so on. The application software often requires bigger hard drives to host various files. Therefore, the Ubuntu Linux server may need an 8GB hard drive, 512MB RAM, a CD-ROM, and a USB port.

Creating virtual machine: Log on to the virtual server. Create a new virtual machine. Enter the hardware information specified in the above. During the installation process, you will be prompted to specify network configuration. Since the virtual machine will be used for the networking class, make sure to create two network cards; one is specified with the bridge mode and the other is specified with the NAT mode. After the virtual machine is created, enable the network cards, CD-ROM, and USB port.

Installing guest operating system: Since the networking class requires the Ubuntu Linux server, you need to download the package from the Web site: http://www.ubuntu.com/getubuntu/download.

Make that the server version is downloaded. Burn the downloaded file to a DVD-R disk. Insert the DVD into the host computer's CD-ROM drive. Then, the installation process can be started. The installation is straight forward. When asked if you would like to install the Apache, PHP, and MySQL packages, click Yes to install these packages to the guest operating system.

VMware Player installation: After the virtual machine with guest operating system is installed, it can be copied to each of the computers in the lab and distributed to the students. VMware Player is needed to run the virtual machine. You can download VMware Player from the Web site: http://www.vmware.com/download/player.

After VMware Player is installed, the students can use it to open the virtual machine and perform hands-on activities on the guest operating system.

EXAMPLE 2: WEB SERVER DEVELOPMENT ON LINUX FOR ONLINE COURSES

In this example, we are going to discuss the configuration of a Web server. The configuration will be based on the requirements of an online teaching/learning system. In the previous chapter, the requirements for a Web server were examined. In the following, let us summarize the requirements that are related to the Web server.

- Through the Web server, students should be able to browse course materials from off-campus computers with Internet connection.
- Students need to interact with the simulation software hosted by the Web server through the Internet.
- Some engineering courses may need the Web server to host a machine control language to control instruments in an online lab.
- The Web server needs to be set up to allow students to download the application software and course materials.

- The Web server should be constructed to provide university related information, course information, registration information, the information about related services, and the links to the other remotely accessible servers.
- The Web server should be configured to support class Web sites for collaboration. Some class Web sites should also provide interactive GUI tools to allow students to conduct hands-on practice.
- The Web server should support scripting languages such as JavaScript, VB-Script, and other Web programming languages such as Java, PHP and ASP. NET.
- The Web server should support multimedia related activities such as displaying video clips.
- Some Web servers are also required to support network-based software installation. The tools provided by these Web servers can be used to configure HTTP settings.
- The Web server can also be a subject for learning. Students in e-commerce related courses need to learn how to set up a Web server for running a business online.

As described above, the Web server can be either in a stable condition to support online courses, or in an unstable condition for students to get hands-on practice on setting up a Web server. We will look at the Web server configuration for both conditions.

Configuration of Web Servers for Hands-On Practice

To support hands-on practice in e-commerce related courses such as Internet computing, client-server computing, and application development, each student will create his/her own Web server for hands-on practice. Since most of the configuration work will be done by the students themselves, the requirements for the configuration are minimal. In the lab, we only need to conduct basic installation.

As one of the servers provided by the Linux operating system, the Apache Web server supports Web sites. We will use the Apache Web server in this example.

The installation of a Web server is a simple process. However, to make a Web server fully functioning, the other Internet based services such as ftp, finger, and other security measures should also be implemented. The following is a general procedure for setting up a Web server on the Linux operating system:

- The first task is to make sure that the Internet connection is established and the Linux operating system is installed and the Web browser is working properly.

- Next, verify if the specified version of the Apache Web server is included in the Linux operating system. If not, you will need to search for the appropriate version on the Internet. For example, you may search for the RPM package:

  httpd-2.0.46-25.ent.i386.rpm

  On the Linux operating system, the Apache Web server may also be named httpd. Download the software package, and then you are ready to install the Web server.
- The next step is to install the Apache Web server. Suppose that you have downloaded the RPM package; as an example, the following command can be used to install the Web server:

```
rpm -Uvh /mnt/cdrom/httpd-2.0.46-25.ent.i386.rpm
```

  Similarly, you can install ftp, xinet, telnet, and other packages.
- After the Apache Web server is installed, your next task is to start the service. You may run the following command to start httpd:

```
service httpd start
```

- The above command starts the Apache Web server. However, once the server shuts down the service httpd will stop and will not be able to automatically restart after the system is rebooted. To make httpd automatically restart after the computer system is rebooted, enter the command:

```
ntsysv
```

  You can find httpd by using the down arrow key. Then, enable httpd by pressing the space bar. Similarly, you can start other services. After this step, the basic installation is completed. The students can further develop their Web servers based on the hands-on practice requirements.

Configuration of Web Servers for Supporting Web Sites

To create Web sites to support classes, you first need to make sure that the Apache Web server is installed by following the above steps. Then, you may configure the Web server using the following steps:

- To store Web pages, you need to create a folder in the directory /var/www/html and then copy all the files for your Web pages to that folder.
- Among the Web page files, there should be an index.html file in the folder inside the directory /var/www/html. index.html is the default Web page. You may modify the index.html file so that it displays specific information about an individual class. Links to the other Web pages should also be added to the default Web page.
- Test the Web page by starting the Web browser, and enter the URL:

  http://localhost

- If the default Web page is successfully displayed, you can test it through a computer on the local area network and through a computer on the Internet by using the command:

  http://servername.edu

  Similarly, you can configure the Web server to display the information about the university, registration, courses, and so on.

Class Web Site Access Control

To control the access to a class Web site, you can configure the file /etc/config/httpd.conf. For example, to allow everyone to run CGI scripts, enter the following code with the pair of tags <Directory> and </Directory>.

```
<Directory "var/www/cgi-bin">
    AllowOverride None
    Options ExecCGI
    Allow from all
</Directory>
```

By editing the /etc/config/httpd.conf file, you can also allow users to access or deny users from accessing a specific file and to use a specific method to access or deny it from accessing a class Web site.

Configuration of Virtual Hosts for Multiple Class Web Sites

When there are multiple Web sites that need to be created for several classes, a single Web server is able to handle multiple Web sites by using virtual hosts. Each virtual host can use its own IP address, and it can be configured within the pair of tags <VirtualHost> and </VirtualHost> in the file /etc/config/httpd.conf. For example, to create three virtual hosts for the Web sites of three classes ENG3331, ISC3325, and ACC3316, you may write the following code in the configuration file:

```
<VirtualHost www.eng3331.whu.edu>
    DocumentRoot  /var/www/html/eng3331
    ServerName  www.eng3331.whu.edu
    ServerAdmin  webmaster@whu.edu
    ScriptAlias  /cgi-bin/  /var/www/html/eng3331
    Errorlog  /usr/var/www/html/logs/error _ log
    Custmlog  /var/www/html/logs/access _ log  common
</VirtualHost>

<VirtualHost www.isc3325.whu.edu>
    DocumentRoot  /var/www/html/isc3325
    ServerName  www.isc3325.whu.edu
    ServerAdmin  webmaster@whu.edu
    ScriptAlias  /cgi-bin/  /var/www/html/isc3325
    Errorlog  /usr/var/www/html/logs/error _ log
    Custmlog  /var/www/html/logs/access _ log  common
</VirtualHost>

<VirtualHost www.acc3316.whu.edu>
    DocumentRoot  /var/www/html/acc3316
    ServerName  www.acc3316.whu.edu
    ServerAdmin  webmaster@whu.edu
    ScriptAlias  /cgi-bin/  /var/www/html/acc3316
    Errorlog  /usr/var/www/html/logs/error _ log
    Custmlog  /var/www/html/logs/access _ log  common
</VirtualHost>
```

The above code sets three Web sites and the Web pages are stored in three separate directories on a single Web server.

Installation of Linux Operating System by Using HTTP

During lab construction, you may need to install the Linux operating system on many computers in the lab. The Linux distributions such as Red Hat and SUSE provide some tools to assist network-based installation. If SUSE Linux is to be installed, we can use the tool AutoYaST to accomplish the task.

- Prepare an XML file that contains all the installation specifications. The GUI tool AutoYaST module can be used to create the XML file.
- Make sure that the network server can communicate with the computer on which the Linux operating system is to be installed. You will also need to create a directory that contains all the installation files.
- You may install the Linux operating system through Preboot Execution Environment (PXE) which downloads the SLES 9 installation kernel and initrd to the target system. Or, if the network server does not support PXE, you may insert the SUSE Linux installation CD or DVD and restart the computer.
- When the GRUB screen appears, select Installation. When prompted, you can specify the display resolution and select HTTP as the installation source.
- Enter the installation server IP address and the directory that contains the Linux operating system files. Based on the specifications in the AutoYaST file, the installation process will automatically install the Linux operating system on the target computer system.

Similar to the AutoYaST file, the kickstart file provided by Red Hat can also be used for network-based installation. These tools are especially useful for setting up a medium or large computer lab for hands-on practice.

Supporting Java Servlets on Apache Web Server

Sometimes, a Web server is required to execute Java Servlets which are more powerful than a CGI program to avoid starting a new process each time the server receives data from an HTML form. The following is a general procedure to support Java Servlets on the Appache Web server:

- First, you need to install Java Development Kit (JDK) version 1.2 or later.
- You also need to install Apache Tomcat which is a server that runs Java Servlets.
- Make sure that the Apache httpd source files are installed.
- Download and install Jakarta-Tomcat-Connector mod_jk which enables the communication between the Apache Web server and Tomcat.
- Configure httpd and Tomcat to specify the communication between these components.
- Test if the communication between Tomcat and httpd works.

If the test is successful, your Web server will be able to support JavaServer Pages (JSP) and Java Servlets which are the key components for today's e-commerce.

To run simulation and to control instruments through the Web, you may need more in-depth knowledge. A lot of studies have been done in the area of Web-based simulation. For running an x-ray simulation on the Apache Web server, readers can find more details in the paper by Stepanov (2004). Readers can also find another Web-based simulation study done by

Islam and Piasecki (2003). For the Web-based instrument control, readers may find information from the book by Fjeldly and Shur (2003).

CONCLUSION

This chapter has investigated how the open source products are used in the construction of servers to support an online teaching/learning system. It first provided an overview about the client-server architecture. It compares various types of client-server structures. A medium to large online teaching/learning system should be constructed on a three-tier client-server structure.

This chapter briefly introduced the open source operating systems. Linux was identified as a suitable open source operating system for supporting an online teaching/learning system. Then, this chapter examined several major Linux distributions that provide the enterprise-level versions of the Linux operating system. It discussed the system management tools provided by Linux and what can be done with these tools to manage the online teaching/learning system. After the discussion of the management of the Linux operating system, an example was given to illustrate some of the commonly performed configuration tasks to build a Web server.

REFERENCES

Atkinson, R., Cummings, R., Phillips, R., & Pospisil, R. (1999). Course server software for online teaching. In *Proceedings of NET*Working'99 Conference*. Retrieved October 26, 2007, from http://www.users.bigpond.net.au/atkinson-mcbeath/roger/pubs/confs/atkinson-nw99.html

Ayala, G., & Paredes, R. (2003). Learner model servers: Personalization of Web based educational applications based on digital collections. In D. Lassner & C. McNaught (Eds.), *Proceedings of World Conference on Educational Multimedia, Hypermedia and Telecommunications 2003* (pp. 432-435). Chesapeake, VA: AACE.

Boer, A. (2002). A delivery server infrastructure for multimedia distance learning services. In P. Kommers & G. Richards (Eds.), In *Proceedings of World Conference on Educational Multimedia, Hypermedia and Telecommunications 2002* (pp. 178-179). Chesapeake, VA: AACE.

Buchanan, W., & Wilson, A. (2000). *Advanced PC architecture*. Indianapolis, IN: Addison-Wesley Professional.

Debian. (2007). *About Debian*. Retrieved October 16, 2007, from http://www.debian.org/intro/about

Fansler, K. W., & Riegle, R. P. (2004). A model of online instructional design analytics. In *20th Annual Conference on Distance Teaching and Learning*. Retrieved January 26, 2007, http://www.uwex.edu/disted/conference/Resource_library/proceedings/04_1069.pdf

Fjeldly, T. A., & Shur, M. S. (Eds.) (2003). *Lab on the Web: Running real electronics experiments via the Internet*. Hoboken, NJ: John Wiley & Sons.

Hoagland, D., Brewer, S. D., & Hoogendyk, T. A. (2002). *Linux in higher education: Two applications that improve student learning*. Paper presented at the Massachusetts Education Computing Conference (MECC), West Barnstable, MA.

Hunt, C. (2002). *Linux network servers*. Alameda, CA: Sybex.

IBM. (2007). *The Linux experience*. Retrieved October 16, 2007, from http://www.cgselearning.com/marketing/linux/movie.html

Islam, A. S., & Piasecki, M. (2003). *A future Outlook: Web based Simulation of Hydrodynamic models*. Paper presented at AGU Fall Meeting, San Francisco, CA.

Kavanagh, P. (2004). *Open source software: Implementation and management*. Burlington, MA: Digital Press.

Knopper.Net (2007). *What is KNOPPIX?* Retrieved October 16, 2007, from http://www.knopper.net/knoppix/index-en.html

Novell. (2007). *SUSE Linux Enterprise*. Retrieved October 16, 2007, from http://www.novell.com/linux

Red Hat. (2007). *Red Hat home page*. Retrieved October 16, 2007, from http://www.redhat.com

SPARC International. (1994). *SPARC architecture manual Version 9*. Upper Saddle River, NJ: Prentice Hall PTR.

Stepanov, S. (2004). How to make x-ray simulation software working on WWW: A simple recipe based on seven years of experience. In *Proceedings SPIE, 5536* (pp.165-170).

Vetter, S., et al. (2005). *Advanced POWER virtualization on IBM eServer p5 servers: Architecture and performance considerations.* IBM Redbooks. Retrieved June 16, 2006, from http://www.redbooks.ibm.com/abstracts/sg245768.html?Open

Chapter VI
Database Development for Online Courses

INTRODUCTION

In the previous chapter, we discussed the issues related to the server operating system which is used to host other application software such as a learning management system and database management system. The discussion in the previous chapter indicates that, for the learning management system, a database is required for storing course and student information. This chapter will first explore some of the open source database management systems. Several commonly used open source database management systems will be introduced. The features of the database management systems will be compared. We will examine how these features are used to store the course and student information and to support the management of the online teaching/learning system.

The next topic in this chapter is about database design for an online teaching/learning system. Within this topic, we will first review the database development cycle. Then, we will go through some general database procedures which consist of three stages, conceptual design, logical design, and physical design. We will discuss issues such as collcting information about the requirements for the new database, design a data model to meet the requirements, and discuss issues related to physical design.

After the discussion of database design, we will look at the development and implementation of a database for the online teaching/learning system. We will discuss the selection of a database management system (DBMS), converting the data model to a relational database, creating and implementing database objects, and so on.

The next topic is about database management. Once the database is developed, it is required that the database be well maintained for supporting the online teaching/leaning system. We will look at the tasks to be performed by the database administrator including user management, database backup and recovery, database performance tuning, and database security related management.

Lastly, this chapter will give an example of installing and configuring MySQL on a server with the Linux operating system. It will examine the system requirements and demonstrate the procedure of downloading and installing MySQL. This example will show how the Linux operating system supports MySQL and the database operation in the Linux environment. The second example in this chapter is about setting up PHP and MySQL development environment.

BACKGROUND

An online teaching/learning system usually supports hundreds of or thousands of courses each semester. These courses generate a large number of data including course materials, student information, assignments and grade-related information. Semester after semester, the data generated by these courses are accumulating. To be able to store and manage the large number of current and historical data, it is required that a reliable database should be developed to meet the requirements of the online teaching/learning system. Many open source database management system packages are available for developing databases that can be used to store and track data for online courses.

The subject related to developing databases for online teaching/learning systems has been widely studied. Ratna, Samuel, and Bayuaji (2002) developed a synchronous Web-based learning system on which Web Chat was used as interactive media. The Web Chat program was supported by the open source database MySQL and the PHP scripts. The system provided Web-based real-time communication between instructors and students. It also provided management tools to control the real-time communication process. In another study, Potter and Hicks (2004) integrated the open source database application into the social studies classes and the classes of other subjects. By using the open source database application, they were able to develop a well-designed database with minimal cost.

Performance tuning is one of the tasks in database management. The experimentation system developed by Pozniak-Koszalka and Helwich (2005) can be used to test the efficiency of a relational database. Their experimentation system is particularly useful for improving the efficiency of Internet applications and open source database management systems such as MySQL.

MySQL is one of the largest open source database management systems. There are many publications about the design and implementation of databases with MySQL. Readers can find a lot of tools and hands-on information about MySQL in the book by Tahaghoghi and Williams (2006). The book covers the installation and configuration of MySQL, and the use of MySQL to accomplish various tasks such as database design, database security management, Web-based database application, and programming with PHP and Perl.

The combination of MySQL and Linux provides a versatile open source based application development environment. The book by Rosebrock and Filson (2004) is about setting up an open source based LAMP (Linux, Apache, MySQL, and PHP) platform for building dynamic Web-based applications. All these four LAMP components are the key components of an open source based online teaching/learning system. It is very convenient for the reader to get information about the four key technologies in one source while developing Web-based applications.

Many of the e-learning projects are supported by MySQL. Mentioned by Horton and Horton (2003) in their book, MySQL is used to create database servers hosted by the Linux operating system. While combined with the Web server, MySQL supports many Web-based applications, such as providing data for Web forms and reports used by online classes.

Database itself is a major topic covered by curriculums such as computer science, computer information systems, and many other IT related fields. As a general introduction about database design, development, and implementation from the academic and practical points of view, readers can find a wide coverage of database theories in Kroenke's (2006) book where MySQL is examined as one of the major database management systems. The book also discusses the database server technology, database application development, and new technologies such as XML.

In this chapter, our discussion will emphasize open source database software, especially the MySQL package. We will deal with issues in the areas of database functionalities, the role played by a database in an online teaching/learning system, the management of a database system to keep the online teaching/learning system running smoothly, and the advantages of using an open source database management system. This chapter will start with the introduction of the major open source database management systems.

OPEN SOURCE DATABASE MANAGEMENT SYSTEMS

As the center of an information system, databases are created to store and manage the information for an online teaching/learning system. If the online teaching/learning system is supported by an open source operating system and an open source learning management system, then an open source database management system (DBMS) such as MySQL will be the perfect match for those open source technologies. Beside MySQL, there are many other open source database management systems that can be used to support the online teaching/learning system.

A database management system provides a database development and management platform. With the database management system, developers can design and create databases to store and track the course and student information, support Web-based applications, analyze students' performance, and other knowledge management tasks. To meet the teaching and learning requirements, the database management system should include the following components for database development and management:

- **Database server:** This component supports network based database operations and provides a network based database development environment. A database server can distribute data across a network to remote applications and other databases. Especially, it can support the Web database application and allows multiple users to log on to the same database simultaneously.
- **Database management:** This component can be used to create and manage database objects such as databases, tables, users, roles, indexes.
- **Query editor:** It can be used to develop and execute queries to extract data stored in a database. It can also be used to create SQL statements for database management and populate the database with data.
- **Data transformation utilities:** They can be used to move data into and out of a database to other data sources such as relational databases, spreadsheet files, text files, XML files, and other forms of data sources.
- **Data analysis utilities:** They can be used for data analysis tasks such as developing and managing data warehouses, conducting an Online Analytical Processing (OLAP) analysis, data mining and other statistical descriptions of data for decision support.
- **Network utilities:** They can be used to perform network related configurations for remote access and for communication among network devices.
- **Debugging utilities:** They can help with exception handling in SQL code and other database troubleshooting tasks.
- **Programming interface:** This interface can be used to extend the basic SQL functionalities by providing environments to develop programs with PHP, Perl, Python, Ruby, Java, or other programming languages.
- **Database application development utilities:** Some of the database management systems also include utilities to develop database applications such as reports, forms, and Web pages.

Many open source database software packages are currently available. Most of the above components are included in the major open source database software packages such as MySQL. With the above components, an open source database management system can fully support an online teaching/learning system. The open source database solution is an efficient and low cost alternative to a system built with commercial products. In the following describes several popular open source database management systems such as MySQL, PostgreSQL, Berkeley DB, and so on. We will examine the features provided by these database management systems and compare them side by side to see what advantages they have.

MySQL

MySQL is the most popular open source database management system. According to the information provided by MySQL (2007), in 2007, there were over 11 million installations around the world and over 50,000 downloads per day. Many enterprise-level companies such as Google and Yahoo are powered by MySQL for their Web-based business. MySQL is also powerful enough to meet the needs of many online teaching/learning systems. The following are some of the features provided by MySQL:

- MySQL is fast since one of MySQL's design goals is to make it the fastest database product.
- MySQL is also a versatile product. It supports most of the database management system components, such as enterprise database servers, database managers, network access, expert advisory services, advanced graphing, distributed database systems, administration GUI tools, and so on.
- MySQL runs on more than twenty platforms, including Linux, Windows, Mac OS, Novell Netware, and UNIX.
- MySQL complies with the Atomicity, Consistency, Isolation, and Durability (ACID) transaction standard for transaction reliability.
- MySQL has high safety features such as various ways to control database access. Based on the user name, the host name of a computer, and the table name, MySQL can control the access even down to the column or row level. It also supports the secure network protocols Secure Sockets Layer (SSL) and the Secure Hash Algorithm (SHA).
- MySQL supports various remote data access methods such as Open Database Connectivity (ODBC), Java Database Connectivity (JDBC), Object Linking and Embedding Database (OLE DB), and ActiveX Data Objects.NET (ADO.NET).

- To implement more sophisticated application logics, MySQL supports the programming languages such as Java, C/C++, Delphi, Perl, Python, and PHP. The recent version of MySQL also supports XML functions.
- With MySQL, the database administrator can perform tasks such as user account management, database replication and clustering, database backup and restoration, and performance tuning.

With these features, MySQL is a fully functioning database management system that can be used to manage the information generated by an online teaching/learning system. When a server is installed with the Linux operating system, MySQL is often the choice for creating a database server for network based information management. Later, we will look at more detailed information on the design and implementation of databases with MySQL for supporting an online teaching/learning system.

PostgreSQL

PostgreSQL is another open source database management system based on the research project originally developed by the Computer Science Department at the University of California, Berkeley. According to PostgreSQL (2007), this package is an advanced database management system. It is highly reliable, stable, and extensible, and it has much lower maintenance and tuning requirements.

Among the enterprise-level companies, Red Hat and Skype are powered by PostgreSQL for information processing. PostgreSQL is also powerful enough to handle tasks for supporting online classes. Although PostgreSQL is not as popular as MySQL, it has its own special features described in the following:

- PostgreSQL is highly compliant with SQL2003 standard. PostgreSQL implements a larger part of SQL2003 commands than MySQL does.
- PostgreSQL can also run on different platforms such as Linux, Mac OS, and various UNIX platforms. As for Windows, however, only recent versions of PstgreSQL support the Windows platform.
- The remote access methods supported by PostgreSQL are ODBC, JDBC, and ADO.NET.
- The programming languages supported by PostgreSQL are C/C++, Perl, Python, PHP, and so on.
- PostgreSQL also supports the ACID transaction standard for transaction reliability.
- PostgreSQL has several ways to control database access. It can limit the access of the database by using criteria based on the schema, function, network

segment, user identification, and other identification strings. It also supports the secure network protocol Secure Sockets Layer (SSL) and authentication methods such as MD5, crypt, password and Kerberos.

- PostgreSQL provides many database management tools that allow database administrators to manage user accounts, to backup and restore databases, and to do database performance tuning.

With the support from the open source community, PostgreSQL has been developed into a robust and versatile database management system. Many of the information management tasks for an online teaching/learning system can be done with PostgreSQL.

Berkeley DB

Unlike MySQL and PostgreSQL, Berkeley DB is an open source embedded database library. To be used, Berkeley DB needs to be embedded in one of the programming languages such as C, C++, Java, Perl, Python, Ruby, and so on. It can also be used with the application products such as sendmail, the Apache Web server, the OpenLDAP server, and many UNIX based products. The features of an embedded database like Berkeley DB are summarized in the following:

- Berkeley DB is simple and fast. It takes a small amount of memory and can be loaded into memory in a very short time.
- For better performance, an embedded database like Berkeley DB is usually not a relational database and does not use SQL. This type of database is often built on a flat file.
- The administration of an embedded database is relatively easy. There is no user account to manage and no need to set up permissions for access database objects.
- After being embedded in an application product, an embedded database can be shipped with the application product so that the users of the application product do not need to install and implement a database for the application product.
- Being an embedded database, Berkeley DB lowers cost for database implementation. It does not require additional hardware and software.
- An embedded database like Berkeley DB is flexible, and it can be configured to be optimized for a specific application.

To be used with a specific application, Berkeley DB is a good choice for a fast, scalable, and reliable database that supports data management.

There are many other open source database management systems. Some of them are powerful enough to manage an online teaching/learning system. Further discussion of those open source database management systems is beyond the scope of this book. Next, we will look at the issues related to database development to support an online teaching/learning system.

DATABASE SYSTEM DEVELOPMENT

In an online teaching/learning system, the database stores and manages the course and user information. It must be specially designed and developed to meet the requirements by the online teaching/learning system. In general, the database development process involves several major phases including:

- **Requirement investigation:** To meet the requirements of an online teaching/learning system, it is important to find out what exactly the requirements are. The database designers and developers need to thoroughly understand the underlying online teaching/learning system.
- **Database design:** Based on the result of the requirement investigation, the database design team should set up database design goals and create a logical data model and a physical design plan to meet the design goals.
- **Database development:** The development of a database requires careful planning and skills. The issues related to converting a data model to a relational database, populating the database, developing database applications, setting database security, and testing the database should be considered in the development phase.
- **Data analysis:** As the data of teaching and learning are cumulated, they can be analyzed to identify students' learning behavior and to predict the trend in learning and teaching. The data analysis service should be configured and tested to support the data analysis.
- **Database management:** Once the database is in place, the next task is to keep it running in good condition so that online teaching and learning will not be interrupted by database failure. The data stored in the database should be well protected. It is critical to keep the database secure and no database objects should be accessed or modified by an unauthorized person.

It takes a great deal of effort to accomplish each task in the database development process. To better understand the entire process, let us take a closer look at each database development phase to find what tasks should be accomplished and who are involved in the development process.

Requirement Investigation

Since teaching and learning in higher education institutions are so diversified, each online teaching/learning system has its own specific requirements. Therefore, the first task in the database development process is to investigate the specific requirements for the database to be developed. At this phase, the database development team needs to answer these questions: How will the future database be used in the online teaching/learning process? What are the teaching and learning activities supported by the future database? What are the rules and limitations enforced by the university? To find the answers to these questions, the database development team needs to identify the information that will be stored and kept track of. To be able to collect all the above information, the database development team should interview the key players of the online teaching/learning system. They should also examine the documents such as registration forms, class schedules, and course catalogs. They need to understand how the data are used in the online teaching/learning process so that they can design the database to support the teaching and learning activities. To figure out how the data will be used in the teaching and learning activities, they need to observe the data flow in the teaching and learning process. After the information is collected, the database development team will interpret, categorize, and document the information to get ready for the database design.

Database Design

The next phase in the database development process is the design phase. The database designers of the development team need to represent the collected information with database objects and identify the attributes to describe each database object. They also need to identify the relationships among those database objects. With the database objects and relationships among them, the database designers can develop a data model which is the blue print for the future database. After the initial data model is created, the database designers need to verify if the future database will meet the database requirements. Usually, the initial data model is not ready to be used for creating the database physically. It may take several rounds of modifications before the design goals can be achieved logically. The database designers and the key players of the online teaching/learning system should work together to go over the data model for verification. If there should be a modification of the database structure, it is much easier to do it on the data model. It is much harder to make any change on the database structure once the database is physically created and populated with data. Both the database designers and the key players should be satisfied with the data model before the database can be physically implemented.

Since the 1970's, several data modeling techniques have been developed. The following are some of the commonly used data modeling techniques.

- The entity-relationship model (E-R model) introduced by Chen (1976) is one of the widely used modeling tools. This data model consists of entities, attributes, and relationships to represent the logical structure of a database. The word "entity" is a generic term for a database object such as Student, Course, Enrollment, and so on. Attributes are characteristics used to describe a database object. For example, the attributes such as Student Id, First Name, Last Name, Major, and so on are used to describe the database object Student.
- Another widely used modeling tool is the Unified Modeling Language (UML), which includes components such as class, attribute, relationship, and operation. A class is equivalent to an entity in the E-R model. As a general-purpose modeling language, UML can be used in data modeling. Although it is slightly difficult to represent database objects with UML, it is convenient for those who already know UML to develop databases. Besides, UML has more functionalities to represent database activities than those of the E-R modeling technique.
- ICAM Definition Languages (IDEF) is also commonly used for data modeling. In the family of IDEF, IDEF1X is accepted by the federal government as the representation technique for data modeling. The IDEF1X data modeling technique can be used to produce a graphical data model which represents database objects, attributes, relationships among database objects, and database structures. The use of IDEF1X has several advantages. IDEF1X provides icons to represent E-R model components such as entities, attributes, relationships, and domains. Most of the data model logical structures can be represented with IDEF1X icons. It is relatively easy to convert the data model that complies with the IDEF1X standard to a physical database.

In the above, three commonly used data modeling techniques are introduced. An entity or class representing a database object can be further normalized to avoid data modification anomalies. Interested readers can find more detailed information about normalization in the Hillyer's (2007) article on the MySQL Web site.

Before you can implement a database physically, some of the issues related to physical implementation of the database should be carefully considered. The consideration of the database's physical implementation is the subject of physical design. For the physical design, the database designers need to think about things such as using the client-server architecture for hosting the network based database system, how users access the data stored in the database, and the selection of servers and storage devices for the ever growing data sets. For the physical design, the consideration should also include the selection of devices to handle various types of multimedia data generated by the multimedia course materials.

Database Development

The next phase is to develop and implement the database for the online teaching/learning system. The first task in this phase is to select a database management system (DBMS). With the DBMS, the database development team can convert the data model to a relational database. In the relational database, the entities and attributes are implemented with tables which are constructed with columns and rows to store and organize the data. The relationships among the entities are implemented with integrity constraints.

The choice of the DBMS depends on whether the functionalities provided by the DBMS can meet the requirements of the future online teaching/learning system, the cost of the database acquisition and management, and the capability of the network and server devices for hosting the database. For a full featured online teaching/learning system, the chosen DBMS should be able to support all the database management, data analysis, and data storage requirements. As mentioned earlier, several open source DBMS products are available to meet the above requirements. When compared with the commercial DBMS products, the open source DBMS products will cost much less. Also, these open source DBMS products are all supported by the open source operating systems such as Linux. As we can see, the combination of MySQL and Linux or the combination of PostgreSQL and Linux can meet the DBMS selection criteria.

Usually, a database construction project is large and complex. It is worth the effort to plan the project before the construction can be started. To successfully construct the database, the database development team may consider the factors such as:

- The technicians, supporting staff members, and faculty members involved in the project, and the tasks that should be accomplished by these people.
- The availability of the required computer hardware and software, and network devices.
- The need for the database developers to verify if the network architecture and the Internet services are ready to handle the traffic in and out of the database.
- The need to verify if the security measures are enforced on the server computer system and on the network which will host the network based database.
- The need to develop a timeline and a task list to indicate when and how the database construction will be conducted.

Each online teaching/learning system is different. A database construction plan may have more or less items than that in the above list. The plan will guide the database development team to implement the database on schedule and meet the specific requirements of the online teaching/learning system.

The database construction process includes downloading and installing the open source DBMS software package, creating database objects with the DBMS, configuring database objects to implement the relationships and to meet the requirements, creating programming units to enforce constraints and to implement the university's regulations, and testing and verifying if the database can perform as it is supposed to with sample data sets. The database development team including the developers, designers, database administrator, support staff, and faculty should be involved in the testing process. Based on the testing results, the database will be modified. After the database is tested and confirmed by the people involved in the database testing, it is time to populate the database tables with the data generated by the online teaching/learning system.

Once the database is implemented and populated with data, the database developers can now develop some database applications such as forms and reports which serve as a graphical interface between the front-end users and the database objects. These database applications will help front-end users to interact with the database. The database developers will also install and test some client-side software to see if a student is able to remotely access the database through the Internet.

In the above, we have briefly discussed the tasks to be performed during the database development phase. Usually, database construction is done by a group of well-trained IT professionals. The tasks of testing and troubleshooting also need highly skilled technical personnel to get the job done. For a university, if there are not enough qualified in-house technical personnel for the database construction project, it is possible to out source the database construction project to a consulting company when the budget is allowed. If the budget is limited and the database construction has to be done by the in-house technical personnel, make sure that they are given enough time to work on the project.

Data Analysis

Not only the data stored in the database can be used to keep track of student information and course information, they can also be used to analyze the trend in learning and teaching, and students' learning behavior. An enterprise-level DBMS usually provides data analysis services to help instructors and administrators to better understand the teaching and learning in their institutions. The topics of data analysis may include Online Analytical Processing (OLAP), the data mart or data warehouse, and data mining.

Database Management

Once the database is in place, the maintenance of the database is done by the database administrator. Usually, database administrators perform tasks such as user account management, data transformation, database backup and restoration, and performance tuning. They are also responsible for security management. Next, we will discuss database management in more detail.

DATABASE MANAGEMENT

As mentioned earlier, the database stores and controls all the information generated by the online teaching/learning system. Any database error will have a great impact on the online classes, students, and instructors, or even the entire university. Therefore, it is necessary to address the issues on how to manage user accounts, database availability, database performance, database security and reliability in order to support the operations of the online teaching/learning system. The following are some of the tasks that need to be carried out to keep the database running smoothly:

- **Database routine maintenance:** This task may include checking log files and auditing records to detect runtime problems, turning the database on and off for maintenance, troubleshooting database problems, documenting changes during maintenance, breaking up deadlocks which may happen during database operations, and assisting students and instructors in accessing the database. For large network based databases, database administrators may also perform tasks such as partitioning databases and managing network utilities for distributed databases.
- **Database security management:** Database security is one of the top priorities in database management. It may include configuring user accounts and permissions, and updating the database with security patches.
- **Database backup and restoration:** To prevent the loss of data, the database administrator needs to have a database backup and recovery plan. There should be enough storage space to store the backup, and the storage devices should be accessible during the recovery process. Also, to improve database reliability and performance, the database can be replicated to multiple servers linked in a distributed computing environment.
- **Database performance tuning:** Database administrators configure and tune database parameters to ensure that databases run with optimal performance. They detect problems that cause a slowdown in database performance.

- **Data analysis management:** If the data analysis service is provided by the database, the database administrator may also need to manage the resources for data analyses, such as managing the data warehouse or data mart, Online Analytical Processing (OLAP), and data mining processes. The database administrator also needs to plan a schedule to transfer data from the online transaction processing (OLTP) database to the data warehouse or data mart.

Performing these tasks requires a variety of knowledge in many database related fields. Various database management tools have been developed to assist the management of databases. There are many open source database management tools available. Open source database management systems such as MySQL and PostgreSQL provide some database management tools of their own. There are also third party database management tools. In the following, we will look at some of the commonly used open source database management tools.

MySQL Migration Toolkit

Once a database is created, the database administrator needs to populate the database with data which may be manually entered into tables or migrated from other data sources. MySQL Migration Toolkit is a data migration utility that helps the database administrator to quickly migrate data or database objects from various data sources to the MySQL database. It allows the database administrator to complete a data migration job with a wizard-driven interface. The wizard-driven interface walks the database administrator through each step of the migration process. In such a way, it can make the migration task less stressful and prevent mistakes. The following are some of the tasks that can be accomplished by using MySQL Migration Toolkit:

- With MySQL Migration Toolkit, the database administrator can quickly transfer the database objects created with commercial DBMS products to the MySQL database. Migration modules can be used to handle data migration from each of the major commercial DBMS products, such as Oracle and Microsoft SQL Server. These migration modules can also be customized to optimize the migration performance and to deal with some special data types such as geographical data. MySQL Migration Toolkit is a Java based utility, so it is platform free. This means that, by using MySQL Migration Toolkit, the database administrator can migrate a database hosted by other platforms to a database hosted by the Linux platform.
- In a migration process, the database administrator can transfer data in real time or transfer a database snapshot created earlier. MySQL Migration Tool-

kit not only can transfer data, but also can transfer the structures of database objects such as tables, views, indexes, foreign key constraints and so on. It can even restore a database application to match the earlier version of database snapshots. MySQL Migration Toolkit also allows users to create their own Java based migration procedures.

- By using MySQL Migration Toolkit, database migration can be done among servers linked by a network to avoid migration bottleneck and it can be controlled remotely through a desktop computer that has MySQL Migration Toolkit installed.
- Using MySQL Migration Toolkit can reduce migration risks for a complex migration process. MySQL Migration Toolkit provides an eight-step migration methodology to ensure the migration process is done properly. The migration methodology allows the database administrator to select database objects for migration. It also allows schema creation, data mapping, and data transfer.
- In addition to the wizard-based interface, MySQL Migration Toolkit allows the database administrator to customize the migration process manually to optimize the migration process. The database administrator can manually edit the scripts generated by the wizard for the special needs of the migration process.
- MySQL Migration Toolkit provides the database access utility JDBC which can be used to connect database applications to the database hosted by MySQL. In addition to JDBC, users can also add native database access modules written in the C language to improve performance.
- For migration reports, MySQL Migration Toolkit provides a comprehensive report utility that can be used to report the number of database objects that have been migrated. The report utility can also display information about the database objects that have been migrated successfully and those that have not.

Once the data or database objects have been migrated into the database, the database is ready to support the online teaching/learning system. To keep the database running in a healthy condition, tools are needed for database administration. The following discusses some of the database administration utilities.

MySQL Administrator

MySQL Administrator is one of the built-in GUI based utilities used for managing and monitoring MySQL database servers. It allows the database administrator to perform the database management and maintenance tasks described in the following:

- **Administering users:** By using MySQL Administrator, the database administrator can create, update, and delete user accounts. He/she can grant and remove users' privileges of accessing database objects and of executing SQL statements. MySQL Administrator also allows the database administrator to hieratically view the users' privileges based on the types of privileges.
- **Configuring services:** With MySQL Administrator, database administrators can configure, start, stop, and restart database services. They can also view the current status of a service.
- **Viewing database log:** To diagnose server problems and track database changes, the database administrator can use MySQL Administrator to view various log files such as error logs, binary logs, and the logged information of a service. MySQL Administrator can also be used to view the log files of database replication.
- **Database backup and recovery:** By using MySQL Administrator, the database administrator can create various types of database backups and use these backups to restore failed databases.
- **Database performance tuning:** MySQL Administrator allows the database administrator to tune performance by adjusting performance related parameters such as those server start-up parameters.
- **Database monitoring:** Through MySQL Administrator, the database administrator can dynamically monitor the health indicators of the MySQL environment. These indicators may include memory usage, connection usage, hit rates, hard disk space, tablespace, log files being used, the status of server variables, and the number of running queries.
- **Database replication:** To improve the reliability and performance of a database, MySQL Administrator can be used to set up database replication on multiple servers. Also, the database administrator can view the map of replication master and slaves.

With the GUI based MySQL Administrator, the database administrator can reduce management errors, improve the availability of the database, increase productivity, and create a more secure management environment. MySQL Administrator makes database management simpler and more efficient.

MySQL Query Management

MySQL Query Browser is a query management utility that can be used for creating, executing, and optimizing SQL queries. The queries can be visually managed by the drag-and-drop tool included in MySQL Query Browser. MySQL Query Browser provides the following components to assist the management of queries:

- MySQL Query Browser provides many visual tools. There is the Query Toolbar that can be used to run commands for creating, modifying, executing queries, and viewing the query history. The creation of a query can be done with the visual tools. The tables and columns involved in the query can be dragged down from the object browser to the query area, and then the user can edit the code generated by MySQL to fit his/her needs. Also, in the master-detail structure, the data from the master query will be automatically passed to the detail query.
- Script Editor is a programming environment where one can create, edit, and debug SQL scripts. The debugger included in Script Editor can be used to set breakpoints to pause the execution of the SQL statements and scripts, and to control the execution process with step-in and step-out functionalities.
- After a SQL query or script is executed, Results Window displays the results of the execution and allows the comparison of the results by multiple SQL statements. Multiple results can be compared vertically or side-by-side. The results can also be compared hierarchically in a master-detail style. Results Window can even explain the execution results to the user.
- Through Object Browser, the database administrator can explore the structures and relationships of database objects. The database administrator can also select a database object to query and edit, create a new database object, modify or delete a database object, add a bookmark to a commonly used query, and browse previously used queries for reuse by dragging them to the query area.
- By using Table Editor, the database administrator can create, modify, and delete tables. He/she can add and remove columns in a table, and can specify the default character set used by a table. Table Editor allows the database administrator to enforce the foreign key constraints between two tables. It also allows the database administrator to specify the storage engine for hosting a set of tables.

The above discussion shows that MySQL Query Browser is a sophisticated query management utility. All the SQL management tasks can be done by using MySQL Query Browser. It creates a flexible and efficient query management environment.

MySQL Workbench

MySQL Workbench is a database design tool. With it, the database designer can design a database at conceptual, logical and physical levels. MySQL Workbench allows the database designer to create database schemas, perform data migration, create documentations, and visually represent the components in a relational database. The designer can specify a set of notations for the database model. By using MySQL Workbench, the database designer can import or export the model. The zoom feature in MySQL Workbench allows the designer to view the entire model or the details in a specific portion of the model. MySQL Workbench can be used to perform synchronization among database models and generate SQL scripts for database models. It can also be used to perform database reverse-engineering which recovers a database model from a set of SQL statements and program source code.

SQL Session Management

Once a database is created, the database developer will create some database applications such as forms and reports to allow front-end users to interact with the database. A session is created on the database server while a database application is connecting to the database. A session associates a sequence of requests to a login user and manages the user's requests to improve performance. If a database application is Web-based and uses the HTTP protocol to deliver requests through the Internet, the request management becomes a difficult task since HTTP is a stateless protocol which does not remember the previous requests. However, when the user interacts with the database, it is important to have the knowledge of the previous requests, for example, in the activities of online banking. Session Management of MySQL can keep the information consistent across multiple requests of a session to support the state-maintaining Web-based applications.

In addition to the utilities provided by the DBMS packages, there are many third party open source or free database management tools. To name a few, Toad for MySQL and Zmanda are these types of database administration tools. Both are versatile and powerful.

Toad for MySQL

Quest Software provides the free tool Toad for MySQL which can be used to empower MySQL database development and improve the database administrator's productivity. Toad for MySQL provides the MySQL developer and administrator with utilities that are able to create and execute queries and other SQL statements, automate database routine maintenance, manage database objects, import data in or export data out of a database, and view database statistics. It also provides a database searching tool for searching, extracting and comparing objects stored in a database. Toad for MySQL can be easily incorporated with MySQL to create a computing environment that users are familiar with. According to Quest Software (2007), Toad for MySQL has the following features:

- For query development, Toad for MySQL provides the SQL Editor utility which provides an environment for SQL statement development. With SQL Editor, the database developer can create and modify SQL statements, view and edit data, view the structure of a database table, recall a SQL statement, record a sequence of commands entered through a keyboard and generate a micro for later use, navigate a large SQL file with Code Navigator, and so on.
- For assisting the database design, Toad for MySQL provides the E-R Diagram for developing E-R data models. It provides an environment for creating entities and attributes. It also allows the database developer to create relationships. The created diagrams can be sent to the Query Builder to quickly convert a data model to a corresponding relational database.
- To help with the administration of MySQL databases, Toad for MySQL provides the Database Browser for viewing, modifying, and managing database objects. It provides filters and grouping utilities for searching and organizing the database objects. With the Database Browser, one can view and edit data from multiple tables that are related through relationships. Toad for MySQL provides several utilities to compare database objects; for example, the Diff Viewer is used to compare files and data definition language (DDL) SQL statements such as CREATE and ALTER. Another utility Schema and Data Compare can be used to compare database objects and data for data migration and synchronization. To help with session management, Toad for MySQL has the utility Session Monitor for viewing the information of real-time sessions. The Flush and Reset utility provided by Toad for MySQL can be used to flush and reset the commands issued to a server.
- To support data management, Toad for MySQL allows the adding of line numbers in a data grid for quickly locating certain rows. For data grid search, it also provides the Data Search functionality for searching a word or phrase in a data grid. Another useful data management functionality is the integration of an external spreadsheet package such as Microsoft Excel with Toad for MySQL for data importing or exporting or for creating a report.
- Toad for MySQL supports the creation of reports in many ways. It provides the Schema Report Generator which can generate HTML based reports about a database. The reports also include the links to more detailed information. Toad for MySQL also provides the Data Report Designer which can be used to design, create, and distribute live reports.
- Another useful utility provided by Toad for MySQL is the Project Manager which allows the database administrator to perform database management

tasks at a central location. For daily maintenance, the database administrator can use the To-Do Item functionality to create a to-do item list with due dates. An item on the list will turn red if the due date is past, so the database administrator will notice that.

- Toad for MySQL allows the database administrator to schedule a list of tasks that can be done automatically at the scheduled time. It allows MySQL to automatically generate reports, execute queries and scripts, import data from or export data to external spreadsheet files, and automatically e-mail the findings to the business community.

From the description above, we can see that Toad for MySQL is a comprehensive MySQL database development and administration tool. With the graphical interface, the accomplishment of the above tasks can be simplified.

Zmanda

Zmanda is a backup and recovery management utility specially designed for the open source database management system MySQL. Zmanda provides a comprehensive backup and recovery solution for MySQL. According to Zmanda (2007), it provides the graphical interface for the backup and recovery operations. It can perform the online backup of MySQL databases. It can handle multiple database storage engines and manage them intelligently. With the backup, Zmanda can recover a failed database at any point in time. It is easy to use and flexible. The following are some of the backup and recovery tasks that can be accomplished by Zmanda.

- Zmanda can perform database backup in several ways. The database administrator can schedule a full backup to make a complete copy of a database, or schedule an incremental database backup to record the changes to the undergoing database, or choose to make faster raw backup of a MySQL database.
- The scheduling of backup is flexible. Zmanda allows the database administrator to start an immediate backup or postpone scheduled backups.
- Zmanda can optimize the backup performance by matching the storage engine and the undergoing MySQL.
- Zmanda provides great support for network based database systems. It allows the database administrator to remotely backup a MySQL database behind a firewall. This feature is ideal for an online teaching/learning system.
- Whenever it is needed, Zmanda allows the database administrator to conduct activities such as compression or encryption of the undergoing MySQL backup for reducing data storage occupation and enforcing security measures.

- Zmanda provides notification service. It can e-mail the database administrator about the status of the backup and allows the database administrator to view MySQL backup reports via RSS feed.
- Zmanda also provides backup monitoring service. The database administrator can monitor and browse backups through the Internet.
- As backups accumulate, storage space will quickly run out. It is necessary to delete the older backups. Zmanda allows the database administrator to create a retention policy on the retention duration and deletion of backups that have expired.
- With Zmanda, the recovery of a MySQL database can be granulated to any point in time or to any particular transaction such as the transaction right before the database failure to prevent data loss.

These features show that Zmanda is a good companion of MySQL. It can greatly reduce the time and effort spent on database backup and recovery.

The tools Toad for MySQL and Zmanda are used to take care of different tasks. These tools are not against each other. Toad for MySQL can be used by database designers to create database models with the E-R diagram. Database application developers may also find Toad for MySQL useful. They can use it to create and test SQL code. Database administrators can use Toad for MySQL to transport data in and out of a database and schedule routinely performed maintenance tasks. On the other hand, database designers and developers usually do not use Zmanda because it is a tool for database administrators who are in charge of database backup and recovery. Both of these tools can be easily incorporated with MySQL. Some of the tasks handled by these two third party tools can also be done by the MySQL built-in utilities. However, these two tools may give database administrators a better environment to work on their projects.

The features described above indicate that MySQL is a fully functioning database management system with minimal cost. It is a great choice for supporting an online teaching/learning system.

EXAMPLE 1: DBMS INSTALLATION AND CONFIGURATION ON LINUX

In the above, we have discussed some open source database management systems and the related database management issues. As mentioned earlier, these open source database management systems can all be installed on the server with the Linux operating system. The following example will illustrate how to install and configure the MySQL database management system on the Linux operating system.

Before the installation, make sure that the Linux operating system and the network are working properly and the technician who will perform the installation has the root privilege. Depending on the usage of MySQL, its installation on Linux may require the RAM as small as 512 MB and several gigabytes of hard drive space. To support a large database, MySQL can also use over 16GB RAM on a 64-bit multi-processor system with multiple hard drives configured with the RAID 10 architecture. The technician should also make sure the version of Linux is supported by the latest MySQL software package.

After the technician has verified that the requirements for hardware and software are all met, it is the time to download the MySQL package from the MySQL.com Web site. There are several types of installation packages. One can download the package in the RPM format, or the package in the tar format, or the package of source code. The installation of the RPM package is fast and easy. However, the RPM installation will place the configuration files everywhere, so it is difficult to find these files. Although it is a bit more complicated, the installation of the tar package will keep the configuration files in a folder that is easy to find. In the following we will take a look at the installation for both types of packages.

First, suppose that you have downloaded the MySQL tar.gz installation package such as mysql-version_number.tar.gz from MySQL's Web site. The version_number represents a version of MySQL. Extract the compressed tar.gz file with the desktop management GUI tool KDE or GNOME, or with the following command for extracting and installing the installation package.

```
# tar -xzf mysql-version _ number.tar.gz
# cd mysql-version _ number
# ./configure --prefix=/usr/local/mysql-version _ number
# make
# make install
```

Next, you will set up a configuration file to specify some management and security options. You may modify some of the pre-made configuration files to fit your needs. For MySQL, the name of a pre-made configuration file often starts with my, such as my-huge.cnf, my-large.cnf, my-medium.cnf or my-small.cnf. These configuration files are designed for different types of servers. For example, for a small server, you may choose to modify the my-small.cnf file. You can copy the selected pre-made configuration to your configuration file directory and rename it as /etc/my.cnf. Assign the root to the owner of the file and assign the read/write privilege to the user root. By using the vi editor, you can add new user accounts to the file or enable the innodb option which provides MySQL with a ACID compliant storage engine which provides commit, rollback, and crash recovery capabilities.

After the configuration of the my.cnf file, you should create the mysql database with the command, `mysql _ install _ db` and start the MySQL database server with the command, `mysqld _ safe` and connect to the newly created MySQL server with the root account. After the MySQL server is started for the first time, you can set the password for the root account. After the new password is set, restart the server and the MySQL server is ready to use.

For the RPM type installation, there are two types of packages, the server installation package and the client installation package. The server installation package has everything while the client installation package is only for accessing the MySQL server installed on another computer. If you have downloaded the PRM installation packages, you can make a standard installation of both server and client RPMs with the command below.

```
rpm -i MySQL-server-VERSION.glibc23.i386.rpm
rpm -i MySQL-client-VERSION.glibc23.i386.rpm
```

Before files are installed, RPM will verify the integrity and authenticity of the packages. The data of the server RPM package will be placed in the /var/lib/mysql directory. During the installation, the login user account mysql will be created by the RPM installation package. The RPM installation package will also configure the file /etc/init.d/ to specify that the server will be started automatically at the boot time. If the installation is successful, your MySQL database server should be up and running after the installation process is completed. At this time, you should assign a password for the login account mysql to secure the MySQL server. Once the MySQL database server is running, the database designer and developer can go ahead to design and develop databases for the online teaching/learning system.

EXAMPLE 2: SETTING UP PHP AND MYSQL DEVELOPMENT ENVIRONMENT

The integration of PHP and MySQL provides a development environment for developing a Web based application. PHP is a scripting language and is used to develop dynamic Web pages. MySQL provides support for dynamic Web pages. To develop a PHP-and-MySQL development environment, you need three application software packages, the Apache Web server, MySQL, and PHP. The installation of the Apache Web server and MySQL has been covered before. The following briefly describes the installation of PHP.

The first task is to download PHP from the Web site:

http://www.php.net/downloads.php

Since the installation file is formatted as a .gz file, you can extract the PHP installation file with the `tar -xzf` command. The next step is to compile the file with the command `./configure`. Use the `make` command to create an executable file for the installation and execute the command `make install` to install the PHP package. After the initial installation, the PHP modules should be added to the Apache Web server. Then, run the `make` and `make all` commands again to complete the installation.

After PHP is installed, to allow PHP to access MySQL, a link to /chroot/mysql/tmp/mysql.sock from /chroot/httpd/tmp should be created with the command `ln`. These two files must be physically placed on the same file system. To test the installation of PHP, you may create a .php file with the following content.

```
<?
phpinfo();
?>
```

The built-in function phpinfo returns the information about PHP as well as MySQL. Copy the file to a web directory and open the file in a Web browser. The detailed information about the installed PHP should be displayed on the Web page. If MySQL is running properly, you should also see a MySQL section displayed on the Web page.

CONCLUSION

In this chapter, we have discussed the issues related to the open source database management systems. Three typical open source database packages have been introduced. MySQL is one of most used open source database management systems, PostgreSQL is one of the advanced open source database management systems, and Berkeley DB is an open source embedded database. We then discussed database development. The first stage of database development is the design stage. For the three phases of the database design process, we discussed collecting database requirement information, developing a data model, and planning for the physical implementation of a database. After the discussion of database design, we talked about the issues of converting a data model to a relational database. The discussion also included database implementation and testing. The next topic we dealt with was database management. DBMS packages such as MySQL provide many sophisticated database management tools. We investigated some of the open source database management tools provided by MySQL. We also looked at some of the third party database management tools such as Toad for MySQL and Zmanda. The last part of the chapter provided an example to illustrate how the open source DBMS MySQL can be installed on the Linux operating system. As pointed out in this chapter, these open source database management systems and management tools can meet the needs of an online teaching/learning system.

Once a database is in place, our next task in the online teaching/learning system development process is to develop a learning management system on top of the database. The development of a learning management system will be covered in the next chapter.

REFERENCES

Chen, P. (1976). The entity-relationship model - toward a unified view of data. *ACM Transactions on Database Systems, 1*(1), 9-36.

Hillyer, M. (2007). *An introduction to database normalization.* Retrieved November 16, 2007 from http://dev.mysql.com/tech-resources/articles/intro-to-normalization.html

Horton, W., & Horton, K. (2003). *E-learning tools and technologies: A consumer's guide for trainers, teachers, educators, and instructional designers.* New York: Wiley.

Kroenke, D. M. (2006). *Database processing: Fundamentals, design, and implementation.* Upper Saddle River, NJ: Prentice Hall.

MySQL. (2007). *Why MySQL?* Retrieved November 6, 2007 from http://www.mysql.com/why-mysql

PostgreSQL. (2007). *About.* Retrieved November 6, 2007 from http://www.postgresql.org/about

Potter, K., & Hicks, D. (2004). Open-source database applications as collaboration and technology integration tools in teacher education. In C. Crawford et al. (Eds.), *Proceedings of Society for Information Technology and Teacher Education International Conference 2004* (pp. 2549-2550). Chesapeake, VA: AACE.

Pozniak-Koszalka, I., & Helwich, M. (2005). Experimentation System for Evaluating MySQL Database Management System Efficiency. In *Proceeding (454) Databases and Applications - 2005.* Innsbruck, Austria.

Quest Software. (2007). *Toad for MySQL features*. Retrieved November 20, 2007 from http://www.toadsoft.com/toadmysql/Features.htm

Ratna, A.A.P., Samuel, J., & Bayuaji, L. (2002). Web-Chat PHP based system using MYSQL database as interactive communication media on Daskom On-Line. In *Proceeding (367) Information Systems and Databases*. Tokyo, Japan.

Rosebrock, E., & Filson, E. (2004). *Setting up LAMP: Getting Linux, Apache, MySQL, and PHP working together*. Alameda, CA: Sybex.

Tahaghoghi, S. M. M., & Williams, H. (2006). *Learning MySQL*. Sebastopol, CA: O'Reilly Media, Inc.

Zmanda (2007). *Zmanda open source backup*. Retrieved November 20, 2007 from http://www.zmanda.com

Chapter VII
Class Management

INTRODUCTION

In the previous chapter, we discussed the issues related to the database which is used to store student information and course information. After the network, server, and database have been set up properly, our next task is to develop a learning management system to support class management. In this chapter, we will examine the open source tools used for class management. Learning Management System (LMS) software is commonly used to support course setup, management, and assessment. The first part of this chapter will focus on various open source learning management systems. Some commonly used open source LMS software packages will be introduced. We will investigate how these LMS software packages can be used to manage classes and course materials.

After the general introduction to the LMS software packages, our emphasis will be on open source LMS management. We will first look at the responsibilities of different groups of people related to LMS management such as those of the online teaching support team, computer service team, and faculty members. Then, we will discuss some popular open source LMS packages and the configurations of the commonly used LMS tools to meet the requirements of online teaching and learning. In this chapter, we will also discuss the issues related to open source LMS administration and security management.

Many LMS software packages can provide tools for developing multimedia course materials and tools for collaboration. Moodle provides blogs, Wiki, forums, and chats for collaboration. It provides content management, quiz management, and peer assessment to support teaching. It assists course development with the modulated construction by creating plugins. This chapter will provide more information about these tools.

The last part of this chapter will give an example of the installation and configuration of the open source LMS Moodle on Linux. In this example, we will investigate the requirements for installing Moodle on Linux, and then practice how to download and install Moodle. The installation process will illustrate the configuration of Moodle to meet the requirements of the online teaching/learning system. The second example is about setting up Sakai on linux for an online teaching/learning system.

BACKGROUND

An online teaching/learning system usually supports a large numbers of classes. It needs enterprise-level learning management system software to schedule, track, and report information of online courses. A learning management system (LMS) software package is designed to handle these tasks. The topics related to using learning management system software have been widely studied. As a general introduction, Horton and Horton (2003) discussed strategies on selecting an LMS and the alternatives to the LMS. Itmazi and Megías (2005) discussed the major LMS products such as WebCT, Blackborad, and so on. Cole's (2005) book covers a great amount of detail about Moodle as an open source learning management system. It illustrates how Moodle works and how to use the powerful tools such as assignments, forums, journals, quizzes, surveys, chat rooms, and workshops. It also provides some tips on online teaching with Moodle and Moodle administration.

Due to the fact that LMS plays a major role in supporting online teaching and learning, LMS has been studied in-depth in various academic fields. Numerous papers have discussed it. Briefly, we can group these papers into three categories, teaching with LMS, LMS management, and developing LMS enrichment tools.

In the area of teaching with LMS, we can find many papers published in recent years. To name a few, Marko and Honkaranta (2007) investigated how the LMS tools and computer skills affect teaching at the university level. Their survey revealed mixed results on using the advanced tools offered by LMS. There is another report on using adaptive LMS with augmented reality by Lim, Xu, and Jin (2005). By combining the virtual reality with LMS, they created a virtual learning environment.

As for LMS administration, Lassila and Pöyry (2007) discussed the use of the Software and a Service (SaaS) environment to support online teaching and learning. Such a service can help students and instructors to take advantage of LMS supported online teaching and learning. From their case study, they discovered that e-learning is more efficient if a service-centered approach is adopted by both developers and universities.

Training and technical support are main tasks in the management of LMS. Finkelstein (2007) discussed these important issues. He and others developed a learner-centered training and support program that could meet the requirements by both the new users and those who changed from the old system to the new system. Finkelstein (2007) presented both the successful and unsuccessful experiences of changing from one LMS to another and showed that their training program could train a large number of instructors in a short time.

In the area of developing LMS enrichment tools, we can also find many studies published in recent years. For example, Casillo, Chianese, Moscato, and Penta (2006) illustrated a process to develop authoring tools for a generic leaning management system. These authoring tools can efficiently develop and manage the content for multimedia based courses. To further extend the functionality of a learning management system, Wu, Zhao, Peng, and Xue (2006), proposed a concept model designed for spoken language tests in an e-learning system. Based on the concept model, they created the Spoken-English-Test-Oriented (SET-Oriented) architecture for content authoring, online learning, tests and assessments.

In this chapter, we are going to focus on the topics of open source LMS software packages. We will discuss issues in the areas of teaching with LMS and the administration of LMS. The discussion will start with the introduction of the major open source LMS packages.

OPEN SOURCE LEARNING MANAGEMENT SYSTEMS

As described earlier, LMS plays a key role in supporting online teaching/learning systems. Most university online courses are supported by general purpose LMS software packages. As the demand increases from the universities, the LMS market is growing rapidly. Hundreds of learning management systems and Web-based training management software packages have been developed. Among these LMS products, there are over 30 major LMS vendors, some of them produce commercial LMS products and others provide open source products. To meet the teaching and learning requirements, a mature LMS product often includes the following components:

- **Instruction management:** LMS provides tools for instructors to plan and manage their classes. With these tools, instructors are able to decide how to present their course materials and how to schedule their classes.

- **Course delivery management:** LMS often provides tools for online help and provides remote access tools for students to view, explore, and download online course materials. It also provides tools to allow instructors and students to communicate with each other.
- **Student management:** LMS includes tools for managing students' accounts and students' grades.
- **Skill assessment:** Tools are often included for managing online assignments, quizzes, and exams.
- **Multimedia course material development:** To support the development of Web-base course materials. Some of the LMSs may provide authoring tools for multimedia course content development.
- **LMS management:** To keep a learning management system running smoothly, managing tools are also provided for security measures, online registration, system backup, and crash recovery.
- **Personalization management:** Tools are often provided for students to personalize their study. Students can personalize their learning environments, schedule their learning activities, and develop personal blogs.
- **Collaboration management:** A sophisticated LMS should include tools for collaboration. Many LMS vendors include forums, chats, virtual whiteboards, video conferencing, and text messengers for collaboration.

Over a dozen open source LMS software packages are currently available. A lot of them include all the components listed above and more. These open source LMS software packages can handle the tasks of creating teaching materials and managing online courses. Due to the advantages of open source products, a large number of universities are currently using open source LMS products to support their online teaching/learning systems. According to the figures provided by Moodle (2008), there are over 400,000 users from 193 countries using Moodle in over 75 languages. Together with other open source LMSs, the open source LMS market is large and the demand for open source LMSs is high. These open source LMSs provide a high quality and low cost solution for supporting online teaching/learning systems. In the following, we are going to examine some of them, including Moodle, ATutor, Claroline, ILIAS, Sakai, and so on. These packages are major players in the open source LMS market. We will first have a summary of these open source LMS packages:

Moodle

Moodle is the largest open source LMS sponsor and supporter. According to the Web site moodle.org (Moodle, 2008), it can currently scale from a single user site to a university of 200,000 students. Moodle is supporting millions of students and courses, and the number keeps growing. Moodle is the second largest LMS provider and its market share is only slightly below the commercial product Blackboard. Moodle provides similar functionalities as those supported by Blackboard or WebCT. According to the analysis done by Munoz and Duzer (2005), Moodle's end of semester evaluation composite scores is slightly higher than Blackboard. Also, Moodle is free and Blackboard is charging an annual license fee. Blackboard provides professional service while Moodle's service depends on programmers worldwide. Moodle provides rich features and useful functionalities to support learning management tasks. The following are some of them:

- Moodle is supported by open source operating systems such as Linux and FreeBSD. This feature guarantees the smooth operation of Moodle on Linux.
- Moodle is supported by open source database management systems such as MySQL and PostgreSQL. Moodle can also store and query information on external databases.
- Moodle supports constructive learning. It allows students to comment on course content or contribute course content through Wiki.
- Some knowledge management tools for the management of content, surveys, and glossaries are included in Moodle. Moodle can also be used as a performance analysis tool. It can be used to analyze teaching efficiency and student performance.
- With Moodle, we can create a truly diversified learning environment. Moodle supports over seventy five languages. It allows students to choose their own languages and specify their own time zones. These are great features for supporting globalized universities.
- Moodle supports modulated construction for creating new functionalities by using plugins. These plugins can be used to improve course Web site management and user management. They can also be used to enhance services and enrich course content.
- Moodle has strong support for class management. Tools are provided by Moodle for scheduling classes, posting course descriptions, presenting multimedia course content, and importing student data and course materials from other LMS software packages such as Blackboard and WebCT.
- Students can access course Web sites created on Moodle through various Web browsers. Since Moodle provides tools for course Web site management, it can be used to schedule online courses and manage activity modules, quizzes and grades. Moodle also provides remote access tools to assist students for

remotely accessing course materials and participating in collaboration activities.

- Moodle provides collaboration environments for online teaching and learning. Many commonly used collaboration tools such as forums, chats, blogs, Wiki, peer assessment, and workshops are supported by Moodle.
- Moodle provides tools for managing students' accounts. It supports several authentication schemes such as LDAP or various other standard methods. To protect the data transmitted over the Internet, Moodle provides several data encryption, certification, and decryption utilities.

With these features, Moodle can meet the basic requirements for course management by an online teaching/learning system. Moodle is deployed by higher education institutions on a very large scale. By hosting Moodle on the Linux operating system, we can create open source based fully functioning online teaching/learning systems. Later, we will look at more detailed information on setting up Moodle for supporting an online teaching/learning system.

Sakai

Sakai is a new Java based open source LMS developed jointly by several higher education institutions such as University of Michigan, Indiana University, MIT, and Stanford, and many individual users and developers. The Sakai project was started in early 2004 and its first version was released in March 2005. Later, major technology companies such as IBM, Sun, and Unisys joined the Sakai project. According to Sakai (2007), in 2007, there were over 250 institutions using or testing Sakai for their online teaching/learning systems. The rapid increase of its popularity among higher education institutions is due to its collaboration features. The following are some of the collaboration features included in Sakai:

- Sakai is designed to be a platform for research and group projects. It has greatly improved the interactivities among researchers, instructors, and students.
- To meet the requirements by an online teaching/learning system, Sakai allows users to modify the settings of the tools and services provided by Sakai.
- Based on the role of the user, Sakai can be configured so that each individual user can be assigned a set of tools for a specific project.
- Sakai provides many commonly used collaboration tools such as live chats, forums, and Wiki, and threaded discussions.
- For instructors and students to share documents in a private folder, Sakai provides the Drop Box Tool that allows the participants of the Drop Box to upload multiple files at once to a private folder for other participants to share.

- With the Really Simple Syndication (RSS) reader, the News Tool allows users on a Sakai worksite to view the continuous updates from other blogs, event listings, or other frequently changing worksites.
- The Email Archive Tool is used to archive the e-mails received on a class worksite and the list of e-mail addresses is sent to all the participants. It can also automatically generate worksite e-mail addresses.
- Message Center included in Sakai can be used to facilitate the one-on-one and group communication.
- Another widely used collaboration tool is Resources. The Resources Tool can be used to create course materials in various formats, link to other Web sites, and display course materials on the Sakai worksites. With the Resources Tool, worksite owners can control permissions on content posting, deleting, and reading in a specific folder.

Like the other LMS software packages, Sakai also includes the commonly used course management tools and services. The following are some of them supported by the Sakai package.

- Sakai allows students to remotely access the course materials stored on a class Web site and download them to their home computers.
- The Announcements Tool included in Sakai can be used to inform students about important events and schedule change.
- The Assignments Tool provided by Sakai allows instructors to create and grade online assignments. A special feature of the Sakai Assignments Tool is that it allows an instructor to download all the submissions by students at once.
- The Gradebook in Sakai is used to store students' scores for homework, quizzes, projects, and exams. It allows instructors to grade in various ways such as letter grades, pass or fail, or numerical scores.
- Sakai provides the Home tool which is a portal page for each class and project worksite. The Home tool allows instructors to customize their class Web sites.
- The Melete Modules tool included in Sakai is a lesson builder tool that allows instructors to develop course materials.
- Sakai allows each student or instructor to create his/her own online worksite with the My Workspace tool.
- The Membership Tool is useful for joining or un-joining several worksites which the user has the permission to access.
- The Schedule Tool allows the instructor or the owner of a worksite to post the schedule in the calendar format. The created schedule will be integrated

with the My Workspace schedule. It can also be merged with the schedules of other worksites.

- With the Site Info Tool, the user can access and modify the worksites' information such as the participant list and tool manual. This tool can also be used to publish and duplicate a worksite and import course materials to a worksite.
- Sakai provides the Syllabus Tool for instructors to create syllabi. It also allows instructors to link to the pre-existing syllabi. It can control whether the syllabi can be viewed by the public or by the students in a specific class only.
- The Synoptic Tool is useful for displaying the most recent information. It can be used to configure the display time period and the number of items to display. This tool can also be used to detect the first time that a user visited a worksite.
- To assist in creating online exams and quizzes, Sakai provides the Tests and Quizzes tool for instructors. This tool can be used to generate tests in various formats such as multiple choice, true/false, short answer, matching, or filling-in-the-blank questions. The tool provides many ways to manage online tests and exams, such as importing test questions from an external test bank, randomly selecting test questions, and creating a test bank to store test questions. An interesting feature is that it supports audio based test questions.
- In Sakai, worksite owners can upload files or an entire directory to their worksites through WebDAV. WebDAV is the technology that makes a folder in a remote worksite appears on the user's local computer. The user can drag files and folders from the local computer to the remote worksite or verse versa.
- Sakai's Worksite Setup Tool is a worksite development tool that can be used to create projects and course Web sites. It is also a worksite management tool used to add or remove tools and change access permissions. Like the Site Info Tool, this tool can also publish and duplicate a worksite and import materials to a worksite.

With these features, Sakai is certainly a sophisticated LMS product. It is worth it to give Sakai a try to see if Sakai can be used as a low cost alternative for supporting an online teaching/learning system. The setup of Sakai is relatively easy. It supports Java JDK/JRE, Tomcat, and Maven. Once the Java package, Tomcat, and Maven are downloaded and installed, you can download and install Sakai. Sakai is supported by Linux, Solaris, and Windows. The database management system used by Sakai is HSQLDB and it is pre-configured. It is not necessary to configure the server operating system and database management system for hosting Sakai. If other database management systems such as MySQL and Oracle are used to support Sakai, additional configurations are required.

Claroline

Like Moodle, Claroline is another leading open source LMS package. According to Claroline (2008), the Claroline LMS package has been used by 95 countries with more than 150 downloads per day. Claroline is constructed with open source products such as PHP and MySQL. Most of the commonly used operating systems such as Linux, Mac OS and Microsoft Windows support Claroline. The design goal of Claroline is to follow teachers' pedagogical experience and needs. It allows the instructor to create a course-centered platform. For each course, it creates a course space equipped with a set of management tools which will perform the following tasks:

- **Creating online course materials:** Claroline provides tools for writing course descriptions, online exams, and exercises. The questions in an exercise can be written in various formats. The tools can also track students' performance on these exams and exercises.
- **Developing learning paths:** The tools provided by Claroline can be used to integrate course materials, exercises, and imported learning modules needed by learning activities. It creates a sequence of learning activities and combines learning materials and exercises according to the learning activities.
- **Document management:** The tools provided by Claroline can be used to create HTML documents. The tools can create folders and sub-folders to store these HTML documents. Users can also use these tools to publish documents in various formats such as text, PDF, HTML, and so on.
- **Group management:** To enhance collaboration, Claroline provides some tools for creating groups and adding the other tools to each of these groups. The tools can also help with configuration of group settings and facilitate the collaboration among students and instructors.
- **Assignment submission:** Tools are provided by Claroline for students to submit their assignments from home or answer the questions posted online. Students can also post questions and opinions for others to discuss.
- **Online collaboration:** Claroline provides various online collaboration tools such as chats, forums, and Wiki. Some of the tools can be used for synchronous conversations which allow real-time discussion. The others can be used for asynchronous conversations which allow students to join the discussion at anytime and anywhere. The topics for discussion can also be posted on Wiki, which allows students and instructors to add and edit the content on a Web site.
- **Course organization:** To manage course content and classes, several tools can be used to add events in a course calendar, post announcements on a course

Web site, and send notices to students or group members. The tools can also be used to display the calendars of all related courses and set up links to other courses and resources. These tools can be used to manage a course schedule with tasks and deadlines.

- **Data analysis:** A useful tool is provided by Claroline for the analysis of statistical data. The statistic tool can track students' usage of a course Web site. Based on the analysis generated by the tool, the instructor can supervise the students' progress.

Most of Claroline's tools are easy to use. Based on the requirements of a learning activity, some of these tools will be integrated with the course materials to form a platform which provides a flexible learning environment.

ATutor

ATutor is another open source software package for managing e-leaning systems. As a Learning Content Management System (LCMS) software package, ATutor is designed to focus more on the learning content and less on the course and user management than an LMS package does. ATutor has built-in content authoring, assessment, and collaboration support. It has good online help for new users, and it supports multi-lingual usage. Based on the analysis done by Commonwealth of Learning (2003), when dealing with the learning content, ATutor had a higher overall score than that of Moodle. As pointed out by Commonwealth of Learning (2003), ATutor had a smaller user base as it was quite new to the market in 2003. ATutor is currently supported by over 15 languages. The following are some of the features provided by ATutor.

- ATutor is relatively easy to install or update, and it can easily retrieve and import previously developed learning modules to extend its functionalities.
- ATutor allows instructors to quickly assemble, package, and re-distribute online learning content based on the objectives of a course and the learning styles of the students who are participating in the class. Based on different teaching and learning scenarios, ATutor can re-organize the learning environment settings, tools, modules, privileges, and groups to make the learning and teaching more effective.
- ATutor provides assistive technology to help students, instructors, administrators, and users with disabilities to access the learning content. To improve accessibility, it also allows the access to all learning content through keyboards and provides text alternatives for all visual elements. Together with a screen reader called ATalker which can read aloud ATutor interface and feedback

messages, these features allow a blind person to listen to access the learning content. ATutor also provides the tool ASLpah.ca for the new technology called "signlinking" representing the sign language version of hyperlinking.

- ATutor is built to work with mobile devices such as cell phones, personal data assistants (PDAs), and so on.
- Like many other LMS packages, ATutor provides a tool called AForm to help instructors to create course materials such as online forms, tests, or surveys. In addition, the tool prompts the course material developer to add text alternatives for maximum accessibility. ATutor provides a Web service called AChecker to verify if the developed course content meets the international accessibility standards.
- By adopting the IMS/SCORM Content Packaging specifications, ATutor can be used to create re-usable learning modules. It can also import or export the IMS/SCORM compatible learning modules from or to other packages. Instructional Management Systems (IMS) is a standard for interoperability of learning systems and learning content, and Shareable Content Object Reference Model (SCORM) is a standard on how individual instruction elements should be integrated.
- ATutor conforms to XHTML 1.0 which is a HTML-like language designed to work with XML. This will ensure that the learning content in different documents and in different languages can be displayed consistently.
- ATutor provides a list of collaboration tools, ACollab for supporting group activities, AChat for supporting online real time communication, and AComm which is a Java-based instant messaging and whiteboard tool.

Many of the features provided by ATutor are creative and cannot be found in other LCMS software packages. When combined with LMS packages, ATutor is a powerful package to support online teaching/learning systems.

ILIAS

ILIAS is another well known open source Web-based LMS. Like other LMS software packages, it provides tools for course management, course material development, collaboration management, evaluation and assessment. ILIAS can run on every server that supports PHP and MySQL. According to ILIAS (2007), ILIAS provides the following features to support an online teaching/learning system:

- **Individual personal desktop:** The individual personal desktop tool is provided for each user of ILIAS. On the personal desktop, the user may find useful information such as the personal profile and individual learning progress.

It also displays course related information such as the list of courses, group members, class announcements, and learning resources. On the desktop, users can also find the utilities for helping desktop management such as bookmark management, calendars, and the utilities for configuring the password and system language.

- **Course management:** The tools provided by ILIAS for course management can handle jobs such as the management of learning resources, timing based events, access control, enrollment setting, and announcements to classes. Some of the tools can also be used to track each student's learning progress.
- **Collaboration management:** A set of tools from ILIAS are used for collaboration management such as chats, forums, podcasting, file sharing, and group management utilities.
- **Exam and evaluation management:** ILIAS provides a set of tools for generating exams and assignments. Questions generated for exams and quizzes can be in various formats such as multiple choice, numerical score, filling-in-the-blank, and matching formats. The exam questions are re-usable and can be randomly selected for each different exam. ILIAS also provides course evaluation tools such survey and report tools for collecting students' feedback, analyzing the feedback, and presenting the result of the analysis by a report.
- **Learning content management:** To be portable and accessible, ILIAS supports various standards such as IMS and SCORM. It provides tools to import, export, and create XML documents. ILIAS uses the OpenOffice plugin called eLAIX to convert a text document and Word document to an ILIAS learning module. The converted learning module is editable by ILIAS. The other learning resource management functionalities may include the support of Web site management, file management, RSS Reader, and Google Maps.
- **LMS administration:** To manage users and resources, several tools provided by ILIAS can be used to perform tasks such as role based access control, PayPal-Payment, and multiple session management. ILIAS provides various authentication schemes such as LDAP, SOAP, RADIUS, and Shibboleth. A Web service interface is also provided by ILIAS for supporting data exchange and machine-to-machine interaction over the network.

In the above, we have discussed five open source LMS/LCMS packages. Each of them has its own special features. In general, they provide adequate tools and services to support an online teaching/learning system. Table 7-1 describes the usage of these five LMS/LCMS packages.

As mentioned earlier, there are over 30 major LMS vendors. Detailed description about their products is beyond the scope of this book. These open source LMS packages have been deployed in a very large scale among higher education institu-

Table 7-1. Usage of LMS/LCMS

LMS/LCMS	Usage
Moodle	Moodle has been used by universities for many years. It is capable of handling the learning management tasks for large scale institutions. It has been shown that Moodle is reliable enough for handling the daily operations of supporting an online teaching/learning system. Like most of the open source products, there is no customer support team to depend on. This requires LMS administrators and technicians to be highly trained so that they can solve problems by themselves. For many small and medium-sized universities, this could be a problem since they may not have technical personnel who are familiar with Linux and Moodle. On the other hand, due to its large user base, the information about troubleshooting commonly seen problems may already be posted on the Moodle discussion forums. A person with some training should be able to follow the instruction posted on the forums to solve a problem. As troubleshooting is concerned, Moodle should be one of the best choices among open source LMS products.
Sakai	Even though Sakai has a short history, its popularity has increased dramatically. Sakai is designed to enhance collaboration which is one of the weaknesses of online teaching and learning. Many new online collaboration ideas have been implemented on Sakai. Sakai is also strong in the functionalities traditionally provided by a LMS. If collaboration is highly required and the university has efficient technical support, Sakai is the choice.
Claroline	Claroline is designed with a course centric approach. With Claroline, it is easier to integrate the learning tools with courses and the administration of an individual course is simple. Students may find Claroline easy to navigate. When dealing with an online teaching/learning system that does not need a versatile learning management system, Claroline can be considered.
ATutor	Unlike other LMS products, ATutor is LCMS which focuses on the management of content. It provides the learner with the right content at the right time. ATutor is often used with a LMS product. When using ATutor with a LMS, the combination can provide a lot more services than using a LMS alone.
ILIAS	One of the great features provided by ILIAS is the individual personal desktop. This allows each user to individualize the learning resources. The choice of ILIAS will depend on if the features provided by ILIAS are essential or if the LMS administrator and other technical personnel are familiar with ILIAS.

tions. It has been proven that open source technologies such as the Linux operating system and one of the above LMS packages can support a fully functioning online teaching/learning system.

MANAGING OPEN SOURCE LEARNING MANAGEMENT SYSTEMS

Keeping a learning management system running properly is critical to the success of teaching online courses. The management of a learning management system is the joint responsibilities of the online teaching support team, computer service team, and faculty members. The teaching support team's responsibility is to set up the teaching site and assist faculty members and students. The tasks that may be performed by the teaching support team are shown below:

- The teaching support team is responsible to post course descriptions, degree plans, course rotation plans, class payment, support team member information, and faculty member information on the university Web site. The information may need to be updated each semester.
- Before each semester starts, the teaching support team posts class schedules on the university Web site. The team is responsible for making sure that the class registration constraints are set and the online registration system is working properly.
- The team needs to post the instruction of the usage of the online teaching/learning system such as how to log on, how to use the online communication tools, how to use the multimedia tools, how to submit assignments, and how to collaborate with the instructors and other students.
- Before a semester starts, the team should upload the students' accounts to the classes that they are going to take. The team will also need to upload the students' accounts to the online labs and remote access service. Also, the team needs to make sure that the faculty members' accounts are working properly.
- If the course materials are archived and stored in a centralized database, the team will help the faculty members to upload the archived course materials. In addition, the team can assist the faculty members in setting up exams and quizzes, collaboration tools, and video conferencing equipment.
- The team needs to provide training for the faculty members on how to use multimedia tools to create online teaching materials. The team also manages the multimedia tools to keep them in good condition.
- During the semester, the team performs daily maintenance tasks such as troubleshooting, providing technical support, adding students to and removing students from classes, developing new teaching sites, creating exams and quizzes for the faculty members, distributing surveys, and organizing Web conferences. The team should also perform tasks such as upgrading the learning management system, setting up new services, and installing new teaching tools.
- At the end of the semester, the teaching support team will help the faculty members to set up makeup exams and quizzes or reset the course materials for the students who received incomplete grades. The team will also archive the course materials and store the archives in a central database for future use.

The technicians from the computer service department will take care of the network, computer system hardware and software, and security related tasks. The following is the list of tasks that can be accomplished by the computer service team:

- The computer service team is responsible for managing the university's directory service. The tasks may include creating and managing the students' accounts in the directory service so that students can use the same accounts to log on to the classes supported by the LMS, VPN, e-mail, and other services.
- Keeping the server that hosts the LMS running smoothly is another responsibility of the computer service team. This team will perform tasks such as software and hardware installation and upgrade, security patch installation, service configuration, and server troubleshooting. System backup and recovery are also the tasks to be performed by this team.
- The management of the university's network system is one of the responsibilities of the computer service team. The tasks include maintaining network devices, enforcing network security measures, and troubleshooting network related problems.
- The computer service team also takes the responsibility for managing the online computer labs. Before a semester starts, the team updates or reconstructs the online computer labs to meet the demands of the online courses. During the semester, the team will perform tasks such as troubleshooting lab problems and assisting instructors in developing hands-on practice materials.
- Technical support on using network devices, computer systems, and lab equipment is also provided by the computer service team. Both instructors and students need help on using the network and computer systems. Especially, when using the online computer labs for hands-on practice, students are often given the administrator's privilege. They may make mistakes and crash the servers and the network built in the lab.
- Database maintenance and administration can also be part of the responsibility of the computer service team. The team needs to install and configure the database to support the LMS. The team also performs database administration tasks such as user management, database performance tuning, database backup and recovery, data protection, and data storage device management.
- The computer service team also provides training on how to use network devices, computer hardware and software. The training may include providing pre-written instructions and post them online and offering workshops for demonstration and hands-on practice. The training can also include individual help sessions for the instructors and the teaching support team members.

In many cases, the faculty members are involved in online teaching/learning system management. The management tasks performed by the faculty members may include the following:

- The faculty members will design lab activities and provide the requirements for software and hardware configuration and network setup. It is important for the teaching support team and the computer service team to set up the online teaching/learning system to meet these teaching requirements.
- The faculty members will work together with the computer service team to design, upgrade or rebuild the online computer labs.
- They will be asked to verify if the newly created classes on the LMS and the newly built online computer labs meet the requirements of teaching and hands-on practice. They will give feedback to the teaching support team and the computer service team for further improvement.
- The faculty members will also provide some technical support to help students to remotely access the LMS, upload assignments, use online computer labs for hands-on practice, and so on.

Now that we have looked at the management responsibilities of the online teaching support team, computer service team, and faculty members, next we will discuss the issues related to LMS management. Although our discussion will be mainly around the Moodle LMS, it also applies to other LMSs. As mentioned earlier, the management of an LMS may include tasks such as creating user accounts, managing collaboration services, managing evaluation instruments and grades, managing classes, and LMS configuration.

Creating User Accounts

Most of the open source LMSs may provide various ways of user authentication. A user can be authenticated by e-mail authentication, Lightweight Directory Access Protocol (LDAP) authentication, or self-registration authentication. Brief descriptions about these three authentication methods are given below:

- **E-mail authentication:** For sending messages to e-mail servers, most of the current e-mail systems have no user authentication. Lacking authentication for e-mail is security vulnerability. By altering an e-mail's header, a spammer can make spam e-mail to appear as though they come from many different original sender addresses. In such a way, the e-mail recipient's spam filter is fooled and accepts the spam e-mail. Some of vulnerable computer systems on the Internet can also be used by spammers to launch spam e-mail. The e-mail authentication technology is used to prevent spam attacks by verifying the sender's real IP address and determining if the sender should be trusted.

- **LDAP authentication:** LDAP is a widely used authentication method. The authentication information about users and network resources is stored in a directory. The stored information can be used by many server-side services such as the remote access VPN server, the e-mail logon service, the learning management system, the database management system, and so on. When a user is trying to log on to a computer system linked to the network where the LDAP server is installed, LDAP performs the user id lookup and verification. If the information provided by the user matches the information stored in the directory service, the user can then log on to the computer system. The information stored in the directory can be altered or deleted by the network administrator.
- **Self-registration authentication:** This authentication method allows users to create their own accounts. This technology has been used by many online shopping vendors to allow customers to create their own accounts. An online teaching/learning system can also benefit from this technology. By using self-registration, students can add themselves to the classes with their own permission. The self registered students can view the course content and requirements for a period of time without registering a class, and then decide if they want to register the class or not. The self-registration method is also a great way for group activities. Students can register themselves in the groups they want to join. Self-registration can be configured to allow students to register themselves under certain conditions such as meeting the course prerequisites and financial clearance. It can also set the time period during which students need to make a decision if they want to register a class or not. Self-registration can also be configured to allow a user to register as a student whose account has limited accessibility.

Sometimes, the combination of these authentication methods is used to create a more flexible and secure authentication method. For example, the self-registration method is often combined with the LDAP authentication method. For example, only users who are university employees and students can register themselves in a class that they want to preview. In such a way, they have more flexibility to preview classes and online classes are better protected.

When creating user accounts for students, you will be prompted to select the authentication method. Based on the above discussion, you can select the authentication that meets the requirements by the online teaching/learning system. Other information needed for creating a user account will be the e-mail address. Often, the LMS will send a confirmation e-mail to the user for whom the account is created. Once the user is confirmed, the account will become active. Student accounts often have the following permissions.

- Student accounts should allow students to remotely log on to the registered class sites created on the LMS.
- They should allow students to read and download course materials from the class sites.
- Through the Internet, students should be able to view and listen to the multimedia course content.
- To communicate with instructors and other students, each student should have an e-mail account created on the LMS.
- Students should be able to submit their assignments, take exams and quizzes, and view their grades online.
- Collaboration tools such as forums, chats, virtual whiteboards, Wiki, or text messengers should be added to a student's account so that the student can interact with instructors and other students.
- Students should also be able to participate in video conferences. They should be able to use video conference tools such as VoIP phones, virtual whiteboards, and so on.

Instructor accounts need more privileges; they often require LMS administrators to create accounts for instructors and add the instructors' accounts to the courses they are going to teach. In addition to the permissions given to a student, the configuration of instructor accounts should add the following permissions:

- Instructors should be allowed to use the multimedia tools provided by the LMS to create multimedia course materials.
- Instructor accounts should be configured to allow the instructors to set up their own classes, such as creating folders and links for assignments, lab manuals, lecture notes, syllabus, and so on. They should also be allowed to upload course materials to these folders and configure how these course materials should be used by students.
- Instructors should be permitted to create exams and assignments. For example, they should be able to set the due dates for assignments. They should be able to set up the exam logon time, the exam duration, the exam format, the password for the exam, and the instruction for taking the exam.
- Instructors should be able to grade students' assignments, exams, and hands-on lab activities. They should be allowed to post student grades and write comments. They can decide if a student can resubmit his/her assignment.

They also should have the power to return the assignment to a student for modification.

- A person with the instructor's privilege should be able to configure the collaboration tools such as forums, chats, Wiki, and workshops. He/she should also be able to determine who should get the subscription from a forum. The students who have the subscription will automatically get all the new posts through e-mail.
- An instructor should have the privilege to set up a video conference such as distributing the invitations to the students, setting the video conference logon time, allowing students to use the virtual whiteboard or other collaboration tools provided by video conferencing software. During the online conversation with the students, he/she can let the students take control of the microphone or the pen on the virtual whiteboard.

For each semester, the LMS administrator may need to create thousands of student accounts. If something needs to change in the student accounts, it may require the LMS administrator to modify thousands of student accounts. An easy way to accomplish this task is to create a student role. Each time a new student account is created, the student role will be added to the student portfolio. Should anything need to be changed, the LMS administrator only needs to change the settings in the role once. Similarly, the LMS administrator can create an instructor role for instructors.

Managing Collaboration Service

Collaboration tools are used for group activities, tutoring, online discussion, and posting information. An open source LMS often provides several collaboration tools such as forums, chats, or Wiki.

A forum is an asynchronous collaboration tool, which means that students who participate in a forum do not have to log on to the LMS at the same time. With a forum, students can participate in a discussion through the Internet. Some of the open source LMSs also allows students to subscribe the content of a forum. The content of the forum will be e-mailed to the subscribers regularly. Usually, a forum can be configured in one of the following options:

- **Single discussion mode:** This forum option allows one and only one discussion in the forum. With this option, all the students participate in the same discussion.

- **Individual post discussion mode:** This forum mode allows each individual student to create one discussion. With this option, each student can post his or her own statement or question which accepts multiple responses.
- **Multiple discussion mode:** This option allows multiple discussions to be created and each discussion can have multiple students participating in it. It also allows each student to create one or more discussions.

Usually, students participating in a forum can have three different types of permissions. The following describes these three permission types:

- Students are only permitted to read the discussions and replies by others; they cannot post their own discussions and replies.
- Students are permitted to reply to the discussions posted by others, but they are not permitted to post their own discussions.
- Students are permitted to post discussions and can reply to the discussions posted by others.

Instructors should be able to set these permission types for students in a class based on the teaching requirements. There are other forum configurations that can be done to meet the teaching requirements. The following are some of them:

- A forum can be configured so that a discussion posted by a student can be rated by other students and the instructor. Further, it can be configured on how the discussion can be rated and who can rate the discussion. A forum can be configured to only allow the instructor to rate the post. If a forum is configured to allow both the instructor and the students to rate the post, the rating by the other students and the instructor can be used to grade the post. The instructor who does the configuration can decide if the rating should be stored in the grade book. The instructor can also decide which time period the other students can rate the post.
- The person who does the configuration can decide if the students and the instructor who participate in a forum can upload attachments. If so, how many attachments and the maximum size of each attachment are allowed to be uploaded to the forum. The decision will be based on how much storage space is available on the hard disk.
- A forum can be configured so that it can be viewed in many different ways. It can be configured to allow all the students and the instructor to view their own posts as well as the posts by others. It can also be configured to allow some students to post their own discussions and view the rating from the instructor but not the ratings or replies by the other students.

- A forum can also be configured to distribute subscriptions in different ways. The distribution of subscriptions can be configured to only allow a specific group of students and the instructor to receive the subscriptions. It may also allow everyone who participates in the forum to receive the subscription. It can also be configured on how to distribute the subscriptions. Most commonly, e-mail is used to distribute subscriptions.

Once a forum is configured and made available to the class, e-mail will be sent to each student to inform them that the forum is available for discussion. The instruction on how to participate in the forum should also be attached to the e-mail to help students get started. The instructor may post the initial discussion to welcome students in his/her class. The daily maintenance of the forum will be the joint effort of both the teaching support team and the instructor. The following are some tasks they usually perform:

- Archiving the content of the forum is often performed by the LMS administrator who can specify the content and time period for archiving.
- There should also be a policy about the content posted on the forum. For example, the posted content should be related to the course materials and the students participating in the forum should not debate negatively on each other.
- Some forums can also be configured to test students with some basic questions before allowing them to participate in the forums. Doing so will make sure that the students understand the content posted on the forum.
- Some forums can be scheduled to allow instructors to have some one-on-one tutoring time with some students who are falling behind.
- A forum can be configured to assign a group of students to their own discussion. For each group, the members of the group can have more permissions than the general public.

Similar to a forum, there is another collaboration tool called Wiki. A Wiki is a Web-based document jointly developed by students, instructors and others who know the topic well. The discussion about Wiki is given next.

Unlike a forum which is for online discussion, a Wiki is a well defined Web-based document to present course content knowledge. The cover page of a wiki contains a list of subjects. Each subject on a Wiki can be followed by many sub-titles and each sub-title covers a specific topic related to the course content. Each topic has detailed descriptions about the knowledge covered by the course and links to resources related to the knowledge. The knowledge not only is contributed by the instructor, but also contributed by the students. By using Wiki, the students are encouraged to be actively involved in creating a class document that covers the knowledge, skills, and learning experience. The following provides some information related to the management of Wiki.

- The configuration of Wiki allows the LMS administrator to specify different user accounts. There may be three types of user accounts. The instructor account allows the instructor to edit a Wiki page and the students to view the content on the Wiki page. The student account allows each student to have his/her own Wiki page. Both the owner of the Wiki page and the instructor can edit the content on that Wiki page. The group account allows each group to have its own Wiki pages. All the group members and the instructor can edit the group Wiki pages. There should be a policy on who should edit what. A Wiki site can be centrally controlled by the instructor, or it can be the complete responsibility of the students, or anything in between.
- Wiki pages can be managed in many ways. Each wiki page can be set with different permissions. For example, it can be set to have both text and graphical content. It can be enabled or disabled. It can also be set as read-only or to allow readers to read and write.
- The LMS administrator can configure Wiki so that it can automatically detect the disconnected links. If there is a Wiki page that is not linked to any other page or it is empty, the LMS administrator can configure Wiki to automatically remove the delinked or empty Wiki page.
- Wiki can be set to backup pages to a database and recover the Wiki pages if an intentional or unintentional damage should occur. The LMS administrator can decide how many old backups to keep and how long to keep these backups. The LMS administrator can also decide which backup file to use for recovery.
- The Wiki pages on a Wiki site can be linked and presented in various ways to help readers to find the content they are looking for. A map or a page index can be created to allow readers to view the Wiki pages by following the links. The LMS administrator can also create links to the most recently updated pages, the newly added pages, the most often changed pages, and the most visited pages.
- Wiki pages can also be configured to allow readers to download the files linked to the Wiki pages and export some of the Wiki pages in the HTML or compressed zip file formats.

In the above, we have briefly discussed the forum, an asynchronous collaboration tool which allows students to communicate without logging on to the forum at the same time. To have online live conversations, students can use synchronous collaboration tools such as chats or text messengers. The following is a brief discussion of chats.

Chats provide communication in real time. There are two types of chats, the text based chat and the graphic based chat. The popular text messenger is a type of text based chat. The graphic based chat room is created in a 2D or 3D graphical environment. The chat room is a virtual environment which allows individuals to participate in group activities or built their own work space. Some of sophisticated chat rooms are also integrated with audio and video functionalities. The management of chats includes the following tasks:

- For most of the LMSs, the LMS administrator can configure one or more chat rooms for different purposes. A chat session can start at a specific time and end at a pre-determined time. There can be one chat session from the beginning to the end of a semester, or multiple chat sessions created for different time periods. The LMS administrator can schedule the chat sessions.
- A chat can also be configured to send a reminder to the students and remind them to participate in the chat at a specific time.
- A chat can be set to record messages posted on it during a chat session. The LMS administrator can decide at what time to release the recorded chat messages to the public.
- The information about the chat participants such as the participants' names and the time the participants joined the chat session can be viewed on the chat Web page.
- Some of the LMSs can integrate chats with other synchronous collaboration tools such as VoIP phones.
- The chat should be set so that the instructor can control at what time students can post their questions and how many questions can be posted at one time. In such a way, the instructor can better control the class.

A graphic based chat room takes a lot of computing recourses. It is not a practical solution if the Internet connection has a lower transmission rate. For many universities, text based chats are often used to share information among students and instructors.

In the above, we have examined several collaboration tools commonly included in an open source LMS package. To assist the LMS management, we have considered some issues related to the management of these collaboration tools. One usage of LMS is to evaluate students' performance and give grades to the students based on their performance. Next, we will discuss the issues related the management of evaluation instruments and grades.

Evaluation Instruments and Grade Management

An LMS package often provides various evaluation instruments. Exams are the main instruments used to evaluate students' performance. The configuration of exams involves the following tasks:

- The exam creator, either the instructor or the LMS administrator, need to set the exam time based on the requirements.
- The number of attempts permitted should also be set. Some sample online exams should allow students to try as many times as they want.
- When creating an exam, one should specify the grading method. The commonly used measures for evaluating students' performance are numerical scores, letter grades, pass and fail grades, and percentage grades. If multiple attempts are allowed, the exam creator can also decide which attempt should be graded.
- An exam should be configured on how to inform students about their grades. If it is a multiple choice exam, students can get their numerical scores as soon as they have submitted their answers. For other types of exams or assignments, the instructor can decide the type of grade to use and may write comments as feedback.
- Each exam can have its own password. The password is useful when the instructor needs to control how to distribute the exam. For example, if the students are required to take a proctored test at a specified location, the password can be used to make sure that only the students who show up at the specified location can take the test.
- For some hands-on based exams, the LMS administrator can specify a set of computer IP addresses so that students can take their hands-on practice based exams from those computers.
- The order of questions on an exam can be randomized so that each test looks different from the others. In such a way, there is less chance for one student to copy another student's answers.
- For a sample exam, the answers should be provided for students so that they can correct their mistakes.
- To re-use the questions on a real exam, you can configure the exam so that the answers to the exam questions are hidden from the students. After the students finish the exam, all they can see are their exam scores, but not the details such as which answer is incorrect and what the correct answer is.

After students submit their assignments or exams, their work will be evaluated and they will receive the grades. The grades can be given in several ways. They can be in the letter scale such as A, B, C, D, F, or in the numerical scale from 0 to 100. Additionally, the instructor can also provide comments along with the letter grades or numerical scores. Many open source LMS packages provide grade management tools to help instructors. The following are some of the commonly used functionalities of a grade management tool:

- A grade management tool can be configured to store and track students' scores for the classes they are taking. Some of the grade management tools also provide analysis tools to help students improve their performance.
- A grade management tool can be used to implement a grading policy. Usually, the instructor weighs the homework, projects, and exams differently. For example, the homework may get 20 percent, projects 20 percent and exams 60 percent of the total grade for a class. The grade management tool can be used to implement the instructor's grading policy.
- Students' grades should be well protected. They need to be backed up frequently. The process of backup and recovery can be done by importing and exporting students' grades to or from spreadsheet files. The grade management tool can be used to accomplish this type of task.
- The instructor can scale scores in different ranges. The commonly used scale range is from 0 to 100. However, with the grade management tool, the instructor can scale the scores in any range he/she wants such as from 200 to 800.

Grade management tools can greatly help instructors to better manage students' grades. Tracking and analyzing students' grades are often tedious and time consuming. A well developed grade management tool can reduce the grading time significantly. Like the grade management tools, class management tools can also greatly improve the efficiency of teaching. We will discuss class management next.

Class Management

Class management is another job that can be done by an LMS. The tasks of class management include student roster management, student group management, permission management, backup and recovery of course materials, and so on. The following are the descriptions of these management tasks:

- **Student roster management:** The management of student rosters includes adding, updating, or removing student accounts. Daily maintenance of student rosters may also include changing permissions assigned to students and helping students log on to class Web sites.

- **Student group management:** Students enrolled in an online course can be grouped in many ways. A group can be configured so that the students in the group can only work with their own group members, or the group can be created to allow the group members to work within the group as well as to view the other groups' content.
- **Permission management:** Permission management deals with permissions to access certain course content. Some course materials may need to be released based on certain conditions such as completing the required assignments; some course materials may be released during a certain time period.
- **Backup and recovery of course materials:** Backing up course materials is one way to prevent the loss of course content. The management tools provided by an LMS package will allow the administrator to configure the schedule of the backup, the type of the backup, and the device to store the backup. In case that the course materials get lost, the backup can be used to recover the course materials. A recovery management tool can be used to specify which backup to use and how the recovery should be conducted.

In the above, we have discussed various tools used for class management. In addition to the management of classes, the LMS itself also needs to be configured to support the teaching and learning activities. We will consider the LMS configuration next.

LMS Configuration

Often, an online teaching/learning system has its own specific requirements on the LMS. To meet these specific requirements, the LMS administrator needs to reconfigure the LMS. There are several areas that can be reconfigured such as the e-mail setting, the security setting, the language setting, the themes of GUI, and so on. The following is a brief description of the configuration in these areas:

- **E-mail setting:** E-mail is part of an LMS package. The configuration of e-mail may include setting up the e-mail server, adding e-mail users, and setting passwords for the e-mail users. The LMS administrator may also set the limit for the number and size of e-mail attachments.
- **Security setting:** The security management may include the LMS user account management and LMS login management. By following the security policy, the auto login features may need to be blocked. The login audit should be enabled.
- **Language setting:** The language setting can be used to specify the language to be used by the class site, the list of languages the students can use, the time zone, and the country.

- **GUI setting:** The LMS administrator can configure the class site GUI to specify the name of the site, the cover page format, the technical support information, the class name and the instructor's name. The themes of GUI can be configured to meet the teaching and learning requirements.

In the above, we have discussed the LMS configuration related issues. At this point, several major management tasks for supporting an online teaching/learning system have been examined. In the following, we are going to practice how to install and configure an LMS package such as Moodle on the Linux operating system.

EXAMPLE 1: MOODLE INSTALLATION AND CONFIGURATION ON LINUX

All of the major open source LMS packages are supported by the Linux operating system. As the largest open source LMS, Moodle is also supported by Linux. The following is an example that illustrates the installation of Moodle on the Linux operating system.

Normally, the installation of Moodle on Linux is done by a technician who has the root account. Before the installation is started, make sure that the server computer system is configured so that it can communicate with other computers on the same network and the Internet connection is working properly. Before installing Moodle, you also need to make sure that MySQL and PHP are installed. The Apache Web server should be installed and configured. You may need to check Moodle's Web site to find out which version of Linux is required by the latest version of the Moodle package. After you have verified that the server operating system is working properly, download the Moodle installation .tgz file from Moodle's Web site. Extract the compressed .tgz file with either the desktop management GUI tool such as KDE or GNOME, or with the following command:

```
mkdir  moodle
mv moodle_file.tgz  moodle
cd  moodle
tar -xvzf  moodle_file.tgz
```

To make Moodle accessible through the Internet, the directory moodle created with the above command should be copied to the Web server directory /var/www/html. The installation of Moodle requires that the directory /var/www/html can be read, written, and executed. The following command can do just that:

```
cd /var/www
chmod 777 html
```

The next step is to install Moodle. There is the installation script install.php. You can run the installation script at your Web server's Web site:

http://your_web_server/install.php

The installation process starts with the of language selection. The next screen displays the setting of PHP.

To run the installation script (install.php), just try to access your Moodle main URL using a Web browser, or access it directly. If you have not done so, you need to create a folder to store the Moodle data with the following command:

```
cd /var/www/
mkdir moodledata
chmod 777 moodledata
```

You can choose to use GUI tools to create the data directory. The next screen is about the configuration of MySQL. You need to create a new database for Moodle and your own user password to replace the default password with the following command:

```
CREATE DATABASE moodle;
USE moodle;
GRANT ALL PRIVILEGES ON moodle.* TO 'moodleuser'@'localhost' IDENTIFIED
BY 'moodleuserpassword';
FLUSH PRIVILEGES;
quit
```

Restart MySQL. If the configuration of the database is successful, go back to the installation page to view the database configuration information.

The last screen is about site settings. It allows you to configure the cover page format, the content to be displayed, and the Web master's contact information. Save the configuration of the site. You can now view the newly created Moodle Web site. For accessing the online computer lab for hands-on practice, Moodle can be configured to integrate the Linux Terminal Server for online computer lab access.

EXAMPLE 2: SETTING UP SAKAI ON LINUX

Sakai can be easily integrated into the existing LAMP packages. In this example, suppose that the LAMP packages have been installed through the examples in the previous chapters. The tasks to set up Sakai may include the following:

- Configure the Java computing environment
- Configure Tomcat
- Configure Maven
- Download and the install Sakai package
- •Configure Sakai and the Web page
- Configure the database

There are different versions of the Sakai installation package. For the small scale implementation, not all the tasks in the above are necessary.

Configuration of Java

The first step is to check if Java is installed on the host computer. If not, you can download the J2SE Development Kit (JDK) from the Web site:

http://java.sun.com/j2se/1.5.0/install.html

After JDK is installed, one needs to configure the environment variables so that the working directory is linked to the JDK software. If the Sakai Demo version is chosen for installation, the configuration of Tomcat and Maven can be skipped. The Demo version can be used for small companies.

Configuration of Tomcat

Tomcat can be used as the Java Servlet container. It can also post Web pages. One can download Tomcat from the Apache Web site:

http://tomcat.apache.org/download-55.cgi

Download, unpack, and install Tomcat. The configuration of Tomcat may include the following tasks:

- Specify the environment variables.
- Configure Tomcat to accept UTF-8 URLs.

- Re-direct users automatically to the Sakai application by creating an index.html file in the webapps/ROOT directory.

Configuration of Maven

Maven is a tool that is used to build and manage Java projects. Maven can be downloaded from the Web site:

http://maven.apache.org/maven-1.x/start/download.html

Download, unpack, and install Maven. The configuration of Maven may include the following steps:

- Specify the environment variables.
- Create a build-property file for building the Sakai package.

Installation of Sakai

Maven is used to build and deploy Sakai source code. The following are the main steps used for Sakai installation:

- Download the Sakai source code from the Web site: http://www.sakaiproject.org/portal/site/sakai-downloads.
- Unpack the Sakai source code in the specified directory.
- Start Maven in the specified directory to build Sakai. Maven will detect all the dependency files, download these files, and deploy Sakai to Tomcat.
- Start Tomcat to run Sakai.

Configuration of Sakai

After Sakai is deployed, the default configuration of Sakai should be modified for different environments. The following are some of the main configuration tasks.

- Make sure that Tomcat can read and write to Sakai's home directory such as $CATALINA_HOME/sakai.
- If needed, modify the Sakai properties file sakai.properties.
- Configure Sakai to work with application software such as the e-mail server or HTTP proxy.
- Test Sakai to make sure that it is running properly.

Configuration of Database

Suppose that MySQL is the database management system installed on the host computer. To integrate Sakai with MySQL, the following tasks may need to be accomplished:

- Design and implement a database for Sakai on MySQL.
- Create Sakai users and groups in MySQL, and make sure that adequate privileges are assigned to the groups.
- Configure MySQL to specify the database server, remote access, character sets, user authentication, data transaction, and the connection to Tomcat.
- Transfer the data from other data sources into the database for Sakai.
- Test Sakai to verify if the database for Sakai is working properly.

After the configuration procedure is completed, an enterprise-level leaning management system is ready to go. Further tests may also be needed with a set of courses. After that, the Sakai leaning management system can be released to the public.

CONCLUSION

In this chapter, the issues related to open source LMS packages have been discussed. First, we looked at some open source LMS packages. Five commonly used open source packages, Moodle, ATutor, Claroline, ILIAS, and Sakai were introduced. After we discussed the functionalities provided by these five LMS packages, we investigated the tasks related to LMS management. The management tools included in LMS packages were described. The last part of this chapter demonstrated how to install and configure Moodle and Sakai on the open source operating system Linux.

REFERENCES

Casillo, P., Chianese, A., Moscato, V., & Penta, A. (2006). IDEA: A developing tool of learning resources for LMS environments. *Advanced Learning Technologies, 2006. ICALT 2006* (pp. 571-572).

Claroline. (2008). *About Claroline.* Retrieved July 26, 2008, from http://www.claroline.net/about-claroline.html

Cole, J. (2005). *Using Moodle: Teaching with the popular open source course management system.* Sebastopol, CA: O'Reilly Media, Inc.

Commonwealth of Learning. (2003). *COL LMS open source.* Retrieved June 7, 2008, from http://www.col.org/colweb/webdav/site/myjahiasite/shared/docs/03LMSOpenSource.pdf

Finkelstein, A. (2007). Practicing what you preach: A learner-centered learning management system (LMS) training and support program for faculty. In C. Montgomerie & J. Seale (Eds.), *Proceedings of World Conference on Educational Multimedia, Hypermedia and Telecommunications 2007* (p. 2403). Chesapeake, VA: AACE.

Horton, W., & Horton, K. (2003). *E-learning tools and technologies: A consumer's guide for trainers, teachers, educators, and instructional designers.* Indianapolis, IN: Wiley.

ILIAS. (2007). *ILIAS learning management.* Retrieved November 7, 2007, from http://www.ilias.de

Itmazi, J. A., & Megías, M. G. (2005). *Survey: Comparison and evaluation studies of learning content management systems.* Retrieved June 6, 2008, from http://elearning.ppu.edu/jamil/Docs/MICRO.pdf

Lassila, A., & Pöyry, P. (2007). Online education and learning management systems from service-centered perspective. In *Proceedings of the 6th IASTED International Conference on Web-Based Education* (pp. 210-215). Chamonix, France.

Lim, C., Xu, R., & Jin, J. (2005). E-Learning via augmented reality on adaptive LMS. In G. Richards (Ed.), *Proceedings of World Conference on E-Learning in Corporate, Government, Healthcare, and Higher Education 2005* (pp. 2199-2204). Chesapeake, VA: AACE.

Marko, A., & Honkaranta, M. (2007). Bridging the gap between advanced distributed teaching and the use of learning management systems in the university context. *Advanced Learning Technologies, 2007. ICALT 2007* (pp.293-294).

Moodle. (2008). Moodle community. Retrieved June 6, 2008 from http://moodle.org

Munoz, K. D., & Duzer, J. V. (2005). Blackboard vs. Moodle: A comparison of satisfaction with online teaching and learning tools. Retrieved May 7, 2006, from http://www.humboldt.edu/~jdv1/moodle/all.htm

Sakai. (2007). Sakai project. Retrieved November 7, 2007, from http://sakaiproject.org/index.php?option=com_content&task=view&id=103&Itemid=208

Wu, Y., Zhao, W., Peng, X., & Xue,Y. (2006). A concept model for computer-based spoken language tests. *Telecommunications, 2006. AICT-ICIW '06*. (p. 4).

Chapter VIII
Security Management

INTRODUCTION

During the operation of an online teaching/learning system, security is a top priority. As an online system, the teaching/learning system is vulnerable to Internet hackers and hundreds of malicious viruses. A security related problem can cause significant damage to the online teaching/learning system. This kind of damage can possibly shut down the entire system or even spread viruses to the university's network and infect other systems on the network. To ensure the health of the online teaching/learning system, great effort has to be made to ensure the system's security. In this chapter, we will investigate issues on securing the online teaching/learning system.

The first topic to be discussed in this chapter is the possible vulnerabilities that may affect the security of the online teaching/learning system. Security problems can happen in various components of the online teaching/learning system such as the network, Web service, server computer systems, client computer systems, database systems, and so on. Several security vulnerability detection methods and open source vulnerability detection tools will be introduced in this chapter.

Based on the requirements of the online teaching/learning system, the university's rules, and the possible vulnerabilities, a security policy should be created by a team of network managers, instructors, and university administrators. The security policy serves as a guideline on what to do about the issues related the availability, reliability, integrity, and confidentiality of the online teaching/learning system. The policy will decide on the protection, authentication and authorization policies.

To enforce security measures, we will need security management tools. For various security management tasks, there are many open source tools that are available. In this chapter, we will take a look at the commonly used open source security management tools. We will discuss features provided by these tools and how they are used to enforce security measures and how to implement the security management plan.

The last part of this chapter will give an example to demonstrate security management on the Linux operating system. Linux has several powerful security management tools. We will practice how to configure these tools and how to use these tools to enforce the security measures. The second example in this chapter is about setting MySQL security.

BACKGROUND

Security of an e-learning system has caused, in general, a great deal of concern among researchers. The enforcement of security policies often requires great effort from a team which consists of computer service personnel, university administrators, faculty members, and online teaching support staff members. Weippl (2005) addressed the security concern among higher education institutions and demonstrated how administrators can be trained to use the virtual e-learning environment. For pre-college education, Yang and Dark (2005) discussed an information security risk assessment project for a K12 school corporation in their paper. They implemented the risk assessment project to analyze and evaluate the risks in the instructional technology systems. Another security evaluation study was reported by Dark (2003) who gave an overview of security evaluation, evaluation design, evaluation implementation, and evaluation management.

Riola (2006) discussed the security issues related to the wireless network used to support online teaching. Riola (2006) addressed the wireless network implementation and security issues in supporting technology based teaching. For the issues related to the mobile e-learning security, readers can also find information from Weippl's (2004) paper.

Gokhale (2002) discussed the issues related to the analysis of security vulnerabilities, the development of appropriate security policies, and the enforcement of the security measures. El-Khatib, Korba, Xu, and Yee (2003) presented ways to protect e-learning projects by enforcing appropriate security measures.

A large number of books and articles have been published to help readers to identify security vulnerabilities, develop security policies, and enforce security measures. For example, the book by McNab (2004) demonstrates how to identify security vulnerabilities. The book by Peltier (2004) shows the reader how to develop well-defined security policies. The book by Kaeo (2003) explains how to carefully carry out and test security policies. Various security technologies have been developed to define, configure, and manage security measures. The book by Fung (2004) examines network security technologies and various levels of network security structures.

Readers can also find security related information on open source products. The book by Smith (2005) provides detailed information about the security tools included in the Linux operating system. The book by Turnbull (2005) explains how to protect e-mail servers, Web servers, file servers, and so forth, hosted by the Linux operating system. To learn more about the open source security management tools, readers can refer to the book by Howlett (2004). The book introduces security tools for setting up firewalls, identifying security vulnerabilities, monitoring network traffic, tracking and analyzing security data, and encrypting data transmitted over the network.

In this chapter, we will mainly discuss security tools and security management that are related to the open source products used by online teaching/learning management systems. In particular, we will focus on the security management of the Linux operating system, MySQL database management system, and Moodle learning management system. We will also examine the tools provided by the Linux operating system as well as third party security management tools.

VULNERABILITY ASSESSMENT

Like e-commerce and many Web-based applications, an online teaching/learning system faces many security threats from Internet hackers and viruses. Although the Internet is the main source of security vulnerabilities, security problems can also occur on internal networks, operating systems, database management systems, learning management systems, as well as many other application software packages. The following are some factors that may cause security weaknesses:

- The Web server and the services hosted by the Web server are the most vulnerable components in an online teaching/learning system.
- The database management system and the remote access service provided by the database management system can be a factor of the security vulnerability, especially when the database management system is not using the operating system authentication.
- The operating system and the directory service provided by the operating system can be a factor that contributes to the security vulnerability. The improperly secured publicly shared files and directories hosted by the operating system are security concerns.

- The learning management system and its remote access services can also be a factor that may cause security problems.
- The improper configuration of network devices, protocols, and services will lead to some serious security problems.
- Wireless network access points and data transmission through air can post some security threats, especially if those data that are not adequately encrypted.
- Downloading software and installing the downloaded software from the Internet may cause computer virus infection.
- Weak security policies can lead to inadequate security measures when trying to protect the online teaching/learning system from hacker attacks and computer virus infection.

Security problems are mainly due to hacker attacks and computer viruses. Although most hacker attacks come from the Internet, there are also some dangerous internal hackers. The following are some of the commonly seen hacker attacks:

- Hackers often launch a denial-of-service (DoS) attack which is one of the simplest and most commonly used methods. A denial-of-service (DoS) attack floods a network with useless network traffic which takes away the bandwidth of the victim network. In such a way, it overloads the network service and causes the service to shut down.
- Hackers can log on to a server by trying many different password combinations. They can use some of the free software to try a large number of passwords rapidly.
- Hackers may use spyware to attack. They can set up some Web sites and wait for people to browse and interact with their application software, or download their free files. The interactivities with the application software or the downloaded files will bring the spyware to people's computers. Then, the spyware secretly collects information about the people and their computers, and transmit the collected information to the hackers' Web sites or e-mail addresses. Once a hacker steals the password and user information from a victim computer, he can set a spam relay from the victim computer system to harm other computers on the network without being caught.
- Hackers can also use publicly available accounts provided by Web servers, database servers, learning management systems, and operating systems. These publicly available accounts are used for the initial configuration for the convenience of system administrators. These accounts often have well known user names and passwords. If the passwords are not changed before the public can see the accounts on the network, the hackers can log on to the system as the

administrator and create accounts for themselves. From there on, the entire system will be under the hackers' control. Even through an anonymous account which has no administrator's privilege, a hacker may still peek through the file structure to collect some information about the users and the structure of the file system.

- Hackers can sniff a wireless network without being physically wired to the network. Some of the wireless network devices have no protection by default for quick installation. If they are not reconfigured, these devices will allow hackers to access the network without proper authentication. On the wireless network, when a computer is booted up, it sends a broadcasting message to search for an access point nearby. A hacker can capture the broadcasting message to obtain the sender's information. With the sender's information, the hacker can figure out how to access the victim computer system to collect other valuable information. The hacker can set up a rogue access point to offer a connection to the victim computer which is looking for a connection. Once connected, the victim's data will be transmitted to the rogue access point. Then, the hacker will be able to read all the unencrypted data or decrypt the encrypted data.
- There are many free network monitoring tools available on the Internet. A hacker can download and install one of these tools to capture the network traffic. If the data are not encrypted, the hacker can read all the information, even the user name and password, carried by a network transmission protocol. Unfortunately, most of the earlier network transmission protocols including the well known FTP and HTTP carry clear text over the Internet.
- The Web interactive components such as ActiveX controls and Java applets, as well as many scripts can also cause some serious security problems. Hackers can use these programs to bypass a firewall to penetrate into a private network. Sometimes, a hacker makes a malicious package available on a Web site and pretends the package can help users in some ways. Once this type of file is opened on a computer, the hacker will take control of the computer.
- Another way that a hacker can damage an online teaching/learning system is to utilize software bugs. These software bugs create security holes that allow the hacker to collect information about users, computer systems, and networks. Some of these software bugs can even give the hacker some privilege to perform certain activities such as delete, modify, or copy files on a victim computer.
- Hackers may be able to convince the online application tools provided by a database management system or learning management system to run malicious scripts which are designed to cause some significant damage.

Most of the security problems caused by hackers can be prevented by carefully configuring the operating system and application software. Make sure that the publicly available accounts are reconfigured or removed. The network administrator also needs to make sure that the communication ports, network protocols, and network devices such as routers and remote access servers are properly configured to prevent hackers' penetration. The network administrator should update the system timely with security patches and service packs as soon as they are available. He/she should make sure that a strong password policy is implemented. The system administrator and the database administrator should ensure that users do not get more privileges than they are supposed to.

Firewalls are the first defense of an online teaching/learning system. A firewall can be used to protect the university's network from offensive Web sites and malicious hackers. In many ways, a firewall can prevent hackers' attacks. It can be used as a filter to restrict certain network packets and protocols. It can also identify security vulnerabilities by comparing the incoming network traffic with the trusted information. The policy for utilizing Internet resources should be defined and implemented by using the firewall.

To protect data transmitted over the Internet, most of the newly created Web-based software includes security technologies such as Secure Sockets Layer (SSL) for establishing an encrypted link between a Web server and a browser. To transmit confidential data over the Internet, it is the user's responsibility to make sure that the security technologies are used for the transmission.

To prevent hackers from logging on to the system by trying a large number of passwords, the system should enforce a strong password policy and limit the number of times a user can enter incorrect passwords. Once the number of wrong passwords passes a certain limit, the system will freeze the logon for some time before the logon process can restart again.

One of the effective ways to detect a hacker's intrusion is to implement a well defined auditing policy. The auditing policy should include the auditing of the logon and the access of confidential files. There are many open source tools that can be used to identify security vulnerabilities. Later, we will look at some security management tools that enforce security measures so that we can prevent hackers from damaging our systems.

In addition to hackers' attacks, an online teaching/learning can also suffer from computer virus infection. The computer virus infection can damage the system in many ways, from losing files to paralyzing the entire system. The following are some types of computer viruses and the damages they can cause:

- **Boot virus:** This type of virus can be triggered by a computer boot process. During the boot process, the virus can damage a computer system by overwriting or replacing the boot program. In such a way, the virus can load itself into memory so that the computer cannot perform normal booting. Instead, the user will see a message on screen sent by the virus. The well known viruses Disk Killer and Stone are boot viruses.

- **Program virus:** This kind of virus becomes active when a computer is running an executable file such as a file with the extension .BIN, .COM, .EXE, .OVL, .DRV, .DLL, or .SYS. The virus can be loaded into memory and infect other executable files that are started after the infected file. Once an infected program is copied to other computers, it can infect the programs hosted by the other computers. Some of the commonly known program viruses are Sunday and Cascade.
- **Trojan horse virus:** Similar to a program virus, a Trojan horse virus is an executable file. The difference is that the Trojan horse does not load itself to memory. Instead, it claims that it is a game or it can do some helpful things such as eliminating viruses on your computer and wait for someone to download and open it. Once opened, the virus may do something annoying to the user or it may wipe out the entire hard disk. The commonly known Trojan horse viruses are Beast and Bifrose.
- **Stealth virus:** This type of virus infects a computer in a stealthy way and is very difficult to detect. It can hide itself in a regular file and modify the file size so that the size is the same as that of the original file to avoid the detection by antivirus software. Some of the stealthy virus can even temporarily replace the infected file with a copy of uninfected file to trick the antivirus software. There are several stealthy viruses. The commonly known ones are Joshi and Whale.
- **Polymorphic virus:** Like a stealthy virus, this type of virus also tries to hide its identity. It can change its appearance in each different infection. Antivirus software may not be able to detect all types of viruses. Therefore some forms of polymorphic viruses may be able to survive and continue to damage the system. It is difficult to remove this type of virus from an infected system. Cascade and Virus 101 are known polymorphic viruses.
- **Macro virus:** This type of virus becomes active when one opens an infected file which includes macros. Files like word processing files or spreadsheet files may include macros to perform certain activities and can be infected by the macro virus. If the infected file is copied to another computer, the files with macros on the other computer can also be infected. Some of the known macro viruses are WM/Helper.C;D;E and W97M/Ekiam.
- **Java or ActiveX virus:** This type of virus can be spread through Web browsers. Once a user clicks a button or a link behind which the virus is hiding, the virus takes control of the victim computer through the currently opened Web page.

This kind of virus can perform dangerous operations such as extracting any information from the computer or executing any instruction. There are some commonly known viruses of this type such as JS.Exception and Bubbleboy.

- **E-mail virus:** This type of virus can be spread through e-mail messages. It can automatically mail itself to all the e-mail entries in the e-mail address book on the victim computer system. When infected e-mails are carried to other computers, they will infect the e-mail entries stored on the other computers. It is difficult to clean up the damage caused by e-mail viruses. These viruses can often cause huge loss of time, man power, and money. Some of the known e-mail viruses are W32/Mytob.gen@MM and Mimail.
- **Worm:** A worm is a type of virus that often infects a network. Once a worm virus gets on a network, it scans the network and tries to find a security hole on the computers connected to the network. Then, from the newly infected computer, the worm continues to probe the network to find other security holes. The worm can harm the network by consuming the bandwidth of the network. Unlike other computer viruses that often need to be carried by another program to replicate themselves. The worm can propagate itself without being carried by another program. Some known worms are W32/Bolgimo.worm and Supernova Worm.

Any of these viruses can do significant damage to an online teaching/learning system once it is infected. Adequate security measures must be enforced to prevent viruses from infecting the computers and networks. Users, technicians, administrators must be highly alert about potential virus infection. They must do the best they can to prevent virus infection from happening. The following shows how viruses can infect computer systems and private networks, and provides some tips that can help reduce the chance of computers being infected by viruses:

- **File downloading:** Downloading and installing files is the main way of introducing the Trojan horse virus, Java and ActiveX virus, and many other viruses. While trying to complete assignments, students may need to download some scripts, patches, multimedia tools, free software, Java applets, and so on. Downloading files from unknown Web sites makes the online teaching/learning system very vulnerable to various viruses. Be careful when downloading and installing files from the Internet. Make sure to download files only from trusted Web sites. Users should be informed about dangerous Web sites and about the instruction on how to clean infected files.
- **Web server and Web browser:** Web related technologies such as Web browsers and Web servers are probably the most vulnerable to virus attacks. Web-based technologies are entrances for many different types of viruses. Through

Web browsers, viruses can be downloaded to a client or server computer system. A Web server may support the interactive services such as ActiveX controls and Java applets which may potentially allow viruses or other malicious software to enter a private network. By penetrating ActiveX controls or Java applets, many of the viruses can bypass a firewall used for protecting the private network. A Web server also supports scripts to be executed on the server. Viruses can hide in scripts. Once the scripts are executed by the Web server, the viruses hidden in the scripts will infect the Web server as well as the private network. The FTP service supported by many Web servers can be another security hole. Many of the viruses can be potentially transferred to a victim computer system through FTP. Some of the viruses can hide in multimedia files and desktop application files such as spreadsheet and word files. Once these files are opened by a Web browser, the computer system will be infected by the viruses.

As we can see, Web related technologies are very vulnerable to viruses. Therefore, by the default installation, Web servers turn off the services that support ActiveX, Java applets, scripts, and so on. This may cause inconvenience for students who need to interact with class Web sites. The students may have to turn on these services so that they can access their online teaching materials. However, they may want to configure the Web browser to prompt first before they can start these services.

Users have to be very careful not to download and execute files from unknown sources. It is the Web server administrator's responsibility as well as the user's responsibility to update the Web server and Web browser with the latest security patches. Also, the user should make sure not to follow links provided by unknown sources.

- **Application software:** Running application software such as multimedia software, database management systems, learning management systems, as well as desktop applications can also post some security risk. Some viruses, such as macro viruses and worms, are designed to damage these kinds of application software. Those viruses can be introduced into a database by executing virus infected macro or SQL procedures. E-mail is the vulnerable application software that can spread viruses which can be carried by e-mail messages. When a user opens an e-mail message that has a virus, the user's computer will be infected. The widely installed media players can also make computer systems vulnerable. Through a media player, the Trojan horse and other viruses can be passed on a victim computer system. Like media players, instant messaging may also cause some security vulnerabilities. Instant massaging can transfer files over the Internet. By doing so, worms can sneak into a private network and replicate themselves on the network through an Internet Relay Chat (IRC) channel.

As described above, most of the application software related virus infections are due to the vulnerabilities of the Internet exposure. There are several things that students and faculty members can do to reduce the vulnerabilities caused by the application software. To prevent viruses from being introduced by e-mail, users should be careful not to open untrusted e-mail. The e-mail server administrator can configure a filter at the gateway to eliminate e-mails from suspicious origins. The user should not accept communication requests from unknown sources. Security vulnerabilities can also be reduced if the remote access services of the application software are properly configured. Make sure not to assign more privilege to users than they really need.

In the above, we have discussed various security vulnerabilities that may exist in an online teaching/learning system. Some security measures have been suggested to reduce the vulnerabilities. To decide where, when, and how to implement the security measures at the enterprise level, a security policy should be carefully developed. The next topic is about security policies.

SECURITY POLICIES

A security policy is a set of rules and practices about what to protect and how to protect it. To protect an online teaching/learning system, the security policy should be created by a team that consists of the system and network administrators, the institution's leaders, application developers, faculty members, and instructional support staff members. In such a way, the requirements for security in different areas will be taken care of by the security policy.

The creation of the security policy starts with collecting information such as the current regulations and rules imposed by the university and the current security practice performed by the computer service department. The security policy development team should evaluate how security problems will impact the operation of the online teaching/learning system. The team needs to identify the information that should be protected and provide a list of possible security vulnerabilities. The team will prioritize the vulnerabilities and provide a guideline on how to deal with these security vulnerabilities. The team should propose a list of proper security measures to be enforced for protecting the sensitive information. The team needs to consider the level of technical difficulties and the cost for enforcing these security measures. Also, the team should develop a privacy policy for publishing personal information on the course Web sites.

When creating the security policy, the team should consider the issues related to confidentiality, integrity, and availability of the online teaching/learning system:

- **Confidentiality:** Keep confidential information from being viewed by unauthorized individuals.
- **Integrity:** Prevent the confidential information from being intentionally or unintentionally altered.
- **Availability:** Make sure that the authorized users can view and modify the information whenever they need to.

For each of these areas, the security policy development team should provide a list of regulations to be enforced on the online teaching/learning system and for the users. These regulations also serve as a guideline for the system developer and system administrator to follow. The following shows some possible regulations that can be enforced to reduce security vulnerabilities in each of the areas.

Confidentiality

To improve confidentiality on the online teaching/learning system, the security policy can specify the following regulations:

- The security policy should be clear on rules related to system authentication. The policy should be specific on who should be given the privilege to access what information and who should be given the privilege to access which computer systems and network devices.
- The security policy should provide a guideline on how to protect data from being accessed by unauthorized individuals. It should specify what data should be encrypted and how to encrypt these data.
- The security policy should include a strong password regulation to harden users' passwords.
- The security policy should also include rules on how to monitor and audit the online teaching/learning system. The rules should specify who can perform the monitoring and auditing procedures.

Integrity

To prevent the data from being intentionally or unintentionally altered by unauthorized individuals, the security policy should include a set of regulations to define what data can be modified by a user and how to protect the data transmitted over the network. The following lists some of the regulations:

- The security policy will define the authorization of who should be allowed to do what. After a user logs on to the online teaching/learning system, the user can only perform those activities that are allowed by the authorization regulations.
- The security policy will recommend the protocols and encryption methods used to transmit data over the Internet.
- The security policy should also include the procedures to prevent hackers from stealing or altering sensitive information.

Availability

To make sure that the information is available to qualified users, availability rules should be specified in the security policy. The following are some of the regulations commonly included in the security policy:

- The security policy should specify the time frame that certain information should be available to the qualified users. For the online teaching/learning system, the course materials, assignments, and exams are available only in certain time periods.
- The security policy can also specify where the information will be available to the qualified users. Some universities require students to take tests at specified locations where the tests can be proctored.
- The security policy may specify how to deliver the information to the qualified users. Web, e-mail, collaboration and multimedia tools are often used to deliver different types of information.

Once the security policy is created, it will take a lot of team effort to implement the security policy. The successful implementation of the policy largely depends on how well the users are educated and how well they understand and follow the policy. A precise and concise security policy can greatly help the understanding. Not only the users and technical personnel need to be educated, but also the university's administrators. It is also required that the security policy be updated to meet the current requirements. Even though the security policy is developed with team effort, it may not be perfect. After the security policy is put into place, a procedure is needed to evaluate and monitor how the security policy is carried out. Also, as time changes, there will be some updates to the security policy to meet new requirements.

When developing an online teaching/learning system, the security policy should also include the privacy policy which is a set of rules about how personal information may be used on the course Web sites. The privacy policy may contain the following regulations:

- What private information should be collected and stored on an online teaching/learning system?
- Which level of privilege is allowed to access which level of personal information?
- How can the private information be accessed (read only, read and write, or downloadable from a Web page)?
- How long is the private information available to a qualified person?

The privacy policy can be applied to exams, assignments, projects, and student grades. For example, instructors are allowed to access students' grades for one semester. They can read, modify, and print their students' grades from the course Web sites. A student can only read his/her own grades. However, the privileges cannot be given to the general public, other students, and other staff members. Also, before a Web master can publish a student's name, photo, and other personal information, he/she should have the student's approval.

Depending on the university's rules, the privacy policy may be different for one university to another. The security policy team has to be very protective of the personal information. Any leaking of personal information may cause a serious consequence.

OPEN SOURCE SECURITY MANAGEMENT TOOLS

To enforce the security measures defined in the security policy, the use of security management tools is often required. There are many open source security management tools available for free download. Some of these tools are comprehensive and the others are designed to accomplish a specific task. Among these security management tools, some are specially designed to handle the security management tasks for an operating system, some are for a database management system, some are for a learning management system, some are for a network protocol, and so on.

Usually, an open source operating system such as Linux includes various security management tools. Most of the time, these built-in security management tools are adequate to handle the daily security management tasks. There are also many third party security management tools which can be installed on an open source operating system. The security management tools can be used to identify security vulnerabilities, set up firewalls, provide authentication and authorization services, monitor and audit user behavior, detect and remove viruses, clean up infected files, and so on. The following summarizes the tasks done by various security management tools.

Security Assessment Tools

To detect security holes, various tools are available to scan networks and operating systems. The following are tasks that can be done by various scanners:

- **Port scanner:** As the name indicates, a port scanner can be used to check if there are any open ports. If the port scanner finds any currently active open ports, it writes a detailed report about the open ports. There are several open source port scanners available for free download, Nmap (2007) is one of such open source port scanners. It is a ping scanning tool. It can determine which computer is currently running on the network and perform decoy port scanning.
- **Web scanner:** A Web scanner can be used to test the configuration of a Web server. It can test security vulnerabilities through remotely logging in and searching for scripts with known vulnerabilities. It can also perform brute force account testing to see if there is an account with a default password or an account with an easy-to-guess password. Nikto (2007) is one of such open source Web server scanners. It can scan multiple Web components. Nikto can test against Web servers and identify dangerous files and CGIs. It can also be set to automatically update vulnerability information to keep the scanner updated.
- **Virus scanner:** A virus scanner can be used to scan files to check if a file is potentially a virus. Once the virus scanner detects a file that is likely to contain a virus, it will send out a message to warn the user. Virus scanners can detect viruses hiding in hard drives as well as in computer memory. There are many open source virus scanners designed to detect viruses such as dialers, Trojans, and many other kinds of malware. Clam AntiVirus or ClamAV (2007) is an open source virus scanner. ClamAV is often shipped with the Linux operating system. It is especially useful to detect viruses on an e-mail server. It also provides an advanced database updater for scripted updates. It will scan for viruses as e mails before they can be saved to mailboxes. It can also be configured to perform routine scans on files. ClamAV can be installed on various operating systems such as Linux, Windows, and UNIX. It provides flexible and scalable scanning functionalities. It is fast and provides on-access scanning which becomes active after an operation system starts and interacts with application programs until the operating system is shut down. Clam AntiVirus stands in between the operating system and the application

to make sure that no virus can pass through. A multi-threaded daemon is used to carry out the scanning in the background so that the scanning process will not interrupt other computation tasks. It does virus database updates multiple times per day to keep the information about virus up-to-date. Clam AntiVirus is able to deal with almost all mail file formats and a large number of archive formats such as zip, tar, gzip, bzip2, and so on. It supports many different types of executable and portable files compressed with UPX, FSG, Petite, and so on.
- **Firewall scanner:** A firewall scanner can be used to test firewall configuration. It can identify different levels of security vulnerabilities on both proxy-based and filter-based firewalls. Some of the more advanced firewall scanners can also balance the usability and security based on the level of vulnerability. Most of the firewall scanners are able to generate a detailed report about the testing result. Both ClamAV (2007) and Nmap (2007) include utilities for scanning firewalls.

Some of the security vulnerability detection tools combine various scanners and other functionalities to test the security vulnerabilities in multiple areas. With these comprehensive tools, the security management team can test the security architecture for an enterprise against the well-known vulnerabilities. These comprehensive tools often include reporting utilities to produce detailed reports about the testing. The following are some of the open source comprehensive security vulnerability testing tools:

- **Foundstone WSDigger:** Foundstone WSDigger (WebHosting.Info, 2005) was released by McAfee as an open source security vulnerability testing tool. This is a security assessment tool that can be used to scan a large distributed network system. It automates penetrating-style Web service security testing. It includes sample attack plug-ins for SQL injection, cross-site scripting, and X-PATH injection attacks and it is updated with the latest vulnerability information and threat correlation. Users are welcome to develop and share their own plug-ins. Foundstone WSDigger allows the user to run a checklist and let the user determine the severity of a threat so that critical vulnerabilities can be fixed first.
- **Nessus:** Nessus (Tenable Network Security, 2007) is considered by many IT professionals as one of the best free network vulnerability scanner available. Even though Nessus is a closed source product now, it is still free except the latest plug-ins. Over 11,000 free plugins have been developed for Nessus. Nessus can perform local and remote security checks. It also provides client-server architecture and an embedded scripting language for writing plug-ins.

With a variety of plug-ins, Nessus can effectively strengthen an enterprise's security by complying with the internal policies and external regulations.

Among the tools mentioned above, Nessus is the top choice among vulnerability scanners. Not only is it capable of detecting a large number of network vulnerabilities, it also provides an adequate report system. With its GUI interface, Nessus is also very easy to use.

Identifying security vulnerabilities is an important and complex task. It is difficult to perform this type of task manually on an online teaching/learning system. The open source tools described above can greatly help the security manager to quickly and efficiently identify security problems.

Antivirus Tools

As described earlier, an online teaching/learning system is vulnerable to various viruses. It is necessary to install antivirus software to protect the system. With the protection of antivirus software, the risk of virus damage can be reduced significantly. Every client computer and server computer should have antivirus software installed before these computers are connected to the Internet. To help students install antivirus software on their home computers, most of the universities provide antivirus software which can be downloaded from the universities' Web sites.

If an online teaching/learning system is run with the Linux server operating system, there are very few virus attacks on the server. Therefore, not many open source antivirus software packages are available for the Linux operating system. However, most of the client computers at students' homes have Windows based operation systems. There are a large number of viruses designed to attack these operating systems. A lot of antivirus software is developed for Windows operating systems, some of them are open source products, some of them are freeware, and others are commercial products. Most of the antivirus software packages used by universities are commercial products. Usually, a university has a package deal with an antivirus software vendor. However, some open source or free antivirus software packages can also provide protection as well. In the following, we will look at some of the open source or free antivirus software packages:

- **ClamWin:** ClamAV that was mentioned earlier provides an open source virus scanning toolkit. It also provides antivirus software called ClamWin (2007), which is an open source antivirus program for Windows based operating systems. Due to its powerful antivirus engine, ClamWin has a high virus detection rate and it provides a flexible scan scheduling toolkit. Like ClamAV, the database used to store virus information is updated promptly. In addition,

ClemWin can be added to Microsoft Outlook to remove virus-infected attachments automatically.

- **AVG Antivirus Protection:** AVG Antivirus Protection (Grisoft, 2007) is award winning comprehensive antivirus software for various Windows based operating systems. It has a free edition, AVG Anti-Virus Free, for the protection of personal computers. According to AVG, AVG Anti-Virus Free was the number one downloaded program on CNET Donwload.com and it was the first most popular antivirus program based on the Editor's Choice of CNET. The AVG antivirus program can provide real-time protection and remove all major threats on an infected system. It is easy to use and is very efficient. The AVG antivirus program can be easily installed and uninstalled on a personal computer. Through the wizard provided by the program, one can create a rescue disk, remove viruses, and restore system files. The AVG antivirus program can also schedule automatic scanning, change program configuration, and specify the unwanted program exceptions.
- **Avast! Antivirus:** Avast! Antivirus is another award winning antivirus program provided by Alwil (2007) for desktop computer and server protection. It also provides a free edition. The recent free edition is Avast Home Edition 4.7.1098, which can be downloaded from CNET Download.com. According to Alwil (2007), there were forty millions of registrations and the software was rated with five stars by the CNET editors. The Avast! package allows users to scan files. It provides protection for text messaging, P2P communication, and e-mail. It provides the network traffic with intrusion detection. The Avast! package also provides Web Shield which monitors and filters HTTP traffic. It includes scanners such as the NNTP scanner for scanning Usenet Newsgroup traffic. The NNTP scanner can also scan operations on files. The boot-time scanner can be used to scan files stored in hard disks, CDs, flash drives, and floppy disks. When a computer system is infected by the known viruses, Avast! can be used to remove these viruses.
- **Avira AntiVir PersonalEdition:** Avira AntiVir PersonalEdition by Avira (2007) is another free antivirus program which supports real-time protection. Avira Antivir supports various 32-bit and 64-bit operating systems such as Linux and Windows. It can also be used to protect PDAs and network based applications such as e-mail and share points. It provides personal firewall, antispam, and antiphishing functionalities. It can recognize infected files. It checks the Internet downloads and blocks the infected Web sites. The security manager can customize a scanning process. With this program, the security manager can schedule the scanning process in a flexible way. This program provides a scanning report in a spreadsheet file and provides options for the security manager on how to deal with the scanning result.

Among the antivirus tools described above, both AVG Antivirus Protection and Avast! Antivirus are award winning products. However, AVG Antivirus Protection is much easier to use. Therefore, the choice goes to AVG Antivirus Protection.

In an online teaching/learning system, students' home computers are often used as client computers. It is the security manager's responsibility to help students to protect their home computers with antivirus software. Often, a Web page is developed for each online class to inform the students on how to download and install the antivirus software provided by the university. The Web page also provides the latest information about virus attacks and other security related issues.

Adware/Spyware/Scumware Remover

Adware is advertising software that is integrated with host application software. If the user accepts the adware during the installation of the application software, it will be installed on the user's computer system. Once installed, adware will often display banners or annoying pop-up windows on the user's screen. Spyware is software that secretly sends the user's surfing activities to advertisers and others who may be interested in collecting market data. While the user is surfing some commercial Web sites or downloading some free software, the spyware can be installed without the user's knowledge. The spyware can slow down the victim computer's performance. Similar to the spyware, scumware is software that steals information on the network traffic without the user's knowledge. In addition, scumware can replace an online advertisement provided by a Web site with its own, or adding its own advertisements. Manually uninstalling adware, spyware, or scumware may not fully remove these software programs. It often requires the user to have a tool called adware/spyware/scumware remover to completely remove these types of programs. There are several well developed open source or free adware/spyware/scumware removers that can accomplish the task. As mentioned earlier, there are very few antispyware packages developed for the Linux operating system due the fact that Linux is less vulnerable to adware, spyware, or scumware. However, it is necessary for the client computers with Windows based operation systems to have adware/spyware/scumware remover software. The following are some of them:

- **Spyware Doctor Starter Edition:** Spyware Doctor produced by PC Tools (2007) is well known enterprise-level commercial antispyware. Its cut-down version Spyware Doctor Starter Edition is free. Spyware Doctor Starter Edition offers scanning and removing capabilities, scheduled scans, and free signature file updates. As a cut-down version, it only offers some active protection. Spyware Doctor Starter Edition is available as free software offered by Google.

- **Microsoft's Windows Defender:** For students' client computers run by various versions of Windows operating systems, Microsoft's (2007) Windows Defender is a good choice for removing spyware. Windows Defender is free and is often bundled with Windows operating systems, or one can download it from Microsoft Web site. Although it consumes more processing power, it provides solid real-time protection.

All of the above antispyware can get the basic job done to protect the computer systems with Windows based operating systems. The differences among these packages are minor. Often, the antispyware that provides better protection and spyware removal capability will consume more processing power and vice verse. However, for most of the newer personal computers, the processing power is adequate to support any of these antispyware programs.

Firewall Management Tools

A firewall is the software used to protect computer systems connected to a private network. To protect an online teaching/learning system constructed on a private network, an enterprise-level firewall program is often installed on the network gateway server. A personal firewall program can also be installed on an individual computer system for further protection. The personal firewall program should be installed on a student's home computer which is used as the client computer on the online teaching/learning system. The firewall program will check each incoming network packet to decide if the packet should be forwarded to its destination. The firewall can be configured to accept only the packets from trusted domains and network protocols. It can also be configured to accept only the network packets with proper authentication certifications. It will drop those unwanted packets defined by the security policy. The firewall is considered one of the crucial components for implementing the security measures. Several open source or free firewall management products are available to help the security manager to configure the firewall so that the security policy can be implemented properly. The following describes some of the firewall management products.

- **IPCop firewall:** The IPCop firewall (IPCop, 2007) is an open source firewall management program. It is known for its efficiency, versatility, and ease of installation. It is a powerful Linux based firewall with an easy access Web interface. One of the advantages of IPCop is that it can run on old computers so that one can turn any surplus computer system to a firewall host. It can serve as a demilitarized zone (DMZ) which is a neutral zone between a university's private network and the Internet. The DMZ can prevent outside users from directly accessing the data in a private network. IPCop also supports many other security related functionalities such as the intrusion detection system, IP Security (IPSec) VPN service, Dynamic Host Configuration Protocol (DHCP) server, Network Address Translation (NAT) service, time server, Web proxy, and so on. With these functionalities, IPCop is a full featured firewall package that will meet the security requirements of an online teaching/learning system.

- **Sunbelt-Kerio Personal Firewall:** The free version of Sunbelt-Kerio Personal Firewall by Sunbelt Software (2007) provides reasonable protection. Unlike some of the firewall programs which only provide one-way protection, Sunbelt-Kerio Personal Firewall supports two-way firewall protection that protects incoming and outgoing network traffic. Two-way protection can prevent a hacker's intrusion and make valuable data stay inside the private network. The free version of Sunbelt-Kerio Personal Firewall includes firewall functionalities such as the packet filter, network and host intrusion prevention system, file integrity verification, and the control of application launch and communication. It generates reports about the statistics of blocked activities and attacks. It supports automatic updates and provides logging capabilities.
- **Comodo Firewall:** Comodo Firewall (Comodo, 2007) is another well designed free firewall program. Comodo Firewall is designed to prevent hacker attacks and spyware, and identity theft for both computer systems and networks. Comodo Firewall has the ability to support Internet Connection Sharing. It provides two-way protection of the threats from both inside and outside. It also provides the host intrusion prevention system to protect the operating system files and to block the installation of any malware. Comodo Firewall provides the GUI to assist firewall configuration. It monitors real-time network traffic and updates the information about the newest threats.

There are many other free firewall management tools that can meet the requirements of an online teaching/learning system. In addition to these third party firewall products, an operating system often includes a firewall program which can also get the job done. Among the firewall management tools mentioned above, the IPCop firewall is often considered by many IT professionals as a better choice due to the rich features included in the tool.

Spam Filter

Spam is unsolicited bulk e-mails sent to people's e-mail inboxes. It is really annoying to receive a large number of junk e-mails every day. A spam filter is the e-mail preview utility software that can identify spam e-mails and remove them from uses' e-mail inboxes. Spam e-mails can be identified by checking the sender's email address, the key words, or the criteria set by e-mail users or security managers. Some of the Internet service providers (ISPs) also use spam filters to prevent spam e-mails. Most of the e-mail servers include some forms of spam filters. There are also some third party spam filters, and many of them are free or open source products. The following describes some of them.

- **SpamAssassin:** SpamAssassin (2007) is an open source spam filter produced by the Apache Software Foundation. According to SpamAssassin (2007), it is the winner of the 2007 InfoWorld "Best of Open Source Software" BOSSIE Award. The installation and configuration of SpamAssassin is relatively simple. SpamAssassin allows users to add their own rules for spam filtering. With SpamAssassin, it is relatively easy to add the user's and the site's specific policies to the e-mail server. Since SpamAssassin can identify spam signatures in many different ways, it is difficult for spammers to find ways to deliver their spam e-mails. SpamAssassin can be used with many e-mail server systems such as procmail, sendmail, postfix, qmail, and so on.
- **Mozilla Thunderbird spam filter:** The Mozilla Thunderbird spam filter is another well known open source spam filter developed for the e-mail system Mozilla Thunderbird (Mozilla, 2007). The spam filter is built in the Mozilla Thunderbird system. When you install the Mozilla Thunderbird e-mail system, the spam filter will be automatically installed. The filtering process is carried out based on the rules defined by the user as well as the theory of Bayesian spam filtering. Its adaptive filter can be trained by the user to identify junk e-mails. As time goes on, the trained adaptive filter becomes more and more efficient. The Mozilla Thunderbird spam filter will be automatically updated by the Mozilla Thunderbird e-mail system. This spam filter is a very efficient system by taking only a little system processing power. Once spam e-mails are identified, the spam filter gives the user options on how to deal with the junk e-mails. The user can manually remove the junk e-mails or configure the filter to automatically move them to the junk folder.
- **MailWasher:** MailWasher (2007) is a free spam filter with an interesting approach. It is easy to install and configure. It is also easy to use by configuring it to check e-mails at a certain time and send an audio and video notice when a new e-mail arrives. It allows the e-mail client to preview an e-mail before downloading the e-mail to the client's personal computer. Such an approach can prevent spam e-mails and other unwanted files from harming the user's computer. When MailWasher identifies a possible spam e-mail or virus, it will display a warning message to caution the user. It allows the user to place an e-mail in the blacklist where the e-mail will automatically bounce and be

deleted, or place an e-mail in the friends list where the e-mail address will always be accepted. The filter provided by MailWasher can be configured to filter out potential spammers' addresses.

Among the three spam filter tools, SpamAssassin is the winner due to its rich features and ease of use. It is also easy to add customized rules to SpamAssassin.

As spammers spread more and more spam e-mails, every user's e-mail inbox is flooded with junk e-mails. It is a tedious task to remove a large number of junk e-mails. All the spam filters mentioned above can significantly reduce the number of spam e-mails. The security manager should install a spam filter on each of the e-mail server and encourage each e-mail client to do the same.

Rootkit Detector

A rootkit is a type of technique that can be used to hide malware such as viruses and spyware so that the malware cannot be detected by antivirus scanners. The stealth malware hidden by using the rootkit technique is very difficult to detect and can cause great damage to a computer system or a network. A rootkit can be used by a hacker to access a computer system or even take full control of the system. Facing the rootkit threat, a new type of security software called rootkit detector has been created to deal with the malware hidden with the rootkit technique. Among these rootkit detection programs, some are open source or free software. The following briefly describes some of the open source or free rootkit detectors:

- **OSSEC:** OSSEC (2007) is an open source host-based intrusion detection system. One of its functionalities is rootkit detection. OSSEC includes the open source rootkit detection software called Rootcheck. Security managers can use Rootcheck to scan host systems for known rootkits. Rootcheck is also able to alert the presence of unknown rootkits. Once a rootkit is detected, Rootcheck will generate a report to provide the information about the finding. While integrated with OSSEC, it provides additional services such as file integrity checking, real-time alerting, system monitoring, correlation analysis, and so on. The installation of Rootcheck is simple, and it runs on various operating systems such as Linux, Mac OS, and different versions of UNIX.
- **Rootkit Hunter:** Rootkit Hunter (2007) is another open source rootkit scanner. This rootkit scanning tool can be used to identify rootkits and other stealthy malware by running various tests such as MD5 hash comparison and checking wrong file permissions. It also checks the default files used by rootkits, suspected strings and hidden files. Rootkit Hunter runs on the Linux operating system distributed by various Linux distributions.

- **Panda AntiRootkit:** Panda AntiRootkit is free software that not only detects rootkits but also removes them. The capability of removing rootkits makes Panda AntiRootkit a valuable product. Panda AntiRootkit can reveal the hiding technique of rootkits at a lower level so that it is able to detect known and unknown rootkits hidden in files, drivers, and computation processes. After rootkits are indentified, Panda AntiRootkit removes them by deleting all rootkit associated registry keys to prevent them from functioning. The Exhaustive Scan Monitor provided by Panda AntiRootkit can be used to monitor the presence of rootkits in drivers and boot processes. Panda AntiRootkit has a reporting utility to generate reports about the findings.

In the above, we have examined several rootkit detectors that are able to discover the malware hidden by the rootkit technique. It is often necessary to use these rootkit detectors with full featured antivirus software to completely remove the detected malware from the victim system. Among the above rootkit detectors, both Rootkit Hunter and OSSEC are good choices. Rootkit Hunter is designed to run on Linux and UNIX machines. OSSEC has more intrusion detection functionalities.

So far, we have discussed security management tools for detecting security vulnerabilities, dealing with viruses, removing adware, spyware, and scumware, managing firewalls, filtering spam e-mails, and detecting rootkits. We have looked at some commonly used open source or free tools. Most of these tools are available for download from the third-party vendors' Web sites. In addition to these third-party security management tools, the open source operating systems such as Linux also provide some security management tools. The following examples will demonstrate some of the security management functionalities supported by the Linux operating system.

EXAMPLE 1: ENFORCING SECURITY MEASURES ON LINUX OPERATING SYSTEM

As an enterprise-level operating system, Linux includes many tools to enforce security measures. The security management tools in the Linux operating system are used to protect system files, user information, confidential data, networks, and application programs such as database management systems, Web servers and Web sites, leaning management servers, e-mail servers, clients, and so on. The following are some of the tasks performed by these security tools:

- Create and configure user accounts to enforce the requirements of the security policies.

- Enforce the account lockout policy set by the security policies.
- Build firewalls according to the security policies.
- Verify if the strong password policy has been followed.
- Disable unnecessary or insecure user accounts and services.
- Enable security monitoring, log warning, and auditing services to check security events.
- Set access restrictions for shared files, folders, and disks.
- Block vulnerable network protocols and communication ports.
- Encrypt the data transmitted over the local area network or the Internet.
- Enforce security measures for Web servers, Web services, Web sites, and virtual directories.
- Harden network communication protocols.
- Configure restrictions for remote access.
- Verify if the certificate and its public key are valid.
- Backup the systems regularly and clean the infected files.

To practice how to carry out these tasks with the tools included in the Linux operating system, we will work on two examples. The first example demonstrates how to encrypt network traffic on Linux, and the second one shows how to configure a filter to block unwanted protocols and computer systems from which others may access your system.

The first example will demonstrate how the network traffic can be easily captured by the free downloaded network monitoring software Ethereal. It will also show how the Secure Sockets Layer (SSL) protocol can be used to protect the data transmitted over the network. This demonstration requires that the Web server should be working properly on the host computer system. Some of the Linux distributions such as Red Hat Linux include the network monitoring tool Ethereal. If not, users can download it from the Web site http://ethereal.brothersoft.com/. After Ethereal is downloaded and installed on the host computer, at the # prompt, you can start Ethereal by entering the command:

```
ethereal
```

After Ethereal is started and is set to capture the network traffic, from another computer that can access the Web server through the Internet or local area network, you can try to access the default Web site supported by the Web server. After browsing the default Web site, you can perform some interactive activities such as logging on to a Web account or search for a specific word. Stop Ethereal's capturing process. You will be able to find the account information or the word you are trying to search in the captured data. This is because the protocol http carries the data in the plain text format. To protect the information from being read by unauthorized individuals, you can use SSL to encrypt the data before transmitting the data through the Internet. To do so, consider the following steps:

- Suppose that you want to search for a word on the default Web site. You should make sure the search engine is working properly. For example, on Red Hat Linux, you need to configure and start the htdig service.
- Download and install a version of the SSL program. For example, if an RPM package is downloaded, you can run the following command to install a SSL program on a personal computer with the x86 platform.

```
rpm -Uvh mod _ ssl-version _ number.ent.i386.rpm
```

- After the SSL program is installed, start Ethereal and set it to the capture mode. From the computer that can access the Web server, start the Web browser and enter the URL.

  http://*Web_server_URL*/htdig/*Web_page*.html

- After searching for a few words, you can stop Ethereal's capture process.
- Examine the captured data by Ethereal. This time, you will not be able to find the http packets in the captured data.

Our next example is about configuring IP filtering tools such as iptables to block users from using certain network protocols from a certain computer to access the host computer. Suppose that you would like to block the user on the computer with the IP address 10.1.1.1 (or using this IP address on another computer that can access your host computer.) from accessing the Web server. You can follow the steps below to implement this security measure:

- The first step is to verify if the iptables is functioning on your computer by entering the following command:

```
iptables --list
```

- Once you have confirmed that the iptables is working properly, enter the following command to drop the request from the computer with the IP address 10.1.1.1 to the Web server on the host computer:

```
iptables --append INPUT --source 10.1.1.1 --destination-port 80 -jump
drop
```

- Test the filter by accessing the Web server from the computer with IP 10.1.1.1. The access request should be dropped.
- To clean up the rule that you have just set for the iptables, enter the following command.

```
iptables --flush INPUT
```

EXAMPLE 2: SETTING MYSQL SECURITY

After MySQL is successfully installed, the database administrator will work on the security related issues before the database can be made available to the public. The default installation of MySQL may have some security vulnerabilities if not modified. For example, the following are some potential problems if:

- The default database administrator account is left unchanged.
- The MySQL process is shared with other processes running on the host Linux operating system.
- The remote access is not modified to have data encryption protection.
- The anonymous user accounts are not disabled.
- The sample databases are left running on MySQL.

Database Service Isolation

To improve security, the chroot utility is used to isolate the database service from other processes. The following are some possible measures used to strengthen MySQL's security.

1. To make sure that MySQL is handled by a group of trusted users, the system administrator should created a user group and assign the database administrator accounts to this group with adequate privileges.
2. The MySQL installation process can be configured so that it is ready for creating MySQL the database administrator accounts. For example, compile the MySQL installation file with configurations, such as specifying the path to the working directory and the temporary directory, setting the privileges to run the MySQL daemon, and setting the parameter --with-mysqld-ldflags = -all-static which specifies that MySQL is linked statically.

3. After the compilation, set the chroot environment by creating directories corresponding to the root directories such as /dev, /etc, /tem, /usr, /libexec, /httpd and so on, in the chroot directory such as /chroot/mysql/.
4. Install MySQL in the working directory, for example, /usr/local/mysql. Copy the installation files from the working directory such as /usr/local/mysql to the chroot directory /chroot/mysql/usr/local/mysql.
5. To remove the default accounts, edit the file /chroot/mysql/etc/group to remove all the default account except the group users created in step 1.
6. During normal operation, to dispose of unwanted output streams of a process, you need a device file /dev/null to discard all the data written to it. Create the file /dev/null with the command mknod in the directory /chroot/httpd.

Security for Remote Access

First, you need to disable other remote access services such as Telnet and the default database remote access service. The technology SSH can be used to enhance the security of remote access. SSH can hide the information carried by a packet to protect it from hackers. The following are the steps to set up the SSH service.

1. Download and install the SSH server and client package on the server machine.
2. Test the SSH server on server machine.
3. Install the SSH client package on a client machine and test the connection to the SSH server.
4. Use the network monitoring utility to capture the network traffic and verify that the data are encrypted and hidden from hackers.

Database Administrator Accounts

After MySQL is installed, the default user names and passwords should be changed immediately. By default, there is no password for the database administrator account. In the command terminal, you can use the mysqladmin password command to change the passwords. The default account name for the database administrator is root. It should be changed so that it is harder for hackers to penetrate the database system with the brute-force method.

Anonymous User Account

To improve database security, the anonymous user account should be removed from MySQL. After you log on to MySQL, use the command DELETE to delete the anonymous user account and then flush the privileges to remove the privileges assigned to the anonymous user account.

Sample Databases

For security reasons, the sample databases installed with MySQL should also be removed. The command DROP DATABASE can be used to accomplish this task.

After performing the above tasks, MySQL is now much secure. Depending on the usage of MySQL, many other security measures can also be added.

In the above, two simple examples have been to illustrate the security configuration on Linux. The complete converge of Linux operating system management is beyond the scope of this book. Interested readers can find more detailed information in any of the books about Linux security, such as the book by Barrett, Silverman, and Byrnes (2003).

CONCLUSION

In this chapter, we have discussed the issues related to the security management for an online teaching/learning system. To meet the security requirements, we need to first identify the security vulnerabilities in the online teaching/learning system. Two major sources that cause a system to be insecure are hacker attacks and virus infection. This chapter has listed the ways that hackers can attack the online teaching/learning system. It also discussed how different types of viruses can damage the online teaching/learning system. To protect the online teaching/learning system, this chapter suggests that a team including users, developers, and administrators should develop a well defined security policy. The security policy must address the issues related to system confidentiality, integrity, and availability. The implementation of the security policy often requires the assistance of security management tools. There are hundreds of such tools available. This chapter focuses on the open source and free tools and categorizes these tools into different categories. Several products in each category have been used to illustrate that these open source and free security management tools are adequate for handling the tasks of identifying security vulnerabilities and enforcing security measures. Through two examples, this chapter showed that the built-in security management tools in the Linux operating system can also accomplish security management tasks.

So far, we have discussed most of the components in the client-server system which supports the online teaching/learning system. There is one component that has not been discussed. It is the client component, which is also called the front-end of the client-server system. The next chapter is devoted to the discussion of the client component.

REFERENCES

Alwil. (2007). *Avast! Antivirus v4.7.* Retrieved December 27, 2007, from http://www.avast.com/index.html

Avira. (2007). *Ariva.* Retrieved December 27, 2007, from http://www.avira.com/en/pages/index.php

Barrett, D. J., Silverman, R. E., & Byrnes, R. G. (2003). *Linux Security Cookbook.* Sebastopol, CA: O'Reilly Media, Inc.

ClamAV. (2007). *About ClamAV.* Retrieved December 25, 2007, from http://www.clamav.net

ClamWin. (2007). *About ClamWin Free Antivirus.* Retrieved December 28 2007 from http://www.clamwin.com/content/view/71/1

Comodo. (2007). *Comodo.* Retrieved December 29 2007 from http://www.comodo.com

Dark, M. (2003). Evaluation theory and practice as applied to security education. In C. Ervin & H. Armstrong (Eds.), *Security education and critical infrastructures* (pp. 197-214). Norwell, MA: Kluwer Academic Publishers.

El-Khatib, K., Korba, L., Xu, Y., & Yee, G. (2003). Privacy and security in e-learning. *International Journal of Distance Education, 1*(4), 1-19.

Fung, K. T. (2004). *Network security technologies* (2nd ed.). New York: Auerbach.

Gokhale, A. (2002). *Computer and network security.* In C. Crawford et al. (Eds.), *Proceedings of Society for Information Technology and Teacher Education International Conference 2002* (pp. 2445-2446). Chesapeake, VA: AACE.

Grisoft. (2007). *Tough on viruses and easy on users.* Retrieved December 27, 2007, from http://www.grisoft.com/doc/welcome/us/crp/0

Howlett, T. (2004). *Open source security tools: Practical guide to security pplications, A (Bruce Perens' open source series).* Upper Saddle River, NJ: Prentice Hall PTR.

IPCop. (2007). *IPCop.* Retrieved December 29, 2007, from http://ipcop.org/index.php

Kaeo, M. (2003). *Designing network security* (2nd ed.). Indianapolis, IN: Cisco Press.

MailWasher. (2007). *MailWasher - The reliable free spam blocker*. Retrieved December 29, 2007, from http://www.mailwasher.net

McNab, C. (2004). *Network security assessment: Know your network*. Sebastopol, CA: O'Reilly Media, Inc.

Microsoft. (2007). *Windows Defender*. Retrieved December, 29, 2007 from http://www.microsoft.com/downloads/details.aspx?FamilyId=435BFCE7-DA2B-4A6A-AFA4-F7F14E605A0D&displaylang=en

Mozilla. (2007). *Thunderbird 2*. Retrieved December 29, 2007, from http://www.mozilla.com/en-US/thunderbird

Nikto. (2007). *Submit updates for Nikto databases*. Retrieved December 25, 2007, from http://www.cirt.net/code/nikto.shtml

Nmap. (2007). *Nmap free security scanner*. Retrieved December 25, 2007, from http://insecure.org/nmap

OSSEC. (2007). *About OSSEC*. Retrieved December 29 2007 from http://www.ossec.net/main/about

PC Tools. (2007). *Spyware Doctor*. Retrieved December 29, 2007, from http://www.pctools.com/spyware-doctor

Peltier, T. R. (2004). *Information security policies and procedures: A practitioner's reference* (2nd ed.). New York: Auerbach.

Riola, P. (2006). Wireless security in the classroom. In C. Crawford et al. (Eds.), *Proceedings of Society for Information Technology and Teacher Education International Conference 2006* (pp. 1027-1032). Chesapeake, VA: AACE.

Rootkit Hunter. (2007). *Rootkit Hunter*. Retrieved December 29, 2007, from http://www.rootkit.nl/projects/rootkit_hunter.html

Smith, P. G. (2005). *Linux network security (Administrator's Advantage Series)*. Hingham, MA: Charles River Media.

SpamAssassin. (2007). *The Apache SpamAssassin project*. Retrieved December 29, 2007, from http://spamassassin.apache.org

Sunbelt Software. (2007). *Sunbelt Personal Firewall*. Retrieved December 29, 2007, from http://www.sunbelt-software.com/Home-Home-Office/Sunbelt-Personal-Firewall

Tenable Network Security. (2007). *The network vulnerability scanner.* Retrieved December 25, 2007, from http://www.nessus.org/nessus

Turnbull, J. (2005). *Hardening Linux*. Berkeley, CA: Apress.

WebHosting.Info (2005). *McAfee unveils new open source tool for Web security.* Retrieved December 28, 2007, from http://www.webhosting.info/news/1/mcafee-unveils-new-open-source-tool-for-web-security_0711056156.htm

Weippl, E. (2004). Improving security in mobile e-learning. In L. Cantoni & C. McLoughlin (Eds.), *Proceedings of World Conference on Educational Multimedia, Hypermedia and Telecommunications 2004* (pp. 209-216). Chesapeake, VA: AACE.

Weippl, E. (2005). *Security in e-learning (Advances in Information Security).* New York: Springer.

Yang, D., & Dark, M. (2005). A service learning project of information security risk assessment for K12 school corporations. In C. Crawford et al. (Eds.), *Proceedings of Society for Information Technology and Teacher Education International Conference 2005* (pp. 1672-1677). Chesapeake, VA: AACE.

Chapter IX
Client Computer System and Remote Access

INTRODUCTION

An online teaching/learning system is often constructed on the Web-based client-server architecture. Personal computers at students' homes perform client-side operations. These computer systems share some computation load and should be properly configured so that they can remotely access the servers through the Internet. For the online teaching/learning system, the configuration and management of the client computers present many challenges due the variety of computer types and application software. In this chapter, we will examine various challenges on the client side and look for solutions that can be implemented with open source products.

This chapter begins with the discussion of the Linux open source desktop operating systems. Linux originally created for personal computers is suitable for personal computers and workstations. We will discuss several major Linux desktop operating systems and look at the components included in them.

A desktop environment is software that runs on the computer systems and handheld devices on the client side. In this chapter, information will be given about the open source desktop environment and how to configure the desktop environment to meet the requirements of the online teaching/learning system. Our focus will be on the desktop environment that can be hosted by Linux which is a widely used operating system and is a great choice as the open source solution for supporting the client-side computation needs.

An operating system often includes various desktop application tools for tasks such as handling office applications, multimedia presentations, service management, device management, network configuration, display configuration, file transfer, and so on. This chapter will introduce some of the open source desktop management tools for handling tasks that are often performed on the online teaching/learning system.

For the online teaching/learning system, remote access must be set properly from the client computers at students' homes to the servers on campus through the Internet. In this chapter, we will investigate various ways of providing remote access services and configuring them on the client side. We will also discuss troubleshooting procedures for the Internet remote access.

The last part of this chapter will present examples to illustrate how to configure and test the Internet connection and remote access services on the Linux operating system. It will demonstrate how to use the tools provided by the Linux operating system to accomplish these tasks.

BACKGROUND

Most of the studies related to e-learning are conducted on the client side. Therefore, we can find a large number of publications that deal with the client-side technologies used in Web-based teaching and learning. Hicken (2000) investigated various needs for Web-based applications. He pointed out that different Web access technologies are used for different needs. He explored possible Web access options for various client-side instruments such as desktop computers, hand-held devices, and wireless equipment. He also mentioned the difficulties in developing Web-based applications to meet various needs. Hicken (2000) also discussed some issues related to the development process such as quality control. For the topic related to remote access, Esche (2002) summarized various remote access tools for a remote experiment in engineering education.

Desktop video conferencing can be used to accomplish many tasks in teaching, learning, and class management. Westhoff (2005) reported that the desktop video conferencing technology had been used for the management of the pre-service teacher education classes. The technology was used for the instructor to keep in touch with the students and monitor the students' teaching activities in the classroom. Geibel (1999) conducted a study on teaching and learning in the computer labs and the desktop environment. He presented several solutions with products such as Novell, Microsoft, IBM, and Apple, Sassafras, and Pharos. He also gave an overview of assessment procedures and evaluation technologies.

There are various types of computer systems on the client side. Some of the computers run on commercial operating systems and others run on open source operating systems. The application software installed on these computer systems is usually very different. For the management of the Windows operating system, readers may find the book by Bott, Siechert, and Stinson (2007) informative. The book covers the latest Windows operating system, Windows Vista as well as the application software such as Microsoft Windows Media Player and Microsoft Internet Explorer 7. It includes hundreds of quick solutions, flexible workaround tips, and troubleshooting instructions. The book is well written and easy to follow. It is suitable for students who do not have much system administration experience.

Equivalently, the book by Petreley and Bacon (2005) provides many helpful tips about Linux desktop management. The book covers the two commonly used desktop management systems KDE and GNOME. It demonstrates how to customize the desktop GUI, remote access, Internet connection, print service, e-mail, and boot process to best fit the user's needs.

For a more general approach, the book by Horton and Horton (2003) is not about any specific operating system. Instead, it covers topics such as how to identify the hardware and software needs on the client side. It shows how the learning tools can be used to improve Web-based learning. It discusses the issues related to the installation and configuration of client-side hardware devices and application software. The book also discusses various remote access technologies.

For the online teaching/learning system, remotely accessing the servers located on campus always needs the attention of the students, faculty members, and computer service department. It is critical to keep the remote access service running smoothly. It is also important to make sure that the students are well informed on how to configure their home computers so that they are able to connect to the remote servers through the Internet.

There are several remote access schemes to choose. The Virtual Private Network (VPN) is one of the commonly used technologies that can provide remote access. Snader's (2005) book discusses how the VPN works and how to create a safe and effective VPN service by using the tunneling, authentication, and encryption technologies. For readers who want to know how to set up wireless based VPN services, they may find the book by Shneyderman and Casati (2002) helpful. The book provides information about the mobile VPN technologies and provides the tutorial on developing VPNs in various environments. Through the examples, the book also gives many hands-on tips for creating secure and effective wireless VPN services.

For the more comprehensive coverage of remote access, readers can take a look at the book edited by Kasacavage (2002). This book is helpful for network administrators and IT professionals who are trying to establish secure and efficient remote access services. It examines the necessary remote access needs and provides solutions to meet the needs. It covers technologies and skills on developing remote access services for different platforms.

In this chapter, we will focus on the topics related to desktop management on the client side, including remote access setup on the client side. In particular, we will discuss in detail about the open source desktop management and remote access tools as well as the desktop management for the Linux operating system.

LINUX DESKTOP OPERATING SYSTEM

Linux and other open source operating systems play an important role in personal computers on the client side of an online teaching/learning system. Although many people may assume that Linux is mainly a server operating system, it is actually widely used on personal computers as a desktop operating system. As an operating system for personal computers or some call it a desktop operating system, Linux is often used on the computers in computer labs, offices, or at students' homes. The usage of Linux as the desktop operating system has topped that of Linux as the server operating system. According to DesktopLinux.com's survey in 2007 (Vaughan-Nichols, 2007), 64 percent of Linux desktop operating systems were used on client computer systems and the rest of them were used on workstations and developers' desktop computers. This indicates that the Linux operating system is easy enough to be used by students at home.

In the online teaching/learning system, the requirements for the desktop operating system are related to the desktop environment, Internet connection, e-mail client management, Web surfing, multimedia tools, application development, office application software, and remote access. Many of the open source operating systems can meet these requirements. In particular, since Linux was originally created for personal computers, it can best meet the requirements.

Sometimes, the Linux personal computer operating system is called Linux workstation operating system or Linux desktop operating system. It supports various desktop environments that allow users to handle daily computing tasks such as file management, window management, searching, printing, plug-and-play support, wireless network configuration, laptop enablement, gaming, networking, and using multimedia devices. The Linux personal computer operating system often provides the following functionalities for daily computing activities.

- **Desktop environment:** Usually, each Linux operating system includes several desktop environments for file management and window management. The popular desktop environment such as KDE or GNOME is commonly used as the default desktop environment by various Linux distributions.
- **Multimedia:** The Linux desktop operating system supports various audio and video technologies such as the streaming protocol, multimedia editing

toolkit, drawing toolkit, MPEG video, MP3 audio, DVD player, and so on.

- **Print service:** The print service on a Linux personal computer can be used to set up print options, detect and add network based printers, search for printer drivers, and update the drivers.
- **Wireless support:** Various wireless devices are supported by the Linux operating system. Linux supports a full range of wireless chipsets with various capabilities.
- **Device drivers:** Linux supports a broad range of drivers for network devices, audio and video devices, plug-and-play, boot process, wireless connection, notebook enhancement equipment, and so on. Linux with all major hardware original equipment manufacturers (OEMs) makes sure that these OEMs' hardware can work properly on Linux. All major semiconductor manufacturers such as Intel and AMD verify that their system BIOSs work across the board with Linux on client machines.
- **Graphics:** Linux provides graphic enhancement technologies to support two-dimensional and 3-dimentional graphic features. These technologies can be used to accelerate the performance in window switching, viewing, and zooming. They can deliver three-dimensional graphics and support features such as window translucency and multiple desktops.

Today's Linux desktop operating system is rich not only in desktop management functionalities, but also enhanced with many open source application programs. Many of application software packages have been distributed with Linux. The following are some of them:

- **Firefox:** Firefox is a popular free Web browser created by Mozilla. Firefox supports various desktop operating systems such as Linux, Microsoft Windows, and Mac OS X. Some great features are included in Firefox such as spell checker, download manager, incremental find, tabbed browsing, live bookmarking, and Google search engine. In addition to these features, Firefox also includes over 2000 add-ons such as Adblock Plus for blocking adware, DownThemAll for download management, FoxyTunes for music player management, and Web Developer. Since its first release in 2004, Firefox has taken over 16 percent of the browser market share.
- **Flash Player:** Flash Player is a widely used multimedia player created and distributed by Adobe. The Linux version of Flash is a major addition to the Linux desktop operating system. With Flash, users can develop Flash-based Web sites.
- **RealPlayer®:** RealPlayer is a media player that can work on a number of multimedia formats such as MP3, MPEG-4, QuickTime, and so on. The recently

upgraded RealPlayer for the Linux desktop operating system also supports the Windows Media formats and the Banshee music player which can be used for encoding and decoding various music formats. Banshee can also play, import and burn audio CDs.

- **Beagle:** Beagle is a system search tool for Linux. With Beagle, users can search documents, chat logs, e-mail and contact lists, Web history, source code, music files, and images. The newer version of Beagle can conduct search in multiple domains. Beagle is also a desktop management tool that can index and search personal information.
- **OpenOffice.org:** OpenOffice.org is a suite of office application software. It supports many different operating systems including Linux, Solaris, Windows, and so on.
- **Lotus Notes:** Lotus Notes application software is produced by IBM. It is used to view, edit and print notes. It is also used for planning monthly reports, editing reports, and tracking social contracts. IBM fully supports Lotus Notes for Linux.
- **Linux Terminal Server Project (LTSP):** LTSP allows many thin client terminals to simultaneously access a server. A thin client terminal displays and handles the input and output of application software on the server.
- **Mono:** Supported by Novell, Mono is a project that implements the .NET framework on Linux. Mono provides .NET compatible tools such as the C# compiler and Common Language Runtime. Mono can be used to create cross-platform application software.

With these attractive features and added application software, the Linux desktop operating system has been accepted by many personal computer manufacturers such as Dell, HP, and Lenovo. As the demand for the Linux desktop operating system keeps growing, these companies pre-install the Linux desktop operating system on some of their new personal computers.

There are some popular distributions of the Linux operating system designed for personal computers. The following describes these distributions.

Ubuntu Linux

Ubuntu (2007) is a Linux distribution mainly for desktop-oriented operating systems. The goal of Ubuntu is to make it an easy-to-use, free, and versatile Linux operating system. Ubuntu is regularly updated every six months with 100 percent free software. Ubuntu is specially designed to best fit in different desktop environments. For example, Kubuntu is designed for the KDE desktop environment, Xubuntu is for the Xfce desktop environment, and Eubuntu is for the school environment. The analysis of DesktopLinux.com's survey (Vaughan-Nichols, 2007) shows that the Ubuntu family was number one in the year 2007; it took up 30 percent of the Linux desktop operating system share. For personal use, Ubuntu's share is even higher in the year 2008; it is more than 55 percent of the Linux desktop operating system share. Its popularity is due to the following factors:

- **Usability:** Ubuntu includes various tools for desktop management. For the convenience of users, Ubuntu allows them to integrate e-mail, searching, and calendaring. Ubuntu provides the latest Web browsing technologies such as inline spell check support in Web forms, built in phishing detectors, and enhanced search engine management. Ubuntu is also great for dealing with multimedia materials. For example, the photo editing tool F-Spot supports 16 commonly used file types and enables users to import photos from various devices such as a hard drive, camera, or iPod. Ubuntu provides a comprehensive media player to run audio and video files. In addition, Ubuntu also provides sophisticated system administration tools such as sudo for system administration, the Ubiquity installer for live hard disk installation without restarting the computer. The Ubuntu installation program supports migration from Windows. The desktop components for the Windows operating system such as bookmarks, settings, and wallpapers can be imported into Ubuntu for immediate use. Users can also install Ubuntu on a Windows partition and import Windows users' configurations into Ubuntu.
- **Accessibility:** Accessibility and internationalization are also the advantages of Ubuntu. It is easy to edit and share files in other formats including Microsoft Office, Word Perfect, KOffice or StarOffice. It is a great feature for the online teaching/learning system due to the software and hardware variation of the client side. Ubuntu supports speech and Braille output functionalities for blind people, and provides a screen reader and magnifier tool called Orca which can be used by users with limited vision or no vision to operate the programs on Ubuntu's desktop. Ubuntu provides an on screen keyboard and allows users to customize the keyboard and mouse. It can even stick the modifier keys such as Shift, Ctrl and Alt so that the tasks such as writing upper case words can be made easy. Ubuntu aims to be usable by as many people as possible and therefore it supports over 40 languages.
- **Application software:** Ubuntu provides a variety of application software. It has a complete office productivity suite, OpenOffice.org. Converting various documents to pdf files on Ubuntu is just one click away. It includes the popular Web browser Firefox for Web surfing. It also includes the instant messenger Pidgin and the graphic editor GIMP.

- **Lightweight:** Ubuntu is a lightweight operating system. All the application and system files can fit into a single CD. It is a live CD that does not require the hard disk to function and only requires 256MB memory to run the operating system. If users want to install Ubuntu to hard disks, the live CD will check if the hardware is compatible with Ubuntu and the installation only needs 4GB hard disk storage space. This feature is particularly good for those students who have low-end computer systems.

The above features make Ubuntu a very popular desktop operating system. Many personal computer manufacturers have been offered Ubuntu to be installed on the desktop and laptop computers. These manufacturers also provide technical support of Ubuntu for their customers.

SUSE Linux

SUSE is another major Linux distribution and is a founding member of the Desktop Linux Consortium. SUSE is owned by Novell (2007) which is a well known network software company. The open source version of SUSE Linux, openSUSE is a desktop operating system. SUSE Linux Enterprise Desktop (SLED) is a commercial desktop operating system. According to Vaughan-Nichols (2007), the SUSE Linux family took up 21 percent of the Linux desktop operating system share in 2007, which was only behind the ever-popular Ubuntu family. openSUSE is the most distributed operating system in the SUSE Linux family. The following are some of the features provided by SUSE Linux:

- SUSE Linux allows users to select a desktop environment from several options such as KDE or GNOME.
- SUSE Linux includes application software such as OpenOffice.org. The Novell version of OpenOffice.org is compatible with many other document formats such as Microsoft Office and Adobe PDF.
- SUSE Linux is bundled with several multimedia software packages. It has K3b for CD/DVD burning, Amarok for audio playback, Kaffeine for movie playback, and RealPlayer.
- SUSE Linux can co-exist with Windows operating systems. The SUZE Linux desktop operating system can connect seamlessly to many collaboration services such as Microsoft Active Directory, Novell GroupWise, Lotus Domino, and Microsoft Exchange servers.
- SUSE Linux comes with the security management software AppArmor which protects applications and the operating system from hackers' attacks, virus infection and other security threats.

- SUSE Linux has Xgl which provides a 3-D graphical desktop environment.
- SUSE Linux includes the Beagle integrated desktop search tool which can search keywords in documents, application files, e-mail, recent Web pages, and so on.

The above features demonstrate that SUSE Linux is a good choice for handling computing tasks in an enterprise-level environment which consists of various applications and operating systems. SUSE Linux provides an open source platform that can interoperate with other products such as Microsoft Windows and Microsoft Office. This is why many global companies such as Wal-Mart, BMW, and Casio use SUSE Linux as their Linux solution. For the online teaching/learning system, SUSE Linux is also a good choice for both desktop and server computer systems.

Debian

Debian (2007) is another major Linux operating system. Its main form is the influential open source Debian GNU/Linux. Based on Debian GNU/Linux, many other forms of Linux operating systems have been developed including Freespire, Linspire, Linux Mint, MEPIS, Xandros, as well as the popular Ubuntu. Not including Ubuntu, the other forms of Debian took up 14 percent of the Linux desktop operating system share in 2007 (Vaughan-Nichols, 2007). The following are some of the features that make Debian GNU/Linux a special Linux operating system:

- **All-in-one operating system:** Debian GNULinux is an operating system that can handle the tasks on both the client side and the server side. Unlike other Linux distributions that may have workstation, personal, and server editions or open source and commercial editions, Debian GNU/Linux covers all editions in one package and it is 100 percent free.
- **Application software:** Debian GUN/Linux is well known for its coverage of a wide range of free application software. It comes with 18733 precompiled application software packages. It takes three DVDs to store the packages. These packages are bundled up according to their dependencies for easy installation. With the inclusion of these application software packages, Debian GUN/Linux provides a variety of choices for users to accomplish their tasks ranging from office management, security management, system administration, to application software development. Additionally, these software packages can run on eleven different computer architectures including the x86 architecture and various mainframe architectures such as IBM zSeries.
- **Stability and reliability:** Debian GUN/Linux has a rigorous release cycle which follows strict policies regarding its packages, stability, and the quality

of its releases. When Debian GNU/Linux is used as a server operating system, it is so stable that it may not need to be rebooted for years.

- **Easy maintenance:** With its integrated package management system, users can easily upgrade, install and remove packages in between major releases. The package management system can help maintain dependent packages automatically so that it can eliminate orphan files and incompatible products while updating the system. The entire Debian Linux operating system can be updated over the Internet by executing a single command. System administrators can even use a scheduler to schedule a routine update automatically with the latest programs, tools, and security patches.
- **Modest requirement:** Debian GNU/Linux requires modest computing resources. It does not require faster and bigger computer hardware such as the CPU, RAM, video card, hard disk, and so on. Debian GNU/Linux can be installed on many of the surplus computers. A Pentium-III personal computer with 128 MB RAM and a 4GB hard disk will be sufficient enough to load the Debian package. One of the great features of Debian is that one operating system can be run on several computers.
- **Flexible desktop environment:** Debian GNU/Linux 2.0 allows users to select their favorite desktop environments. It provides nearly all available window managers including KDE, GNOME, Window Maker, and so on.

Due to the fact that Debian is an all-in-one operating system, using Debian in the online teaching/learning system can significantly reduce the system management workload. If both the client and server computer systems are using the same operating system, it will be much easier to perform the tasks such as system configuration, software updating, technical support, and troubleshooting.

As far as the GUI is concerned, the Ubuntu Linux has the edge. The graphical user interface built on Ubuntu Linux is stable and has good performance. Many tools included in the graphical user interface are easy to use. Adding new tools to the GUI can also be easily done. Many of the new Linux users start with Ubuntu Linux.

OPEN SOURCE DESKTOP ENVIRONMENT

The desktop environment included in the Linux desktop operating system plays an important role in desktop management. Once a computer system is booted up, the first thing that the user sees is the desktop environment which is a graphical user interface (GUI). The desktop environment usually includes components such as icons, windows, toolbars, folders, and background wallpapers. It usually provides management tools such as the window manager and file manager. It may also provide a set of script libraries and themes to assist the administrator in managing the desktop. In the desktop environment, users can perform activities such as configuring services provided by operating systems, searching directories and files, dragging and dropping objects on desktops, formatting disks, enabling and disabling services, connecting to the Internet, capturing screen images, starting and stopping application software, and so on. The themes and icons of the desktop environment are designed to help users carry out activities easily.

Nowadays, each operating system supports its own desktop environment. Some of the desktop environments are used by commercial operating systems and others are used by open source operating systems. Most of the students' computers are equipped with desktop environments supported by commercial operating systems such as Windows-based operating systems and Mac operating systems. The desktop environments for these operating systems are designed to be used with a dedicated operating system, which means that it is difficult for users to switch from one desktop environment to another desktop environment on these commercial operating systems. There are also many open source desktop environments created for open source operating systems. The commonly used graphic based desktop environments are K Desktop Environment (KDE) and GNU Object Model Environment (GNOME). Unlike the commercial operating systems, the open source operating systems such as Linux often allow you to choose a desktop environment from several options. For example, the user can decide whether to use KDE or GNOME as the desktop environment for his/her Linux operating system.

The first desktop environment was developed by Xerox. Later, Apple developed its desktop environment for Apple personal computers. The first significant open source desktop environment is KDE which was released in 1996. Later, in the year 1997, another major open source desktop environment GNOME was released. Both KDE and GNOME are developed based on the X Window technology, which is a graphics system created on the client-server structure. The X server is a video management program which provides the graphic service. The server concept here is not the same as the server concept in an online teaching/learning system. Actually, the X server is installed on the host computer which can be the user's desktop computer system. The X client is application software used to display the video image. Through a network, the X client can display the video image on another computer on the same network.

The desktop environment based on the X Window technology may include some of the following components. These components can be configured to interact with one another to form a lightweight desktop environment or a full featured desktop environment:

- **File manager:** The file manager handles the management tasks for files and directories. It displays the files and directories in a hierarchical structure so that users can easily locate the files they are looking for. The file manager also handles basic file operations such as searching, viewing, copying, pasting, and deleting files.
- **freedesktop.org (fd.o):** fd.o handles the shared technology and interoperability for desktop environments such as KDE or GNOME.
- **Inter-application interfaces:** These interfaces allow X clients to communicate with each other.
- **Program manager:** It is a program that can display a start up menu which contains a list of application programs. These application programs can be represented by icons and displayed on the desktop. The program manager allows users to select an application program to run or select a specific service to configure.
- **Synergy:** Synergy allows multiple computers with different operating systems to share a mouse and keyboard.
- **Window manager:** The window manager controls the placement and appearance of various application windows. It keeps track of the currently opened windows. It defines what is going to happen after a mouse clicks. It also has the ability to switch between desktop environments with different appearances. The window manager is the most fundamental component of a desktop environment.
- **XD640:** It is a 640x480 lightweight desktop environment and office suite.

A full featured desktop environment may also provide programs to handle the configuration tasks for screensavers, desktop display, wallpapers, document processing, Web browsers, remote access clients, e-mail clients, networks, portable storage devices, and so on. In addition to the well known desktop environments KDE and GNOME, there are other desktop environments available. The following describes some commonly used desktop environments.

GNU Network Object Model Environment (GNOME)

GNOME (2007) is a powerful, easy-to-use, and free desktop environment. It can meet various computing needs such as those listed below:

- **Personal computing needs:** GNOME includes most of the software packages needed for every day personal computing. It has the Web browser, office suite, and so on. It is easy-to-learn and most of the beginners should have no problem using this desktop environment as soon as they log on to their personal computers. GNOME can handle the files created by Microsoft Windows operating systems. This makes GNOME an ideal choice for a network that consists of operating systems from different vendors, which is the case of our online teaching/learning environment. GNOME allows users to choose from dozens of languages for their desktop environments, which is a great feature for a global online teaching/learning system.

- **Application development needs:** GNOME provides a comprehensive and flexible platform for developers to develop application programs. It supports a variety of programming languages such as Java, C#, Python, Perl, C, C++, and GTK+ which is a platform for creating graphical user interfaces (GUIs) on Windows as well as on UNIX and Linux systems.
- **Remote access needs:** GNOME supports the remote access toolkit. Through GNOME, users can remotely access servers so that they can access online teaching materials or perform hands-on practice. In this way, students can perform remote system administration tasks on the computers installed in the online computer lab.

To meet these needs, GNOME also includes many additional packages to further enrich its functionalities. The following describes some of the packages included in the GNOME desktop environment:

- **Text editors:** GNOME includes some text editor programs such as vi and gedit. gedit is a text editor of the GNOME desktop environment. It can be used to process text with activities such as cut, copy, paste, search, replace, undo, and so on. It is a convenient tool to edit configuration files. It is easier to learn how to use gedit than to use the old-fashioned vi editor, especially, for students who are used to Microsoft Windows operating systems.
- **Desktop management tools:** Several desktop management tools are provided by GNOME. gnome-panel is an important component of the default GNOME desktop. It includes a configurable launcher and taskbar. gnome-screensaver is the official screensaver configuration program provided by GNOME. Alacarte is a menu editor program used for the GNOME desktop. GDM is a display configuration tool that allows users to customize display settings and troubleshoot for the settings. grecord is an application program used for recording sound. GNOME includes several tools for CD/DVD management such as gnome-cd used as an audio CD player, nautilus-cd-burner used as a data CD burner tool, and Sound Juicer used to extract audio from a CD and then convert it into audio files. gnome-screenshot is a tool used to take screenshots.

- **System management tools:** GNOME includes the graphical tool Baobab for disk-space analysis. Gconf-editor allows developers to debug applications and edit hidden and complex settings. GNOME Keyring is a security management tool which verifies the user's name and password. GNOME System Monitor is a tool that is used to monitor the system process and resource. GST is a set of Linux configuration programs used for the configuration of the network, disk, time, run level, and boot loader. GNOME Terminal is a terminal emulator used to execute commands.
- **File management tools:** Nautilus is the default GNOME file manager. In addition, it is also a Web browser and an FTP client. It can also be used to customize GNOME. File Roller is an archive manager which can be used to create, view, and modify archived files. GNOME Search Tool is a file searching tool. Evince is a versatile document viewer for PDF and PostScript documents. Eye of GNOME is an image viewer which can zoom and rotate images, and make background transparent. logview is a log file viewer. Tomboy is a tool that serves as a note-taking manager. It can be used to link personal notes together.
- **Internet tools:** Epiphany is a Web browser included in GNOME. Epiphany supports many advanced features such as tabbed browsing, cookie management, popup blocking, and so on. Ekiga is a VoIP and video conferencing application for GNOME. Many of the high-quality audio and video compression-decompression algorithms are supported by Ekiga.

For the convenience of users, GNOME is designed to help them quickly search files and find application programs. It has a taskbar that displays icons for currently used programs and displays the notification area for background programs to post notices. It is easy to configure the appearance of GNOME with different themes, icons, fonts, and screensavers.

According to Vaughan-Nichols (2007), GNOME is the most used desktop environment installed on Linux in 2007. It took up 45 percent of the free desktop environment market share. Because of its popularity, GNOME is the default desktop environment for several major Linux distributions such as Debian, Fedora, Ubuntu, and SUSE.

K Desktop Environment (KDE)

KDE (2007) is a free, full-featured, and easy-to-use desktop environment. It is designed to handle daily desktop management tasks. It provides various desktop management tools as well as tools for developing desktop management scripts. KDE also serves as the platform for other desktop application software such as KOffice, KDevelop, and so on. KDE was originated by Matthias Ettrich in 1996. That time, Matthias Ettrich was a student at the Eberhard Karls University of Tübingen. The current version of KDE is KDE 4. KDE is supported by a large KDE user and developer community as well as companies such as Novell and IBM. By accepting the freedesktop.org standard, KDE can work with applications from other desktop environments. According to KDE (2007), the KDE desktop environment has the following features:

- KDE provides a management tool called Konqueror which can be used as a Web browser, file manager, or document viewer. Konqueror supports various programming languages and security protocols such as XHTML, Java, and SSL.
- KDE includes a user friendly personal communication suite called Kontact which is a combination of KMail, KOrganizer, KAddressBook, KNotes, KSnapshot, KD3 Burner, and so on.
- KDE has an integrated office suite called KOffice which is a combination of several packages such as KWord, KSpread, KPresenter, Karbon for vector drawing, a database front-end Kexi, and so on.
- KDE offers a development environment called KDevelop which can be used to seamlessly integrate various development tools and programming platforms. It also offers other development tools such as KParts as a high-performance development framework, DCOP for communication between processes, a native I/O framework, an XML-based GUI, and KConfigXT as a programming interface.

These features make KDE a versatile and easy-to-use desktop environment. With KDE, some of the desktop management tasks such as configuring wireless security, customizing desktop display, adding and configuring network printers can be easily carried out. According to Vaughan-Nichols (2007), KDE was the second most used desktop environment by Linux in 2007.

In general, UNIX based operating systems are a bit less user friendly than the operating systems of the commercial vendors Macintosh and Microsoft. This disadvantage has kept UNIX based operating systems from being very popular for the computers used on the client side. The easy-to-use KDE desktop environment will change people's view about the Linux operating system. KDE will find its way to reach out to more users who work on the computers at home and in offices.

Xfce

Xfce (2007) is another free desktop environment for UNIX and UNIX-like platforms such as Linux, Solaris and BSD. Vaughan-Nichols (2007) indicated that Xfce took the third spot after GNOME and KDE in 2007. Xfce is best known as a lightweight desktop environment. It takes less memory and other system resources, and it loads and executes application programs fast. By combining several desktop management components, it is a fully functioning desktop environment. It allows the user to pick a component from the available ones to create a desktop environment that best fits the user's requirements. The following gives a brief description of the components in Xfce:

- **Window manager:** Xfce provides a window manager that can be used to specify the application windows in a multiscreen mode, format desktop display, and manage workplaces. The configuration tasks can be done in a dialog box. The user can edit keyboard shortcuts with the keyboard shortcut editor provided by the Xfce window manager. The window manager also supports features such as transparencies and shadows.
- **File manager:** Xfce provides a file manager called Thunar, which is an efficient and easy-to-use file manager that can be used to search, copy, paste, delete, and print files. In addition, it allows users to rename multiple files at once with specified characteristics. It can even automatically generate new file names for audio files based on the files' tags. It has a fast response time and directory load time.
- **Menu configuration:** Xfce provides menus, applets and application launchers to assist configuration. Via a mouse, Xfce can be fully configured by selecting, dragging and dropping the graphical elements.
- **Application software:** Several commonly used applications are included in Xfce. For example, Xfce has a terminal emulator with tabs, an iCal based calendar, and a mixer to control the volume. Other application software may include the text editor Mousepad, the audio player Xfmedia, the print manager Xfprint, and the CD/DVD burner Xfburn.
- **Multimedia tools:** As a desktop environment, Xfce includes various multimedia tools such as the sound manager, the clock, pixmaps, backgrounds, icons, and so on.
- **Session manager:** The session manager provided by Xfce can be used to start up and shut down functionalities.
- **Settings manager:** Xfce has a settings manager which can be used to configure global Xfce components and general items.

As a lightweight desktop environment, Xfce is suitable for front-end personal computers with low computing power. Its simplicity, efficiency, and similarity to many commercial UNIX desktop environments make it a perfect choice for the online teaching/learning system powered by a version of UNIX.

OPEN SOURCE DESKTOP APPLICATION SOFTWARE

As described above, both the desktop operating system and its desktop environment provide some desktop application tools. There are also many open source comprehensive desktop applications available. Choosing the right application software for desktop management will depend on the factors such as the user's experience of using certain management tools, the flexibility, availability, and usability of the tools, the ease-of-use feature and the look and feel of the GUI environment.

In the online teaching/learning system, running the applications on the client side can improve performance since the workload is distributed to individual client computers. The open source application software can be freely downloaded. It will not add additional cost to students. Running software on a local computer does not generate network traffic. It is convenient for students to run application software on their home computers. Based on the course requirements, students can add or remove the application software as they need.

The following will categorize these open source application software packages by their functionalities and provide information about how to use these application software packages on the client side of the online teaching/learning system. The desktop application software can be organized into six categories shown below.

Office Application Software

Office application software deals with word processing, spreadsheets, presentations, personal databases, graphic editors, math equation editors, and macro toolkits. Almost every Linux desktop operating system includes open source office application software. Often, an office application software suite bundles several office software packages together to deal with multiple office tasks. In addition to the tasks mentioned above, some of the office suites may also include an email client and a groupware package for personal communication. There are many open source and free application suites available including the well-known OpenOffice.org, StarOffice, Koffice, and NeoOffice. The following are the descriptions of these office suites.

- **StarOffice:** Although StarOffice developed by Sun Microsystems (2007) is not completely free for business use, it is the basis of the open source product OpenOffice.org. It includes full-powered word processing, spreadsheet, presentation, drawing, and database capabilities. StarOffice can run on Linux, Windows, and Solaris operating systems. It supports the Microsoft Office formats and allows users to edit and save Microsoft Office files. It adopts the OpenDocument format for global compatibility, and it can convert various documents into pdf files.
- **OpenOffice.org:** OpenOffice.org (2007) is a StarOffice-based open source office application suite. It supports the OpenDucument standard for global compatibility and interchanges data with Microsoft Office. OpenOffice.org is supported by many different operating systems such as Microsoft Windows, Linux, Solaris, BSD, OpenVMS, OS/2 and IRIX. It can handle most of the office tasks. It has a component called Writer which is similar to Microsoft Word. OpenOffice.org includes spreadsheet application software which is similar to Microsoft Excel. In addition, it can automatically define a series for graphing and save spreadsheet directly as pdf files. Similar to Microsoft PowerPoint, OpenOffice.org provides a presentation component called Impress. With Impress, presentations can be saved into Adobe Flash or pdf files. For processing data, OpenOffice.org includes a database application software call Base which is similar to Microsoft Access. Like Access, Base can be used as front-end application software of other database systems including MySQL, PostgreSQL, and even Microsoft Access. OpenOffice.org has a graphics editor called Draw. In addition to the graphics editing functionalities, Draw also has the desktop publishing functionality similar to that of Microsoft Publisher. Math is a tool included in OpenOffice.org for editing mathematic formulas embedded inside other documents.
- **KOffice:** The KOffice (2007) office suite is an open source product by KDE. The newest version of KOffice can be run on Linux, various versions of UNIX, Windows, and Mac OS X. KOffice also supports OpenDocument for wide-range compatibility. KOffice provides several components to handle office related tasks. It has a word processor called KWord which is a frame based application. It is relatively easy to handle a complex graphical layout with KWord. The spreadsheet application included in KOffice is called KSpread. KSpread supports multiple sheets, templates, charts, spell-check, hyperlinks, data sorting, and supports scripting languages such as Python, Ruby and JavaScript, and built-in mathematic formulas, and so on. The presentation component in KOffice is called KPresenter. KPresenter is XML based software, and it can input presentations in various formats including Microsoft PowerPoint, MagicPoint, and OpenOffice.org Impress. Karbon14 is a vector drawing ap-

plication provided by KOffice. It includes a variety of drawing and editing tools. Krita is a bitmap graphics manipulation program for image processing. Similar to Microsoft Access, Kexi is a data management component included in KOffice. Kugar is a report development tool. KFormula is a KOffice tool for editing mathematic formulas. KChart is a chart creation tool supported by KOffice. It can be used to create graphs for KWord and KSpread.

- **NeoOffice:** NeoOffice (2007) is a version of OpenOffice.org specially adapted to Mac OS X. It has office application components including a word processor, spreadsheet, presentation, and graphics. It integrates OpenOffice.org with the Aqua interface of Mac OS X. NeoOffice is also compatible with Microsoft Office. It can import, edit, and save Microsoft Office Word documents, Excel documents, and PowerPoint documents. NeoOffice also supports Microsoft Excel Visual Basic for developing application macros.

The office suites introduced above should be enough to take care of the requirements by various computer systems on the client side. Any of these office suites have enough functionality to handle the daily office computation tasks. These open source office suites can exchange files with commercial office products such as Microsoft Office. All these features make the open source office suites a valuable alternative solution for handling office computation with no additional cost.

Both StarOffice and NeoOffice are based on OpenOffice. They are more or less the same. Both OpenOffice and KOffice are sophisticated office suite products. KOffice is less compatible with the proprietary office suite Microsoft Office which has the largest market share in the office suite market. If KOffice is not already pre-installed with the Linux operating system, one may consider downloading and installing OpenOffice for better compatibility.

Application Development Software

In the online teaching/learning system, many computer science and information systems related courses require students to work on programming related projects and develop various applications. As an open source solution, we can find that most of the open source desktop operating systems support C or C++ programming language for developing applications. In addition, users can download and install Java based application development software. For Web development, users can find open source scripting languages such as PHP, JavaScript, and Perl. In the following, we will briefly go over the components in the Java package and some scripting languages:

- **Java 2 Platform Standard Edition (J2SE):** J2SE is a package used to create, edit, and debug Java code. With J2SE, students can work on their programming assignments and projects. Developers use J2SE to create application software to implement business computation logics and graphical user interfaces (GUIs). J2SE is supported by all kinds of operating systems including Linux, Solaris, Widows, and so on.
- **Java 2 Platform Enterprise Edition (J2EE):** J2EE is a complete Java application development package. In addition to all of the classes in J2SE, J2EE also contains classes that can be used for developing server-side programs. J2EE is often required by courses that need to handle server-side applications such as those multi-tiered and Web-based applications. Courses such as e-commerce application development and Internet computing often require students to develop their projects on the J2EE platform.
- **Java Studio Creator:** This is an integrated development environment (IDE) that is specially designed for developing portals and other Web applications. With Java Studio Creator, students can easily access databases and build streamlined objects for modeling complex business domains, rules, and systems. Java Studio Creator is often required by Web development related courses to develop Web-based solutions.
- **JavaScript:** This scripting language is used for the client-side Web development. It can also create embedded objects for other applications. Like Java, JavaScript is an interpreted language, which makes the JavaScript platform independent. Despite the name, JavaScript is not much related to Java. In fact, JavaScript supports the structured programming syntax in C.
- **PHP:** PHP is a scripting language designed for developing dynamic Web pages. It is a project of the Apache Software Foundation. A Web server such as Apache executes the PHP code and then creates Web pages. The PHP code is often embedded in HTML documents or embedded in client-side GUI applications.
- **Practical Extraction and Reporting Language (Perl):** Perl (2007) is an interpreted general-purpose programming language for Web development, GUI development, system administration, network programming, and so on. Perl has been extensively used to develop high traffic Web sites. One of the features of Perl is that it is able to make portable code across Windows and UNIX. It is also able to link systems and interfaces together even though they are not originally designed to interoperate. Perl has the ability to handle large data sets and can rapidly develop and deploy applications. With these advantages, Perl is widely used in bioinformatics related courses. It is also often chosen to be the programming language for courses related to Internet computing, system development, and network programming. Usually, Perl is

distributed with the Linux operating system. It can also be downloaded from the Web site http://www.perl.com.

- **Python:** Python (2007) is an interpreted, interactive, object-oriented programming language. As an interpreted language, Python is portable across many operating systems such as Linux, Windows, Mac OS X, and various versions of UNIX. Like a scripting language, Python can be embedded in the code generated by other programming languages. Python can be used with 3D animation packages such as Maya for developing games. It is also a choice of programming language in the security industry. Like Perl, Python is often distributed with the Linux operating system as well as other open source operating systems such as FreeBSD, NetBSD, and OpenBSD, and with Mac OS X. Python has been used to develop large projects in YouTube, Google, NASA, and the Air Canada's reservation management system.

PHP, Perl, and Python are known as the three Ps which are the popular packages for developing dynamic Web pages. Together, they form an enterprise-level application development package that can handle all the application development tasks for an online teaching/learning system.

To assist developers in Java projects, various project development tools called integrated development environments (IDEs) have been created for helping developers to develop, tune, debug, and test Java code. The following are some of the commonly used IDEs:

- **BlueJ:** BlueJ is designed for Java programming training. It can also be used as an environment for developing small scale projects. The ease of use is a great advantage of this package. On the other hand, it lacks some components for developing enterprise-level projects.
- **Java Studio Enterprise:** Java Studio Enterprise is an integrated development environment (IDE) used to develop J2EE applications. By using this IDE, students can develop, tune, debug, and test enterprise applications, Web services, portal components, and other J2EE projects.
- **Java Studio Creator:** This IDE is specially designed for developing portals and other Web applications. With Java Studio Creator, students can easily access databases and build streamlined objects for modeling complex business domains, rules, and systems. Java Studio Creator is often required by Web development related courses to develop Web-based solutions.

The use of these IDEs depends on the tasks to be accomplished. For training and developing stand-alone projects, BlueJ can get the job done. For enterprise -level projects, Java Studio Enterprise is the choice. It provides some key components such as Netbeans for developing network based projects. Java Studio Creator will be the choice when a developer is working on Web based applications.

Web and E-Mail Software

The commonly used Web browsers and Web servers are all free. The Linux operating system usually includes this type of software such as the Firefox Web browser and Apache Web server. The Firefox Web browser and Apache Web server were discussed earlier. For email, students can either install the e-mail software Thunderbird for personal e-mail communication or use the Web e-mail such as Gmail or Yahoo Mail.

In the above, we have examined some office application packages, application development tools, and Web and e-mail tools. The multimedia content development tools belong to another other type of application software. These tools will be discussed in the next chapter when we look at the issues related to the development of multimedia course content. Next, we will look at the tools used for remote access.

OPEN SOURCE REMOTE ACCESS TOOLS

In an online teaching/learning system, students need to be able to remotely access servers through the Internet. The commonly used remote access technologies are Virtual Private Network (VPN), Terminal Services, virtual machines, Remote Desktop, and the remote access service provided by application software such as a database management system and a learning management system. The following briefly discuss these remote access technologies and the issues related to client-side configuration:

- **Virtual Private Network (VPN):** A VPN is a commonly used remote access technology utilized to access a university's network. Once students get on the university's network, they will be able to access the servers, network storage devices, computer labs, and other services where they have the permission to access. VPN servers are usually well protected. Therefore, the VPN is a relatively secure remote access method. VPN client software is usually free. Some of the operating systems include the VPN client software. Students can download the VPN software from the vendor's Web site and configure the VPN client on their home computers. After the VPN software is installed, a student can configure the VPN to remotely access the computer lab servers. The open source VPN software OpenVPN is a full-featured SSL VPN solution. OpenVPN is able to accomplish the tasks such as providing the remote access service, setting site-to-site VPNs, enforcing WiFi security, balancing load, managing failover processes, and controlling fine-grained access. If students have Window operating systems on their home computers, they can use the VPN client configuration Wizard to configure their VPN connection. Some of the Linux operating systems also include a graphical tool for VPN client configuration and the others may allow users to configure a VPN with commands.

- **Virtual machine:** A virtual machine is a technology that allows students to securely perform lab activities that require the administrator's privilege. Virtual machines are often installed in a computer lab on campus. The remote access service of a virtual machine allows students to access the virtual machine through the Internet. The virtual machine client software can be downloaded and installed on the students' home computers. The virtual machine client software can be configured to access a specified virtual server. The commonly used virtual machine software packages are Microsoft Virtual Server from Microsoft (2007) and VMware (2007) from EMC. Both of them are free. Xen (2007) virtual machine monitor is an open source virtual machine designed for various computer platforms such as IA-32, x86-64, IA-64 and PowerPC.
- **Remote access to application software:** Many applications such as a database management system (DBMS) or a learning management system (LMS) provide remote access services. The remote access services allow students who have accounts on these applications to remotely access them directly without having user accounts in the host server computer. By doing so, a student can have any type of client computer system at home to access the LMS or DBMS. In an online teaching/learning system, students, instructors, and staff members remotely access the LMS for their daily learning, teaching, and management activities. Properly setting and maintaining the LMS remote access service is crucial for the courses offered online. Normally, the computer service department enables the LMS remote access service, sets up the Web page for remote logon, and manages the accounts of students, faculty, and staff who have the permission to log on to the LMS.

Often, the database administrator needs to remotely access the DBMS for maintenance. Also, many courses in computer science and information systems are involved in database administration and application development based on specific databases. Students are often required to remotely access the databases for their hands on practice. To remotely access a specific DBMS, the students need to download the client software for that DBMS. After the client software is installed and properly configured, the students will be able to access the DBMS for hands-on practice.

EXAMPLE 1: CONFIGURING REMOTE ACCESS ON LINUX OPERATING SYSTEM

Students can remotely access the Linux operating system graphically or through a text-based interface. The text-based remote access is for the students who do not have a high speed Internet connection. In the following, we will consider several commonly used Linux remote access methods.

Secure Shell (SSH)

Through Telnet, one can remotely access a computer system run on the Linux operating system. Telnet is a text-based remote access method. During the data transmission process, the biggest problem is that Telnet carries plain text which can be easily captured by hackers. SSH is a descendent of Telnet and can be used by the user to log on to another computer over the network. After the user logs on to the other computer, he/she can execute commands and manage files. SSH provides strong authentication and secure communication over insecure channels. By using slogin provided by SSH, including password transmission, the content to be transmitted over the network will be encrypted. SSH can also protect the network from hackers' attacks. The following is an example of SSH configuration.

To conduct the experiment, you need at least two computers connected through a network. Make sure that these two computers can ping each other. To examine the effect of SSH, you may need to install a network observation tool such as Ethereal. Usually, SSH is included in the Linux operating system by default. To enable the SSH service, enter the following command:

```
service sshd start
```

To verify that SSH is secure, you can start Ethereal and set it in the capture mode. Suppose that one of the computers on the network has IP 10.1.1.1. Enter the following command from another computer:

```
slogin 10.1.1.1
```

Execute some commands such as entering the command ls to list files in the directory, and then log out. Stop Ethereal and examine the captured content, you will not be able to find any plain text about the user's password, username, and the commands you have just executed.

SSH can also provide graphic based remote access. To do so, you need to install the X-server on the client computer. Usually, the X-server is included in the Linux operating system. For example, the X-server XDMCP is included in the Red Hat Linux operating system.

Desktop Sharing

Both KDE and GNOME desktop environments support desktop sharing. KDE has a desktop sharing tool called kdenetwork which is a graphical tool for both the client and server configuration. GNOME provides a desktop sharing tool called Vino. Once installed and configured, Vino allows users to remotely access the GNOME desktop and perform various tasks. It is very easy to configure Vino. All you need to do is to click Desktop Preferences and Remote Desktop. Then, you can start your configuration by providing the information of the remote host.

In addition to these tools included in the Linux operating system, there are also some third party remote access tools such as RealVNC (2007) and FreeNX (2007). These third party remote access tools are platform independent. They can be used for the Linux operating system, Windows operating system, or the combination of the two.

EXAMPLE 2: SETTING UP BLUEJ FOR JAVA PROGRAMMING TRAINING

As a training tool, BlueJ has been installed in many computer labs to develop Java projects for many courses that use Java as the programming language. To help the user to set up BlueJ on the Linux operating system, you may use the following steps.

1. Make sure that J2SE JDK Version 5.0 or later has been installed on the host computer.
2. Download the BlueJ installation file such as bluej-250.jar from the Web site: http://www.bluej.org/download/download.html
3. Install BlueJ by executing the file bluej-250.jar with the Java installer which is the installation tool built in the JDK package.
4. Change the working directory to the default bluej directory and execute the command ./bluej to start BlueJ.

5. Once BlueJ is started, you may open a sample project to test if the installation is done successfully.

Students, especially those who are new to Java programming, can get a quick start on developing Java projects with the easy-to-use BlueJ. They can greatly benefit from the GUI tools provided by BlueJ to understand the concepts of objected object-oriented programming.

CONCLUSION

This chapter has discussed the issues relate to personal computers on the client side of the online teaching/learning system. Through the discussion of the Linux desktop operating system, we can conclude that the open source desktop operating systems are adequate for handling tasks performed on the client side. The Linux operating system can accomplish the tasks such as desktop management, developing multimedia course content, supporting wireless networks, providing print service, and managing drivers. As one of the major components of the Linux operating system, the desktop environment provides GUIs for file management, window management, and many other tasks. This chapter has shown that the desktop environments such as GNOME and KDE are sophisticated and versatile. These desktop environments should be able to meet the requirements of the online teaching/learning system.

This chapter has investigated the application software often used on the client computers for handling the tasks such as office management and application development. Several major open source office application products such as OpenOffice.org and KOffice were examined in this chapter. These office products are easy to learn and can handle the tasks such as word processing, creating spreadsheets, editing graphics, and presenting documents.

This chapter has shown that the open source office products can exchange files with Microsoft Office. This feature is great for the client side where a variety of office products are used on various platforms.

We must make sure that students can remotely access the servers in the online teaching/learning system. This chapter has concluded that the Linux operating system provides better way for remote access. Linux can support both GUI-based remote access and text-based remote access for the students who do not have a high speed Internet connection. The last part of this chapter is about remote access configuration. By using the examples, we have practiced the configuration of both text-based remote access and GUI-based remote access, and you can see that the configuration is fairly easy.

REFERENCES

Bott, E., Siechert, C., & g Stinson, C. (2007). *Windows Vista inside out*. Redmond, WA: Microsoft Press.

Debian. (2007). *About Debian*. Retrieved December 1, 2007, from http://www.debian.org/intro/about

Esche, S. K. (2002). Remote experimentation - One building block in online engineering education. In *Proceedings of the 2002 ASEE/SEFI/TUB Colloquium*. Retrieved January 27, 2007, from http://www.asee.org/conferences/international/papers/upload/Remote-Experimentation-One-Building-Block-in-Online-Engineering-Education.pdf

FreeNX. (2007). *FreeNX*. Retrieved December 1, 2007, from http://freenx.berlios.de

Geibel, J. E. (1999). Administration of campus computing labs and faculty desktops. In *Proceedings of the 27th Annual ACM SIGUCCS Conference on User Services: Mile High Expectations SIGUCCS '99* (pp. 71-28). New York: ACM.

GNOME. (2007). *What is GNOME?* Retrieved December 1, 2007, from http://www.gnome.org/about

Hicken, A. (2000). Software quality on the Net: From desktops to Internet appliances. In *Proceedings of WebNet 2000* (pp. 729-731). Chesapeake, VA: AACE.

Horton, W., & Horton, K. (2003). *E-learning tools and technologies: A consumer's guide for trainers, teachers, educators, and instructional designers*. Indianapolis, IN: Wiley.

Kasacavage, V. (Ed.) (2002). *Complete book of remote access: Connectivity and security*. Boca Raton, FL: Auerbach.

KDE. (2007). *What is KDE?* Retrieved December 1, 2007, from http://www.kde.org.uk/what.php

KOffice. (2007). *The KOffice project*. Retrieved December 1, 2007, from http://www.koffice.org

Microsoft. (2007). *Microsoft Virtual Server*. Retrieved December 1, 2007, from http://www.microsoft.com/windowsserversystem/virtualserver

NeoOffice. (2007). *NeoOffice*. Retrieved December 1, 2007, from http://www.neooffice.org/neojava/en/index.php

Novell. (2007). *SUSE Linux Enterprise*. Retrieved December 1, 2007, from http://www.novell.com/linux

OpenOffice.org (2007). *Free office suite*. Retrieved December 1, 2007, from http://www.openoffice.org

Perl. (2007). *Perl.com*. Retrieved December 1, 2007, from http://www.perl.com

Petreley, N., & Bacon, J. (2005). *Linux desktop hacks: Tips & tools for customizing and optimizing your OS*. Sebastopol, CA: O'Reilly Media, Inc.

Python. (2007). *Python programming language -- Official Website*. Retrieved December 1, 2007, from http://www.python.org

RealVNC. (2007). *RealVNC*. Retrieved December 1, 2007, from http://www.realvnc.com

Shneyderman, A., & Casati, A. (2002). *Mobile VPN: Delivering advanced services in next generation wireless systems*. San Francisco, CA: John Wiley & Sons.

Snader, J. C. (2005). *VPNs Illustrated: Tunnels, VPNs, and IPsec*. Boston, MA: Addison-Wesley Professional.

Sun Microsystems. (2007). *StarOffice 8*. Retrieved December 1, 2007, from http://www.sun.com/software/star/staroffice/index.jsp

Ubuntu (2007). *About Ubuntu*. Retrieved December 1, 2007, from http://www.ubuntu.com

Vaughan-Nichols, S. J. (2007). *2007 desktop Linux survey results revealed*. Retrieved December 1, 2007, from http://www.desktoplinux.com/news/NS8454912761.html

VMware. (2007). VMware. Retrieved December 1, 2007, from http://www.vmware.com

Westhoff, G. (2005). Connecting with pre-service teacher education students: Using desktop video conferencing for observing student teaching experiences. In C. Crawford et al. (Eds.), *Proceedings of Society for Information Technology and Teacher Education International Conference 2005* (pp. 2364-2366). Chesapeake, VA: AACE.

Xen. (2007). *XenSource: Open source virtualization*. Retrieved December 1, 2007, from http://www.citrixxenserver.com/Pages/default.aspx

Xfce. (2007). *About Xfce*, Retrieved December 1, 2007, from http://www.xfce.org/?PHPSESSID=625bf4038d0df0edfbc8c938676be141

Section III
Course Material Development for Online Courses

Chapter X
Design and Development of Online Course Materials

INTRODUCTION

In the previous chapter, we discussed client computers, desktop operating systems and desktop environments. A desktop environment is the platform where most of the online course materials will be developed. This chapter will focus on course material development with open source technologies. The first part of this chapter is a brief introduction of instructional design and instructional technology theories. We will discuss the development cycle of technology based course materials. The theories of instructional design and instructional technology will be used to guide the development process.

After the introduction, we will look at some of the open source tools that can be used to develop online course materials. We will have some detailed discussion on the open source Web authoring, multimedia, and collaboration tools. We will explore the options we may have and the functionalities provided by these open source tools.

With the available open source teaching material development tools, instructors can develop various types of the online course materials. This chapter will demonstrate how the open source tools are used to create multimedia and collaboration course materials and how to make the course materials available online so that students can access them through the Internet.

BACKGROUND

A large portion of the online teaching and learning research focuses on the development of online course materials. In general, the development process of online course materials is guided by the instructional design theories. Various instructional design models have been created. The book edited by Reigeluth (1999) summarizes the theories and models of instructional design and celebrates the diversity in the field of instructional design. The instructional design models provide a systematic approach to creating course materials. Dick, Carey, and Carey (2004) provide the theories and practice to systematically design instruction. In addition to the elements such as teachers, students, and course materials in a teaching/learning system, they also point out that the learning environment plays a crucial role. For readers who are more interested in the recent development of instructional design theories and practice, they may consider the book by Reiser and Dempsey (2006) who discussed how technologies would affect the future of this field and the trends in the field of instructional design and instructional technology.

Online teaching and learning can be greatly enhanced by using multimedia course materials. A lot of studies have been done in the area of developing multimedia course materials. The book by Lee and Owens (2004) presents hands-on guidance on design, development, and implementation of multimedia course materials. The book provides a number of tools and worksheets to help readers create their own multimedia course materials. More recently, we have Clark and Mayer's (2007) book which points the way for analyzing how students learn and how to correctly use technology to construct a teaching environment that meets students' needs. This book also provides valuable references.

Collaboration is one of the areas that need to be improved in the field of Web-based learning. Various online collaboration tools have been developed. The application of these collaboration tools have studied intensively. For example, Gellerman's (1994) article provides an overview of the role of video conferencing in distance learning. The article also gives some information about the video conferencing technology. For synchronous collaboration and interactive activities, readers may refer to Clark and Kwinn's (2007) book which is very informative. Various tools are often used to assist the development of collaboration course materials. Nokelainen, Miettinen, Tirri, and Kurhila (2002) described how a tool was used in designing and implementing real time online collaboration. Their study showed that the tool developed by them could be used to create a wide range of computer-based course materials.

In an online teaching/learning system, multimedia course materials and collaboration course materials should be made available to students through the Internet. Web is a convenient technology to deliver the course materials to the qualified students. Koontz, Li, and Compora (2006) created a Web-based design model for instruction, the ASSIST-ME Model, to assist the design of online courses. By applying instructional design theories, Brown and Lu (2001) developed a Web-based tutorial system used to assist the teaching and learning in a technology based database system course.

For each online course, instructors have to develop some online course materials in one way or another. Most of the instructors are familiar with the desktop environment where they create online course materials. Developing course materials in a desktop environment is described in Horton and Horton's (2003) book. Their book covers many tools used to create Web-based multimedia and collaboration course materials. In addition to developing course materials for the desktop environment, many technology based courses also require instructors to develop course materials for networks and servers. Sarkar's (2006) book deals with network based course materials. The book discusses strategies and practice for teaching network and hardware related classes. Chao's (2007) book examines online teaching on the server side and hands-on based online teaching. The book also discusses various issues related to setting up online computer labs to support hands-on practice on the server side.

There has been extensive research on the theories and application of instructional design and instructional technology. To enrich the application of instructional technology, this chapter will focus on the use of open source technologies to develop online course materials. Since an online teaching/learning system highly depends on the Internet ready technology-based course materials, the content covered in this chapter will be treated from the technology point of view. The emphasis will be on how the technologies are used to achieve the objectives proposed in the instructional design.

INSTRUCTIONAL DESIGN

To efficiently transfer knowledge from instructors to students, a well defined process is required to design the communication media and the instructional methods. Instructional design theories deal with these design issues. By following the theories of instructional design, the instructor should be able to develop appropriate course materials and select the right teaching methods to achieve the design goals. Various instructional design models are proposed by researchers to systematically carry out the instructional design process. The models can be used to divide the design process into manageable units. One of the often used models is the ADDIE model which includes five phases: Analyze, Design, Develop, Implement, and Evaluate. The descriptions of these five phases are given below:

- **Analyze:** This is the phase where the designers analyzes the learner's needs and characteristics such as the learner's current knowledge level and learning behavior. The designers may also need to investigate the options of how to carry out the instruction, the constraints and the learning environment. For an online teaching/learning system, the learning environment is a Web-based system that often has technical constraints. The future learning environment has to be built around these constraints.
- **Design:** Based on the result of the analysis, the designers will be able to establish measurable instructional goals. The decision on the instructional goals depends on the requirements for the learning outcomes. According to Bloom's taxonomy in the instructional theory (Ornstein & Hunkins, 2003), the learning outcomes can be categorized into three possible domains, the cognitive domain for knowledge, the affective domain for attitude, and the psychomotor domain for skills. Based on the instructional goals, the designers can determine the course content to meet the goals. After the course content is determined, the designers should be able choose an instructional approach that can deliver the content to the learner. They should specify the assessment instruments, the assignments, and the technologies for the instruction. In this phase, the designers should also specify the user interface to assist the learner in accessing the course content and specify the format of the multimedia course content. For the online teaching/learning system, the designers are often a team of instructors and programmers who are responsible for the design of the user interface and multimedia course content.
- **Develop:** In this phase, the course content developers create instructional materials based on the specifications established in the Design phase. For the online teaching/learning system, the developers should include instructors, system administrators, programmers, and online teaching support staff members. The instructors and programmers will work together to convert the course content into multimedia based course materials. The online teaching support staff and system administrators will work together to make the course materials available on the Internet. During the Develop phase, the developers need to make sure that the servers, networks, and remote access all work properly.
- **Implement:** In the Implement phase, the course materials will be delivered to the students. The instructors, system administrators, and technicians will test the newly established course Web site to make sure that the course materials and collaboration tools are in place for the students to access. Once the course content is made available to the public, it is necessary to provide training for the students to learn how to access the course materials, how to submit assignments, how to use the multimedia materials, and how to use the collaboration

tools. Training should also be provided for the faculty members on how to manage the online classes and how to use the multimedia and collaboration tools. The online teaching support staff should be trained on how to schedule the classes, how to manage the online payment system, and how to register the students to the online classes. The training can be done through a seminar, orientation for new students and faculty members, one-on-one help, technical support, and posting instructions on the course Web sites.

- **Evaluate:** This is the phase to verify and determine if the design goals have been achieved. As mentioned in the Design phase, the learning outcomes can be categorized into three domains, cognitive, affective, and psychomotor. Evaluation materials can be designed around these three domains. The evaluation can be done through tests, assignments, and course evaluation which can be used to get feedback from the students. The evaluation result can be used as a guideline for further improvement. Eventually, all the design goals should be achieved.

The ADDIE model approach has been successfully applied to various online teaching and learning projects. Strickland (2008) reported that the ADDIE model was used to develop multimedia course materials, design Web-based training interface, create Pre-Service Teachers' Virtual Space, and so on. In the process of developing course materials for the online teaching system, the ADDIE model can be applied to create the course materials that are suitable for Web-based teaching and learning. Later in this chapter, an example will be given to illustrate how to use the ADDIE model to guide the development of the online course materials.

The theories of instructional design cover a great deal of content. There are dozens of well-known instructional design models that have been proposed. Detailed coverage of these instructional design models is beyond the scope of the book. Interested readers can refer to the instructional design theory literature mentioned in this chapter's Background section.

Closely related to the field of instructional design theory, instructional technology is the field that deals with the use of technology to support teaching and learning. Various technologies are used to link students to course materials, link students to instructors, and link students to students. There are many definitions of instructional technology. Here, the study of instructional technology theories and practice will help us to wisely use technologies to overcome the challenges encountered in the online teaching/learning system. The theories of instructional technology can be used as a guideline to develop solutions for constructing the online teaching/learning infrastructure and for creating teaching and learning materials. Chapter 2 discussed the application of instructional technology for developing an online teaching/learning system. In this chapter, we are going to focus on the application of instructional technology for developing solutions to the problems in creating course materials. To wisely use technology, the developers are generally required to follow the procedure below to develop a technology based solution:

- **Investigation of challenges:** The first step of developing a technology based solution is to investigate the challenges. For example, allowing students to remotely access course materials from anywhere and at anytime can be considered as a challenge. Also, encouraging students to be actively involved in group activities through the Internet can also be a challenge.
- **Exploration of solutions:** At this step, the developers will look for possible technology based solutions. There may be different solutions that can all resolve the problem posed by a challenge. For example, to allow students to remotely access the course materials in a secure way, we may develop a VPN server with a commercial product or with an open source product.
- **Analysis of solutions:** At this step, the developers will take a closer look at the pros and cons of each solution. They should examine the benefits of each solution and the cost to gain the benefits. For example, by using an open source VPN product, students will be able to remotely access course materials from anywhere and at anytime with zero cost. The disadvantage is that an open source VPN product may not have a well written document and it may take longer time to learn how to use the product.
- **Project development:** Based on the result of the analysis, the developers will be able to choose the solution that is the best for overcoming the challenge. Once the technology based solution is chosen, the next task is to develop a detailed plan to implement the project. After the project is implemented, the developers should collect users' feedback for error correction and further improvement.

Now that we have listed the steps of developing a technology based solution, let us follow the steps for developing online course materials.

Investigation of Challenges

To develop online course materials, the first step includes the tasks such as investigating the requirements from faculty members and students. The investigation should collect information on whether there is a demand for online course materials, whether the instructors are ready to teach Web-based courses, and whether the students are willing to learn in a Web-based environment. If the demand is there, the investigation will focus on the challenges for putting course materials online. Before the online course materials can be developed, we must collect information about the requirements for this type of course materials. It is also important to collect information about the students' learning behavior and the instructors' teaching behavior. At this stage, one or a team of project developers will conduct interviews with the potential users such as the students and instructors, administrators, and the technical support team to find out:

- What types of courses need to be online? Are there any courses that may require multimedia and collaboration course materials? Are there any courses that require hands-on practice over the Internet?
- What are the students' and faculty members' knowledge levels for handling the online courses.
- What are the required resources and computer skills for developing the infrastructure to deliver the online course materials?
- What are the necessary computer skills for the students to access the course content through the Internet and to collaborate with the instructors and other students?
- What are the required technology skills for the instructors to create the materials for online teaching and to manage the online classes?
- Approximately, how many students will simultaneously access the online course materials?
- Do the online course materials need to share the computing resources with other online materials?
- What security measures should be enforced to protect the online course materials and the infrastructure for delivering the course materials?
- What are the limitations for the students to use the online course materials?

Exploration of Solutions

Based on the results of the interviews, the team of developers can set up the objectives for the development of the online course materials. After properly defining the project objectives, the team needs to collect information about possible solutions for developing and delivering such online course materials. The following information may be useful:

- There are options on Internet connection. Based on the types of course materials, there may be a need for the high speed Internet connection.
- Remote access technologies will be chosen. Certain remote access technologies may be required by the online course materials.
- Hardware and software may be needed to enforce security measures such as various types of firewalls and antivirus software.

- There are options on network devices, network protocols, network topologies, and wireless technologies.
- There is information for selecting server technologies. The information should include the options of server operating systems, server computer systems, and server-side services.
- There are options on learning management systems and the services provided by the leaning management systems.
- There are options on database management systems and the services provided by the database management systems.
- There is information for the selection of desktop technologies. The information should include desktop operating systems, desktop environments, desktop application software, and so on.
- There is choice of Web servers, Web browsers, Web services, and the functionalities provided by the Web software.
- For the development of multimedia and collaboration course materials, the developers need to consider the options of multimedia devices, multimedia content development tools, and collaboration tools.
- There is choice on the types of graphical user interfaces for the class Web sites, online registration, and many other services.
- There are options on programming languages, application development environments, Web authoring tools, and scripting languages for Web development.

Each online course may also have its own specific requirements for technology. It is the development team's responsibility to document the options for the special needs. After the team has investigated the options, the next task is the find the best solution for the project.

Analysis of Solutions

Many factors can impact the decision on the selection of the technologies to form a solution for the development of the online course materials. The following are some of the factors that the development team should consider:

- The available funding for the project.
- The skills for implementing and managing the project.
- The flexibility and reliability of the selected technologies.
- The security of the technologies selected for the project.
- The time to complete the project.
- The estimated cost of developing the online course materials.
- The time needed to learn how to use the selected technologies.

- The technical support from the vendors, product communities, consulting companies, and computer service department.
- The backward compatibility of the products.
- The market share and trend of the products to be selected.

After the pros and cons are considered, the project developers can decide on the best solution for developing and delivering the online course materials. At this step, the developers need to verify if the selected solution will meet the project objectives.

Project Development

Once the solution is selected, the next task is to develop the project. The first step of the development process is to carefully plan the project. Most projects involve issues related to budget, technical support, purchasing, project timeline, and team organization. A well planned project will lead to successful implementation of the project. In the plan, the project development team should make sure that the budget for the project is allocated, the required software and hardware for the project are available on the market, and the project has gained full support from the administrators. The project plan should draft a timeline to keep track of the progress of the development process.

Before starting to implement a sophisticated project, it is always a good idea to create a model which includes all the technologies and activities involved in the project. The model can be considered the blueprint of the project. There are various model development tools such as Unified Modeling Language (UML) that are available to help create a flow chart and icons to represent the underlying project. With the model, the developers can verify if the goals and objectives of the project can be achieved. It is much easier to make changes in the model than to make changes in the actual project. The instructional design theory often plays an important role for constructing the model and verifying the achievement of the goals and objectives. Usually, it may take several modifications for the project to fulfill its design goals and objectives. Both the technical personnel and instructors should be satisfied with the new project before it can be physically implemented.

During the implementation process, the project model will be converted to the physical project. The development team members will work together to implement the project by following the project's timeline. The instructors and the online teaching support staff will create the course materials that are suitable to be placed on the class Web sites. The technicians will make sure that the remote access service and the network are working properly. The programmers or the application developers will create user interfaces for the project. The application software administrators will make the project related application software such as database management system available to the students. Once the project is in place, serious tests should be done before the project can be released to the public.

The testing process will follow the project model to verify if the goals and objectives can be achieved physically. For example, the instructors will test the newly created online course materials which are designed for teaching and hands-on practice. The testing should make sure that the students can perform all the required activities. The testing results should be recorded for future reference. Based on the testing results, the project development team may need to further modify the project in order to meet the teaching requirements.

After the testing process is completed, the project can be released to the public. To help the students quickly learn how to use the new course materials, the development team must provide training for the students. The training can be done through seminars or through multimedia demonstration and step-by-step instruction on the class Web sites. There should be an evaluation procedure to collect the students' feedback on the usage of the new online course materials. Errors reported by the students should be fixed immediately.

Online teaching and learning is a fast changing field. Once a new technology is invented, there will be a demand for it to be used for the course materials or for improving the current teaching and learning. As a result, the course materials and facilities for teaching and hands-on practice will be updated accordingly. Every semester, there will be some new requirements for the online teaching/learning system. To quickly update the course materials, various tools have been invented to help the instructors and technical personnel to get the job done. The following section will introduce some of the tools.

OPEN SOURCE COURSE MATERIAL DEVELOPMENT TOOLS

There are three types of tools that can be used to develop online course materials. These three types of the tools are Web authoring tools for developing Web pages, multimedia tools for creating multimedia course materials, and collaboration tools for group activities. For the purpose of this book, we will look at some of the open source tools in these areas. We will start with some open source tools for developing multimedia materials.

Multimedia Tools

A multimedia teaching material consists of audio, video, text, and graphics. Multimedia based course materials can greatly improve the quality of teaching, especially for online courses where there is no face-to-face instruction and it is not easy for students to interact with their instructors. While reading the text based online course materials, the students may not know where to pay attention to and may misunderstand the course content. For a lot of hands-on practice related course content such as a lab-based project, a small mistake at the beginning of the lab work can make a whole day's work worthless. With the multimedia development tools, audio and video can be added to the text to improve understanding. For example, a movie can be used to illustrate exactly how a lab experiment should be done. For some ambiguous steps, the students can play the movie repeatedly until they learn how to do the work. There are some open source multimedia tools that are already included in the Linux desktop operating system. These tools can be used for editing multimedia content, drawing graphics, playing and managing MPEG video and MP3 audio files, burning CDs/DVDs, and so on. For example:

- Flash Player distributed by Adobe can be used to develop Flash-based Web sites.
- The media player, RealPlayer for Linux, can work on a number of multimedia formats such as MP3, MPEG-4, QuickTime, and so on.
- Banshee is an audio player that can be used for encoding and decoding various audio formats, and play, import and burn audio CDs.
- Ekiga is a tool used for VoIP and video conferencing for GNOME. It supports many high-quality audio and video compression-decompression algorithms.
- The KDE desktop environment includes the multimedia tools KSnapshot, KD3 Burner and Karbon.
- The Xfce desktop environment includes several multimedia tools such as the Xfce Sound Manager, Xfmedia audio player, Xfburn CD/DVD burner, and so on.

In addition to these built-in multimedia tools, there are many third party open source multimedia tools or free multimedia tools for creating multimedia course materials. With these tools, users can record sound and video, deploy multimedia files, present multimedia course materials online, and capture screenshots. The following is a brief instruction to some of these multimedia tools:

- **VLC media player:** The VLC (2008) media player is an open source cross-platform media player and streaming server. It supports various operating systems such as Linux, Windows, and Mac OS X. It can play on various audio and video formats such as MPEG-1, MPEG-2, MPEG-4, DivX, MP3, and so on. It can also play DVDs, VCDs, and various streaming files.

- **Gadwin PrintScreen screen capture:** PrintScreen is a free product from Gadwin (2008). It can make screenshots in many ways. Users can make a full screenshot or make a screenshot of a specific window. PrintScreen allows users to print a screen instantly, copy the capture to the clipboard, save the capture in a file, or send it to a destination through e-mail. Users can select from six different image formats and use the advanced image features.
- **StationRipper radio recorder:** StationRipper (2008) can be used to record Internet radio broadcasts. It can record up to 600 audio streams simultaneously. It can also record and play iTubes radio and podcasts. In addition to recording and playing songs, StationRipper can also be used to manage the downloaded broadcasts. It can be used to keep track of your favorite radio stations. SrationRipper can keep track of all the downloaded content so that users can easily search for the content they want. During the downloading, it can also automatically skip the duplicated content.
- **FlasKMPEG video convertor:** FlasKMPEG (2008) can be used to convert MPEG video files to other formats. It can be used to decode MPEG1/MPEG2 video and A52/MPEG audio. FlasKMPEG can also be used to encode and decode DVD and VCD audio and video content.
- **Inkscape graphics editor:** Inkscape (2008) is an open source graphics editor. It supports many W3C standard Scalable Vector Graphics (SVG) features such as markers, clones, and alpha blending. Inkscape works with the operating systems such as Linux, Windows, and Mac OS X or other UNIX-like operating systems.
- **DVDx video backup:** DVDx (2008) is open source DVD backup software. It can be used to convert DVD videos to high quality movies in the AVI and MPEG1/2 formats. It can copy DVD movies into other formats such VCD, SVCD, DivX, and WMV. Before the encoding process, DVDx allows users to preview the content. It also provides audio track support.
- **XnView graphic viewer:** XnView (Gougelet, 2008) is a free graphic viewer. It can also be used to convert graphic files. XnView supports over 400 graphic formats. It also supports most of the commonly used operating systems including Linux, Windows, Mac OS X, and many different versions of UNIX. XnView even works on pocket PCs and smart phones.

There are other open source and free multimedia development and management tools that are just as good as those described above. The selection of these tools often depends on the developers' experience with the tools and depends on whether the tools to be selected can handle the job of developing multimedia course materials.

Web Authoring Tools

Web authoring tools can be used to develop a Web site which can be accessed through the Internet. A Web site consists of Web pages that are linked together. Some of the Web pages are used as front-end applications for a database or a learning management system. These types of Web pages may include forms and reports. A Web authoring tool often includes a Web page editor for creating Web pages. With a Web editor, the user can create links and clickable images. A Web editor can also be used to create Web applications such as forms and reports and link them to the data sources at the back end. Web authoring tools generate HTML code which is the markup language that defines the layout of Web pages. Usually, a Web authoring tool allows users to develop Web pages in the What You See Is What You Get (WYSIWYG) editing mode or in the HTML code editing mode. The WYSIWYG editing mode allows users to make Web pages even if they are not experts of HTML. Normally, a Web authoring tool allows users to switch between the WYSIWYG editing mode and the HTML code editing mode. To help users to get a quick start, some Web authoring tools provide templates for some commonly used Web pages. Some of the Web authoring tools are distributed with the Linux operating system. NVU is such a Web authoring tool often distributed with Linux such as Ubuntu Linux and SUSE Linux. Screem is another Web authoring tool supported by Red Hat Linux and other Linux distributions which support GNOME as the default desktop environment. The following describe these two Web authoring tools:

- **NVU:** NVU (2008) is a full featured open source WYSIWYG Web authoring system that works for various operating systems such as Linux, Microsoft Windows, and Mac OS X. With NVU, users can create Web pages and manage Web sites. They can switch between the WYSIWYG editing mode and the HTML code editing mode. NVU works just like those commercial Web authoring software packages such as Dreamweaver. NVU allows users to log on to a Web site and edit the Web pages online. The HTML code generated by NVU will work on commonly used Web browsers. NVU also supports the development of forms, tables, and templates.
- **Screem:** Screem (2008) is another versatile Web page editor written for the GNOME desktop environment supported by Linux distributions such as Red Hat Linux. It can also be used as an XML code editor. Unlike other HTML editors, Screem does not support the WYSIWYG editing environment. Because of this, users can create cleaner and better HTML code than that generated by the WYSIWYG editing environment. On the tool bar, users can select the commonly used elements and insert the markup code of these elements at the place where the current cursor is located.

NVU and Screem can be downloaded directly from their Web sites. With the rich features and the Web site management capability, NVU is often considered a good choice as a Web authoring tool. However, users have also reported some defects in the package; for example, the source code is automatically modified without notifying the user. When using NVU, be sure to save a copy of the source code. There are also many third party Web authoring tools available. Some of them are very sophisticated. The following describes those tools.

- **Aptana Integrated Development Environment (IDE):** Unlike some of the Web authoring tools that focus on HTML code, additionally, Aptana IDE (Aptana, 2008; Kyrnin, 2008) also has a strong support for JavaScript which allows users to create rich Internet applications. Aptana allows users to add their own macros to implement the actions required by a Web page. Through Aptana, users can visualize the specifications of how the text, images, headers, and links on a Web page will be presented. This feature makes the development of JavaScript for dynamic Internet applications much easier. Aptana supports FTP so that the developed Web pages can be uploaded to remote Web sites. Aptana also supports the integrated proxy service which allows Aptana to be used behind a firewall. To help users quickly develop their Web pages, Aptana provides integrated samples to help users who want to create a similar Web page. In Aptana, there are thousands of third party plugins which extend Aptana to a wide range of applications. The applications created with Aptana can be integrated with new technologies such as the iPhone technology. One of the advantages of Aptana is that it supports a very efficient debugging tool. The error and warning messages for HTML, Cascading Style Sheets (CSS), and JavaScript can be displayed in one view. By gathering and organizing the information on Aptana Wiki, Aptana provides an in-application help which supports the HTML code editing mode.
- **Bluefish editor:** Bluefish (2008) is an editor for designing Web pages and Web applications such as forms and reports. Bluefish supports over a dozen programming and markup languages for developing dynamic and interactive activities. These features make it a powerful Web authoring tool for experienced Web designers and programmers. Bluefish also supports the WYSUWYG editing environment. Wizards are provided for creating commonly used Web applications. Bluefish also provides GUI tools for developing HTML tags, tool bars, images, links, and so on. The editing environment of Bluefish has a variety of editing features and a powerful search tool. Bluefish allows users to open over 500 documents simultaneously in its multiple-document interface. It allows users to encode Web pages into more than twenty different languages.

- **HTTrack Website copier:** HTTrack (Kauler, 2008) allows the user to copy an entire Web site from the Web server to a local computer for offline processing. It tracks the Web site's link structure and recursively copies all the images, HTMP code, and directories. On the local computer, the user can browse the site from link to link and update the copied Web site. HTTrack is free software and it supports multiple operating systems such as Linux, Windows, and various versions of UNIX.

Among the above three third party Web authoring tools, Aptana has got a lot of recommendations from users. The users like the Aptana IDE and the fact that it is written in Java which allows the Java programmer to easily extend the functionalities.

There are over a dozen sophisticated open source and free Web authoring tools. Most of them can meet the requirements for developing Web sites for an online teaching/learning system.

Open Source Collaboration Tools

Online teaching/learning systems need collaboration tools to support group projects, interactive learning, and online tutoring services. Various Web-based collaboration tools can be used to meet the needs. Web conferencing is a commonly used collaboration tool. The development of this type of course material often requires team work. An intelligent tutoring system is also a collaboration tool that promotes students and instructors to work together. A leaning management system such as Moodle provides collaboration tools for collaborative online teaching and learning. The collaboration tools included in Moodle are forums, chats, blogs, Wiki, peer assessment, workshops, and so on. In addition to the collaboration tools included in a learning management system, there are also some third party open source collaboration tools. The following are some of them:

- **Drupal:** Drupal (2008) is a versatile and powerful open source Web collaboration and publishing tool. With Drupal, a group of users can publish and manage various contents on a Web site. Drupal is capable of delivering various types of Web 2.0 based applications such as Wiki, forums, newsletters, picture galleries, social networking sites, peer-to-peer networking, core Web content management, community Web portals, e-commerce applications and single or multi-user blogs. Drupal also provides various functionalities such as collaborative authoring, podcasting, file uploading and downloading, and many more. It is often viewed by its users as one of the best Web collaboration tools. Drupal includes over 2000 community-developed modules.

- **WordPress:** WordPress (2008) is a widely used open source blog publishing system. It is known for its easy to use WYSIWYG blog publishing environment which supports various formats and styles of text. It is backed by MySQL for data storage. To help users to get a quick start, WordPress provides templates for some common tasks. To extend the functionalities, WordPress allows plugins to be added to its system. It provides a permalink structure which means permanence in links; this structure is useful for a blog entry to be linked to, from, or cited by outside sources. WordPress is an excellent blog management tool. It can keep track of users who have visited the blog and can block a specific user's IP address. It also provides an integrated link management utility. With WordPress, users can trackback or pingback; this can keep track of who is linking to, or referring to the blog articles.
- **ICEcore:** ICEcore (2008) is an open source integrated collaboration environment. It allows a group of users to share knowledge, collaborate, and communicate. In this integrated collaboration environment, users, functions, tasks, and contents are integrated to form a team project. As an open source tool, ICEcore allows users, technical support teams, and social network experts to work together to create new features for the software. With ICEcore, users can host online discussions, chats, conduct polls, and schedule meetings. ICEcore can also be used to manage the collaboration environment such as setting up teams, editing documents and files, sending quick messages, publishing through blogs, integrating with other applications such as MySQL and openSUSE, scheduling meetings, and setting up networks among teams.

As we can see from the above description, these collaboration tools are versatile and sophisticated. They can be used to create advanced collaboration environments. If the collaboration tools provided by a learning management system are not adequate, we should consider using these open source collaboration tools. Among the open source collaboration tools, Drupal is the one that is easy to use. It also has excellent technical support through its Web site. For more sophisticated collaboration activities, ICEcore is often recommended by users. It has also been mentioned by many users that WordPress is a good tool to create blogs.

Now that we have discussed the open source tools for developing online course materials, let us practice how to create course materials with the tools in the following example.

EXAMPLE: ONLINE COURSE MATERIAL DEVELOPMENT

As described in the previous section, there are many sophisticated open source tools available to assist the development of course materials. This section will demonstrate the course material development process with some of the open source tools. It will demonstrate the process of creating multimedia course materials for hands-on lab activities. We will go over each major step in the ADDIE model and make decisions on selecting the appropriate technologies. A simple example will be used for demonstration purposes. Each instructor may have specific needs on what to cover in the course materials and how to present these materials. With so many choices of open source tools, the use of a specific tool will depend on the requirements, availability, and the user's familiarity with the tool. The ultimate goal is to develop the course materials that meet the requirements of online teaching and learning. It was mentioned earlier that the ADDIE model has five phases, Analyze, Design, Develop, Implement, and Evaluate. Let us start with the Analyze phase.

Analyze

To set up the design goals, we need to first analyze learners' characteristics. The investigation starts with identifying the hands-on requirements for a Linux networking course which covers topics such as network systems, network configuration, network security, network protocols, network equipment, and network troubleshooting. The course includes many lab activities to teach students the hands-on skills. Through the hands-on practice, the students will be able to develop networks to solve business problems. During the hands-on practice, the students will perform the following tasks:

- Get familiar with network utilities such as ping, traceroute, and ethereal.
- Install and configure network equipment such as network interface cards, switches, and routers.
- Design and implement local area networks and wide area networks.
- Configure the network to meet the business requirements such as creating the directory service for managing users, computers, and network equipment at the enterprise level.
- Configure remote access services and network based applications.
- Identify security vulnerabilities and enforce security measures to protect the network system.

In addition to the requirements for hands-on practice, we will also collect information about the students' knowledge, learning behavior, and learning environment.

Suppose that the Linux networking class involved in this study is a sophomore or junior-level course. There are not a lot of prerequisites for the course. For students who have some knowledge about the Linux operating system and some basic programming skills, they should be qualified for this course. Most of the students are motivated to do hands-on practice because hands-on practice helps the understanding of the content, makes the learning more fun, and gives the students more opportunities on the job market. At the sophomore or junior-level, the students are familiar with the university's rules, the university's grading system, and the university's online teaching/learning system. Except for a few individuals, most of the students make adequate effort to study the course materials and to complete the assignments on time.

Most of the lab activities can be done through the university's online teaching/learning system. A learning management system will be used to manage the class and host the course materials. Through the learning management system, the students will be able to view and download the course materials. The students can also submit their assignments to the learning management system and view their grades. For the students who have several computers and have network equipment at home, they may also do their lab work at home and submit their lab reports through the university's leaning management system.

A special online computer lab is developed for the students to complete their lab activities. The students can remotely access the computer lab through the VPN service. The online computer lab is equipped with computers installed with the SUSE Linux operating system. These computer systems are used as servers for network development. Each server hosts three virtual machines constructed with a client-server structure. One of them is installed with the server version of the Linux operating system and the other two are installed with the desktop version of the Ubuntu Linux operating system. Each student will be the administrator of the virtual machine assigned to him/her. After a student logs on to the lab computer assigned to him/her from the home computer, the desktop of the student's home computer will be taken over by the desktop of the computer in the online computer lab. Due to the fact that the students will be the administrators of the virtual machines, these virtual machines will not be used for other classes since the students may crash the virtual machines due to configuration mistakes.

Design

The next phase of the course material development is to design the course materials to meet the teaching and hands-on practice needs. To help the students carry out the hands-on tasks listed in the Analyze phase, we will first identify the design goals. For example, to help the students with the installation and configuration of the network equipment such as network interface cards, the lab manual will be designed to achieve the following measurable objectives:

- After the lab activities, the students should be able to understand how computers communicate through the network.
- The students will be confident that they can make the computers on the Linux network communicate with each other.
- The students should be able to use the network configuration utilities.
- The students should be able to configure the network interface cards for the given IP addresses.
- The students should be able to verify if a network interface card is working properly and be able to troubleshoot configuration errors.

To help the students achieve these hands-on practice objectives, the lab manual should be developed to guide the students on the hands-on practice. The lab manual should be able to do the following:

- Make sure the students understand the objectives of the lab activities.
- If necessary, provide some background information about Linux networking.
- Help the students to be familiar with the lab environment and get ready for the lab activities.
- Guide the students to configure network devices such as network interface cards.
- Demonstrate how to verify the results of the configuration and correct any mistakes that may occur.
- Teach the students how to write lab reports, and assign the homework to students.
- Provide additional reading materials to help those students who would like to have more information about the lab activities.

The content in the lab manual can be either written in text or presented in the multimedia format. Text-base materials are good for presenting the lab objectives and background information. On the other hand, it is difficult to represent technical details with text-based materials. It may need very lengthy descriptions for some simple configuration activities. We need to keep this in mind that most of our students are new to the course content. It is easy for our students to interpret the content in the lab manual differently from that of professionals. And also, since the students are taking the online class, there is no one nearby to quickly point out where the mistake is. Often, most of our students have no idea what causes an error and they begin to try many things which often leads to more serious problems.

Therefore, multimedia materials are often used to present the content that involves technical details. For example, the configuration and verification processes should be illustrated with screen recording which includes all the mouse movements and commands entered in the command terminal. Comments and tips should be added to the recorded video clips. Links to these video clips will be placed in the lab manual along with text-based content.

Develop

In this example, the instructor will play a major role in developing the lab manual. He/she will write the lab manual with the content specified in the design phase and experiment with the hands-on activities included in the lab manual. The instructor should make sure that the activities in the lab manual can be done in the online computer lab flawlessly. The entire lab manual can be developed with OpenOffice. It is possible that the lab assistants will help with the hands-on activities and the online teaching support staff can help with the creation of the multimedia content. Since the screen recording can be easily done with the Linux operating system, the instructor may be able to do all the recording by himself/herself.

Implement

Once the lab manual is created and verified, it is ready to be delivered to the students online. By now, the online teaching support staff should have already created the class Web site and created the link to the lab materials. Either the instructor or one of the online teaching staff members will upload the lab manual to the properly created folder in the learning management system. After the lab manual is uploaded, the instructor should log on through an account with the student privilege to verify if a student can access the lab manual. If there are problems, the instructor, the system administrator, or technicians should fix the problems as soon as possible. In addition, the instructor should provide the instruction in the lecture notes or in the syllabus on how to access the lab manual and what the grading policy is for the lab reports.

Evaluate

In this phase, we will verify if the design goals have been achieved. The lab reports, assignments, and the course evaluation can be used as evaluation instruments. The students' GPAs and survey results can also be used for the evaluation. The results of the evaluation will be used as a guideline for further improvement to achieve the design goals. More details about evaluation will be covered in the next chapter.

The above example has briefly demonstrated the steps in developing the course materials for the Linux networking class, mainly the lab manual. The technical challenge of the project is that we need to record the mouse movements and other activities on screen as video clips and add them to the lab manual. Also, our students should be able to access the lab manual through the Internet and perform the hands-on practice online. As we can see, two types of technologies have been involved in developing the hands-on practice materials. The first type of technology is the infrastructure that can be used to deliver the lab manual and allow the students to perform the lab activities online. This type of technology is the online teaching/learning system that we have covered throughout this book. The second type of the technology is used to create the multimedia course materials, that is, recording the activities on screen in this example. Since the technologies for delivering the course materials have discussed in the other chapters, let us focus on the technologies used to record the screen activities.

There are several open source screen recording tools available. In this example, we will consider some of these tools such as vnc2swf, Wink, and Byzanz. After looking at the features provided by these tools, we will make a decision on which one we will use to make video clips for this example.

- **vnc2swf:** vnc2swf can be used to create flash based video clips. The flash video clips can be embedded in a Web page. vnc2swf is used with Virtual Network Computing (VNC). The VNC technology requires a server computer and a desktop computer. The vncserver program and the network configuration utilities are installed on the server machine. The students can then log on to the vncserver through the virtual vnc client from the client computers at home. With vnc2swf, we can record all the activities on screen including key strokes and mouse movements on the server side. The vnc2swf program generates high quality videos and does not require a lot of computing resources; this means that it will work with some of the older computers. Some of the Linux distributions do not include vnc2swf in their packages. In such a case, users can download vnc2swf from the Web site http://www.unixuser.org/~euske/vnc2swf/ and download the vncserver from http://old.realvnc.com/download.html.
- **Wink:** Wink is also a tool that can be used to capture the activities on screen. It is more than a screen recording tool. With Wink, one can create tutorials and presentations. It can add additional information with hints popping up on a screen cast, which is a great feature for creating a multimedia lab manual. Wink is also available in multiple languages. If it is not distributed with the Linux operating system, users can download Wink from the Web site http://www.debugmode.com/wink.

- **Byzanz:** Byzanz is a simple screen recording applet included in the GNOME desktop environment. With Byzanz, users can record the activities on screen and save the record as an animated gif file. It may not be installed by the default installation process. If so, suppose that Ubuntu Linux desktop operating system is installed on your computer, install Byzanz with the command:

  ```
  sudo apt-get install byzanz
  ```

  After the installation, users will be able to find Byzanz on the pop-up menu by right clicking the GNOME desktop. Then, the screen recording is just one click away.

As described above, screen recording is relatively simple in the Linux environment. If the user only needs some quick screen recording for the lab activities, Byzanz is a good choice for the Linux operating system that is using the GNONE desktop environment. When you are developing full featured tutoring and presentation materials, vns2swf and Wink are the choices for developing video clips for the lab activities.

CONCLUSION

In this chapter, we have discussed the issues related to course material development with open source tools. As illustrated in this chapter, the instructional design theory plays an important role in developing quality course materials that can ensure the teaching requirements are met. The theory of instructional technology provides us with a systematic approach to implementing a technology based system for teaching and learning.

This chapter has shown that there are many choices of open source course material development tools. Through the discussion of the open source tools for developing online course materials, we have discovered that these open source tools are actually very sophisticated and versatile. These tools are sufficient in handling the tasks of creating Web-based multimedia and collaborative course materials. An example has been used to demonstrate the development of a lab manual with the ADDIE model and open source multimedia tools. As illustrated in the example, not only can the open source products be used to construct the online course materials, they are also powerful, sophisticated, and easy to use.

REFERENCES

Aptana. (2008). *Aptana.* Retrieved June 25, 2008, from http://aptana.com

Bluefish. (2008). *About Bluefish.* Retrieved January 12, 2008, from http://bluefish.openoffice.nl

Brown, J., & Lu, J. (2001). Designing better online teaching material. In *Proceedings of the Thirty-second SIGCSE Technical Symposium on Computer Science Education* (pp. 352-356). New York: ACM Press.

Chao, L. (2007). *Strategies and technologies for developing online computer labs for technology-based courses.* Hershey, PA: IGI Publishing.

Clark, R. C., & Kwinn, A. (2007). *The new virtual classroom: Evidence-based guidelines for synchronous e-learning.* San Francisco, CA: Pfeiffer.

Clark, R. C., & Mayer, R. E. (2007). *E-learning and the science of instruction: Proven guidelines for consumers and designers of multimedia learning.* San Francisco, CA: Pfeiffer.

Dick, W. O., Carey, L., & Carey, J. O. (2004). *Systematic design of instruction* (6th ed.). Upper Saddle River, NJ: Allyn & Bacon.

Drupal. (2008). *Drupal.* Retrieved January 12, 2008, from http://drupal.org

DVDx. (2008). *DVDx.* Retrieved January 12, 2008, from http://www.labdv.com/dvdx/index.php

FlasKMPEG. (2008). *FlasKMPEG / Home.* Retrieved January 12, 2008, from http://flaskmpeg.sourceforge.net

Gadwin. (2008). *Gadwin PrintScreen.* Retrieved January 12, 2008, from http://www.gadwin.com/printscreen/?prnscr

Gellerman, E. (1994). Teleconferencing systems facilitate collaboration and distance learning. *T H E Journal (Technological Horizons in Education), 22*(3), 16-22.

Gougelet, P. (2008). *XnView.* Retrieved January 12, 2008, from http://pagesperso-orange.fr/pierre.g/xnview/enhome.html

Horton, W., & Horton, K. (2003). *E-learning tools and technologies: A consumer's guide for trainers, teachers, educators, and instructional designers.* Indianapolis, IN: Wiley.

ICEcore. (2008). *ICEcore (open source).* Retrieved January 12, 2008, from http://www.icecore.com/open.html

Inkscape. (2008). *Open source scalable graphics editor.* Retrieved January 12, 2008, from http://www.inkscape.org

Kauler, L. (2008). *HTTrack Website copier.* Retrieved June 25, 2008, from http://www.httrack.com

Koontz, F. R., Li, H., & Compora, D. P. (2006). *Designing effective online instruction: A handbook for Web-based courses.* Lanham, MD: Rowman & Littlefield Education.

Kyrnin, J. (2008). *Aptana IDE.* Retrieved June 25, 2008, from http://webdesign.about.com/od/freewebeditors/p/aaaptana.htm

Lee, W. W., & Owens, D. L. (2004). *Multimedia-based instructional design: Computer-based training, Web-based training, distance broadcast training, performance-based solutions, Second Edition.* San Francisco, CA: Pfeiffer.

Nokelainen, P., Miettinen, M., Tirri, H., & Kurhila, J. (2002). A tool for real time on-line collaboration in Web-based learning. In P. Barker & S. Rebelsky (Eds.), *Proceedings of World Conference on Educational Multimedia, Hypermedia and Telecommunications 2002* (pp. 1448-1453). Chesapeake, VA: AACE.

NVU. (2008). *The complete Web authoring system for Windows, Mac, and Linux.* Retrieved January 12, 2008, from http://nvudev.com/index.php

Ornstein, A. C., & Hunkins, F. P. (2003). *Curriculum: Foundations, principles, and issues* (4th ed.). Boston: Allyn & Bacon.

Reigeluth, C. M. (Ed.). (1999). *Instructional-design theories and models: A new paradigm of instructional theory, Volume II.* Mahwah, NJ: Lawrence Erlbaum Associates.

Reiser, R. A., & Dempsey, J. V. (Eds.). (2006). *Trends and issues in instructional design and technology* (2nd ed.). Upper Saddle River, NJ: Prentice Hall.

Sarkar, N. (2006). *Tools for teaching computer networking and hardware concepts.* Hershey, PA: Information Science Publishing.

Screem. (2008). *Screem.* Retrieved January 12, 2008, from http://www.screem.org

StationRipper. (2008). *StationRipper: Record Internet radio.* Retrieved January 12, 2008, from http://www.stationripper.com

Strickland, A. W. (2008). ADDIE. Retrieved January 12, 2008, from http://ed.isu.edu/addie/research/Research.html

VLC. (2008). *VLC media player.* Retrieved January 12, 2008, from http://www.videolan.org/vlc

WordPress. (2008). *WordPress.* Retrieved January 12, 2008, from http://wordpress.org

Chapter XI
Implementation and Evaluation of Online Courses

INTRODUCTION

As stated in the discussion of the ADDIE model in the last chapter, implementation and evaluation are part of the development process. Once online course materials are developed, the next task is to deploy the course materials to students. The first topic of this chapter will deal with the issues related to the deployment of online course materials. In this chapter, we will discuss the tasks such as planning and training involved in the deployment process.

Once the online course materials have been deployed, there will be a large number of requests from the students for help on technology and course content related issues. To keep the online teaching/learning system running successfully, we need a strong technical support team including experienced computer service personnel, instructors, and fellow students. This chapter will deal with the issues related to technical support. We will discuss various ways to provide technical support services.

The development of an online teaching/learning system and course materials are often a complex process. Even with the careful design and planning, errors may still occur and there are always things that need to be improved. To correct errors, the first step is to identify the problems. Often, instructors and students are the first to know if there is a problem or something needs to be improved. This chapter will discuss the issues on how to reach out to users such as students and instructors to collect their response and feedback, and how to fix problems as soon as possible to ensure the quality of teaching and learning. The improvement of the online teaching/learning system and course materials will be based on the feedback from the instructors and students. In this chapter, we will also discuss the topics related to course evaluation which will be used as a guideline for further improvement.

BACKGROUND

The topics covered in this chapter involve the implementation and evaluation phases of the ADDIE model. Studies in these two areas are very active. A number of papers have been published on these subjects. Smitherman, Nasseh, and Repp (2005) reported a case study about the deployment of interactive media materials through a wireless network to schools, students' homes, and surrounding neighborhoods. In their paper, they also analyzed the impact of the rich media materials on students' learning and social activities. They described how the teachers and students were prepared for the deployment and how they used the rich media materials.

In another paper, Omwenga, Waema, Eisendrath, and Libotton, (2005) discussed an objectives-driven e-content structuring and deployment model. They presented an intuitive approach to content structuring and sequencing in the subjects of liberal arts, sciences and engineering. In their study, the knowledge presentation objectives were identified, starting from the most abstract to the most specific. These objectives were used to help break up the course content and sequence. From their analysis, they concluded that the objectives were very important and could be effectively used to validate the course content, and they also found that the collaboration among homogenous groups was the most efficient in training of content development.

Every successful online teaching/learning program must be supported by effective technical support. In their paper, Gibbs and Rice (2003) described the difficulty of technical support in K-12 schools. Because the use of new technology dramatically increased the needs of technical support for the classroom teaching, they developed Web-based software to train the teachers with the information on troubleshooting simple hardware and software problems as part of the teachers' professional development. The training provided the necessary skills for the teachers to solve some commonly encountered technical problems by themselves before calling technical support. The features and usage of the Web-based training software is described in their paper.

Support can also be carried out by students and teachers through Web-based communication. Scherff and Paulus (2006) discussed the issues related to the support for new teachers. In their study, a computer-mediated communication technology was used to connect pre-service teachers in their internship training anytime and anywhere. The authors pointed out that both informal learning and highly structured online forums can be used for teacher support.

The evaluation of online teaching and learning is another field that has been well studied by researchers. One of the significant contributions to the evaluation theory of teaching, training, and learning was proposed and refined by Kirkpatrick (1998) and later revised by Kirkpatrick and Kirkpatrick (2005). The Kirkpatrick model of evaluation provides an in-depth and practical guidance for evaluating training and teaching.

Fortier and Michel (2005) discussed the issues related to the performance of computer systems. The theory, concepts, strategies, and technologies provided by Fortier & Michel (2005) can be used to evaluate the infrastructure of an online teaching/learning system and online computer labs. The evaluation of online courses is covered in Khan's (2005) book which provides sequences of check lists for verifying if the e-learning modules, courses, and programs have achieved their objectives. Price, Walters, and Xiao (2006) discussed the use of an online evaluation system that was designed for students to evaluate their instructors.

Achtemeier, Morris, and Finnegan (2003) gathered the principles of the best practices of teaching and learning using online courses and compared them with the evaluation instruments of their institutions and with other online courses. Based on the results of their study, they provided a guideline for the evaluation of online courses.

For the development of a collaborative evaluation system, readers may find useful information in the paper by Tu, Yen, Corry, and Ianacone (2003) who proposed an integrated online evaluation system to allow instructors, their students, and their peers to evaluate their online teaching. Tu, Yen, Corry, and Ianacone (2003) indicated that the instructors and students were in favor such an evaluation system.

The deployment and evaluation of online teaching have been studied extensively. In addition to applying the commonly used implementation and evaluation theories and practice to the open source based online courses, this chapter will provide information on the training of the open source products. It will also introduce some of the evaluation instruments developed with open source tools.

DEPLOYMENT OF ONLINE TEACHING MATERIALS

The goal of the deployment of online teaching materials is to make sure that students are able to access these materials without any hassle. Depending on the requirements by the online courses, the deployment can be carried out in different ways. The course materials can be deployed through course Web sites, or downloaded through a FTP server, or delivered to the students with CDs/DVDs and portable storage devices such as flash drives, or the combination of different methods. The choice of deployment methods depends on the online teaching/learning environments as listed below:

- Some colleges and universities allow students to access course materials through mobile devices such as iPods and smart phones. For those Internet capable mobile devices, deployment through the Web server is a good choice. Otherwise, the course materials can be delivered through portable media such as flash drives to students' personal computers and then loaded to the mobile devices.
- If a university has multiple campuses located in different countries and the conditions of Internet connection vary from campus to campus. In such a case, multiple Web servers may be needed so that the deployment of the course materials can match the environment at the campus level.
- Some environments may require the course materials to be delivered to students' personal computers through portable storage devices such as CDs/DVDs or flash drives, for instance, a university in a rural area where many of the households have no broadband Internet connection. If a Web server is used to deliver the course materials, the text version of the course materials should be available for quick download.
- Sometimes, course content is so large that it is distributed to multiple servers. When deploying these course materials to students, the servers should be properly synchronized and optimized to make all the course materials available for the students.

In many cases, the deployment of course materials requires team effort. There will be some technical challenges and changes in students' learning behavior. Even though some of the course materials work flawlessly, they may encounter various problems after deployed to students. The following are some of the problems that may occur.

- **Class Web site performance:** The class Web sites are running too slowly. This may be caused by an underperformed server and network equipment, improperly configured hardware and software, or slow network connection.
- **Course management:** The course materials may not be available for students due to several factors. There is no course material backup plan, so the course materials cannot be recovered after a disaster. There are some other factors that may also cause the course materials to be unavailable after a disaster; for example, the log files are not properly stored, the restoration process is not

properly configured, and the instructor is not well trained for class management.

- **Client-side configuration:** The users including the students and instructors are not well informed about the client-side configuration for using the online course materials or managing the classes, or the configuration on the client side is so complicated that it requires the users to have in-depth training that they have not had.
- **Remote access connectivity:** A remote access connectivity problem can be caused by user authentication, security constraints on the Web server and Web browser, wrong configuration on either the client side or the server side, and incompatible remote access technology on the client side.
- **Compatibility:** Some newly developed course materials may not be compatible with the LMS server. Also, some of the third party tools may not be compatible with the course materials and the LMS server.

To avoid the deployment problems, the following tasks should be carried out before starting the deployment process:

- The first task is to investigate the deployment environment including the performance of the Web server and the server that hosts the LMS and other application software, the internal network and the Internet throughput, the compatibility requirements for the client-side software, the conflicts caused by security measures, the users' background knowledge about the upcoming project, user authentication and authorization for using certain resources, the language requirements for a multinational online teaching/learning system, and remote access requirements.
- Based on the results of the investigation, the deployment team should draft a deployment plan that includes the strategies to obtain proper resources for the deployment, the deployment implementation schedule, the arrangement of training, the technical support personnel arrangement, and so on.
- The deployment team should find the solution for the compatibility issues and work around the conflicts caused by the security measures. The team needs to take action to resolve the performance related problems. Before the deployment can get started, funding and personnel should be in place. The team also needs to make sure that the users have adequate knowledge of the client-side software configuration.
- It is also important for the open source LMS server and the online computer lab to handle the content created by proprietary products such as Microsoft Office. Students may submit their term papers as Microsoft Word documents.

Also, in the lab, the Linux based network system may need to share network recourses with the Windows network system.

- Before deploying the multimedia course materials or other types of course materials, make sure that the technologies related to these course materials are available. For example, for the multimedia course content, Macromedia Flash should be downloaded and properly configured so that it is ready for the multimedia course content on the Web site, or we should include Macromedia Flash with the course materials on a CD/DVD for the students to use. If the course content is coded in XML, the XML parser should be provided.
- The deployment team should prepare the instruction on the configuration of the client software, remote logon to the LMS, submission of assignments, hands-on activities in the online computer lab, security measure enforcement, group collaboration, communication between students and instructors, taking online exams, using multimedia course materials, and so on.
- The information about tutoring and technical support should be available for the students. The deployment team needs to collect this type of information and make the information accessible to the students.
- To help the students properly set the client computer at home, the deployment team should make a list of requirements for the computer hardware, network equipment, operating system, Web browser, and application software of the personal computers on the client side, and then post the list on the class Web site. The client software installation instruction should also be included.
- The deployment team should develop a training plan that includes the training objectives, formats of training, content to be covered in the training, prerequisite knowledge required by the training, the information about the trainers, as well as the training schedule.
- The instruction on how to report errors to the computer service department should also be available for the students.

After having completed these tasks, the deployment team can release the online teaching/learning system to the students. During the deployment process, the following tasks will be carried out by the deployment team:

- The system administrator who is also one of the deployment team members needs to contact the instructors to find out the requirements for the instructors' accounts and the students' accounts.
- Based on the requirements for the instructors' accounts, the system administrator will properly set up the accounts so that the instructors can start their online class projects by preparing the course syllabi, implementing the online

computer lab, obtain the students' information, and uploading the course materials.

- Based on the enrollment, the online teaching support staff members will help the instructors to develop the class Web sites. For the students who have enrolled in a specific class, the teaching support staff will set up folders and links for the course materials, assignments, grade books, exams and quizzes, group projects, chat rooms, and so on.
- To make the course materials available for the students, the system administrator needs to set up the students' accounts on the LMS server, VPN server, and online computer lab. The students need to be given the proper privilege so that they can access the course materials and perform hands-on practice. For each class, the system administrator needs to create a student role which has the configuration for the students' accounts. Then, the system administrator can add all the students who enrolled in the class to the student role.
- If portable storage is required for the deployment, CDs/DVDs or flash drives should be preloaded with the course materials and the instruction on how to use the course materials.

An e-mail account should be created for each student who is accepted by the university. The e-mail account is so configured that, after the first logon, the student will be able change his/her password. Through e-mail, the students will be informed that the course materials are available on their class Web sites, or on portable storage devices. The students will also be told how to log on to the class Web sites. In addition, the e-mail will include the information such as where and how to get technical support and the links to the training information. After the classes have started, the instructors may send welcome e-mail to their students and pre-class surveys if necessary.

Many of the students are the first time users of the online teaching/learning system. It is very possible that they will need technical support. They may need help on how to use the online teaching/learning system or on how to fix problems, some of which may be caused by their mistakes. The technical support related issues will be discussed next.

TRAINING AND TECHNICAL SUPPORT MANAGEMENT

Once the online teaching/learning system is made available for the students, questions from the students will pour in. To help students reduce the learning stress, it is necessary to provide training and technical support for the students as well as the instructors. In the following, we will first discuss the issues related to training and then the issues related to technical support.

Training

After the course materials are delivered, many students and instructors will need training on properly using Linux and other open source tools. As mentioned in Chapter 1, one of weaknesses of open source products is lack of marketing and user instruction. Open source products are less known by the public. Therefore, training on using the open source products is a key step for the success of the open source based online teaching/learning system.

Many of our students are first time users of the online teaching/learning system. They are not familiar with the setup and the technology used in the system. Even for those students who have taken classes through the online teaching/learning system, the rapid progress of technology can make the current setting of the online teaching/learning system different from last year's setting. It is also true that the instructors, especially the new faculty, need training on class management. Training will help the students, the instructors, and the technical support team to continuously update their skills and knowledge so that they can keep up with the current trend. The training can be carried out in the following formats:

- **Orientation:** Before the classes start, the online teaching support staff or the computer service department can provide an orientation for the new students and new faculty members. During the orientation, the trainers will demonstrate how to use the online teaching/learning system. The new students will learn how to log on to the online teaching/learning system, how to find the class Web sites, how to log on to the online computer labs, how to submit their homework, how to take quizzes and exams, how to collaborate with the other students and communicate with the instructors. The new faculty members will learn how to log on to the online teaching/learning system, how to post course materials, how to set up the online computer labs, how to set up assignments, quizzes and exams, how to grade assignments, quizzes and exams, how to communicate with the students, and how to edit the class Web sites. The trainees will get hands-on practice during the orientation. The trainers will answer questions and help the trainees solve problems. The trainers will make sure that all the trainees successfully complete the training.
- **Training seminars:** During the semester, the online teaching support staff or the computer service department can also offer seminars to teach the faculty members on using the utilities provided by the Linux operating system, LMS, and database server. The short and focused training seminars are offered to

faculty members to help them create multimedia course materials, set up Wiki, configure class blogs, develop video conferences, use hand-writing devices, and so on. In addition to the training seminars on using the utilities, the computer service department may also provide training on the development of hands-on practice course materials and on the online computer lab management.

- **Video conferencing:** Video conferencing is a convenient tool for training. It can be viewed by trainees from anywhere. For those students who cannot come to campus, they can get the training through a video conference. The faculty members who cannot come to a training seminar can also get the training through a video conference. Video conferences can be recorded for later review. The trainees can review the recorded video conferences as many times as they want.
- **Web-based training:** The class Web sites can the place to post the instruction on how to get started, how to troubleshoot commonly encountered errors, how to access course materials, how to use learning tools, how to use collaboration tools, how to use multimedia tools, and so on. The trainees can access these training materials anytime and anywhere. When running into technical problems, the students and instructors can often find solutions posted on these Web sites. The only drawback of Web-based training is that it lacks face-to-face instruction and the trainees won't be able to get their questions answered right away.
- **Workshops:** A professional development workshop is another way to get training. When new technologies are released on the market, many consulting companies will provide training workshops to help IT professionals update their knowledge. The trainers in the workshops are professionals with first-hand experience. Most of the trainees are also IT professionals with many years of experience. The computer service technicians and faculty members can greatly benefit from participating in the professional development workshops. The knowledge gained from the workshops can be used to update the computer labs so that the instructors can teach the up-to-date content knowledge.
- **Books:** Professional development books and other professional development documents can also be used for the training. The computer service technicians and faculty members can study these books to update their knowledge and skills.

For the open source online teaching/learning system, training is crucial for running the system successfully. Due to the fact that there is less marketing effort for the open source products, some of the open source products are not as well known as the commercial ones. The computer service technicians, faculty, and students may be less prepared on using these products. The first thing that needs to be done is to make sure that the technicians in the computer service department and the instructors get well trained. If necessary, some of the computer service technicians and instructors should attend professional workshops to catch up with the current trend in the open source products. A lot of professional training for open source products is available. There is training on the Linux operating system, open source Web servers such as Apache, database management systems such as MySQL, and open source programming languages such as Perl, Python, and PHP. For the Linux operating system, the training may cover the following content:

- Kernel management and development
- User management
- Software management and development
- System initialization
- Process and service management and development
- Remote access service management
- Security management
- Troubleshooting

For the database management system, the training content may include the following:

- Database server administration
- Query languages
- Database programming with PHP
- Databases, tables, and other database objects
- Network based databases
- Troubleshooting

For the Apache Web server, the following training content may be included:

- Apache installation and configuration
- File management
- Web page development
- Apache service startup
- Virtual hosts and aliases
- Web server protection and CGI scripts
- Troubleshooting

For the programming languages, the following training content may be included:

- Programming logic
- Programming language software configuration
- Programming with PHP and HTML
- Dynamic Web page programming
- Application development with PHP and HTML
- Connection to data sources
- Troubleshooting

Depending on the requirements, many other topics can also be included. Professional training can be carried out in various formats such as online or face-to-face workshops.

Basically, there are two types of online professional training, the online training provided by companies that produce the open source products and the online training provided by training companies. The online training provided by product producers is often free. The training materials can be downloaded from the companies' Web sites. The training provided by the training companies often includes multimedia materials as well as the online computer labs for hands-on practice. Most of the online training provided by the training companies is also supervised by qualified trainers. The training companies will charge registration fees when you use their online training materials. Often, this kind of training costs about several hundred to several thousand dollars.

The training companies also provide instructor led face-to-face workshops. The instructors will give lectures and help with lab activities. The instructors' help is necessary for beginners who may make many mistakes during the hands-on practice and do not know how to fix the problems. During a workshop, participants can also learn from each other since some of them have some experience with the open source products. A disadvantage of the face-to-face workshop is the cost. The training companies often charge a large fee for a workshop and participants will also pay for the travel, meals, and lodging.

To catch up with the latest development in the IT industry, the timing for the training is important for the successful implementation of the online teaching/learning system. The course materials and online computer labs are updated frequently due to the fast changing technology in the IT industry. Each semester, there will be new requirements by the online teaching/learning system. Training should be done regularly, say every semester, to keep up with the current technology trend.

Training for the instructors and students should focus on the topics that they need. Before scheduling the training, a survey should be conducted to identify the knowledge and skills that will benefit the students and instructors. The survey can also collect information about possible attendance to a specific training. The result of the survey can be used to set up the training schedule, the format of the training, and the content to be covered by the training. As mentioned earlier, the external professional development training is expensive. The result of the survey can also help to plan the budget for the training and seek new funding for the training. To reduce the cost, some of the training can be done internally and some can be done through the Web. After the decision is made on what to cover in the training and how the training will be carried out, the computer service department can schedule the training for the next semester, post it on the university's Web site and encourage all the students and instructors to participate in the training.

Due to the complexity of the online teaching/learning system, in addition to training, the instructors and students, especially the inexperienced ones, still need technical support to solve individual technical problems. The issues related to technical support will be discussed next.

Technical Support

Technical support is very important for the successful implementation of the online teaching/learning system. Due to the lack of face-to-face help on many technical problems, online and telephone technical support are crucial for reducing the stress of online teaching and learning. Technical support is done in various areas of the online teaching/learning system such as remote access, LMS usage, and online computer labs. The need to cover so many different technologies makes technical support a difficult task. The following are some of the difficulties in technical support.

- The requirements for technology vary from course to course. Each course has its own special needs for what hardware and software to use and how the configuration should be done.
- The technical support team also needs to provide support for various types of computer systems such as the Linux or Windows operating systems on personal computers, or Linux on Sun's UltraSPARC platform. Especially, different platforms on the client side may be used to access the servers and the university does not have much control of the client side.
- Students' knowledge levels are different. Some students may need very detailed help through telephone conversations and others may consider online instruction and help adequate. Some of the students are not afraid to try anything. They may easily reset the existing configuration and disable some of the services in the online teaching/learning system.
- Different courses may have different requirements for security. Some of the technology based courses such as networking courses need the system administrator's privilege for the students. With this kind of privilege, the students

can easily mess up the machines and networks in the computer labs. This can make technical support very difficult.

- The frequently changing course materials and technologies can make technical support very difficult. Once a new technology is implemented or the course materials are updated, there will be a large number of additional requests for help. For example, the students may need assistance in reconfiguring their Web browsers after a new collaboration tool is installed.
- The technical support for various courses poses a great challenge for the technical support team. Unlike the technical support provided by IT companies which only deals with their own products. The technical support for the online teaching/learning system needs to deal with products from different vendors. Especially when the students ask questions related specific course content, the technical support team members may not be familiar with the course content.
- Also, for the open source based online teaching/learning system, many of the open source products do not have well documented manuals for users. Some solutions may be found on the Internet. In many cases, the technical support team members may have to find solutions by themselves.

Facing these difficulties, the technical support team itself needs strong support from the university administrators, instructors, and students. The administrators, instructors, and technical support team should work on financial and knowledge update related issues to get the team ready to support online teaching and learning.

Technical support should have financial support for training, hiring technicians and student workers, purchasing and upgrading software and hardware, and daily maintenance. The financial support depends greatly on the administrators who need to be well educated about the importance of technical support.

The technical support team needs well-trained, skilled, and versatile technicians to handle the job. Besides technicians, the team should include experienced network administrators, system administrators, and database administrators. It should also include the online teaching support staff members who have helped to develop the LMS server and set up the class Web sites. The knowledge update for the technical support team members cannot be neglected. It is necessary to send the team members to external training workshops or classes, and encourage them to be certified in some IT fields. Specifically, the technical support team should prepare the following support for the open source products used in the online teaching/learning system:

- A list of the download sites of the open source products.
- Installation instruction for each of the open source application software such MySQL, PHP, and the Apache Web server.
- Instruction for the configuration of peripherals such as printers, scanners, and so on.
- Description of the Linux operating system's initialization errors and device conflicts, and instruction on how to work around these problems.
- Instruction on how to deal with the Linux operating system's freeze.
- Procedures of diagnosing problems of network services such as DNS, DHCP, NFS, FTP, Samba, and so on.
- Procedures to diagnose the operating system's crash and lockup.
- Procedures to diagnose Internet connection problems.
- Instruction on downloading and installing critical updates.
- A list of e-mail problems and how to fix the problems.
- Instruction on how to troubleshoot performance problems.
- Instruction on the installation of anti-virus and anti-spyware software and on how to solve security problems.
- Instruction on how to protect data.

There are also many other unpredictable problems that the technical support team needs to solve. Once a problem is fixed, the technical support team should record the symptom, the diagnostic procedure, and problem solving procedure for future use.

To get familiar with the course content, the technical support team members may also take some of the courses offered by the university. In such a way, the team members will learn some new knowledge as well as get to know the course content, so they can provide better service.

The instructors are a significant part of technical support. They are the ones who are most familiar with the course content and they are ones who have made the decision on what technologies to use in the classes. The instructors have developed the course materials and the class assignments. Therefore, they should be members of the technical support team, or at least the technical support team needs to consult with them.

The technical support team needs to collect the course syllabi and hands-on practice materials such as lab manuals from the instructors. It is also a good idea to sit down with the instructors to discuss the course requirements and what the instructors expect from technical support.

The instructors' knowledge should also be updated frequently. They should be encouraged to participate in professional development training workshops and professional conferences in the related fields. Funding should be allocated to support these professional development activities, and these activities should be counted as part of their workload. The students will benefit a lot from the up-to-date knowledge of their instructors. The new knowledge and skills will give the students a competitive edge on the job market.

To efficiently provide technical support, some services should be set up. For example, a hot line may be established so that the students can get help 24 hours a day and 7 days a week. For many small and medium-sized universities, a hot line may not be a practical solution. In such a case, a database system can be developed for technical support. An online work order form can be created to take orders from the users. The orders can be categorized according to the subjects of instruction, so a particular order will be sent to the technical support person who specializes in that area. For each technical support request, there will be a record which contains the problem description and how the problem is solved. Later, when the same problem comes up, a technical support person can easily find the solution by searching the database. This kind of information can also be posted on the Internet so that the students and instructors can solve some problems by themselves. This can significantly reduce the workload of the technical support team.

As another service, the technical support team can create and manage a Wiki or discussion group. The team can create some discussion for each area of technical support. The students and instructors are allowed to contribute questions and solutions on the Wiki. In such a way, everyone will be able to contribute to the technical support, and this can significantly reduce the number of requests to the technical support team.

Both training and technical support are part of the implementation phase in the ADDIE model of instructional design. The next phase in the development process is the evaluation phase. The issues related to evaluation will be discussed next.

ONLINE COURSE EVALUATION

The last phase of the ADDIE model is evaluation. Once the new course materials are delivered and the new teaching and learning environment is in place. We will be looking forward to finding out if the students like what we developed, if what we did have made a difference in the online teaching and learning, if the students' learning behavior has changed for the better due to our effort, and how we can make it even better. The evaluation process is used to answer these questions. The goal of evaluation is to assess the effectiveness and to identify the areas for improvement. Through evaluation, we can find out if the students have gained the knowledge and skills through the learning process and if the teaching and learning have benefited from the online teaching/learning system. The evaluation will provide guidance for further improvement of the existing online teaching/learning system and for new projects. The result of the evaluation also serves as the needs assessment for the budget of the upcoming year. The following are some of the evaluation tasks for the online teaching/learning system:

- Find out how the students feel towards the open source based online teaching/learning system.
- Gather information on the effectiveness of the knowledge delivery methods and the online teaching and learning environment.
- Collect feedback from the students on the use of the open source operating system and application software.
- Find out if the open source products are adequate for the online hands-on practice, the development of the multimedia course materials, group collaboration, course material presentation, and class management. Also, verify if the open source products are suitable for online teaching and learning.
- Identify the problems in the open source based online teaching/learning system.
- Identify the needs for further improvement on the infrastructure of the teaching/learning system, class Web sites, course materials, lab manuals, and so on.
- Evaluate the results of learning, the instructional methods used by the instructors, and the efficiency of technical support.
- Check if the objectives of the online computer labs have been achieved.

There are many ways of evaluation. Evaluation models such as the model by Kirkpatrick and Kirkpatrick (2005) provide some guidelines on who, what, when, and where to evaluate. Here, we will start with Kirkpatrick's evaluation model. Then, we will discuss some other evaluation models.

Kirkpatrick's Four-Level Evaluation Model

Kirkpatrick's four-level evaluation model is one of the evaluation models that are used to evaluate the effectiveness of training. This model includes four levels: Evaluation of reaction, evaluation of learning, evaluation of behavior, and evaluation of results (Kirkpatrick, 1998; Kirkpatrick & Kirkpatrick, 2005). These four levels evaluate training in four different aspects.

The first level of this model is the reaction level. It is to find out if the learner likes or dislikes the training program. For the evaluation of an open source based online course, questions in a survey can be designed to find out how the students feel about the course content, the hands-on practice, the open source environment, and the instructor. This level of evaluation is used to determine if the training method, the instructor, and the environment are appreciated by the students. If the students do not have a positive attitude towards the teaching method, the instructor, and the learning environment, this means that the knowledge delivery method and learning environment may not as effective as initially intended. In such a case, something needs to be done to improve the online course. The first level evaluation can be carried out through a class survey, online evaluation form, semester reports, exit interviews, and so on. For the first level evaluation, we may ask the students if they agree with the following statements from the scale of one - strongly disagree, to the scale of five - strongly agree:

- I am doing well with the Linux operating system and other open source tools.
- The class Web site is well organized and informative.
- I like the flexibility offered by the online teaching and learning environment.
- The course materials are valuable in helping me understand the content.
- The class assignments are beneficial.
- I have a good experience with the Web-based collaboration.
- The instructor is helpful.
- The instructor is well prepared.
- I would like to recommend the instructor to other students.
- The performance of the online teaching/learning system is good enough for me.
- I can handle the Web-based hands-on practice.
- The training is helpful for me to get a quick start.
- The technical support service is helpful and efficient.
- Over all, I am positive towards the online course.

Many other questions can be asked. The instructor and the online teaching/learning system development and management team can learn more about the students' feelings towards the course, instructor, and technical support. Based on the result of the evaluation, they can make more effort for the improvement in the areas that the students do not feel positive about.

The second level of this model is the evaluation of learning. The evaluation at this level is to find out if the students have learned the course content. It is to measure if the students' have gained the knowledge and skills as expected and if their attitude has changed positively. The evaluation can be done in various ways. The commonly used methods for the evaluation of learning are pre-post exams, pre-post assessment surveys, homework, lab projects, troubleshooting skills, term papers, grades, and so on. These measurements can be used to find out if the class has had a positive impact on the students' learning and if the learning objectives have been achieved. The pre-post exams and surveys are designed to measure the changes in the students' knowledge, skills, and attitude before and after the class. To measure the gain in hands-on skills, hands-on related items should also be included in the exams, surveys, lab projects, homework, and so on. The exams and lab projects should be designed so that they include items at different difficulty levels.

The third level is about the evaluation of behavior. At this evaluation level, we will find out how well the knowledge and skills learned in the previous classes are applied to the subsequent classes and to real-life problem solving. The third level evaluation can also be used to figure out how the learning has changed the students' behavior in the collaboration with other students and in self-discipline. The third level evaluation may take some time since the students may need opportunities to apply the knowledge and skills they have learned. Therefore, the timing for the evaluation is an important factor. The decision has to be made on when to conduct the evaluation and how often the evaluation needs to be done. Various methods can be used to conduct the third level evaluation, such as surveys, team projects, interviews, internships, demonstrations, and so on. A survey is an easy-to-implement evaluation instrument for this purpose. As an example, the following are some of the statements that can be asked to see if the students agree in the scales of one to five:

- I have been using the knowledge and skills learned from the previous classes a lot.
- I am actively involved in group activities.
- I know how to schedule my time so that I always complete my assignments on time.
- Before going to class, I preview the course content.
- Previewing the course content makes me better understand the lecture.
- While working on my homework, I often use the knowledge I learned from the previous classes.
- The books used in my classes are great references for my internship.

Faculty advisors, instructors, supervisors, and managers can also provide information on how the students use their knowledge and skills and how their behavior has been influenced by the knowledge and skills.

The fourth level of Kirkpatrick's evaluation model is about the evaluation of results. The outcome of this evaluation will reveal if the learning has an impact on the students' careers, professional development, and business environments. The result of the evaluation can also be used for further improvement of upcoming training. Alumni surveys, employee annual evaluation, and employer feedback can be used as the fourth level evaluation tools. Due to the fact that the data for this level of evaluation are often collected from the students who have already graduated, the data collection takes longer time and is more expensive. The data to be collected may include the following achievements which may come from the students' knowledge and skills:

- Helped the company to increase the revenue and profit.
- Helped other individuals to increase their productivity.
- Made contribution to the improvement of product quality.
- Gave new ideas to provide better services for the customers.
- Found ways to reduce cost.
- Was promoted to a leadership position.
- Became technology/business know-how.
- Passed the qualifying exam for my doctoral degree.
- Invented new products and patented these products.
- Published new books or journal articles.

For the fourth level evaluation, it may be difficult to identify exactly which factor results in which achievement since the students' effort, the impact of teaching, the working environment, family influence, and many other factors can also contribute to a student's achievement. This means that we need to carefully design the evaluation instrument to get a better indicator for the success of the teaching and learning. The following are some sample statements in an alumni survey that links the students' achievements to the knowledge and skills gained from taking the courses offered by the university, including online courses:

- I am currently working on a job where I can use the knowledge and skills learned from the courses taken at the university.
- I acquired good problem solving skills by taking the courses at the university.
- With the knowledge and skills learned from the university, I can keep up with the pace of my new job.
- My research ability is good due to the knowledge and skills learned from the university.
- My college education gave me the ability to handle group activities.
- My knowledge, skills, and learning habit acquired at the university make it easier for me to pick up new knowledge and skills at work.
- With the knowledge and skills acquired from taking the university courses, I was competent when I first entered the work force.
- Being able to handle the online courses has prepared me to work in an e-commerce environment.

- I have saved my company lots of money due to my ability to work with Linux and other open source products.
- My university study has given me good analytical skills and I am able to conduct analyses for my company's problems.
- Since I graduated, I have used my solid knowledge and skills in using technology, which contributes a lot to my job.
- Doing projects at the university has made me more creative. My creativity has led to my new invention.
- My hands-on skills acquired during my years of study at the university helped me get a quick start on my job, and I still benefit from them.
- From my own experience as a supervisor, I know that my knowledge and skills gained from my college education are valuable to my employees.
- My study at the university has made me an effective communicator and team player.

In addition to the alumni survey, other evaluation instruments such as entrance exams for higher-level education, supervisor's evaluation, job annual reports, referees' comments on journal papers and book proposals, and qualifying exams in graduate schools can also be used to evaluate the students' achievements. Even though collecting data for the fourth level evaluation is more difficult than that of the other levels, the result of the evaluation provides the most valuable measurement about the teaching and learning from a program.

The Kirkpatrick four-level evaluation model has been successfully applied in many technical training organizations/companies. These technical training companies have developed various evaluation instruments based on the Kirkpatrick four-level evaluation model. Each evaluation level can be specified for a specific evaluation process. These evaluation instruments have been consistently proven valuable as tools for various evaluation processes.

Kirkpatrick's four-level evaluation model has been around for years and it is still one of the effective evaluation methods used today.

Other Evaluation Models

In addition to Kirkpatrick's four-level evaluation model, there are other effective evaluation models. The following are some of the commonly used evaluation models.

Return On Investment (ROI)

ROI (Lee, Son, & Kim, 2004) is a formula that is used to determine the return of a given investment. In terms of accounting, ROI is a simple formula: Return = Profits/Costs. The following are two examples of ROI:

$100/$1,000 = 10% ROI
$-30/$100 = -30% ROI

When ROI is used to evaluate a teaching and learning process, it does not count for factors such as people and time. Evaluating an education system is more complex. Unlike the effectiveness analysis in business, universities are considered non-profit organizations. The effectiveness analysis for education does not consider the money spent on an online teaching/learning system as purely the annual cost. The money spent on education is considered a long term investment. Also, it is difficult to assess the effectiveness by just counting the cost and enrollment. The students' attitude towards learning and problem solving is also an important factor that is not included in the formula. It is not easy to measure these factors. It is true that a university should carefully spend the money on the administrative cost, travel cost, cost of physical facilities, and maintenance cost. The money should be spent wisely on improving the quality of teaching and learning, on student recruitment and retention, on knowledge update for faculty and staff, and so on. Therefore, when applying ROI to an educational program, the measurement of profits includes factors such as increased productivity, a shorter learning curve, improved retention, and greater satisfaction.

Learning Analytics

The analysis of learning (Bersin, 2003) is the process to use business analytics to evaluate the efficiency, effectiveness, and impact of training and e-learning. Learning analytics can be used to provide information to make the training more efficient and more effective. It measures three things: efficiency, effectiveness and compliance. The following are some details about these three areas:

- Efficiency measures the training expenditure per student, per hour, or per course. It also measures the training budget as the percentage of revenue.
- Effectiveness measures the outcomes of the learning such as enrollment rate, students' GPAs, and student retention rate. It also measures the knowledge and skills acquired by the students.
- Compliance measures the diploma or certification acquisition rate.

Through these areas of measurement, we can reveal the relationship between the expense of the training/teaching and the impact of the training/teaching on the students. In addition, the result of the analysis provides justification for the training cost. When properly used, learning analytics can help with the decision on the type, format, and content of training programs.

Balanced Scorecard

A balanced scorecard (Kaplan & Norton, 1992) is an evaluation model that evaluates the financial outcomes as well as the human factors. This evaluation model focuses on four areas: Financial, customer, internal business process, and learning and growth. Each of the areas can be briefly described as below.

- The financial area describes the financial goals which are designed to maximize the return on investment and to best improve efficiency.
- The customer area focuses on the ability to offer high quality products and services to the customer to meet the customer's expectations. Customers' expectations may vary. Therefore, to better serve the customers, the customers will be categorized into different types and each type will be provided with a different kind of service.
- The internal business process area deals with improving business processes. It examines the end results of the business processes such as the production and service to see if these processes achieve the expectations.
- The learning and growth area evaluates the ability of an organization in dealing with change and growth. Learning new knowledge and skills is one way to prepare the students for new challenges.

In the balanced scorecard model, there is a balance among these four areas. Properly balancing these four areas will help organizations to maximize their performance. The balanced scorecard model measures the success of a project by using the project's objectives as the performance indicators. This model provides a comprehensive evaluation by dynamically establishing the relationships among the four areas. The results of the evaluation can be used in many ways. The following are some of the usage of the evaluation results:

- The evaluation results can be used as the guideline for the long term development of the project.
- The results of the evaluation can be used to facilitate an organization to define its development strategy.

- With the results of the evaluation, an organization can assess its performance at all levels and at all locations.
- An organization can use the results of the evaluation to identify the gaps among different levels and locations.
- The results of the evaluation can be used as the guideline for the budget and personnel distribution.
- An organization can also identify the importance of a project among all its projects and determine the priority of support.

The implementation of the balanced scorecard is not a simple task due to the fact that there is not a standard step-by-step approach, especially for a project in education. In general, the first thing to do in the implementation process is to get people involved in a project, get them ready for change, and clarify the vision of the project. Then, the vision needs to be converted to operational goals which are used as performance indicators. With the performance indicators, the evaluator should design matrices including what should be measured and the criteria of success, and then associate each goal with financial resources. The last task for the implementation process is get feedback and adjusting the strategies accordingly.

As one of the key components of the ADDIE model, a well developed evaluation process can really tell us if the project we developed has the end result we intended and if the time has been well spent on developing such a project.

Evaluation can tell us if students really gain the knowledge and skills due to our effort. The evaluation models discussed above can help us achieve the evaluation objectives. By following these evaluation models, we can design a comprehensive and effective evaluation process. Among those models, the Kirkpatrick four-level evaluation model is the one used mostly by many technical training organizations due to its simplicity and success records for many years.

CONCLUSION

This chapter has examined the issues related to implementation and evaluation. In order to develop and implement a successful online teaching/learning system, we need to make sure that the course materials are properly delivered to the students. As pointed out earlier in this chapter, the delivery process often requires team effort and the technologies should be properly put in place. Once the course materials are delivered, many students and instructors need training on properly using Linux and other open source products. This chapter has shown that training can be done in different ways and with different technologies. It has explained why technical support is important after the course materials are delivered to the students, and it has discussed technical support issues in detail. In this chapter, different technical support methods are applied to different teaching and learning tasks. Evaluation is the last topic of this chapter, which concludes that the result of evaluation is an indicator for determining if a teaching and learning project is successful. This chapter has introduced several evaluation models to assist the evaluator in designing and setting up an evaluation process. Among these evaluation models, the Kirkpatrick four-level evaluation model has been given more attention due to the fact that it has been widely used by educational organizations.

REFERENCES

Achtemeier, S. D., Morris, L. V., & Finnegan, C. L. (2003). Considerations for developing evaluations of online courses. *Journal of Asynchronous Learning Networks, 7*(1). Retrieved August 23, 2006, from http://www.aln.org/publications/jaln/v7n1/v7n1_achtemeier.asp

Bersin, J. (2003). E-learning analytics. *Learning Circuits*. Retrieved March 21, 2008, from http://www.learningcircuits.org/2003/jun2003/bersin.htm

Fortier, P. J., & Michel, H. E. (2005). *Computer systems performance evaluation and prediction*. Burlington, MA: Digital Press.

Gibbs, J., & Rice, M. (2003). Web-based software to help meet technical support needs in K-12 schools. In G. Richards (Ed.), *Proceedings of World Conference on E-Learning in Corporate, Government, Healthcare, and Higher Education 2003* (pp. 2157-2159). Chesapeake, VA: AACE.

Kaplan, R. S., & Norton, D. P. (1992). The balanced scorecard: Measures that drive performance. *Harvard Business Review, 70*(1), 71-80.

Khan, B. H. (2005). *Managing e-learning strategies: Design, delivery, implementation and evaluation*. Hershey, PA: Information Science Publishing.

Kirkpatrick, D. L. (1998). *Evaluating training programs: The four levels* (2nd ed.). San Francisco: Berrett-Koehler Publishers.

Kirkpatrick, D. L., & Kirkpatrick, J. D. (2005). *Evaluating training programs: The four levels* (3rd ed.). San Francisco: Berrett-Koehler Publishers.

Lee, Y., Son, C. & Kim, M. (2004). Preliminary analysis of evaluation criteria in e-learning Return On Investment (ROI). In G. Richards (Ed.), *Proceedings of World Conference on E-Learning in Corporate, Government, Healthcare, and Higher Education 2004* (pp. 367-369). Chesapeake, VA: AACE.

Omwenga, E., Waema, T., Eisendrath, G., & Libotton, A. (2005). Development and application of an objectives-driven eContent structuring and deployment model. In P. Kommers & G. Richards (Eds.), *Proceedings of World Conference on Educational Multimedia, Hypermedia and Telecommunications 2005* (pp. 573-578). Chesapeake, VA: AACE.

Price, T., Walters, J., & Xiao, Y. (2006). *A role-based online evaluation system.* Retrieved August 23, 2006, from http://www.iadis.org/Multi2006/Papers/15/F023_EL.pdf

Scherff, L., & Paulus, T. (2006). Encouraging ownership of online spaces: Support for preservice english teachers through computer-mediated communication. *Contemporary Issues in Technology and Teacher Education [Online serial], 6*(4). Retrieved January 12, 2008, from http://www.citejournal.org/vol6/iss4/languagearts/article1.cfm

Smitherman, H., Nasseh, B., & Repp, P. (2005). Case study, sharing digital middletown project experiences and findings: Practical deployment of rich media content for education and entertainment by long distance high bandwidth wireless technology. In P. Kommers & G. Richards (Eds.), *Proceedings of World Conference on Educational Multimedia, Hypermedia and Telecommunications 2005* (pp. 351-354). Chesapeake, VA: AACE.

Tu, C., Yen, C., Corry, M., & Ianacone, R. (2003). Collaborative evaluation of teaching for e-learning. In G. Richards (Ed.), *Proceedings of World Conference on E-Learning in Corporate, Government, Healthcare, and Higher Education 2003* (pp. 325-330). Chesapeake, VA: AACE.

Section IV
Trends and Advances

Chapter XII
Trends and Advances

INTRODUCTION

In this chapter, we will discuss the advances in open source products and the trends in the technologies used for developing online teaching/learning systems. The topics of trends and advances discussed in previous chapters will be summarized in this chapter. We will also look at new features and new ideas in the application of the open source products that will potentially have an impact on the online teaching/learning systems.

The discussion will start with the advances in the network related open source tools. As more and more university courses are taught online, there is an increasing demand for faster and more reliable network technologies. A lot of effort has been made to improve network hardware and software. In this chapter, we will examine some of the new network and telecommunication related technologies and how these new technologies will impact online teaching and learning.

Then, we will look at the advances in server operating systems and services. We will investigate the trends in server software, hardware, and services. We will discuss the new and emerging technologies that can potentially improve servers' performance and reliability.

As more and more course materials are made available online, there will be a higher demand for databases to hold and manage the ever increasing data generated by various online courses. We will discuss the advances in database management systems and Web-based databases.

Learning management systems (LMSs) are rapidly changing. A lot of advances have been made in the LMSs, and many new LMS features are developed to enhance the performance and functionality of the LMSs. In this chapter, we will examine some of the new features and technologies.

The next topic to be discussed in this chapter is about the advances of security related technologies. This chapter will provide some information about the trends in antivirus tools. We will also explore some new development in virtualization, access control, and data encryption.

The area of multimedia software, collaboration software, and other desktop application software is the most improved area. Especially, the open source multimedia and collaboration tools have been made much easier to use. This chapter will introduce some of the advances in this area, and we will take a closer look at some new features of the multimedia software, collaboration software, and other desktop application software.

The last topic in this chapter is about the trends in instructional technology. The advances in the theory and practice of instructional technology will be discussed. Online teaching/learning systems are getting more sophisticated and flexible. We will look into some of the new development in various future learning structures that have been proposed.

The rapid progress of technologies and ideas for online teaching and learning has made a tremendous difference in higher education. As the progress continues, we can expect education institutions to keep on improving their online teaching. This chapter will talk about how students and instructors will benefit from the progress and improvement.

BACKGROUND

Using open source products in e-learning is one of the trends in the area of e-learning technology. The open source products such as Web 2.0, Linux, Moodle, Apache, MySQL, and PHP are gaining popularity among higher education institutions. Many factors are contributing to this movement. Online teaching/learning systems are one of the major costs of universities' operations. By using the open source products, universities can significantly reduce their spending on the online teaching/learning systems. The usability of the open source products has been improved significantly. The Firefox Web browser is such an example. Open source product companies are also making more effort on marketing and on support for their products.

The open source approach will continue to be a main way of inventing new technologies. MacManus (2007) picked the open source movement as the most promising trend for the Web in 2008. He predicted that Web browsers, social networks, mobile Web, open data, open ad networks, and microformats would significantly influence Web-based computing. Torkington (2007) has summarized some trends in the open source approach. One is to strengthen the effort to convince users to adopt the open source products by improving the usability, marketing, and support. The second one is to adopt the business models which embrace the open source strengths. Another trend is to resolve the scaling and platform challenges for Web 2.0. Also, there is a trend to extend open source to the territory of proprietary software, hardware, and data.

Due to the fact that the infrastructure of an online teaching/learning system is based on the Internet technology, innovation in the Internet technology will have a great impact on the way of online teaching and learning. The open source Web 2.0 (O'Reilly, 2005) is such a technology that carries the new e-learning platform called E-learning 2.0. (Downes, 2008) which will make the student be more of the course content producer than the course content consumer.

As online teaching/learning systems are widely accepted by universities, globalization is another trend in e-learning. Enders and Fulton (2002) collected over a dozen research articles on globalization. The researchers discussed the impact of globalization on higher education. They also discussed the changes and challenges that are faced by students, faculty, and the labor market. Aoki (2004) discussed globalization related issues, and the difficulties and opportunities of international collaboration. Paulsen (2005) predicted that globalization and large-scale operation are the trends for online education. On the other hand, do-it-yourself learning (Jarche, 2007) has become a trend in recent years. Do-it-yourself learning encourages learners to decide the subjects they want to learn and search for the information through Google, Wikipedia, and YouTube.

According to Koper (2004), using the semantic Web in education provides a distributed, self-organized and self-directed life-long learning format. With the semantic Web, students and instructors can create and work together in a flexible online teaching and learning environment. Camacho and R-Moreno (2007) proposed a metadata-based model which can automatically modify the learning design to improve learning and allow users to incorporate the course content with new semantic information.

TRENDS IN NETWORK AND TELECOMMUNICATION

The improvement of network technologies often results in a significant change in online teaching and learning. The following improvements in the wireless network and network protocols have the potential to take the online learning and teaching to a new level.

There are several next generation wireless broadband technologies such as WiMAX, Long Term Evolution (LTE), and Ultra Mobile Broadband (UMB) that are already or about to be released soon. These technologies can significantly improve the wireless transmission rate, area coverage, and quality. The following describes some of these technologies which can help online teaching/learning systems to reach more students and improve the quality of online teaching and learning:

- **WiMAX:** WiMAX is a wireless broadband technology that can cover an area as large as 50km radius. The proposed transmission rate is 75 Mbps for downloading and 25 Mbps for uploading. Practically, depending on how far away the transmission center is and how many users are in the same sector, the WiMAX data transmission rate can be lower. The WiMAX technology is in its initial deployment stage. Its mass production is expected to be in 2009.
- **LTE:** LTE is a next generation wireless broadband technology. It can reach users over a 100km away and has the proposed download rate of 100Mbps and upload rate of 50Mbps. Practically, it may not get that fast depending on the distance. LTE is still at the early stage of development. It is expected to be at the mass production stage by the year 2011.
- **UMB:** UMB is the technology that will be ready in 2009. The Internet (TCP/IP) network technology based UMB will run on the next generation radio system. It has a proposed 17-291Mbps download rate and 10-79Mbps upload rate. The coverage range can reach 50km.

In addition to the three mentioned above, there are many other similar wireless broadband technologies. These technologies can significantly improve online teaching/learning systems' mobility, capability, and performance on running Voice over Internet Protocol (VoIP) and real time application tasks.

The newly developed network protocols can also have a great impact on network technologies. The next generation Internet protocol version 6 (Ipv6) is about to replace the current version Ipv4. The current Ipv4 uses a 32-bit binary number for the IP address. In theory, Ipv4 can assign 4 billion IP addresses. Ipv4 is about to run out of all its available IP addresses due to the rapid growth of Internet and mobile devices. Also, in Ipv4, 95% of IP addresses are not efficiently used. Ipv6 will resolve these problems and provide many other features as described below:

- Ipv6 uses 128-bit IP addresses; this is enough to meet all the IP address demands for many years to come.
- With Ipv6, a high-quality path can be established between two hosts to transmit audio and video data.
- Ipv6 is more secure by including the end-to-end security measures which are currently the add-ons to secure Ipv4.

- Ipv6 can simplify network management. It allows peer-to-peer communication which eliminates the need for network configuration.
- Mobile devices can greatly benefit from Ipv6 since it can assign each mobile device a static IP address and no network configuration is required.

Overall, IPv6 is more efficient, easier to use, and more secure. It has better support for mobile and peer-to-peer computing. A future online teaching/learning system can certainly benefit from these features. Interested readers can get more information about Ipv6 from Ipv6's Web site at http://www.ipv6.org.

TRENDS IN SERVER OPERATING SYSTEMS

Like the improvement in the network and telecommunication technologies, server related technologies have also made impressive progress. One of the current trends is to add the virtualization technology to the server. Both the latest SUSE Linux Enterprise Server and Red Hat Enterprise Server have provided virtualization technologies and virtualization management tools. Linux kernel 2.6.20 has included the kernel-based virtual machine for the Linux operating system. To support mission critical applications, more and more server operating systems include the cluster management suite to handle application failovers. A cluster computing system allows more students to simultaneously log on to a server and to work on various tasks.

Breakthroughs in hardware can also bring significant changes in the server technology. Computer hardware has been through many revolutionary changes, especially, in CPU related technologies. Multiple Linux operating systems can run simultaneously on a single multi-core CPU chip. Intel's (2008) nanometer technology can dramatically increase the energy efficiency and performance of processors. A nanometer based CPU can make computation such as gaming and multitasking much faster while using much less energy. More and more servers will also move to use the 64-bit CPU and to host the 64-bit version of the server operating system to support virtualization, more memory, and 64-bit application software such as MySQL.

TRENDS IN DATABASE TECHNOLOGY

The database technology will continue to improve in the coming years. To enhance a database's scalability, extensibility, interoperability, and openness, the Extensible Markup Language (XML) has been adopted and upgraded by almost all major database management software companies. Users are able to store and query XML data in a Web-based database. With a newly developed database management system (DBMS), users are able to modify, insert, or delete content in a XML document. With this kind of DBMS, users can also convert XML data to and from other data formats.

Many DBMSs support the improved data compression functionality for making database backup more efficient and saving more storage space. The data compression tools can also be used to compress historical data stored in a data warehouse.

Parallel processing is one of the features supported by many DBMSs to improve database performance. Some of the newly developed management tools can be used to assist the database administrator in managing parallel processing. More improved tools for handling business intelligence projects will also be widely supported by DBMSs.

TRENDS IN LEARNING MANAGEMENT SYSTEMS

Learning Management Systems (LMSs) are one of the fast changing components in an online teaching/learning system. Today's LMSs are built to support globalized online teaching and learning. Through the Internet, students can access course materials available in multiple languages that are all supported by LMSs. Many of the LMS packages include more sophisticated collaboration tools and multimedia tools such as VoIP to enhance collaboration and develop multimedia course materials. More features will be added to support international collaboration.

There will be better ways to personalize online teaching and learning. The future LMS will be more supportive of personalization which allows students to develop their own blogs and manage their own course materials and class schedule. It will be easier for the LMS to integrate with operating systems, databases, and other application software. The LMS will provide a more sophisticated tutoring system and a more sophisticated learning progress monitoring and analyzing system.

TRENDS IN SECURITY MANAGEMENT

Protecting an online teaching/learning system is the top priority. There will be more security measures to protect sensitive information, fend off viruses, and harden the network against hacker attacks. The virtualization technology used by many Linux operating system distributions can greatly improve security. A virtual machine can be created on a host computer system without leakage. Another way to prevent external attacks is to create internal enclaves for sensitive data and for data management systems. To control the access to computer resources such as application software or devices, the security model Dynamic Access Control is used to design controls for resource access based on users' roles. A decoy server called a honeypot can be established to lure hackers. In such a way, we can catch hackers' information and their behavior, which can help us stop their attacks.

Each year, there will be some new viruses. The antivirus software will continue to add new components to deal with newly created viruses. To improve research on creating new antivirus software, antivirus software companies will share virus information. Security will be strengthened on plug-and-play devices. Software will be developed to automatically perform some of the security tasks to reduce security administrators' workload. Threat Correlation is this type of software. Once the information about a new virus is available, the software will correlate the threat information to the system's vulnerability information previously gathered by the software and decide how to prevent the virus from attacking the system. Various security products such as the firewall, antivirus software, and spam filter can be built together to form a comprehensive unified threat management system. The unified threat management system can simplify security administration. With such a system, the security administrator needs only to deal with the security software which can update all the security measures concurrently.

For data encryption, there are also some new features that have become popular in recent years. Context-based encryption is one of such features. It allows users to create any number of different security sessions for different applications and the security sessions can be configured to have different security levels.

TRENDS IN APPLICATION SOFTWARE

Application software has a direct impact on the quality of online teaching and learning. Multimedia software, collaboration software, and other application software continue to be improved.

Multimedia content includes various formats such as audio, video, animation, and so on. The latest version of the KDE desktop environment includes a cross-platform multimedia API called Phonon which allows users to access all multimedia frameworks through one API. Phonon is used to playback most of the common multimedia formats and stream the media over a network. For instance, Phonon can process multiple audio sources as a single audio stream.

Augmented reality is a virtual environment that simulated the real world. It has been used in various training workshops. Although it is not widely used in online teaching and learning due its cost and its requirement for high network throughput, it has some potential to be used in online teaching and learning once the cost and technical issues are resolved.

Social computing software which is a kind of collaboration software has been used to form an online community for collaborative learning. New social computing software is implemented on the popular open source Internet technology Web 2.0. Social computing has been supported by Web 2.0 which has great potential for online teaching and learning.

The success of Web 2.0 can improve the education of gaming in various areas. First, Web 2.0 enriches online gaming by improving the graphics and richness of the content. It also makes online collaboration easier by improving online communication, player relationship, and media sharing.

The Web 2.0 technology is also used to support context-aware computing which an adaptive mobile computing method. Web 2.0 based context-aware computing can connect user context and community information with the Web service to allow students to access services and multimedia content according to their location, identity, and preferences. In their article, Schmidt and Winterhalter (2004) discussed how context-aware computing can be applied to e-learning.

TRENDS IN INSTRUCTIONAL TECHNOLOGY

One of the trends in the online teaching and learning infrastructure is to increasingly use mobile devices for better mobility. The improvement of the wireless technology allows students to use smart phones, PDAs, iPods, and other Internet mobile devices to access course materials whenever and wherever the course materials are needed. These devices can also be used for real-time Web conferencing. The use of mobile devices has created a new way of learning called personal broadcasting. Podcasting is one of the popular personal broadcasting methods. It allows students to share course information through iPods.

The increasing use of Google, Wikipedia, and YouTube in online teaching and learning is a new trend. By using these technologies, there comes another new learning trend called do-it-yourself (DIY) learning, which is a rapidly growing learning method.

The Web 2.0 technology leads to a new trend in e-learning called E-learning 2.0 which allows users to create and share knowledge with others. Students can form a social network for collaborative learning. E-learning 2.0 is also called social learning (Downes, 2008).

Course content modularization is an approach that divides the course content of all subjects into small unites. Many of the technology based courses share common components. Modularization is particularly useful for teaching this type of course. Based on the requirements of a new course, the small units from different subjects can be reassembled and used to teach the new course. Such an approach can speed up the course material development process and will have a significant impact on online teaching and learning.

In the above, some new technology trends and their application to online teaching and learning are discussed. Some of these technologies have existed for years and continue to be improved and the others are new or still under development. As technology and instruction improve, the quality and performance of online teaching/learning systems will get better and better.

CONCLUSION

In this chapter, some trends in online teaching and learning as well as the supporting technologies have been discussed. The rapidly advancing technologies have been changing the way of teaching and learning and will continue to do so in the future. As described in this chapter, open source products such as the Linux operating system, Web 2.0, and Ipv6 have had and will continue to have a great impact on online teaching/learning systems. We know for sure that there will be new inventions in the coming years and the open source approach will lead the charge.

The theory and practice of instructional technology will continue to be updated to adapt to the fast changing technology, and there is no sign that the progress will slow down. Therefore, university administrators, instructors, students, and IT professionals have to update themselves to keep up with the new trends.

When developing and running an online teaching/learning system, the people who are involved in the project need to closely examine the new trends and adopt the new ideas and technologies that can be used to improve their online teaching and learning.

REFERENCES

Aoki, K. (2004). Globalization of e-learning: Issues and opportunities for International collaboration. In G. Richards (Ed.), *Proceedings of World Conference on E-Learning in Corporate, Government, Healthcare, and Higher Education 2004* (pp. 161-166). Chesapeake, VA: AACE.

Camacho, D., & Rodríguez-Moreno, M. D. (2007). Towards an automatic monitoring for higher education learning design. *International Journal of Metadata, Semantics and Ontologies, 2*(1), 1-10. Retrieved March 17, 2008, from http://www.ii.uam.es/~dcamacho/papers/dcamacho-IJMSO.pdf

Downes, S. (2008). *E-learning 2.0*. Retrieved March 15, 2008, from http://www.elearnmag.org/subpage.cfm?section=articles&article=29-1

Enders, J., & Fulton, O. (Eds.). (2002). *Higher education in a globalising world: International trends and mutual observations: A festschrift in honour of Ulrich Teichler (Higher Education Dynamics)*. Norwell, MA: Springer.

Intel. (2008). *Hafnium-based Intel® 45nm process technology*. Retrieved March 18, 2008, from http://www.intel.com/technology/45nm/index.htm?cid=cim:ggl|xeon_us_quadserver|k78EF|s

Jarche, H. (2007). *The future of learning is DIY*. Retrieved March 15, 2008, from http://www.jarche.com/?p=1047

Koper, R. (2004). *Use of the semantic Web to solve some basic problems in education: Increase flexible, distributed lifelong learning, decrease teacher's workload*. Retrieved March 15, 2008, from http://www-jime.open.ac.uk/2004/6

MacManus, R. (2008). *Most promising for Web 2008: Open source movement*. Retrieved March 15, 2008, from http://www.readwriteweb.com/archives/most_promising_web_2008_open_source.php

O'Reilly, T. (2005). *What is Web 2.0: Design patterns and business models for the next generation of software*. Retrieved March 15, 2008, from http://www.oreillynet.com/pub/a/oreilly/tim/news/2005/09/30/what-is-web-20.html

Paulsen, M. F. (2005). *Online education: Trends and strategic recommendations*. Retrieved March 6, 2008, from http://home.nettskolen.nki.no/~morten/pp/CampusInnovation.ppt#541,1

Schmidt, A., & Winterhalter, C. (2004). User context aware delivery of e-learning material: Approach and architecture, *Journal of Universal Computer Science, 10*(1), 38-46.

Torkington, N. (2007). *Open source trends*. Retrieved March 15, 2008, from http://radar.oreilly.com/archives/2007/04/open-source-trends.html

About the Author

Lee Chao is currently a professor of math and computer science in the school of Arts and Sciences at University of Houston – Victoria, USA. He received his PhD from the University of Wyoming, USA, and he is certified as Oracle certified professional and Microsoft solution developer. His current research interests are data analysis and technology-based teaching. Dr. Chao is also the author of over a dozen of research articles in data analysis and math modeling, and books in the development of computer labs and database systems.

Index

H

I

J

K

L

M

N

O

Breinigsville, PA USA
24 February 2011

256287BV00001B/1-10/P